B

THE BEST OF
Edward Abbey

THE BEST OF
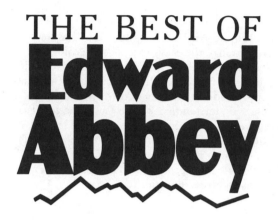
Edward Abbey

Edited and illustrated by
Edward Abbey

SIERRA CLUB BOOKS • SAN FRANCISCO

The Sierra Club, founded in 1892 by John Muir, has devoted itself to the study and protection of the earth's scenic and ecological resources—mountains, wetlands, woodlands, wild shores and rivers, deserts and plains. The publishing program of the Sierra Club offers books to the public as a nonprofit educational service in the hope that they may enlarge the public's understanding of the Club's basic concerns. The point of view expressed in each book, however, does not necessarily represent that of the Club. The Sierra Club has some sixty chapters coast to coast, in Canada, Hawaii, and Alaska. For information about how you may participate in its programs to preserve wilderness and the quality of life, please address inquiries to Sierra Club, 730 Polk Street, San Francisco, CA 94109.

Library of Congress Cataloging-in-Publication Data

Abbey, Edward, 1927–
    The best of Edward Abbey.

    Reprint. Originally published: Slumgullion stew.
New York : Dutton 1984. Selected chapters from
the author's novels and non-fiction originally
published 1954–1982.
    I. Title.
[PS3551.B2A6   1988]   813'.54   87-23568
ISBN 0-87156-786-5 (pbk.)

Cover design by Paul Bacon

Illustrations by Edward Abbey

Printed in the United States of America

10 9 8 7 6 5 4

Acknowledgments for previously published material:

The selection from *Jonathan Troy* first appeared in *Jonathan Troy*, Dodd, Mead, 1954.

The selection from *The Brave Cowboy* first appeared in *The Brave Cowboy*, Dodd, Mead, 1956.

The selection from *Fire on the Mountain* first appeared in *Fire on the Mountain*, Dial Press, 1962.

The selection from *Black Sun* first appeared in *Black Sun*, Simon & Schuster, 1971.

The selection from *The Monkey Wrench Gang* first appeared in *The Monkey Wrench Gang*, Avon Books, 1976.

The selection from *Good News* first appeared in *Good News*, E.P. Dutton, Inc., 1980.

"Cowboys," "The Moon-Eyed Horse," "Havasu," "The Dead Man at Grandview Point," and "Bedrock and Paradox" first appeared in *Desert Solitaire*, McGraw-Hill, 1968.

"The Great American Desert," "Death Valley," "Manhattan Twilight, Hoboken Night," and "Telluride Blues—A Hatchet Job" first appeared in *The Journey Home*, E.P. Dutton, Inc., 1977.

"Anna Creek," "The Outback," "A Desert Isle," "Sierra Madre," "Down There in the Rocks," "Science with a Human Face," "In Defense of the Redneck," "Fire Lookout," and "The Sorrows of Travel" first appeared in *Abbey's Road*, E.P. Dutton, Inc., 1979.

"Down the River with Henry Thoreau," "Watching the Birds: The Windhover," "Of Protest," "My Friend Debris," and "Floating" first appeared in *Down the River*, E.P. Dutton, Inc., 1982.

Selection from *Appalachian Wilderness* first appeared in *Appalachian Wilderness*, E.P. Dutton, Inc., 1973.

ABOUT THE AUTHOR

Edward Abbey was born and raised on a farm in northern Appalachia but has lived since 1947 in the American Southwest. He was educated, more or less, at the University of New Mexico, Edinburgh University, and Stanford University. He is the author of many books including *Desert Solitaire, The Journey Home, Down the River,* and a forthcoming novel *The Fool's Progress.* At present he lives with his wife and two children near the town of Oracle in Arizona. Current literary projects include *Hayduke Lives!,* a sequel to *The Monkey Wrench Gang,* and *The Cowboy and his Cow,* an essay in mythology and meat.

CONTENTS

The Author's Preface
to His Own Book

The *Reader* as literary object has two useful functions: it can serve as a convenient one-volume introduction to a writer's work for those not previously acquainted with it, leading to deeper intimacies; or the *Reader* may suffice to confirm one's doubts and suspended contempt, thus sparing the critic the bother of looking further. I trust that my book will satisfy the expectations of both types of *Reader* readers.

In compiling this one-man show I have endeavored, as an author naturally does, to present what I think is both the best and the most representative of my writing—so far. The emphasis falls on the latter term. Most of my writing has been in the field of the novel, explorations in certain aspects of the human comedy, especially the traditional conflict between our instinctive urge toward fraternity, community, and freedom, and the opposing demands of discipline and the state. The human versus human institutions—a conflict as old as the development of agriculture, urbanism, militarism, and hierarchy. That theme, like a scarlet thread, runs through everything I have written, binding it together into whatever unity it may have. Seeking to develop this theme in dramatic form, the best and most deeply felt of my writing flows toward fiction, toward the creation of symbolic structures, the telling and retelling (always trying to get it right) of one of our oldest stories.

Excerpts from novels, however, make poor material for an anthology. At least in the kind of fiction I have been writing, few of my excerpts or chapters make much sense in isolation; none have the independent coherence of a good short story. Nevertheless, I chose to insert in this *Reader* one episode from each of my novels, not to please or amuse, but in hope of tickling enough interest to lure the potential reader into the ambuscade of the originals. But these episodes are brief and there are only seven of them.

The bulk of the book consists of chapters from four collections of informal, personal (sometimes highly personal) accounts of travel, ideas, people, nature, places, adventures—*Desert Solitaire, The Journey Home, Abbey's Road,* and *Down the River.* I like to call such writing personal history. Most of the selections qualify, I think, as essays, another adequately vast, vague, and self-defining label. We know that in this world there are actually only two kinds of books: (1) good books, and (2) the others. But books require finer labels so that librarians, in a culture built on the babble of numbers and words, may not go clinically insane.

My first book *(Troy)* was published in 1954. According to the calendar on the wall, I am writing these words in the year 1984. Thirty years in the book-writing business—appalling! For so prolonged an effort my output has been small, about a dozen volumes worthy of the title "book" plus the texts for four or five scenic-photography coffee-table compendiums, which I do not count as legitimate books and which in any case nobody reads. (One of those things, if you attached legs to it, would do as a coffee-table in itself.) Of the eleven or twelve legitimate books only one, *The Monkey Wrench Gang,* goes beyond 300 pages. Hardly enough to gain my union card.

Where have the years gone? Why, into the usual vices of the romantic realist: into sloth and melancholy, each feeding upon and reinforcing the other, into love and marriage and the begetting of children, into the strenuous maneuvers of earning a living without living to earn, into travel and play and music and drink and talk and laughter, into saving the world—but saving the world was only a hobby. Into watching cloud formations float across our planetary skies. But mostly into sloth and melancholy and I don't regret a moment of it.

If I had stayed in Hoboken when I had the chance, holed up in the urban hive while acid rain pattered on the roof and drug-crazed killers stalked the alleyways, I would now be the Dostoyevsky of Hudson County, New Jersey. Two of my American heroes are Nelson Algren and Dr. William Carlos Williams. But I left after one year.

Nothing can be more fatuous than a writer writing about his own writing and the serious reader is advised to skip what follows; I intend to go on probing this same vein for several pages more. It may be of interest to other essayists and novelists. I know that *I* like to read such stuff, up to a point, if there is one.

Despite the meagre production (so far), I have been able to earn my keep at writing for nearly fifteen years. I know that it's vulgar and offensive to talk about money—most authors would far prefer to describe their latest sadomasochistic daydreams—but the grim truth is that I have been well rewarded for my plodding work at the typewriter, with an average income in the period referred to of about 20,000 dollars per year. A handsome sum, more than sufficient for a comfortable life in the country. After centuries of dogged striving at least one member of the Abbey clan (Allegheny Mountain branch) has succeeded in climbing to the uppermost rungs of the lower class.

How did this come about?

Not through institutional assistance. My books are never reviewed in *Time* or *Newsweek* or *New York* or *The New Yorker* or the *New York Review* or *Esquire* or *Harper's* or *Atlantic* or *Village Voice* or *National Review* or *Partisan Review* or *Commentary* or *TV Guide* or *Ms.* or *Mother Jones* or *Rolling Stone* or *Ladies' Home Journal* or *Vogue* or *Sewanee Review* or *The Wall Street Journal*. Each of my books, each defenseless child, has been met with a sublime, monumental, crashing silence—a freezing silence. (Some did receive friendly notices in the Sunday *New York Times* and other regional newspapers.)

When not ignored, my books are greeted with what I must recognize as a coolness verging on outright frigidity, particularly by the doctrinaire buzzsaws of chickenshit liberalism: "The author of this book," said one reviewer about *The Monkey Wrench Gang*, "should be neutered and locked away forever." A Miss "S. C.," reviewing *Abbey's Road* for *The New Republic*, attacked me as "smug" and "graceless" because of a careless remark I let drop about Annie Dillard's theological nature writing; the reviewer was so infuriated by that slip that she even ridiculed the publisher's jacket copy. In the moldy, angst-ridden pages of *The Nation* one Denise Drabelle, identified as an "environmental lawyer," whatever that is, described the author of *Down the River* as "puerile, arrogant, xenophobic and dopey." Why? Because I had foolishly confessed, in a casual aside, to sharing in the popular belief that mass immigration from the Latin South (or from any other source) is not a good thing for the working people and material well-being of the United States. And one more critic, in a survey of Western American writers for the *New York Times Magazine*, called me a "smirking pessimist," apparently in response to my novel *Good News*, in which I foresee the collapse of our military-industrial civilization. I could cite other examples but this is enough to indicate the general tenor of the resistance.

A near unanimous indifference sprinkled with peppery pockets of abuse—such has been the overall critical reception of my thirty years of part-time literary travail. No help at all. Am I complaining or boasting? A little of both, but my essential point is this: a serious writer writing what are meant as serious books can survive and even flourish in the face of official indifference and hostility *if* he has something to say and says it well, something which interests a sufficient number of his fellow citizens. Except for that first and highly forgotten novel, not one of my books has failed to sell at least 10,000 copies in its original trade edition and some, like the hated *Abbey's Road* and *Down the River,* are approaching the 40,000 mark and still selling at a modest but steady annual rate. In one form or another, every one of my books (again with the sole and welcome exception of *Jonathan Troy*) has remained in print and available. My smug pride in this fact is self-evident but more importantly I offer my experience to other writers, especially the new, the young, the struggling, as proof that the author need not subserve a mass market or pander to the East Coast literati in order to enjoy a satisfactory audience. There is a middle way, a strait, tricky, but feasible channel between the rocks on the swift river of Mod Am Lit. That should be good news indeed. Be of good cheer, my fellow scriveners! Ignore the critics. Disregard those best-selling paperbacks with embossed covers in the supermarkets and the supermarket bookstores. And waste no time applying for gifts and grants—when we want money from the rich we'll take it by force. The honorable way.

Death before dishonor, as it were.

Live free or die.

That about sums up (and may well conclude) my literary career. Which is not and never was a career anyway, but rather a passion. A *passion!* Fueled in equal parts by anger and love. How can you feel one without the other? Each implies the other. A writer without passion is like a body without a soul. Or even more grotesque, like a soul without a body.

Yes, I am aware that what I have written above requires certain qualifications. I am happy to acknowledge that some of the American writers I most admire—Doctorow, Vonnegut, Heller, Pynchon, for example—have won an enormous audience. I only wish it were far bigger. And others whom I respect—Gaddis, for example, and Wendell Berry, Joan Didion, Peter Matthiessen, Edward Hoagland, Alan Harrington, William Eastlake, Robert Coover, Barry Lopez, Thomas McGuane, Gary Snyder, Galway Kinnell, Annie Dillard, Robert Creeley, Diane Wakowski, to name but a few—have received the official critical acclaim but not (so far) the number of readers they deserve. Never mind. I stand by and upon the central meaning of my words. There is a middle way. You do not have to write endless disquisitions about suburban hanky-panky, Toyota dealers, self-hating intellectuals, male mutilation, lesbians in bearskins, to live and live happily as a writer in America, God bless her.

You do not even need to be psychoanalyzed, Rolfed, estered, altered, gelded, neutered, spayed, fixed, Mooned, acupunctured, meditated, Zenned, massaged, Cayced, yogied, New Aged, astrocharted, holisticized, computerized, megatrended, therapized, androgynized, evangelized, converted, or even, last and least, to be reborn. One life at a time, please.

What *is* both necessary and sufficient—for honest work—is to have faith in the evidence of your senses and in your common sense. To be true to your innate sense of justice. To be loyal to your family, your clan, your friends, and your community. (Let the nation-state go hang itself.) Stand up for the stupid and crazy. Love the earth and the sun and the animals. Read Walt Whitman, Mark Twain, Henry Thoreau, Jack London, B. Traven, Thomas Wolfe (the real Tom Wolfe, not that other one), John Steinbeck, Nelson Algren, and Dr. William Carlos Williams. When you are appointed to the Nobel Prize Committee, vote for Lewis Mumford for literature, Noam Chomsky for truth, and David Brower for peace. And that about covers it. So far.

So far as America is concerned. As for the remainder of the earthly world, we know what's going on out there. The best of our brother novelists and sister poets are in prison or in hiding or in exile, are being "disappeared," tortured, murdered, from Tierra del Fuego to Mexico, from Siberia and Peking to Prague, from Cairo to Capetown, from Hanoi to Istanbul. What should we do about *that?* I don't know.

In such a world, why write? How justify this mad itch for scribbling? Speaking for myself, I write to entertain my friends and exasperate our enemies. I write to record the truth of our time, as best as I can see it. To investigate the comedy and tragedy of human relationships. To resist and sabotage the contemporary drift toward a technocratic, militaristic totalitarianism, whatever its ideological coloration. To oppose injustice, defy the powerful, and speak for the voiceless.

I write to make a difference. "It is always a writer's duty to make the world better," said Samuel Johnson. Distrusting all answers, to raise more questions. To give pleasure and promote esthetic bliss. To honor life and praise the divine beauty of the world. For the joy and exultation of writing itself. To tell my story.

Well now, says the old wolf, *vox clamantis in deserto,* that should keep him busy for a while.

Edward Abbey
March 1984
Oracle, Arizona

Jonathan Troy

(1954)

He was awakened, hearing laughter, in the dark tunnel of the night, caught between frayed dreams, and sat up and stared into the blackness, hearing from the other end of the room now, weaving through the dark, not the wild trill of leaves in laughter which had awakened him, but only the dismal whine, the dim and melancholy wind (like the song of a ghost in the black and ruined farmhouse which rose, shaking and creaking with misery and age, from dark tangles of bramble-briar and hawthorn, hedged in by plum trees grown wild and apple trees grown tall and shaggy and barren, fronting a yard of Queen Anne's Lace and waist-high witch grass, trailing across its black eyes a hairy skein of Virginia Creeper and volunteer columbine, facing the narrow rutty rocky road that once was and in flood-time still is the bed of a creek, pushing up above its sagging walls and black splintered boards a sway-backed roof as cracked and open as a trellis, with the soft-moulded remains of a red-brick chimney where a catbird family nested in the spring and early summer, where a whippoorwill haunted himself in the autumn, beyond the last farm beyond Falling Rock Cabin way up the hollow in the vine-covered hills behind Tanomee, the old farm which nobody wanted any more and which nearly everybody had forgotten except the boy and (in the fall) the red-jacketed hunters from town with their clean shotguns and pipes and wrinkled eyes on the lookout for rabbits, squirrels, Ringnecks, wild turkeys) of his father, old Nat Troy, rolled asleep in his stolen Army blankets and turning in a nightmare, creaking the broken springs, the oboe sound of his father's snores, a sound too familiar and elemental and old, too interveined with the bedrock of his being and existence, with the stream of his history from its black beginning to its gray present, to be more than simply noticed, an awareness indicated, its real and fundamental message already buried in the chamber of his dreams; he could forget and at once did forget the ancestral nightchant, remembering only the vivid and in memory still-immediate skirl of laughter, feeling the deep and thrilled commotion of his heart, the tingling of his hair, the shaking and trembling of his sweating hands, still hearing, in the black vault of silence, the silent echo of the wind in leaves, and sitting up in bed, stiff with shock and surprise, he turned his head toward the open window, searching for something, and saw, framed in the gray rectangle, a diffusion of undersea light—of light shining through a curtain of falling rain—an unexpected vision which drew him out of his bed, naked, and across the littered floor to the window, where he leaned out head and shoulders, shivering slightly, the wild churning in his mind and heart heating his blood, opening his mouth, exciting his loins, and remembered the green sources and the swing of steel blades over a moon-meadow of frozen moonlight and the slim body of the girl—her knees, the grave level gaze of her eyes, the whirling skirt, the wind of speed lifting her hair—and the flight, the trail of laughter and the taunt or dare or challenge coming back to him over the blue ice and through the air—find me!—and he smiled as he remembered, his hands tightening on the window-frame's edge, and leaned farther out, seeing the dead neon of the Blue Bell Bar, the streetlamps glowing through the soft rain, the street empty and wet-shining and carless, and the silent town abandoned to sleep and night, and he thought of the girl waiting for him a mile or so away through the wet air, past all the steel and concrete and bare-limbed urban trees, somewhere on the other side of the hill beyond the Fair; enthralled by the green joy of love and the urgent delight of sex, he thought of her, and watched, from where he was, a little past the end of the first hour in April, the wordless tireless falling of the rain. . . .

The Brave Cowboy

(1956)

She came slowly out of sleep, dreaming of the surrealistic past, hearing in the present and not far away the click of a light switch, light footsteps on the kitchen floor, the scraping sounds of a heavy object in motion. Alarmed, she reached out to touch Paul—he was not there. The weary pain of loss and separation swept over her; in the twilight of consciousness between sleep and awakening she felt the full weight of all the fear and sorrow and loneliness that in her waking hours she had partially suppressed beneath a routine of activity and facile optimism. Again she heard the unfamiliar sounds; unwillingly she opened her eyes and turned her head and saw, under the door to the kitchen, a splinter of yellow light. She was startled, then afraid, caught for a moment in the paralysis of the unknown and unexpected. She wanted to get out of bed but was afraid to make any noise; she caught at her breath, swallowed hard and finally forced herself to speak. She called out:

"Who is it?"—a scarcely articulate croak.

Which brought no answer; the sounds of activity in the kitchen continued: she heard something hard and heavy strike the wooden floor. "Who's there?" she said, louder and clearer.

A moment of silence, then the voice of Jack Burns: "It's me, Jerry. It's Jack. You awake?"

She slid out of bed, gave her hair one quick brush with her hand and went to the door and opened it. There was Jack, grinning wanly at her, blinking in the light; he had his saddlebags on one shoulder, his rifle in his right hand. She stared at him and rubbed her eyes. "Where've you been?" she said. "Were you in jail?"

"I was. In and out. How about—"

"Where's Paul? Is he all right? Has anything happened?"

"Everything's fine. Paul's right where he wants to be. How about makin some coffee? I gotta start off in a few minutes."

"What happened to your face?" she said. "You look awful."

"It's nothin much—just a little trouble."

"But good God, Jack . . ." She hesitated, floundering among her fears and impressions, still not fully awake. "What happened, tell me. Did you break out of jail?"

"You're shiverin," he said; "why don't you put somethin warm on?" She stared at him. "Go ahead—I'll start a fire in the stove and tell you everything that happened. Hurry up; I can't stay long."

She heard his words, became aware then of the chill in the air, of the taut roughness of her skin. She went back in the bedroom and shuffled into her slippers and put a heavy jacket on over her pajamas. When she re-entered the kitchen she found Jack stuffing paper and kindling-wood into the firebox of the stove. "Matches on the shelf," she said, and in a continuation of that reflex act she went to the cupboard and measured four table-spoonfuls of fresh coffee into the coffeepot. Burns lit the paper under the kindling, set several chunks of juniper on top of that and replaced the stove lid; the fire began to crackle and roar. Jerry dipped about four cupfuls of water out of the bucket, then set the pot on the stove; she closed the damper and the fire settled down to a muted, steady rumble. All of this required no more than a few minutes; they worked quickly and without speaking, conscious of the cold and the approaching dawn.

When she had finished Jerry said: "What are you going to do?" She stood close to the stove, catching the first radiations of heat from the old iron. "You did break out, didn't you?"

"Sure," he said, "what else could I do?" He had one foot on a chair, buckling his spurs to his boots.

"Are the police after you now?"

"I hope not. They'll be scramblin around pretty soon, though. There's a good chance they'll be lookin for me right here, too." He stood up and stretched his arms and yawned mightily. "God, it sure is good to be outa that cage!" He relaxed and smiled awkwardly at Jerry—the condition of his face made normal smiling difficult. "How's that coffee comin along?"

"What?" she said. Then: "It'll take a few more minutes."

He picked the saddlebags up from the floor. "I'll go out and saddle up." He opened the back door and looked out into the darkness. "Won't be long," he said; "there's a light blue streak above the mountains now." He could see, through the miles of starlit space, a faint sheen of snow on the crest of the range. Jerry, looking out the doorway over his shoulder, saw the white gleam and shivered again. "Wouldn't wanta be up there now with only my spurs on," Burns said. He grinned at her, lifted the saddlebags to his shoulder, ducked under the top of the doorway and walked out; she watched his thin legs and narrow back retreat in the direction of the corral, fading into the purple night. Feeling cold and desolate, she closed the door, hearing a whinny from the mare at the same time, and went back to the stove and moved the coffeepot to what appeared to be the hottest area on the stove. She stared at the black charred handle of the vessel, at the round lid under it, at the yellow glint of fire visible through the crack between stove lid and center section. She roused herself again, set the skillet on the stove and peeled half a dozen strips of bacon into it. She put another skillet on the stove, poured a little bacon grease into it, and cracked five eggs and let them fry. She tossed the cracked eggshells toward the woodbox and missed; she did not bother to pick them up.

Something has happened, she decided; something terrible has happened.

From outside came the sound of hoofs beating on the hard earth, the soft coaxing voice of Burns, the mare Whisky's answering nicker. Again she heard, as in a dream, the jingle of spurs and the cowboy's steps across the porch.

"Hey, somethin smells mighty good," he said, coming in; he spotted the bacon and eggs on the stove. "Jerry, you're my angel."

"I'm a damned worried angel," she said, setting a plate, knife, fork, two cups, on the table.

"What's wrong?"

"What's wrong? What's right?" The coffee began to perk and bubble; she flipped the eggs over, forked the strips of bacon out of the skillet and onto a doubled-up paper towel. "Sit down," she said. "Soon as you eat I'm going to put something on that massacred face of yours. What on earth happened to you?"

"Is that all that's frettin you?" Burns sat down at the table and gave the plate a spin; he remembered his hat, took it off and set it on the floor beside his chair. "Huh?"

"You men make me sick," she said. "You act like children. Even my son or that mare out there would have better sense. Here you are with your face cut up and running away from the police and there Paul is in the county jail waiting to go to a Federal prison for a year or two. What's the matter with you people?" She dished out the eggs and bacon onto his plate and turned back to the stove to rescue the coffee, already beginning to boil over. "I think you're both crazy, that's all."

"You might be right there," Burns agreed. "Question is—what can you do about it?"

"Don't make me angry," Jerry said; she filled his cup with coffee, then her own. "There's plenty I could do," she added.

Burns gazed sombrely into his black coffee. "Maybe so," he said, "maybe so." The vapor rising from the coffee clouded his face, giving him a temporary intangibility.

Jerry sat down. "What kind of extra trouble is Paul in now?" she asked.

"None that I know of." Burns began to eat. "He helped me get out but there's no call for anybody to learn that."

"What are you going to do now?"

Burns spoke between mouthfuls of bacon and egg. ". . . Up to the mountains. Hide—" He gulped down some of the steaming coffee. "—Hide out maybe a few days. Get some meat, make jerky."

"I can give you some things."

"Can't take canned goods—too heavy, too bulky."

"I baked yesterday. I'll give you some bread."

"That'd be fine, Jerry."

"You say you're going to hide for a few days—what does that mean? What then? Where will you go?"

Burns ate heartily; a touch of egg adorned his beard. "I can go north, west or south. Winter's comin so I guess I'll go south: Chihuahua or maybe Sonora, dependin on how things look."

"What will you do down there?"

"I dunno. Just live, I guess." He swabbed his plate with a piece of bread. "I like Mexico—I have friends there."

"But Jack—" Jerry hesitated. "You'll be back, won't you?"

"Sure. When I'm nothin but a face on the post office wall I'll come a-sneakin back. You'll see me comin down across the mesa out there some evening when things are peaceful."

"Don't talk to me like that. You know you can't go on like this—you're in the Twentieth Century now."

"I don't tune my life to the numbers on a calendar."

"That's ridiculous, Jack. You're a social animal, whether you like it or not. You've got to make some concessions—or they'll hunt you down like a . . . like a . . . What do people hunt down nowadays?"

"Coyotes," Burns said. "With cyanide guns." He finished his coffee and wiped his mouth. "I better get a move on."

Jerry gripped her cup tightly, though it burnt her fingers. "Jack—" she said.

He looked at her over his hand. His lean worn face, beaten and discolored, harsh, asymmetrical, homely as a hound, touched her to the heart. She wanted to reach out to him, laugh and weep for him; instead she forced a smile, saying: "Like some more to eat?"

He stared at her for a long moment before answering. "Thanks, Jerry . . . I've had enough."

"I'll fix you something to take with you."

"That'd be mighty nice of you, Jerry." He pushed back his chair, put on his hat and stood up. "I gotta get goin right away, though."

"Won't take me but a minute." She got up too and started to demonstrate her words. Burns was about to interfere, changed his mind, picked up his rifle and bedroll, and went outside. Jerry finished packing a paper sack with a half loaf of dark bread wrapped in tin foil, with cheese and salami and oranges. She hurried out after him. "Don't run off," she said.

Burns had slipped the rifle into the saddle scabbard and was tying the bedroll on behind the cantle when she came out. "Here," she said, "take this. It's bread."

"Thanks a lot," he said, taking the package and jamming it into the top of the saddlebag. He knotted the last thong, then went to the pump to fill his canteen; she followed him. The air was chill enough to vaporize their exhalations, lending their speech a vague, smoky visibility.

"I want to give you back the money," she said.

Burns unscrewed the cap of the canteen, held it under the spout and began pumping. Jerry picked up a can full of water and poured the water slowly into the top of the pump. "You have to prime this damn thing," she said. Flecks of ice glittered in the starlight.

"I forgot." He pumped the handle up and down and after much groaning and gasping the pump started to give water, splashing over the cowboy's hand and over the canteen.

"I don't need the money, you know. Not really . . ." She turned to go back to the house. "I'll get it."

"I could use the ammunition," he said at last. "And I'll take back half the money." Jerry started toward the porch. "No more," he said after her.

She went inside; Burns walked to his outfit and hung the canteen on the saddlehorn. He waited; the mare snorted and twitched her ears, pawing the ground, eager for the dawn and the ride. He looked to the east: the mountains seemed darker now, the snow almost blue; above the rim the sky was fading in waves of green and yellow, a hint of the sun burning below the horizon. But far in the west the night still held, deep and brilliant with the ice-blue crackling points of light from the stars.

Jerry hurried out of the house toward him, the bandoleer in her hands. "All right, I kept half the money. Now take it."

He accepted the bandoleer without a word.

"I almost forgot," she said. "I want to do something for your face."

"My face is hopeless," he said, trying to grin. "What can you do for it?"

"That broken tooth may give you trouble."

"Broken tooth?"

"You might at least let me wash the blood off your cheek."

"That ain't blood, that's skin. I washed everything off that would come off before I got here."

"Where?"

He smiled painfully. "In an irrigation ditch."

"That's what I thought," she said. "Come on inside; there's warm water on the stove."

He patted the mare on the shoulder and the horse turned nervously and blew some of her foggy breath in his face. "Jerry, I gotta vamoose. Me and Whisky got a long ways to go." Awkwardly he faced the mare. "Ain't that right, girl?" he said, slapping and rubbing the gleaming shoulder.

"Don't start loving up that damned horse in front of me," Jerry said. "Anything else you need?"

Burns put a hand on the pommel, a foot in the stirrup, ready to mount. "No," he said, and stopped to think. "Well I don't have any tobacco. They took it—"

"Wait," she said, "just one more minute!" And shuffled in her slippers as fast as she could back into the kitchen.

"They took it all away from me . . ." Burns concluded, addressing the kitchen door. He surveyed the eastern horizon again, then turned his narrowed and anxious eyes toward the house and past it and looked up the road that led toward the city.

Jerry came out of the kitchen. "Here," she said, a little breathlessly, "here's some of Paul's old pipe tobacco."

"I ain't got a pipe, Jerry," he said softly. "Could you find any cigarette papers?"

"I know, I know," she said. "No, I couldn't find any papers. But here's a pipe he never uses." She gave Burns a handsome briar pipe with a slender stem. "I know he wouldn't miss it," she added, as the cowboy hesitated; "it's one I bought him for his birthday. Please take it, Jack."

"Well . . . okay," he said. "I'm sure obliged to you. To both of you. Just hope this fancy tobacco don't spoil me." He put the pipe and tobacco inside his shirt. "Pockets all fulla junk," he explained sheepishly.

"Jack—"

"Yeah?" Again he prepared to mount, his foot in the stirrup, his back toward her.

"Jack . . ." She stepped forward and touched his shoulder and he faced her again, waiting. "Kiss me," she said.

"I want to," he said. But he made no move. "I want to."

"What are you afraid of?"

"I don't know. Nothin, I guess." He reached out then and embraced her and kissed her gently and quickly on the lips. "What I'm afraid of," he said slowly, "is me. That's all."

"We're both afraid of the same thing, then," Jerry said. She smiled at him while her vision dimmed. "You'd better go," she managed to say.

"What's so funny?" He returned her smile with a stiff, uncertain grin.

"You'd better go, Jack."

"Yes," he said. "I know." He released her and turned and pulled himself up, a little wearily, into the saddle. He adjusted the bandoleer on his back, tugged at the forebrim of his hat.

"Goodby, Jack."

"Goodby, kid," he said. "Say goodby to the boy for me." He touched Whisky with the reins and she turned, facing the mountains. "Take care of your old man," he said. "When I come back I wanta see you both out here." The mare pranced and whinnied and shook her head, impatient, indignant, eager for flight.

"Yes," Jerry said. "I hope so. God, I hope so."

"I'll see you in a year or so. Maybe sooner."

"Yes," she said; she shivered in the keen air, blinking the mist out of her eyes. "Be careful, Jack."

"Adios," he said, and flicked the mare with the leather, and at once she began to trot, then canter, away from the house and corral and toward the mountains. Burns reined in a little and slowed her to a brisk trot. Jerry, watching, saw him turn in the saddle and wave back at her. Weakly she pulled one hand out of a jacket pocket and held it up for him to see, but he had already turned and straightened and was facing the east.

She stood in the bleak gray light, huddled and cold in the jacket and her pajamas, and watched Jack Burns ride away: she saw him cross the embankment by the big irrigation ditch and disappear for several minutes and heard or thought she heard the rattling dance of Whisky's iron shoes across the wooden bridge; she saw horse and rider reappear on the higher ground beyond the ditch, figures already greatly diminished by the perspective of distance; she saw them slowly mount the rise to the edge of the mesa and there, where she knew there was a fence although now it could not be seen—the light obscure and shifting—she saw the cowboy dismount and work at something in front of the horse, then remount and ride on; she saw them, the man and his horse, fade, melt, diminish by subtle gradations of light and dimension into that vast open expanse of stone and sand and space that swept on, mile after mile after mile, toward the dark mountains.

From a cottonwood tree near the ditch came the whirring call of a grouse hen, the cawing of approaching crows. Jerry shivered, urged her cold aching limbs into motion and returned to the kitchen. She had water to carry, she remembered, a breakfast to make ready for her son, lunches to pack, dishes to wash, a job in the city at nine o'clock—no end of things to do. . . .

Fire on the
Mountain

(1962)

The sun was hanging close to the shoulder of the mountain when Lee and I regained the old wagon road and measured its final few switchbacks up to the bench of level ground where the corral and cabin stood. We saw the sorrel stallion, barebacked and glossy, staked out in the little dry park in front of the corral. A thread of smoke dangled over the cabin chimney and Grandfather himself, when he heard our horses, appeared in the open doorway.

"Evening," he said. "I thought you boys would show about now. I got three cans of beans and a panful of corned beef warming up on the stove."

"That'll do for a start," Lee said.

We dismounted and unsaddled our horses. I was tired. In fact the saddle, as I lugged it to the corral fence, seemed to weigh approximately five hundred pounds.

"You can just turn old Blue loose, Billy," Grandfather said. "He'll stick close to Rocky. You might brush him down a little."

Lee picketed his horse. We curried our animals with juniper twigs and then went into the cabin, following the scent of food. The inside of the cabin was neat and clean, furnished with an iron cot, a table and chairs, a cupboard full of canned goods, a kerosene lamp, and other supplies, including a sack of grain suspended on baling wire from the rafters to make life more difficult for the mice. A pot of coffee simmered on the stove.

"That smells good," Lee said.

"Ain't quite ready yet," the old man said, stirring the corned

16

beef with a fork. He handed me the empty water bucket. "Billy, would you mind filling that? We'll be ready to eat as soon as you get back."

"Yes sir." I swallowed my disappointment, took the bucket, left the cabin and walked along the footpath toward the spring at the head of the ravine. The path led downward along the base of a cliff, winding among boulders big as boxcars and under tall stately yellow pines, until it reached a sort of glen or grotto in a deep fold of the mountainside. The air felt cool, the light was green and filtered down in there—I thought of the lion. I knelt by the sandy basin of the spring and drank from my cupped hands before filling the pail. The glen was very quiet; I could hear no breeze, no bird cries, no sound at all except the gentle purr of the water as it glided over moss-covered rocks and sank out of sight into the mud and weeds below the spring.

I returned to the cabin, the bucket of water pulling down my arm and shoulder. Grandfather was dishing out the food into tin plates and pouring the coffee. Lee stood near the corral, feeding grain to the horses.

"Come and get it!" Grandfather shouted. To me he said, "Put the water on the stove, Billy, and bring your plate outside. Too hot to eat in here."

The three of us sat on the grass against the cabin wall, in the shade, and faced the sunlit world below. We were silent for a while and too busy to admire the spectacular view, eating what I thought was probably the best meal I had ever had in my life. Later, after second helpings all around, full and comforted, we set our plates aside and began to talk and look at things again.

"How could I forget my cigars."

"Have a tailormade," Lee said, offering a cigarette to the old man.

Grandfather examined the cigarette. "They say women enjoy these things."

"That's right," Lee said, "and I enjoy women." He offered his pack to me. "Cigarette, Billy?"

I hesitated. I wasn't allowed to smoke, of course. Besides, I preferred the corncob pipe I had hidden in my suitcase back at the ranch-house.

"Put them back," Grandfather said. "Don't give the boy one of those."

"Why not?"

"It's a filthy, evil, despicable habit, a disgrace to the human race." Grandfather lit his cigarette and took a deep drag. "He's too young. Put them back."

They smoked. I pulled a stem of grass and chewed on it and looked. There was much to look at from where we sat. With the great mountain at our backs, we had a full and open view to the north, east and south—one-half the known world. I could see four different mountain systems, not counting the one holding me up, the lights of two cities, and about seven thousand square miles of the desert in between. I saw the San Andres Mountains rolling north, the Sacramento Mountains beyond Alamogordo forty miles away to the northeast, the Guadalupe Mountains some eighty miles due east and the Organ Mountains and the hazy smudge of El Paso far to the south, with the deserts of Chihuahua spreading toward infinity beyond.

The sun dropped lower. We watched the shadow of Thieves' Peak creep across the plain toward Grandfather Vogelin's ranch, toward the village of Baker, toward the Guadalupe Mountains, reaching out to meet the curtain of darkness coming toward us from the east.

"Grandfather?"

"Yes?"

"Did you ever climb that mountain?"

"What mountain?"

"The one above us. Thieves' Mountain."

"No, can't say I did. And I never will. This cabin here's high enough for me. About as close to Heaven as I ever want to get. You can bury me here."

"We'll need dynamite for that," Lee said.

"Here Lies John Vogelin: Born Forty Years Too Late, Died Forty Years Too Soon," Grandfather said.

"Why forty years too soon?"

"I figure in forty years civilization will collapse and everything will be back to normal. I wish I could live to see it."

"Why? You'd be right back where you started from."

"I'd like that. That's the place to end up."

"Don't you want to get ahead?" Lee grinned at me.

"I'd rather stay behind. I already got a head."

"You already got a behind, where your head ought to be."

"Don't confuse me. It took me seventy years to figure this much out. Who's going to water the horses?"

Nobody spoke. I stared out at the approaching union of light and dark. Lee and Grandfather stared at me.

"Okay," Grandfather said, "we'll try again: who's going to wash the dishes?"

"I'll water the horses," I said.

"Fine. If you start right away you'll still have time to wash the dishes."

"I'll light the lamp for you," Lee said, "when you're through watering the horses. So you don't have to wash the dishes in the dark."

"Thanks," I said. "But us real cowboys always wash our dishes in the sand."

Lee was silent.

"Lee, you lose," Grandfather said. "You wash the dishes. The boy's whipped you again. Billy, you'll find another old bucket inside the corral."

"Why can't I just take the horses down to the spring?"

"That boy asks a lot of questions," Lee said.

They stared at me hopefully.

"All right," I said, "why not? That's all I asked. Wouldn't it be easier to take the horses to the spring than to carry the water back here to the horses?"

"A bucket of water is lighter than a horse," Lee pointed out.

"The horses can walk," I said.

"But they're tired."

"Will you please answer my question?"

The old man smiled and patted my knee. "You're right, Billy, it should be easier to do it your way. But the horses don't like it down in there. And the trail is too tight for all three at once; you'd have a rough time. And besides, think what a mess three big horses, full of water and grass and grain, would make of one little spring which is barely big enough to dip a pail into. We drink out of that spring too."

"I guess you're right, Grandfather. I should've thought of that." I stood up.

"Someday we'll cover the spring, run a pipe from it down to a water trough the horses can get to."

"How long have you been using this place?" Lee asked, winking at me. "How many years, John?"

"You shut up and wash your dishes."

I walked to the corral, found the bucket and started down the path to the spring. Lee and the old man rose to their feet, stretching. "We'll give you a hand, Billy," Grandfather said, "as soon as we clean up."

"Yes sir."

The twilight was moving in. I had to go carefully to find my way, for the trail seemed awfully vague in the deep shadows under the cliff. When I reached the spring the tree toads were bleating, a dismal noise and a sure sign of night. There was no other sound, except the murmur of the flowing water. A few fireflies twinkled in the gloom above the weeds.

The long day in the desert sun had drawn a lot of water from my body. I was thirsty again. I squatted close to the spring, scooped up a double handful of water and drank. I dipped up more and bathed my face.

When the last tinkle of falling drops had died away I became aware of a deep and unexpected silence. The toads had gone silent and the water seemed to run more quietly than before. Even the fireflies had disappeared. I waited for a moment, listening to the silence, then reached cautiously for the bucket and dipped it into the water as quietly as I could, afraid to make too much noise. Looking around in all directions I could see nothing, nothing but the damp weeds, the wall of rock, the grand trunks of the yellow pines, the dusky woods. I looked up.

I should not have looked up. On the brink of the crag above

the spring I saw a pair of large eyes gleaming in a sleek head, saw a dark powerful shape of unforeseeable hugeness crouched as if to leap. I could not move, I could not make a sound. I stared up at the lion and the lion stared down at me. Paralyzed, I squatted by the spring, gripping the water bucket, unconscious of the ache in my muscles, and waited for death to fall upon me.

My grandfather called through the silence, from the far-away cabin out of sight and out of reach beyond the twilight: "Billy?"

I tried to answer but my throat was numb. The lion watched me.

My grandfather called again: "Billy? Where are you?"

This time the lion turned its massive head and with yellow, luminous eyes looked blandly, without curiosity or fear, up the pathway.

I heard the old man's boots scraping on the stones of the path, coming toward me, and at last the big cat stirred itself and rose and vanished, all at once, suddenly, with uncanny grace and stillness, into the night and the forest.

Grandfather called me for the third time, coming closer, and now I thought I could answer. "Here," I croaked. "I'm here." I managed to stand up, the heavy bucket frozen in my grip. As the old man came toward me down the path I took a few leaden steps to meet him.

He stared at my face. "What happened to you?"

I told him.

He put one arm around my shaking shoulders and with his other hand unwrapped my fingers one by one from the handle of the water bucket. Carrying the water himself, he led me up the pathway among the boulders to the cabin where Lee waited for us in the welcome glow of the lamp.

"What's wrong?" Lee said, wiping a tin plate with a bandana.

"He saw it."

"Saw what?"

"The lion."

"Ah . . ." said Lee. He looked at me and smiled, his deep eyes tender. "You're a lucky boy." He gripped my arm. "How about a cup of your grampaw's coffee?"

"Yes," I said calmly. "I can drink anything."

A little later all three of us went back to the spring, with both buckets, and looked around. Lee even climbed up to the ledge above the spring but by that time it was too dark to see any tracks. We went back up the trail, watered the horses, built a little squaw fire outside between the cabin and the corral, and unrolled the sleeping bags which the old man kept in the cabin. We sat around the fire for a while after that, watching the moon over the eastern ranges, and talked of the lion, the lost horse, the next day's work, in which Lee announced he would not be able to join—he was leaving us in the morning. But he promised to come back to the ranch in two or three days.

"What does a mountain lion sound like?" I asked.

"Well," Grandfather said, "like a woman. Like a woman screaming. How would you describe it, Lee?"

Lee considered. "Compadres, a lion does sound something like a woman. Like a vampire-woman wailing for her demon lover."

"Are we going to hunt the lion, Grandfather?"

"No, we'll let well enough alone. If we don't hunt him why he won't hunt us. Besides, it's the only lion left on the place. I can't afford to lose him."

"Do you think he's watching us now?"

"I wouldn't be surprised."

Nobody said anything for a minute or so. The moon crept up into the stars. I added more sticks to the fire.

Grandfather stretched his arms and yawned. "I don't know about you fellas but I am tired. Anybody want to sleep on the cot inside?"

Lee grinned. "Is there room for all three of us?"

"Not with me in the middle there ain't."

"Then let's all sleep out here."

"By the fire," I said.

"You boys do that," Grandfather said, "but somebody might as well use that cot. I've been sleeping on the ground for about seventy years now, give or take a few."

"You ought to be used to it," Lee said.

"I'm used to it. But I never did like it much." Picking up his bedroll, the old man walked toward the cabin door. "Goodnight, gentlemen."

"Goodnight," we said.

Lee and I shook the scorpions and black widow spiders out of the sleeping bags, spread them on the ground close to the fire, removed our boots and hats and crawled inside. We did not use our saddles for pillows. A saddle is hard enough just to sit on.

At first I lay on my side, gazing at the coals of the burning pine. Then I lay on my back and stared straight up at the stars. The flaming blue stars. Out in the little park the horses stumbled around, munching grass, and I heard one of them staling on the hard ground. A meteor stroked quietly across the sky.

"Lee?"

"Yes?"

"Up there on the peak: Was it—something like the lion?"

He did not answer at once. "Would you mind repeating that question?"

"What you found up there—was it something like the lion?"

"Oh. Yes. Yes, Billy. It was something like the lion."

I thought about that as I looked straight up at the stars. The marvelous stars. A marvelous day. The stars became dimmer as I watched them, as if they were drifting farther and farther away from us. I closed my eyes and slept and dreamed of the missing pony, fireflies, a pair of yellow burning eyes. . . .

FROM

Desert Solitaire

(1968)

Cowboys

June in the desert. The sun roars down from its track in space with a savage and holy light, a fantastic music in the mind. Up in the mountains the snow has receded to timberline—Old Tukuhnikivats and the other peaks take on a soft spring green along their flanks; the aspen is leafing out. The roads up into the meadows and forests are open again and all the Moab cattlemen who hold grazing permits up there (and some who don't) are moving their stock out of the desert and into the national forest, where the animals will stay until September and the return of the snow.

Springtime on the mountains. Summer down here.

Yesterday I helped Roy Scobie clear his cows out of Courthouse Wash, which runs mostly to the west of the park and through the south end of it. We started early, about six, after a hot breakfast in the morning twilight. Three of us—Roy, his Basque hired man Viviano Jacquez, myself.

Roy is a leather-hided, long-connected, sober-sided old man with gray hair, red nose and yellow teeth; he is kind, gentle, well-meaning, but worries too much, takes things too seriously. For instance, he's afraid of having a heart attack, falling off the horse, dying there on the sand, under the sun, among the flies and weeds and indifferent cattle. I'm not inferring this—he told me so.

What could I say? I was still young myself, or thought I was, enjoying good health, not yet quite to the beginning of the middle of the journey. I listened gravely as he spoke of death, nod-

26

ding in an agreement I did not feel. His long yellow fingers, holding a cigarette, trembled.

Roy's no Mormon and not much of a Christian, and does not honestly believe in an afterlife. Yet the manner of death he fears does not sound bad to me; to me it seems like a decent, clean way of taking off, surely better than the slow rot in a hospital oxygen tent with rubber tubes stuck up your bodily orifices, with blood transfusions and intravenous feeding, bedsores and bedpans and bad-tempered nurses' aides—the whole nasty routine to which most dying men, in our time, are condemned.

But how could I tell him so? What did I know of it? To me death was little more than a fascinating abstraction, the conclusion to a syllogism or the denouement of a stage drama. What do old men who don't believe in Heaven think about? I used to wonder. Now we know: they think about their blood pressure, their bladders, their aortas, their lower intestines, ice on the doorstep, too much sun at noon. But so do the others.

I met Roy and Viviano at a place called Willow Seep near the upper end of Courthouse Wash and there we began the drive. We were only about ten miles from the stockpens near Moab, but would have to check out all the side canyons along the way.

We unloaded the horses from Roy's truck, gave them each a little grain, saddled up, and moved out with the old man in the middle. A fine morning—a sweet cool stark sunlit silent desert morning—before the heat moved in and the deerflies, the sweat, the dust and the thirst came down on us.

Not far down the canyon we found the first small bunch of cows and calves. They saw us coming and trotted off in various directions through the brush, making things more difficult than was really necessary. In the cool of the morning they were feeling lively; also, not having seen a man or a horse all winter, they were half-wild. The little calves had never seen *anything* like us and were, understandably, terrified.

We collected them all after a time and got them moving together down the wash, pushing them steadily but not fast. Only half the cows wore Roy's brand and earmarks but in accordance with custom we herded everything we found toward Moab; the other ranchers would do the same and in the stockpens each man would sort out his own property from the rest. Any cow without a brand—"slick"—belonged to the finder. (Many a famous cattle outfit had been started with no more than a rope and a good horse.) Cooperation is necessary because in this part of Utah there are not many fences. The cattle wander far over the open range, driven by hunger and thirst, and forget who they belong to. Why no fences? Because in much of the canyon country there is no ground to dig postholes in—nothing but solid rock.

Old Roy had something on his mind. When the sun burst out above the canyon rim, flaring like a white scream, and its hot breath burned my neck, I knew what he was thinking about.

The cattle plodded before us, slowing down as the heat rose, reluctant to keep moving. When they stopped we yelled and whistled at them, beat their gaunt hipbones with our bridle reins, kicked them in the ribs. They jogged ahead, half-trotting, and the green dung streamed down their legs. Ugly brutes, bound for a summer in the high meadows and then the slaughter house—too bloody good for them, I was thinking.

Side canyons appeared. Viviano took one, I took the other, while Roy stayed with the bunch we already had. The canyon I faced was choked with brush, impossible to ride through; the prickly pear grew knee-high in great clumps hairy with spines, scrub oak obstructed the path, the branches of juniper and pinyon pine struck at my face, knocked my hat off. I had to tie the horse and go in on foot. The heavy air was swarming with flies and the numerous trails in the thickets were well beaten and dusty, strewn with cow droppings. Real cattle country all right. I picked up a club, went on, stooping under the tangle. The canyon was short and boxed in and at the head was a cow and her calf; I drove them out and back to the main canyon. I was glad to get on my horse and rejoin Viviano and Roy.

Viviano was happy that morning. He sang and whistled continually, winked and grinned when he caught my eye and charged after straying cattle like a maniac, spurring his thin-skinned palomino through the brush, up over rocks, down mud-banks and between trees with what looked to me like complete indifference to life and limb, the vulnerability of the flesh. Not showing off, for I'd seen his exhibitions of recklessness at other times, but simply out of high spirits, for the fun and the hell of it.

Viviano Jacquez, born in the Pyrenees somewhere (he never cared to tell me more), had been imported with his parents into Utah to herd sheep for some congressman's favorite constituent, then drifted from job to job until he came to Roy Scobie's combination dude and cattle ranch. He's a good cowboy, I suppose; at least he knows the basic skills of the trade: can shoe a horse, rope and brand and castrate a calf, fix a flat tire, stretch barbed wire, dynamite a beaver dam or lay out an irrigation ditch. His English is about fifty percent profanity, rough but intelligible, and he can sing, play the guitar, and read your fortune in the cards, the rewards of what I would call his liberal education. He is short, dark and savage, like most good Basques, with large brown glamorous eyes that seem to appeal to the ladies; from thirteen to thirty-five he pursues them all, and if I can believe his lies, makes out with every one.

What else about him? This: he does not understand American clock time and has no sense of responsibility; he is completely and dependably totally unreliable. But, in his favor, he is inexpensive; he is economical; he works full-time seven days a week for room and board and a hundred dollars a month. Employers like that; but it would be false to say that Viviano is exploited. How can you exploit a man who enjoys his work? He'll work for nothing, almost, if necessary, requiring only a token wage or salary in recognition of his professional status.

Not that he never bitches and grumbles. When he isn't singing or whistling or telling lies in some woman's ear he complains loud and bitterly about his pay, the long hours, the lousy food, the skunks under the bunkhouse, the treacherous and conniving women, the stupid dudes. He threatens to quit, gets drunk and disappears for a couple of days. But always comes back. Or has so far.

Poor Viviano with so much to his credit has one problem which he'll never be able to outlive. Two or three beers and he reveals it to me. He has been infected by the poison of prejudice. Infected and victimized. With his dark skin and Spanish accent he is often taken for a Mexican, which he resents, because he despises Mexicans. He also despises Indians. Even his own heritage: "dumb Basko" he once called himself. Inadvertently when drunk he exposes the wistful desire to somehow disappear and merge into the pale-faced millions who own and operate America.

Useless to try and reassure him that he has more to lose than gain by such assimilation; somewhere, in a way we all know, his pride was damaged and his confidence shaken. In our occasional rambles through the beer halls of Moab I have not seen him rebuffed in any way; but he may be alert to signals of rejection too subtle for me. In any case, at one time or another, perhaps unknown even to Viviano himself, the damage was done. And his reaction is the typical one; he responds to prejudice by cultivating a prejudice of his own against those whom he feels are even lower in the American hierarchy than he is: against the Indians, the Mexicans, the Negroes. He knows where the bottom is.

Too late to make a liberal out of Viviano Jacquez.

The sun climbed noon-high, the heat grew thick and heavy on our brains, the dust clouded our eyes and mixed with our sweat—Viviano's white teeth gleam through a kind of pancake makeup of sweat and dirt when he laughs at me or at the hard-mouth beast I'm riding. The cows groan against the forced migration as if they know where it will eventually bring them. I think of the second movement from Beethoven's Eroica. *Marcia funebre.* My canteen is nearly empty and I'm afraid to drink what little water is left—there may never be any more. I'd like to cave in for a while, crawl under yonder cottonwood and die peacefully in the shade, drinking dust. . . . I look aside covertly under my hat brim at old man Scobie who thinks he is going to have a heart attack and fall off his horse: he rides steadily forward, eyes sad and thoughtful, watching the green rumps of his cattle, cigarette hanging from his lower lip, flicking the reins casually back and forth across the mane of his equally thoughtful, abstracted horse. Lunchtime maybe? I think, glancing at the sun. But nobody says anything about lunch.

Some of the cows bunched up in the shade under an overhang in the canyon wall. They refused to move. Their calves stumbled close to them, bawling piteously. The drive was starting to drag. Have mercy on us all, I thought. But Viviano like a sun-crazed madman rode savagely into the cattle, screaming and whistling, lashing at the cows with a length of rope. "Crazy son of my bitches," he was screaming, "let's pick up the feet!"

Roy raised a hand. "That's all right, Viviano," he said, "we'll take a break now. Don't want to run them little beeves right into the ground."

Good man, I thought, heading at once for the nearest shade, where I tied my horse to a log, unsaddled, and dropped. I was too hot and tired at first even to care about food or water. Viviano and Roy joined me, unhurried, lay down in the shade nearby and lit up cigarettes. Above us was the green canopy of the cottonwood tree filtering the light to a tolerable dimness. A few red ants crawled over my belly; I didn't care. *Tengo sed,* I said to myself. I finished my water. But appeasing thirst brought back hunger. Who brought the lunch? I began to worry, realizing for the first time that no one had said a word about it yet. I didn't say anything either. But I was worried.

"I'm worried," old Roy said.

Tengo mucho hambre, hombre—I'm worried too. How did it go in that other language? *Faim? J'ai faim? Je suis famine?* I looked toward Viviano. He was already asleep, the fancy twenty dollar Stetson over his eyes, a pair of flies circling above his open mouth. For a hatband he wore a sterling silver chain—in the mouth a golden tooth. The goddamned lady killer.

"You know what happened to Ernie Faye?" Roy said, evidently addressing me though he was staring up at the leaves.

"No," I said; "what happened to him?"

"You wouldn't know him; this happened three years ago." Roy paused. "He was picking peaches one day in his own backyard, taking it easy, and he had a stroke. When his wife went out to look for him he was on the ground on top of a bushel basket and he was dead. A big strong man, too. Sixty-six years old. That's for a fact."

"It happens. Did you bring any lunch, Roy?"

"Lunch?" He continued to stare at nothing. Thinking. Worrying. "Sixty-six years old," he said.

"It happens. But only once."

"Once is enough."

"Did you bring any lunch?"

"Lunch?" At last he turned his head to look at me. "Well no, I didn't. You hungry?"

"A little bit, now that you mention it."

"Sorry we didn't bring anything. We'll eat good when we get back."

"That's all right," I said. "I'll survive, maybe."

But Roy had lost interest in the subject. He wasn't listening to me. The vacant look was in his eyes as he resumed the study of his problem. After a while he let his head drop back against his saddle and closed his eyes. The red nose, the gray hair, the yellow teeth and fingers, a white stubble of whiskers on his bony jaw, his leathery flat cheeks—he looked like an old horse all right but still tough and viable. He was only about seventy years old.

Old Roy is a good man in most ways, but he has his troubles. I'd been spending some of my days off at his ranch, doing a little work around the place in return for room and board. (There's a girl there, one of the paying guests.) I was sharing a bunkhouse room with Viviano one night when I heard the shuffling of feet, the sound of a mumbling voice. It was very late; Viviano was sound asleep. I got up and stepped outside and saw Roy walking by in his long underwear and boots, a revolver in his hand, talking to himself. What's up? I asked him. Insomnia, he said. I said, Try getting a little sleep. I tried, he said, and I can't. What's the gun for? Skunks, he said—they been at the chickens again.

Well they're no chickens here, I said. No but there's skunks and they're living right under that room where you're sleeping. And he walked away, unhappy and preoccupied.

He has troubles, God knows. He fights with his wife—third or fourth wife—and has difficulties with the bank, with his horses, with his hired help, with the ranch machinery. Mortgaged over his head, he tries to economize by getting by with old trucks and a second-hand tractor, and by hiring cheap and irresponsible help like me and Viviano. He thinks he is saving money by always paying Viviano one month late. Worst of all he skimps on food.

His pack trips are notorious for their frugality. He does the cooking, of course, so that someone else is morally obliged to wash the dishes, and so that he can control the consumption of supplies. "One egg or two?" he'll ask at breakfast time, when you are hungry enough to eat the skin off a bear. Slowly, his old yellow hands shaking, he shovels two little Grade C eggs onto your plate. Then he says, "You want any bacon with that?"

He tries to justify his miserliness with food by pretending that he is observing some time-honored Western tradition. "It's a fact," he will claim, "them old timers never ate much when they was out working on the range. A man rides better on a hard stomach. It's a fact. But we'll eat good when we get back."

The lying old bastard. He hopes that by starving his employees they won't live long enough to collect their wages. The paying guests don't fare much better and as a result seldom come back for a second season at Roy Scobie's Redrock Ranch. It's a beautiful ranch and his pack trips take them into an unknown world—but they don't often return. As a small businessman Roy is getting smaller every season. Bankruptcy and heart attacks loom ahead.

I've endeavored to warn him. He is interested in my opinion and listens at first with some care. Then his attention wanders. The habits of a lifetime are impossible to break. When we bed down at night, out in the open, he always looks for a slab of sandstone to spread his bedroll on. "Rock is softer than sand," he explains. "That's for a fact." His words trail off into the vague mumble, "Slept on rock all my life, goddamnit. . . ." The empty stare follows: a foolish thrift is driving him to ruin and all he cares about is his heart; he is thinking about falling off his horse again like Ernie Faye fell off the ladder picking peaches. Dead on the rock.

I can help him with that question, too, I sometimes think; I have a supply of classic philosophical lore ready to offer at the slightest provocation. Our life on earth is but the shadow of a higher life, I could tell him. Or, Life is but a dream. Or, Who wants to live forever? Vanity, vanity. Recall Sophocles, Roy: Lucky are those who die in infancy but best of all is never to have been born. You know.

All kinds of ideas spring to mind but an instinctive prudence makes me hold my tongue. What right have I to interfere with an old man's antideath wish? He knows what he's doing; let him savor it to the full. He'll never have another chance as good as this. Each man in his humor. Every cobbler gets clobbered at last, etc. Let him shamble through the dark at night in his underwear, looking for the black skunk with the white stripe down its back, the ultimate enemy.

The weird silence woke me up. I looked around. Everything seemed to be withering in the heat, blasted and shrunken under the furnace of the sun. I dreamed of water and wondered if it would be worth the effort to dig a hole through the ceramic mud of the canyon floor. While I debated the matter in my head, Roy opened his eyes, staggered up, glanced blearily at me to see that I was awake, nudged Viviano in the ribs with the toe of his boot. "Let's get on, boys," he said.

We saddled our horses and got on. On with the death march, *marcia funebre*, the stations of the cross, *el jornado del muerto*. The cows faced us stubbornly, their red eyes full of hatred. The poor little white-faced calves trembled on their shaky legs, hides coated with dust, hind-ends crusted with sunbaked excrement. *Miserere.*

Roy moved his horse stolidly against them, implacable. Viviano, undaunted by the heat and still showing off, sprang on his horse—yes, literally vaulted into the saddle—and rode yelling and flailing and whistling into the herd. (One leap and he was in the saddle; five beers and he was on the floor.) I climbed onto my horse like a man dragging himself through a bad dream, got both feet in the stirrups and rode after the others. After a few minutes of milling struggle the weary beasts gave up and headed down the canyon, moving in the right direction toward their fate.

Not that their fate was so terrible: a summer in the high mountain meadows eating flowers, far above the heat and hay fever of the desert; I envied them. The cows would live to breed again, those that didn't eat too much larkspur; the new crop of calves had a life expectancy of at least one full year; only the yearling steers would be shipped off in the fall to meet the hook and the hammer. I nursed my sympathies, saving them chiefly for myself, who could better appreciate them and deserved them more—hungry, tired, dirty and thirsty as I was.

More side canyons came into view—Two-Mile, Sleepy Hollow, and others without names—and we had to separate, explore each one in search of the outlaws and the fugitives, drive them out of the thickets where they were shaded up and add them to the herd.

There is water in Sleepy Hollow, a big pool under a seep in the canyon wall, fenced off from the cows. We paused for a few minutes to drink and refill canteens, then moved on. No time for a swim today. The drive continued.

As the herd became bigger the dust and the heat got worse. The cattle complained but we were merciless. One old cow, followed by her calf, slipped aside into the tamarisk and lay down. Since she was on my flank of the drive I had to get her out. Again I had to dismount and go in on foot, fighting my way through the brush and clouds of gnats and the vicious yellow-backed flies. The cow didn't want to get up; she preferred the shade. I beat her with the club, kicked her in the ribs, yanked at her tail. At last, groaning and farting with exaggerated self-pity, she hoisted her rear end, then her front end, and plodded off to rejoin the gang. When I got back to my horse I was too tired to climb immediately into the saddle; it seemed easier for a while to walk and lead the horse.

Second movement, seventh symphony, Beethoven again—the slow, ponderous dirge. Had the sun moved at all? Not that I could tell. But as I came up with the others, Viviano, grinning through his dusty face, yelled at me:

"Around the bend, only nine son of bitch more, we get the Jesus Christ out of here."

"Good," I said but something in my face must have given me away; Viviano laughed, spurred his horse and dashed off singing.

I parked my beast for a minute close to a mudbank and hauled myself onto the saddle the easy way. But dropped the reins and nearly fell off retrieving them. Recovered. Both feet in stirrups, I took a few gulps of water and proceeded.

Puddles of quicksand lay ahead of us. We drove the herd around to the side but one cow, stubborn and stupid, managed to get into the stuff. Deliberately, I was sure. The sand quivered like jelly beneath the cow's hooves, broke open, sucked at the plunging feet. Panicked, the cow struggled through, splashing mud and sand. Safe. As we went on I looked back and saw the holes the cow had made fill up and brim over with water, like suppurating sores.

More quicksand. This time we weren't so lucky. The pool extended clear across the canyon floor from one sheer wall to the other. We rushed the herd through but one cow, the same one as before, got herself bogged down. Really trapped this time. Belly-deep in the soup, willing to give up, she neither struggled nor bellowed. This cow didn't want to fight anything anymore.

The sun beat down on our backs and the sweat trickled into our eyes. Roy and Viviano discussed the situation briefly; we went to work. Keeping their mounts clear of the quicksand, they each tossed a loop over the cow's head, drew the knot firm around her neck, taking in the slack, and dallied each rope to the horns of their saddles. As the ropes tautened and the horses prepared to pull, I slogged into the mud and tugged at the cow's tail to give her hindquarters whatever lift I could.

We were ready. Roy and Viviano urged their horses forward; the horses squatted, braced, heaved; the ropes squeaked under the strain. For a moment nothing seemed to be happening. Then something was happening. Like a cork from a bottle the cow was being drawn from the suction of the quicksand. She struggled feebly, the horses swung ahead, the mud made a violent raw gasping noise, exploded, and out she came.

Roy and Viviano stopped and gave me some slack; I removed the ropes from the cow's neck as she stood trembling on firm ground. Her eyeballs protruded like a pair of onion bulbs; the tongue, purple in hue and coated with scum, hung loosely from the side of her mouth like a rag of spoiled meat. It was the longest tongue I had ever seen outside of a butcher's shop.

"Seventy dollars worth of cow," Roy explained, coiling his rope. "A fact. Couldn't hardly afford to leave it there."

The cow had still not moved. Viviano rode up and lashed it across the rump. "Heeyah!" he shouted, "lez go man, Jesus Christ!" The cow stumbled toward the herd, Viviano pressing it hard. "Heeyah! goddamn!" Whacking it across the rear with his heavy, wet rope. "Goddamn son of bitch cow!"

The herd began to move, the choking dust filled the air. I climbed on my horse, loading the poor brute down not only with my own weight but with two bootfuls of mud and water.

An hour later we descended the jump-off, a stairway of stone ledges in the canyon floor where trickles of water oozed down over mats of algae, through slick sculptured grooves and into the sandy basins below. The cattle clattered and skidded on the bare rock; sparks flew from the iron-shod hooves of the horses. Lagging behind, I stopped to admire a tiny spring bubbling out of the the sand above the ledges, well off to one side of the trail. The water was so clear, so perfectly transparent, that only the dance of grains of sand in the bottom of the spring, where the flow came up through a fissure in the rock, revealed that it was under pressure and in motion. I took a quick drink—cool and sweet—and rode on through the blessed shade of the canyon walls; the sun had finally dropped below the rim. Life began to seem plausible again after an afternoon of doubt.

We went on for another mile and emerged abruptly and to me unexpectedly into full day again, the glare of the sun and the scalding heat. We were in the mouth of the canyon. Ahead lay the highway, the Colorado River, the outskirts of Moab. We pushed the cattle on over the bridge, across the cement and asphalt, and into the big corrals in the fields beyond. We unsaddled the horses and brushed them and turned them loose in the pasture. Free at last, frolicking like colts, they galloped after one another in circles, lay down and rolled in the dust, got up and galloped some more. I knew how they felt.

Roy's truck was parked near the stockpens. We adjourned the field for a pitcher of beer in Moab. It was, of course, only the usual Mormon 3.2—for which may God forgive them—but never had beer tasted better, or been drunk by more deserving men. Old Roy treated us each to a bag of peanuts and talked a little about tomorrow's work: trucking the cattle up to his allotment on the southern slope of Tukuhnikivats. A tedious job in which I would not participate—back to the Arches for me, I reminded him. Roy's expression saddened; he would have to hire someone to take my place for the day, someone who would probably expect to be paid in United States hard dollars. He looked away and into the emptiness, thinking again; the smoke from his forgotten cigarette rose slowly into the haze beneath the ceiling.

Stop that, I wanted to tell him. *Stop that thinking.* I wanted to put my arm around his old shoulders and stroke his thin gray hair and tell him the truth about everything, the entire wild beautiful utterly useless truth. But I didn't.

Viviano ordered a second pitcher of beer, got up suddenly from his chair, tripped over my outstretched legs and fell flat on the floor. He pulled himself slowly to his feet and scowled about through the gloom to see if anyone had noticed; nobody had. Nobody could have cared less. I should have apologized and helped him get up but I didn't. He tramped bitterly, soggily, toward the men's room and disappeared in a dim, rancid, yellowish light. He was a cowboy, *muy macho, mucho hombre.* Very sensitive.

*   *   *

Years later, still wandering in circles, I will come back to the Arches and the canyon country and inquire about my old acquaintances. Where are they? I will ask and the people will say to me:

Viviano Jacquez? You mean that little Mexican that worked for Roy Scobie? Well, who knows? Some say he went to Ouray, Colorado, to work in a silver mine; some say he married Scobie's cook, that white girl from Oklahoma, and they went to California; some say he went back to sheepherding; some say he went to Spain.

And old Roy? You didn't hear? Well he had to sell out a couple years after you left. He went down to Arizona and started an Indian jewelry store near Sedona. He's dead now. He was hanging a picture on the wall of his store and had a heart attack. He was standing on a chair at the time.

The Moon-Eyed Horse

When we reached Salt Creek we stopped to water the horses. I needed a drink myself but the water here would make a man sick. We'd find good water farther up the canyon at Cigarette Spring.

While Mackie indulged himself in a smoke I looked at the scenery, staring out from under the shelter of my hat brim. The glare was hard on the eyes and for relief I looked down, past the mane and ears of my drinking horse, to something near at hand. There was the clear shallow stream, the green wiregrass standing stiff as bristles out of the alkali-encrusted mud, the usual deerflies and gnats swarming above the cattle tracks and dung.

I noticed something I thought a little odd. Cutting directly across the cattle paths were the hoofprints of an unshod horse. They led straight to the water and back again, following a vague little trail that led into the nearest side canyon, winding around blackbrush and cactus, short-cutting the meanders of the wash.

I studied the evidence for a while, trying to figure everything out for myself before mentioning it to Mackie, who knew this country far better than I ever would. He was a local man, a Moabite, temporarily filling in for Viviano Jacquez, who'd had another quarrel with old Roy Scobie and disappeared for a few days.

"There's a horse living up that canyon," I announced; "a wild horse. And a big one—feet like frying pans."

Slowly Mackie turned his head and looked where I pointed. "Wrong again," he said, after a moment's consideration.

40

"What do you mean, wrong again? If it's not a horse it must be a unicorn. Or a centaur? Look at those tracks—unshod. And from the wear and tear on that trail it's been living out here for a long time. Who runs horses out here?" We were about twenty miles from the nearest ranch headquarters.

"Nobody," Mackie agreed.

"You agree it's a horse."

"Of course it's a horse."

"Of course it's a horse. Well thank you very much. And no shoes, living out here in the middle of nothing, it must be a *wild* horse."

"Sorry," Mackie said. "Wrong again."

"Then what the hell is it?"

"Old Moon-Eye is what you might call an independent horse. He don't belong to anybody. But he ain't wild. He's a gelding and he's got Roy Scobie's brand on his hide."

I stared up the side canyon to where the tracks went out of sight around the first bend. "And this Moon-Eye lives up there all by himself?"

"That's right. He's been up in that canyon for ten years."

"Have you seen him?"

"No. Moon-Eye is very shy. But I heard about him."

Our mounts had raised their heads from the water; shifting restlessly under our weight, they seemed anxious to move on. Mackie turned his horse up the main trail along the stream and I followed, thinking.

"I want that horse," I said.

"What for?"

"I don't know."

"You can have him."

We rode steadily up the canyon, now and then splashing through the water, passing under the high red walls, the hanging gardens of poison ivy and panicgrass, the flowing sky. Where the trail widened I jogged my horse beside Mackie's and after a while, with a little prodding, extracted from him the story of the independent horse.

First of all, Moon-Eye had suffered. He had problems. His name derived from an inflamed condition of one of his eyes called moonblindness, which affected him periodically and inflamed his temper. The gelding operation had not improved his disposition. On top of that he'd been dude-spoiled, for old Roy had used him for many years—since he made a poor cow horse—in his string of horses for hire. Moon-Eye seemed safe and well-behaved but his actual feelings were revealed one day on a sightseeing tour through the Arches when all his angers came to a boil and he bucked off a middle-aged lady from Salt Lake City. Viviano Jacquez, leading the ride, lost his temper and gave the horse a savage beating. Moon-Eye broke away and ran off into the canyons with a good saddle on his back. He didn't come back that night. Didn't come back the next day. Never came back at all. For two weeks Viviano and Roy tracked that horse, not because they wanted the horse but because Roy wanted his saddle back. When they found the saddle, caught on the stub of a limb, the cinch straps broken, they gave up the search for the horse. The bridle they never recovered. Later on a few boys from town came out to try to catch the horse and almost got him boxed up in Salt Creek Canyon. But he got away, clattering over the slickrock wall at an angle of 45 degrees, and was seldom seen afterward. After that he stayed out of box canyons and came down to the creek only when he needed a drink. That was the story of Moon-Eye.

We came at noon to the spring, dismounted, unsaddled the horses and let them graze on the tough brown grass near the cottonwoods. We dipped our cupped hands in the water and drank, leaned back against a log in the cool of the shade and ate some lunch. Mackie lit a cigarette. I stared out past the horses at the sweet green of the willows and cottonwoods under the hot red canyon wall. Far above, a strip of blue sky, cloudless. In the silence I heard quite clearly the buzzing of individual flies down by the creek, the shake and whisper of the dry cottonwood leaves, the bright tinkling song of a canyon wren. The horses shuffled slowly through the dead leaves, ripping up the grass with their powerful, hungry jaws—a solid and pleasing sound. The canyon filled with heat and stillness.

"Look, Mackie," I said, "what do you suppose that horse does up in there?"

"What horse?"

"Moon-Eye. You say he's been up that dry canyon by himself for ten years."

"Right."

"What does he *do* up in there?"

"That is a ridiculous question."

"All right it's a ridiculous question. Try and answer it."

"How the hell should I know? Who cares? What difference does it make?"

"Answer the question."

"He eats. He sleeps. He walks down to the creek once a day for a drink. He turns around and walks back. He eats again. He sleeps again."

"The horse is a gregarious beast," I said, "a herd animal, like the cow, like the human. It's not natural for a horse to live alone."

"Moon-Eye is not a natural horse."

"He's supernatural?"

"He's crazy. How should I know? Go ask the horse."

"Okay, I'll do that."

"Only not today," Mackie said. "Let's get on up and out of here."

We'd laid around long enough. Mackie threw away the butt of his cigarette; I tanked up on more water. We mounted again, rode on to the head of the canyon where a forty-foot overhang barred the way, turned and rode back the way we'd come, clearing out the cattle from the brush and tamarisk thickets, driving them before us in a growing herd as we proceeded. By the time we reached the mouth of the canyon we had a troop of twenty head plodding before us through the dust and heat, half of them little white-faced calves who'd never seen a man or a horse before. We drove them into the catchpen and shut them up.

Tomorrow the calves would be branded, castrated, ear-marked, dehorned, inoculated against blackleg, and the whole herd trucked to the mountains for the summer. But that would be a job for Mackie and Roy, not for me; for me tomorrow meant a return to sentry duty at the entrance of the Monument, the juniper guard and the cloud-formation survey.

As we loaded the horses into the truck for the return to the ranch I asked Mackie how he liked this kind of work. He looked at me. His shirt and the rag around his neck were dark with sweat, his face coated with dust; there was a stripe of dried blood across his cheek where a willow branch had struck him when he plunged through the brush after some ignorant cow.

"Look at yourself," he said.

I looked; I was in the same condition. "I do this only for fun," I explained. "If I did it for pay I might not like it. Anyway you haven't answered my question. How do *you* like this kind of work?"

"I'd rather be rich."

"What would you do if you were rich?"

He grinned through the dust. "Buy some cows of my own."

I hadn't forgotten the moon-eyed horse. A month later I was back at the spot by Salt Creek where I'd first seen the tracks, this time alone, though again on horseback. We were deep into the desert summer now and the stream had shrunk to a dribble of slimy water oozing along between sunbaked flats of mud.

As before I let my pony drink what he wanted from the stream while I pondered the view from beneath the meager shelter of my hat. The alkali, white as lime, dazzled the eyes; the wiregrass looked sere and shriveled and even the hosts of flies and gnats had disappeared, hiding from the sun.

There was no sound but the noise of my drinking mount, no sight anywhere of animate life. In the still air the pinkish plumes of the tamarisk, light and delicate as lace, drooped from the tips of their branches without a tremor. Nothing moved, nothing stirred, except the shimmer of heat waves rising before the red canyon walls.

I could hardly have picked a more hostile day for a venture into the canyons. If anyone had asked I'd have said that not even a mad horse would endure a summer in such a place. Yet there were the tracks as before, coming down the pathway out of the side canyon and leading back again. Moon-Eye was still around. Or at any rate his tracks were still here, fresh prints in the dust that looked as if they might have been made only minutes before my arrival.

Out of the heat and stillness came an inaudible whisper, a sort of telepathic intimation that perhaps the horse did not exist at all—only his tracks. You ought to get out of this heat, I told myself, taking a drink from the canteen. My saddle horse raised his dripping muzzle from the water and waited. He turned his head to look at me with one drowsy eye; strings of algae hung from the corner of his mouth.

"No," I said, "we're not going home yet." I prodded the animal with my heels; slowly we moved up into the side canyon following the narrow trail. As we advanced I reviewed my strategy: since Moon-Eye had learned to fear and distrust men on horseback I would approach him on foot; I would carry nothing in my hands but a hackamore and a short lead rope. Better yet, I would hide these inside my shirt and go up to Moon-Eye with empty hands. Others had attempted the violent method of pursuit and capture and had failed. I was going to use nothing but sympathy and understanding, in direct violation of common sense and all precedent, to bring Moon-Eye home again.

I rounded the first bend in the canyon and stopped. Ahead was the typical scene of dry wash, saltbush and prickly pear, talus slopes at the foot of vertical canyon walls. No hint of animal life. Nothing but the silence, the stark suspension of all sound. I rode on. I was sure that Moon-Eye would not go far from water in this weather.

At the third turn in the canyon, two miles onward, I found a pile of fresh droppings in the path. I slid from the saddle and led my pony to the east side of the nearest boulder and tied him. Late in the afternoon he'd get a little shade. It was the best I could do for him; nothing else was available.

I pulled off the saddle and sat down on the ground to open a can of tomatoes. One o'clock by the sun and not a cloud in the sky: hot. I squatted under the belly of the horse and ate my lunch.

When I was finished I got up, reluctantly, stuffed hackamore and rope inside my shirt, hung the canteen over my shoulder and started off. The pony watched me go, head hanging, the familiar look of dull misery in his eyes. I know how you feel, I thought, but by God you're just going to have to stand there and suffer. If I can take it you can. The midday heat figured in my plan: I believed that in such heat the moon-eyed outlaw would be docile as a plow horse, amenable to reason. I thought I could amble close, slip the hackamore over his head and lead him home like a pet dog on a leash.

A mile farther and I had to take refuge beneath a slight over-hang in the canyon wall. I took off my hat to let the evaporation of my sweaty brow cool my brains. Tilted the canteen to my mouth. Already I was having visions of iced drinks, waterfalls, shade trees, clear deep emerald pools.

Forward. I shuffled through the sand, over the rocks, around the prickly pear and the spiny hedgehog cactus. I found a yel-lowish pebble the size of a crab apple and put it in my mouth. Kept going, pushing through the heat.

If you were really clever, I thought, you'd go back to Moon-Eye's watering place on Salt Creek, wait for him there, catch him by starlight. But you're not clever, you're stupid, I reminded myself: stick to the plan. I stopped to swab the sweat from my face. The silence locked around me again like a sphere of glass. Even the noise I made unscrewing the cap from the canteen seemed harsh and exaggerated, a gross intrusion.

I listened:

Something breathing nearby—I was in the presence of a tree. On the slope above stood a giant old juniper with massive, twisted trunk, its boughs sprinkled with the pale-blue inedible berries. Hanging from one of the limbs was what looked at first glance like a pair of trousers that reached to the ground. Blinking the sweat out of my eyes I looked harder and saw the trousers transform themselves into the legs of a large animal. I focused my attention and distinguished through the obscurity of the branches and foliage the outline of a tall horse. A very tall horse.

Gently I lowered my canteen to the ground.

I touched the rope and hackamore bunched up inside my shirt. Still there. I took the pebble from my mouth, held it in my palm, and slowly and carefully and quietly stepped toward the tree. Out of the tree a gleaming eyeball watched me coming.

I said, "That you, Moon-Eye?"

Who else? The eyeball rolled, I saw the flash of white. The eye in the tree.

I stepped closer. "What are you doing out here, you old fool?"

The horse stood not under the tree—the juniper was not big enough for that—but within it, among its branches. There'd be an awful smashing and crashing of dry wood if he tried to drive out of there.

"Eh? What do you think you're up to anyway? Damned old idiot. . . ." I showed him the yellowish stone in my hand, round as a little apple. "Why don't you answer me, Moon-Eye? Forgotten how to talk?"

Moving closer. The horse remained rigid, ears up. I could see both eyes now, the good one and the bad one—moonstruck, like a bloodshot cueball.

"I've come to take you home, old horse. What do you think of that?"

He was a giant about seventeen hands high, with a buckskin hide as faded as an old rug and a big ugly coffin-shaped head.

"You've been out here in the wilderness long enough, old man. It's time to go home."

He looked old, all right, he looked his years. He looked more than old—he looked like a spectre. Apocalyptic, a creature out of a bad dream.

"You hear me, Moon-Eye? I'm coming closer. . . ."

His nineteen ribs jutted out like the rack of a skeleton and his neck, like a camel's, seemed far too gaunt and long to carry that oversize head off the ground.

"You old brute," I murmured, "you hideous old gargoyle. You goddamned nightmare of a horse. . . . Moon-Eye, look at this. Look at this in my hand, Moon-Eye."

He watched me, watched my eyes. I was within twenty feet of him and except for the eyes he had yet to reveal a twitch of nerve or muscle; he might have been petrified. Mesmerized by sun and loneliness. He hadn't seen a man for—how many years?

"Moon-Eye," I said, approaching slowly, one short step, a pause, another step, "how long since you've stuck that ugly face of yours into a bucket of barley and bran? Remember what alfalfa tastes like, old pardner? How about grass, Moon-Eye? Green sweet fresh succulent grass, Moon-Eye, what do you think of that, eh?"

We were ten feet apart. Only the branches of the juniper tree separated us. Standing there watching the horse I could smell the odor of cedarwood, the fragrance of the tree.

Another step. "Moon-Eye. . . ."

I hesitated; to get any closer I'd have to push through the branches or stoop underneath them. "Come on, Moon-Eye, I want to take you home. It's time to go home, oldtimer."

We stared at each other, unmoving. If that animal was breathing I couldn't hear it—the silence seemed absolute. Not a fly, not a single fly crawled over his arid skin or whined around his rheumy eyeballs. If it hadn't been for the light of something like consciousness in his good eye I might have imagined I was talking to a scarecrow, a dried stuffed completely mummified horse. He didn't even smell like a horse, didn't seem to have any smell about him at all. Perhaps if I reached out and touched him he would crumble to a cloud of dust, vanish like a shadow.

My head ached from the heat and glare and for a moment I wondered if this horselike shape in front of me was anything more than hallucination.

"Moon-Eye. . . . ?" Keep talking.

I couldn't stand there all afternoon. I took another step forward, pressing against a branch. Got to keep talking.

"Moon-Eye. . . ."

He lowered his head a couple of inches, the ears flattened back. Watch out. He was still alive after all. For the first time I felt a little fear. He was a big horse and that moon-glazed eye was not comforting. We watched each other intently through the branches of the tree. If I could only wait, only be patient, I might yet sweet-talk him into surrender. But it was too hot.

"Look here, old horse, have a sniff of this." I offered him the pebble with one hand and with the other unsnapped a button of my shirt, preparing to ease out the rope when the chance came. "Go on, have a look. . . ."

I was within six feet of the monster.

"Now you just relax, Moon-Eye old boy. I'm coming in where you are now." I started to push through the boughs of the juniper. "Easy boy, easy now. . . ."

He backed violently, jarring the whole tree. Loose twigs and berries rained around us. The good eye glared at me, the bad one shone like a boiled egg—monocular vision.

"Take it easy, old buddy." Speaking softly. I had one hand on the rope. I stepped forward again, pushing under the branches. Softly—"Easy, easy, don't be scared—"

Moon-Eye tried to back again but his retreat was blocked. Snorting like a truck he came forward, right at me, bursting through the branches. Dry wood snapped and popped, dust filled the air, and as I dove for the ground I had a glimpse of a lunatic horse expanding suddenly, growing bigger than all the world and soaring over me on wings that flapped like a bat's and nearly tore the tree out of the earth.

When I opened my eyes a second later I was still alive and Moon-Eye was down in the wash fifty feet away, motionless as a statue, waiting. He stood with his ragged broomtail and his right-angled pelvic bones toward me but had that long neck and coffin head cranked around, watching me with the good eye, waiting to see what I would do next. He didn't intend to exert himself unless he was forced to.

The shade of the tree was pleasant and I made no hurry to get up. I sat against the trunk and checked for broken bones. Everything seemed all right except my hat a few feet away, crushed into the dirt by a mighty hoof. I was thirsty though and looked around for the canteen before remembering where I'd left it; I could see it down in the wash, near the horse.

Moon-Eye didn't move. He stood rigid as stone, conserving every drop of moisture in his body. But he was in the sun now and I was in the shade. Perhaps if I waited long enough he'd be forced to come back to the tree. I made myself comfortable and waited. The silence settled in again.

But that horse wouldn't come, though I waited a full hour by the sun. The horse moved only once in all that time, lowering his head for a sniff at a bush near his foreleg.

The red cliffs rippled behind the veil of heat, radiant as hot iron. Thirst was getting to me. I stirred myself, got up painfully, and stepped out of the wreckage of the juniper. The horse made no move.

"Moon-Eye," I said—he listened carefully—"let's get out of here. What do you say? Let's go home, you miserable old bucket of guts. Okay?"

I picked up my flattened hat, reformed it, put it on.

"Well, what do you say?"

I started down the slope. He raised his head, twitched one ear, watching me. "Are you crazy, old horse, standing out here in the heat? Don't you have any sense at all?"

I did not approach him directly this time but moved obliquely across the slope, hoping to head him down the canyon toward the creek and the trail to the corral. Moon-Eye saw my purpose and started up the canyon. I hurried; the horse moved faster. I slowed to a walk; he did the same. I stopped and he stopped.

"Moon-Eye, let me tell you something. I can outrun you if I have to. These Utah cowboys would laugh themselves sick if I ever mentioned it out loud but it's a fact and you ought to know it. Over the long haul, say twenty or thirty miles, it's a known fact that a healthy man can outrun a horse."

Moon-Eye listened.

"But my God, in this heat, Moon-Eye, do you think we should? Be sensible. Let's not make fools of ourselves."

He waited. I squatted on my heels and passed my forefinger, like a windshield wiper, across my forehead, brushing off the streams of sweat. My head felt hot, damp, feverish.

"What's the matter with you, Moon-Eye?"

The horse kept his good eye on me.

"Are you crazy, maybe? You don't want to die out here, do you, all alone like a hermit? In this awful place. . . ." He watched me and listened. "Them turkey buzzards will get you, Moon-Eye. They'll smell you dying, they'll come flapping down on you like foul and dirty kites and roost on your neck and suck out your eyeballs while you're still alive. Yes, they do that. And just before that good eye is punctured you'll see those black wings shutting off the sky, shutting out the sun, you'll see a crooked yellow beak and a red neck crawling with lice and a pair of insane eyes looking into yours. You won't like that, old horse. . . ."

I paused. Moon-Eye was listening, he seemed attentive, but I sensed that he wasn't really much interested in what I was saying. Perhaps it was all an old story to him. Maybe he didn't care.

I continued with the sermon. "And when the buzzards are through with you, Moon-Eye—and you'll be glad when *that's* over—why then a quiet little coyote will come loping down the canyon in the middle of the night under the moon, Moon-Eye, nosing out your soul. He'll come to within fifty yards of you, old comrade, and sit for a few hours, thinking, and then he'll circle around you a few times trying to smell out the hand of man. Pretty soon his belly will get the best of his caution—maybe he hasn't eaten for two weeks and hasn't had a chance at a dead horse for two years—and so he'll come nosing close to you, tongue out and eyes bright with happiness, and all at once when you're hardly expecting it he'll pounce and hook his fangs into your scrawny old haunch and tear off a steak. Are you listening to me, Moon-Eye? And when he's gorged himself sick he'll retire for a few hours of peaceful digestion. In the meantime the ants and beetles and blowflies will go to work, excavating tunnels through your lungs, kidneys, stomach, windpipe, brains and entrails and whatever else the buzzards and the coyote leave."

Moon-Eye watched me as I spoke; I watched him. "And in a

couple of weeks you won't even stink anymore and after a couple of months there'll be nothing left but your mangled hide and your separated bones and—get this, Moon-Eye get the picture— way out in eternity somewhere, on the far side of the sun, they'll hang up a brass plaque with the image of your moon-eyed soul stamped on it. That's about all. Years later some tired and dirty cowboy looking for a lost horse, some weary prospector looking for potash or beryllium will stumble up this way and come across your clean white rib cage, your immaculate skull, a few other bones. . . ."

I stopped talking. I was tired. Would that sun never go down beyond the canyon wall? Wasn't there a cloud in the whole state of Utah?

The horse stood motionless as a rock. He looked like part of that burnt-out landscape. He looked like the steed of Don Quixote carved out of wood by Giacometti. I could see the blue of the sky between his ribs, through the eyesockets of his skull. Dry, odorless, still and silent, he looked like the idea—without the substance—of a horse. Plato's horse: pure horseness.

My brain and eyes ached, my limbs felt hollow, I had to breathe deliberately, making a conscious effort. The thought of the long walk back to my saddle pony, the long ride back to the pickup truck, made my heart sink. I didn't want to move. So I'd wait too, wait for sundown before starting the march home, the *anabasis* in retreat. I glanced toward the sun. About four o'clock. Another hour before that sun would reach the rim of the canyon. I crawled back to the spotted shade of the juniper and waited.

We waited then, the horse and I, enduring the endless afternoon, the heartbreaking heat, and passed the time as best we could in one-sided conversation. I'd speak a sentence and wait about ten minutes for the next thought and speak again. Moon-Eye watched me all the time and made no move.

At last the sun touched the skyline, merged with it for a moment in a final explosive blaze of light and heat and sank out of sight. The shadow of the canyon wall advanced across the canyon floor, included the horse, touched the rocks and brush on the far side. A wave of cooling relief like a breeze, like an actual movement of air, washed through the canyon. A rock wren sang, a few flies came out of hiding and droned around the juniper tree. I could almost see the leaves of the saltbush and blackbush relax a little, uncurling in the evening air.

I stood up and emerged from the shelter of the broken tree. Old Moon-Eye took a few steps away from me, stopped. Still watching. We faced each other across some fifty feet of sand and rock. No doubt for the last time. I tried to think of something suitable to say but my mouth was so dry, my tongue so stiff, my lips so dried-out and cracked, I could barely utter a word.

"You damned stupid harr. . . ." I croaked, and gave it up.

Moon-Eye blinked his good eye once, twitched his hide and kept watching me as all around us, along the wash and on the canyon walls and in the air the desert birds and desert bugs resumed their inexplicable careers. A whiptail lizard scurried past my feet. A primrose opened its petals a few inches above the still-hot sand. Knees shaking, I stepped toward the horse, pulled the ropy hackamore out of my shirt—to Moon-Eye it must have looked as if I were pulling out my intestines—and threw the thing with all the strength I had left straight at him. It slithered over his back like a hairy snake, scaring him into a few quick steps. Again he stopped, the eye on me.

Enough. I turned my back on that horse and went to the canteen, picked it up. The water was almost too hot to drink but I drank it. Drank it all, except a few drops which I poured on my fingers and dabbed on my aching forehead. Refusing to look again at the spectre horse, I slung the canteen over my shoulder and started homeward, trudging over the clashing stones and through the sand down-canyon toward my pony and Salt Creek.

Once, twice, I thought I heard footsteps following me but when I looked back I saw nothing.

Havasu

One summer I started off to visit for the first time the city of Los Angeles. I was riding with some friends from the University of New Mexico. On the way we stopped off briefly to roll an old tire into the Grand Canyon. While watching the tire bounce over tall pine trees, tear hell out of a mule train and disappear with a final grand leap into the inner gorge, I overheard the park ranger standing nearby say a few words about a place called Havasu, or Havasupai. A branch, it seemed, of the Grand Canyon.

What I heard made me think that I should see Havasu immediately, before something went wrong somewhere. My friends said they would wait. So I went down into Havasu—fourteen miles by trail—and looked things over. When I returned five weeks later I discovered that the others had gone on to Los Angeles without me.

That was fifteen years ago. And still I have not seen the fabulous city on the Pacific shore. Perhaps I never will. There's something in the prospect southwest from Barstow which makes one hesitate. Although recently, driving my own truck, I did succeed in penetrating as close as San Bernardino. But was hurled back by what appeared to be clouds of mustard gas rolling in from the west on a very broad front. Thus failed again. It may be however that Los Angeles will come to me. Will come to all of us, as it must (they say) to all men.

But Havasu. Once down in there it's hard to get out. The trail led across a stream wide, blue and deep, like the pure upper reaches of the River Jordan. Without a bridge. Dripping wet and making muddy tracks I entered the village of the Havasupai Indians where unshod ponies ambled down the only street and the children laughed, not maliciously, at the sight of the wet white man. I stayed the first night in the lodge the people keep for tourists, a rambling old bungalow with high ceilings, a screened verandah and large comfortable rooms. When the sun went down the village went dark except for kerosene lamps here and there, a few open fires, and a number of lightning bugs and dogs which drifted aimlessly up and down Main Street, looking for trouble.

The next morning I bought a slab of bacon and six cans of beans at the village post office, rented a large comfortable horse and proceeded farther down the canyon past miniature cornfields, green pastures, swimming pools and waterfalls to the ruins of an old mining camp five miles below the village. There I lived, mostly alone except for the ghosts, for the next thirty-five days.

There was nothing wrong with the Indians. The Supai are a charming cheerful completely relaxed and easygoing bunch, all one hundred or so of them. But I had no desire to live *among* them unless clearly invited to do so, and I wasn't. Even if invited I might not have accepted. I'm not sure that I care for the idea of strangers examining my daily habits and folkways, studying my language, inspecting my costume, questioning me about my religion, classifying my artifacts, investigating my sexual rites and evaluating my chances for cultural survival.

So I lived alone.

The first thing I did was take off my pants. Naturally. Next I unloaded the horse, smacked her on the rump and sent her back to the village. I carried my food and gear into the best-preserved of the old cabins and spread my bedroll on a rusty steel cot. After that came a swim in the pool beneath a great waterfall nearby, 120 feet high, which rolled in mist and thunder over caverns and canopies of solidified travertine.

In the evening of that first day below the falls I lay down to sleep in the cabin. A dark night. The door of the cabin, un-latched, creaked slowly open, although there was no perceptible movement of the air. One firefly flickered in and circled my bacon, suspended from the roofbeam on a length of baling wire. Slowly, without visible physical aid, the door groaned shut. And opened again. A bat came through one window and went out another, followed by a second firefly (the first scooped up by the bat) and a host of mosquitoes, which did not leave. I had no netting, of course, and the air was much too humid and hot for sleeping inside a bag.

I got up and wandered around outside for a while, slapping at mosquitoes, and thinking. From the distance came the softened roar of the waterfall, that "white noise" as soothing as hypnosis. I rolled up my sleeping bag and in the filtered light of the stars followed the trail that wound through thickets of cactus and up around ledges to the terrace above the mining camp. The mosquitoes stayed close but in lessening numbers, it seemed, as I climbed over humps of travertine toward the head of the water-fall. Near the brink of it, six feet from the drop-off and the plunge, I found a sandy cove just big enough for my bed. The racing creek as it soared free over the edge created a continuous turbulence in the air sufficient to keep away all flying insects. I slept well that night and the next day carried the cot to the place and made it my permanent bedroom for the rest of July and all of August.

What did I do during those five weeks in Eden? Nothing. I did nothing. Or nearly nothing. I caught a few rainbow trout, which grew big if not numerous in Havasu Creek. About once a week I put on my pants and walked up to the Indian village to buy bacon, canned beans and Argentine beef in the little store. That was all the Indians had in stock. To vary my diet I ordered more exotic foods by telephone from the supermarket in Grand Can-yon Village and these were shipped to me by U.S. Mail, delivered twice a week on muleback down the fourteen-mile trail from Topocoba Hilltop. A little later in the season I was able to buy sweet corn, figs and peaches from the Supai. At one time for a period of three days my bowels seemed in danger of falling out, but I recovered. The Indians never came down to my part of the canyon except when guiding occasional tourists to the falls or hunting a stray horse. In late August came the Great Havasupai Sacred Peach Festival and Four-Day Marathon Friendship Dance, to which I was invited. There I met Reed Watahomagie, a good man, and Chief Sinyala and a fellow named Spoonhead who took me for five dollars in a horse race. Somebody fed my pick a half-bushel of green figs just before the race. I heard later.

The Friendship Dance, which continued day and night to the rhythm of drums made of old inner tube stretched over #10 tomato cans while ancient medicine men chanted in the background, was perhaps marred but definitely not interrupted when a drunken free-for-all exploded between Spoonhead and friends and a group of visiting Hualapai Indians down from the rim. But this, I was told, happened every year. It was a traditional part of the ceremony, sanctified by custom. As Spoonhead told me afterwards, grinning around broken teeth, it's not every day you get a chance to wallop a Hualapai. Or skin a paleface, I reminded him. (Yes, the Supai are an excellent tribe, healthy, joyous and clever. Not only clever but shrewd. Not only shrewd but wise: e.g., the Bureau of Indian Affairs and the Bureau of Public Roads, like most government agencies always meddling, always fretting and itching and sweating for something to do, last year made a joint offer to blast a million-dollar road down into Havasu Canyon at no cost whatsoever to the tribe, thus opening their homeland to the riches of motorized tourism. The people of Supai or at least a majority of them voted to reject the proposal.) And the peach wine flowed freely, like the water of the river of life. When the ball was over I went home to my bunk on the verge of the waterfall and rested for two days.

On my feet again, I explored the abandoned silver mines in the canyon walls, found a few sticks of dynamite but no caps or fuses. Disappointing; but there was nothing in that area anyway that required blowing up. I climbed through the caves that led down to the foot of Mooney Falls, 200 feet high. What did I do?

There was nothing that had to be done. I listened to the voices, the many voices, vague, distant but astonishingly human, of Havasu Creek. I heard the doors creak open, the doors creak shut, of the old forgotten cabins where no one with tangible substance or the property of reflecting light ever entered, ever returned. I went native and dreamed away days on the shore of the pool under the waterfall, wandered naked as Adam under the cottonwoods, inspecting my cactus gardens. The days became wild, strange, ambiguous—a sinister element pervaded the flow of time. I lived narcotic hours in which like the Taoist Chuang-tse I worried about butterflies and who was dreaming what. There was a serpent, a red racer, living in the rocks of the spring where I filled my canteens; he was always there, slipping among the stones or pausing to spellbind me with his suggestive tongue and cloudy haunted primeval eyes. Damn his eyes. We got to know each other rather too well I think. I agonized over the girls I had known and over those I hoped were yet to come. I slipped by degrees into lunacy, me and the moon, and lost to a certain extent the power to distinguish between what was and what was not myself: looking at my hand I would see a leaf trembling on a branch. A *green* leaf. I thought of Debussy, of Keats and Blake and Andrew Marvell. I remembered Tom o'Bedlam. And all those lost and never remembered. Who would return? To be lost again? I went for walks. I went for walks. I went for walks and on one of these, the last I took in Havasu, regained everything that seemed to be ebbing away.

Most of my wandering in the desert I've done alone. Not so much from choice as from necessity—I generally prefer to go into places where no one else wants to go. I find that in contemplating the natural world my pleasure is greater if there are not too many others contemplating it with me, at the same time. However, there are special hazards in traveling alone. Your chances of dying, in case of sickness or accident, are much improved, simply because there is no one around to go for help.

Exploring a side canyon off Havasu Canyon one day, I was

unable to resist the temptation to climb up out of it onto what corresponds in that region to the Tonto Bench. Late in the afternoon I realized that I would not have enough time to get back to my camp before dark, unless I could find a much shorter route than the one by which I had come. I looked for a shortcut.

Nearby was another little side canyon which appeared to lead down into Havasu Canyon. It was a steep, shadowy, extremely narrow defile with the usual meandering course and overhanging walls; from where I stood, near its head, I could not tell if the route was feasible all the way down to the floor of the main canyon. I had no rope with me—only my walking stick. But I was hungry and thirsty, as always. I started down.

For a while everything went well. The floor of the little canyon began as a bed of dry sand, scattered with rocks. Farther down a few boulders were wedged between the walls; I climbed over and under them. Then the canyon took on the slickrock character—smooth, sheer, slippery sandstone carved by erosion into a series of scoops and potholes which got bigger as I descended. In some of these basins there was a little water left over from the last flood, warm and fetid water under an oily-looking scum, condensed by prolonged evaporation to a sort of broth, rich in dead and dying organisms. My canteen was empty and I was very thirsty but I felt that I could wait.

I came to a lip on the canyon floor which overhung by twelve feet the largest so far of these stagnant pools. On each side rose the canyon walls, mainly perpendicular. There was no way to continue except by dropping into the pool. I hesitated. Beyond this point there could hardly be any returning, yet the main canyon was still not visible below. Obviously the only sensible thing to do was to turn back. Instead, I edged over the lip of stone and dropped feet first into the water.

Deeper than I expected. The warm, thick fluid came up and closed over my head as my feet touched the muck at the bottom. I had to swim to the farther side. And here I found myself on the verge of another drop-off, with one more huge bowl of green soup below.

This drop-off was about the same height as the one before, but not overhanging. It resembled a children's playground slide, concave and S-curved, only steeper, wider, with a vertical pitch in the middle. It did not lead directly into the water but ended in a series of steplike ledges above the pool. Beyond the pool lay another edge, another drop-off into an unknown depth. Again I paused, and for a much longer time. But I no longer had the option of turning around and going back. I eased myself into the chute and let go of everything—except my faithful stick.

I hit rock bottom hard, but without any physical injury. I swam the stinking pond dog-paddle style, pushing the heavy scum away from my face, and crawled out on the far side to see what my fate was going to be.

Fatal. Death by starvation, slow and tedious. For I was looking straight down an overhanging cliff to a rubble pile of broken rocks eighty feet below.

After the first wave of utter panic had passed I began to try to think. First of all I was not going to die immediately, unless another flash flood came down the gorge; there was the pond of stagnant water on hand to save me from thirst and a man can live, they say, for thirty days or more without food. My sun-bleached bones, dramatically sprawled at the bottom of the chasm, would provide the diversion of the picturesque for future wanderers—if any man ever came this way again.

My second thought was to roar for help, although I knew very well there would be no other human being within miles. I even tried it but the sound of my anxious shout, cut short in the dead air within the canyon walls, was so inhuman, so detached as it seemed from myself, that it terrified me and I didn't attempt it again.

I thought of tearing my clothes into strips and plaiting a rope. But what was I wearing?—boots, socks, a pair of old and ragged blue jeans, a flimsy T-shirt, an ancient and rotten sombrero of straw. Not a chance of weaving such a wardrobe into a usable rope eighty feet long, or even ten feet long.

How about a signal fire? There was nothing to burn but my clothes; not a tree, not a shrub, not even a weed grew in this stony cul-de-sac. Even if I burned my clothing the chances of the smoke being seen by some Hualapai Indian high on the south rim were very small; and if he did see the smoke, what then? He'd shrug his shoulders, sigh, and take another pull from his Tokay bottle. Furthermore, without clothes, the sun would soon bake me to death.

There was only one thing I could do. I had a tiny notebook in my hip pocket and a stub of pencil. When these dried out I could at least record my final thoughts. I would have plenty of time to write not only my epitaph but my own elegy.

But not yet.

There were a few loose stones scattered about the edge of the pool. Taking the biggest first, I swam with it back to the foot of the slickrock chute and placed it there. One by one I brought the others and made a shaky little pile about two feet high leaning against the chute. Hopeless, of course, but there was nothing else to do. I stood on the top of the pile and stretched upward, straining my arms to their utmost limit and groped with fingers and fingernails for a hold on something firm. There was nothing. I crept back down. I began to cry. It was easy. All alone, I didn't have to be brave.

Through the tears I noticed my old walking stick lying nearby. I took and stood it on the most solid stone in the pile, behind the two topmost stones. I took off my boots, tied them together and hung them around my neck, on my back. I got up on the little pile again and lifted one leg and set my big toe on the top of the stick. This could never work. Slowly and painfully, leaning as much of my weight as I could against the sandstone slide, I applied more and more pressure to the stick, pushing my body upward until I was stretched out full length above it. Again I felt about for a fingerhold. There was none. The chute was smooth as polished marble.

No, not quite that smooth. This was sandstone, soft and porous, not marble, and between it and my wet body and wet clothing a certain friction was created. In addition, the stick had enabled me to reach a higher section of the S-curved chute, where the angle was more favorable. I discovered that I could move upward, inch by inch, through adhesion and with the help of the leveling tendency of the curve. I gave an extra little push with my big toe—the stones collapsed below, the stick clattered down—and crawled rather like a snail or slug, oozing slime, up over the rounded summit of the slide.

The next obstacle, the overhanging spout twelve feet above a deep plunge pool, looked impossible. It *was* impossible, but with the blind faith of despair I slogged into the water and swam underneath the drop-off and floundered around for a while, scrabbling at the slippery rock until my nerves and tiring muscles convinced my numbed brain that *this was not the way.* I swam back to solid ground and lay down to rest and die in comfort.

Far above I could see the sky, an irregular strip of blue between the dark, hard-edged canyon walls that seemed to lean toward each other as they towered above me. Across that narrow opening a small white cloud was passing, so lovely and precious and delicate and forever inaccessible that it broke the heart and made me weep like a woman, like a child. In all my life I had never seen anything so beautiful.

The walls that rose on either side of the drop-off were literally perpendicular. Eroded by weathering, however, and not by the corrosion of rushing floodwater, they had a rough surface, chipped, broken, cracked. Where the walls joined the face of the overhang they formed almost a square corner, with a number of minute crevices and inch-wide shelves on either side. It might, after all, be possible. What did I have to lose?

When I had regained some measure of nerve and steadiness I got up off my back and tried the wall beside the pond, clinging to the rock with bare toes and fingertips and inching my way crabwise toward the corner. The watersoaked, heavy boots dangling from my neck, swinging back and forth with my every movement, threw me off balance and I fell into the pool. I swam out to the bank, unslung the boots and threw them up over the drop-off, out of sight. They'd be there if I ever needed them again. Once more I attached myself to the wall, tenderly, sensitively, like a limpet, and very slowly, very cautiously, worked my way into the corner. Here I was able to climb upward, a few centimeters at a time, by bracing myself against the opposite sides and finding sufficient niches for fingers and toes. As I neared the top and the overhang became noticeable I prepared for a slip, planning to push myself away from the rock so as to fall into the center of the pool where the water was deepest. But it wasn't necessary. Somehow, with a skill and tenacity I could never have found in myself under ordinary circumstances, I managed to creep straight up that gloomy cliff and over the brink of the drop-off and into the flower of safety. My boots were floating under the surface of the little puddle above. As I poured the stinking water out of them and pulled them on and laced them up I discovered myself bawling again for the third time in three hours, the hot delicious tears of victory. And up above the clouds replied—with thunder peals.

I emerged from that treacherous little canyon at sundown, with an enormous fire flaring in the western sky and lightning overhead. Through sweet twilight and the sudden dazzling glare of lightning I hiked back along the Tonto Bench, bellowing the *Ode to Joy*. Long before I reached the place where I could descend safely to the main canyon and my camp, however, darkness set in, the clouds opened their bays and the rain poured down. I took shelter under a ledge in a shallow cave about three feet high—hardly room to sit up in. Others had been here before: the dusty floor of the little hole was littered with the droppings of birds, rats, jackrabbits and coyotes. There were also a few long gray pieces of scat with a curious twist at one tip— cougar? I didn't care. I had some matches with me, sealed in paraffin (the prudent explorer); I scraped together the handiest twigs and animal droppings and built a little fire and waited for the rain to stop.

It didn't stop. The rain came down for hours in alternate waves of storm and drizzle and I very soon had burnt up all the fuel within reach. No matter. I stretched out in the coyote den, pillowed my head on my arm and suffered through the long night, wet, cold, aching, hungry, wretched, dreaming claustrophobic nightmares. It was, all the same, one of the happiest nights of my life.

The Dead Man at Grandview Point

Somnolence—a heaviness in the air, a chill in the sunlight, an oppressive stillness in the atmosphere that hints of much but says nothing. The Balanced Rock and the pinnacles stand in petrified silence—waiting. The wildlife has withdrawn to the night, the flies and gnats have disappeared, a few birds sing, and the last of the flowers of summer—the globemallow—have died. What is it that's haunting me? At times I hear voices up the road, familiar voices . . . I look; and no one is there.

Even the tourists that creep in and creep out in their lumbering, dust-covered automobiles reveal a certain weariness with desert travel, a certain longing to be elsewhere, to be where it's high, cool, breezy, fresh—mountain or seashore. And they should. Why anyone with any sense would volunteer to spend August in the furnace of the desert is a mystery to me; they must be mad, these brave tourists, as I am mad.

Each day begins clean and promising in the sweet cool clear green light of dawn. And then the sun appears, its hydrogen cauldrons brimming—so to speak—with plasmic fires, and the tyranny of its day begins.

By noon the clouds are forming around the horizon and in the afternoon, predictable as sunrise and sunset, they gather in massed formations, colliding in jags of lightning and thunderous artillery, and pile higher and higher toward the summit of the sky in vaporish mountains, dazzling under the sunlight. Afterward, perhaps, comes a little rain—that is, a violent cloudburst above some random site in the desert, flooding arroyos and washes with torrents of mud, gravel and water in equal parts, a dense mixture the color of tomato soup or blood that roars down the barren waterways to the river, leaving the land an hour later as dry as it was before. The clouds melt away, the thunder fades and the sun breaks through again, blazing with redoubled intensity upon sand and rock and scattered, introverted shrub and tree. Rainy season in the canyonlands.

One morning I am requested via the shortwave radio to join a manhunt. Not for some suspected criminal or escaped convict but for a lost tourist whose car was found abandoned in the vicinity of Grandview Point, about fifty miles by road from my station in the Arches.

Grateful for the diversion, I throw canteens and rucksack into the government pickup and take off. I go west to the highway, south for three miles, and turn off on another dirt road leading southwest across the mesa called Island in the Sky toward the rendezvous. There I find the other members of the search party holding a consultation: Merle and Floyd from park headquarters, the county sheriff and one of his deputies, a relative of the missing man, and my brother Johnny who is also working for the Park Service this summer. At the side of the road is a locked and empty automobile, first noted two days earlier.

Most of the surface of this high mesa on which our man has disappeared is bare rock—there are few trails, and little sand or soft earth on which he might have left footprints. There are, however, many gulches, giant potholes, basins, fissures and canyons in which a man could lose himself, or a body be hidden, for days or years.

There is also the abyss. A mile from where we stand is the mesa's edge and a twelve-hundred-foot drop straight down to what is called the White Rim Bench. From there the land falls away for another fifteen hundred feet to the Colorado River. If he went that way there won't be much left worth looking for. You could put it all in a bushel sack.

Learning from the relative—a nephew—that the missing man

is about sixty years old, an amateur photographer who liked to walk and had never been in the Southwest before, we assume first of all that the object of the search is dead and that the body will be found somewhere along the more than twenty miles of highly indented rimrock that winds northwest and northeast from Grandview Point.

The assumption of death is made on the grounds that an airplane search by the sheriff failed to find any sign of the man, and that at least two days and possibly more spent in the desert in the heat of August with only what water (if any) he could carry is too much for a man of sixty, unfamiliar with the terrain and the climate.

We begin the search by dividing as evenly as we can the area to be investigated. Assigned the southernmost sector, my brother and I drive down the road another five miles to where it dead-ends close to the farthest reach of the mesa—Grandview Point itself. Here we share our water supply and split up, Johnny hiking along the rim to the northwest and I taking the opposite way.

All morning long, for the next four hours, I tramp along the rim looking for the lost tourist. Looking for his body, I should say—there seems little chance of finding him still alive. I look in the shade of every juniper and overhanging ledge, likely places to find a man besieged by thirst and sun. I look in the gullies and fissures and in the enormous potholes drilled by wind and sand in the solid rock—deep pits like wells, with perpendicular sides . . . mantraps.

At times I step to the brink of the mesa and peer down through that awful, dizzying vacancy to the broken slabs piled along the foot of the wall, so far—so terribly far—below. It is not impossible that our man might have stumbled off the edge in the dark, or even—spellbound by that fulfillment of nothingness— eased himself over, deliberately, in broad daylight, drawn into the void by the beauty and power of his own terror.

"Gaze not too long into the abyss, lest the abyss gaze into thee," said Nietzsche. He would, wouldn't he?

I watch also for a gathering of vultures in the air, which might be a helpful clue. Not for *him,* of course, now perhaps beyond such cares, but for us, his hunters.

The sun burns in a lovely, perfect sky; the day is very hot. I pause when necessary beneath pinyon pine or juniper for rest and shade and for a precious drink of water. Also, I will admit, for recreation: to admire the splendor of the landscape, the perfection of the silence.

The shade is sweet and desirable, but the heat very bad and early in the afternoon, out of water, I give up and return to the truck. My brother is waiting for me and by the lost expression on his face I understand at once that he has found our man.

We radio the rest of the party. Johnny and I wait in the shade of the truck. They arrive; we wait another hour until the undertaker, who is also county coroner, comes from Moab with his white ambulance, his aluminum stretcher and his seven-foot-long black rubber bag. Johnny leads us to the body.

The route is rough and long, across rocky gulches and sandstone terraces impassable to a motor vehicle. We walk it out. About a mile from the road we come to a ledge rising toward the rim of the mesa. Near the top of the rise is a juniper, rooted in the rock and twisted toward the sky in the classic pose of its kind in the canyon country. Beneath the little tree, in the shade, is the dead man.

Coming close we see that he lies on his back, limbs extended rigidly from a body bloated like a balloon. A large stain discolors the crotch of his trousers. The smell of decay is rich and sickening. Although the buzzards for some reason have not discovered him, two other scavengers, ravens, rise heavily and awkwardly from the corpse as we approach. No canteen or water bag in sight.

The nephew makes a positive identification—I can't imagine how. But the coroner-undertaker nods, the sheriff is satisfied, and together with the deputy the three of them begin the delicate, difficult task of easing the swollen cadaver into the unzippered rubber bag.

Johnny and I retrace what we can of the dead man's course. There is no discernible trail on the slickrock but by walking around his final resting place in a big half-circle we cut sign— intersect his tracks—in a ravine a hundred yards away. There on the sandy floor we find his footprints: where he had entered the ravine, where he became panicky and retraced his way not once but twice, and where he had struggled up an alluvial bank to the ledge. From that point he could see the juniper with its promise of shade. Somehow he made his way to it, laid himself down and never got up again.

We return to where the others are waiting, gathered about the black bag on the stretcher, which the undertaker is in the act of zipping shut. The sheriff and the deputy are scrubbing their hands with sand; the undertaker wears rubber gloves.

We are not far from Grandview Point and the view from near the juniper is equally spectacular. The big jump-off is only a few steps south and beyond that edge lies another world, far away. Down below is the White Rim; deeper still is the gorge of the Colorado; off to the right is the defile of the Green River; look- ing past Junction Butte we can see the deep gorge where the two rivers join to begin the wild race through Cataract Canyon; be- yond the confluence lies the wilderness of the Needles country, known to only a few cowboys and uranium prospectors; on the west side of the junction is another labyrinth of canyons, pinna- cles and fins of naked stone, known to even fewer, closer than anything else in the forty-eight United States to being genuine *terra incognita*—The Maze.

Far beyond these hundreds of square miles of desiccated tableland rise the sheer walls of further great mesas comparable in size and elevation to the one we stand on; and beyond the mesas are the mountains—the Abajos and Elk Ridge forty miles south, the La Sals and Tukuhnikivats forty miles east, the Henrys fifty miles southwest.

Except for the town of Moab, east of us, and the village of Hanksville near the Henry Mountains, and a single occupied ranch on this side of the Abajo Mountains, the area which we overlook contains no permanent human habitation. From the point of view of political geography we are standing on one of the frontiers of human culture; for the man inside the rubber sack it was land's end, the shore of the world.

Looking out on this panorama of light, space, rock and silence I am inclined to congratulate the dead man on his choice of jumping-off place; he had good taste. He had good luck—I envy him the manner of his going: to die alone, on rock under sun at the brink of the unknown, like a wolf, like a great bird, seems to me very good fortune indeed. To die in the open, under the sky, far from the insolent interference of doctor and priest, before this desert vastness opening like a window onto eternity—that surely was an overwhelming stroke of rare good luck.

It would be unforgivably presumptuous to pretend to speak *for* the dead man on these matters; he may not have agreed with a word of it, not at all. On the other hand, except for those minutes of panic in the ravine when he realized that he was lost, it seems possible that in the end he yielded with good grace. We see him staggering through the fearful heat and glare, across the tilted ledge toward the juniper, the only tree in sight. We see him reach it, at great cost, and there, on the brink of nothing and everything, he lies down in the shade to rest. He would not have suffered much after that; he may have died in his sleep, dreaming of the edge of things, of flight into space, of soaring.

We are ready to go. A few flies are already circling above the dark shape on the stretcher. A few dark birds are floating on thermals far out over the chasm of the Colorado, somewhat below the level of the mesa. It is possible from here to gaze down on the backs of soaring birds. I would like to stay for a while and watch the birds but the others are ready to go, the sun is very hot, the corpse is stinking, there is not enough shade for us all under the one small tree, and the world—the human world—is waiting for us, calling us back. For the time being.

There are eight men here, alive. More or less alive. Four pick up the stretcher and begin the march back to the road and the ambulance. The other four walk alongside to relieve when needed. We soon need relief, for the weight is greater than it looks, and the rock, sand, brush and cactus make walking with a load difficult. The sun is pitiless, the smell is worse, and the flies are worst of all, buzzing in swarms around the putrid mass in the rubber sack.

The dead man's nephew, excused from this duty, walks far ahead out of earshot. We are free as we go stumbling and sweating along to say exactly what we please, without fear of offending.

"Heavy son of a bitch. . . ."

"All blown up like he is, you'd think he'd float like a balloon."

"Let's just hope he don't explode."

"He won't. We let the gas out."

"What about lunch?" somebody asks; "I'm hungry."

"Eat this."

"Why'd the bastard have to go so far from the road?"

"There's something leaking out that zipper."

"Never mind, let's try to get in step here," the sheriff says. "Goddamnit, Floyd, you got big feet."

"Are we going in the right direction?"

"I wonder if the old fart would walk part way if we let him out of that bag?"

"He won't even say thank you for the ride."

"Well I hope this learned him a lesson, goddamn him. I guess he'll stay put after this. . . ."

Thus we meditate upon the stranger's death. Since he was unknown to any of us we joke about his fate, as is only natural and wholesome under the circumstances. If he'd meant anything to us maybe we could mourn. If we had loved him we would sing, dance, drink, build a stupendous bonfire, find women, make love—for under the shadow of death what can be wiser than love, to make love, to make children?—and celebrate his transfiguration from flesh to fantasy in a style proper and fitting, with fun for all at the funeral.

But—we knew thee not, old man. And there is, I suspect, another feeling alive in each of us as we lug these rotting guts across the desert: satisfaction.

Each man's death diminishes me? Not necessarily. Given this

man's age, the inevitability and suitability of his death, and the essential nature of life on earth, there is in each of us the un-speakable conviction that we are well rid of him. His departure makes room for the living. Away with the old, in with the new. He is gone—we remain, others come. The plow of mortality drives through the stubble, turns over rocks and sod and weeds to cover the old, the worn-out, the husks, shells, empty seedpods and sapless roots, clearing the field for the next crop. A ruthless, brutal process—but clean and beautiful.

A part of our nature rebels against this truth and against that other part which would accept it. A second truth of equal weight contradicts the first, proclaiming through art, religion, philoso-phy, science and even war that human life, in some way not easily definable, is significant and unique and supreme beyond all the limits of reason and nature. And this second truth we can deny only at the cost of denying our humanity.

We finally reach the road, which I had begun to fear we would never see—the death march seemed everlasting—and shove stretcher and burden into the undertaker's ambulance, a white Cadillac glittering with chrome and powdered with the red dust of Utah. He slams shut the doors, the undertaker does, shakes a few hands and drives off, followed by the nephew driving the dead man's car.

The air is clean and sweet again. We can breathe. We rest for a while in the shade of the other cars, passing around water bags, smoking, talking a little. Someone tells a bad joke and the party breaks up. We all go back the thirty-five miles to the highway and from there by separate ways to our separate places, my brother south to Blanding, myself to the Arches.

Evening now, a later day. How much later? I'm not quite sure, I can't say, I've been out here in the heart of light and silence for so long that the numbers on a calendar have lost their meaning for me. All that I can be certain of at this moment is that the sun is down, for there is Venus again, planet of beauty and joy, glowing bright and clear in the western sky, low on the horizon, brilliant and steady and serene.

The season is late—late summer on the high desert. The thunderstorms have been less frequent lately, the tumbleweeds are taking on the reddish tinge of their maturity, and the various grasses—bluestem, fescue, Indian ricegrass, grama grass—which flourished after the summer rains have ripened to a tawny brown; in the slanting light of morning and evening the far-off fields in Salt Valley, where these grasses are most abundant, shine like golden velvet.

The nighthawks, sparse in numbers earlier, have gone away completely. I haven't seen one for a week. But not all the birds have left me.

Southwest, toward Grandview Point and The Maze, I can see V-shaped black wings in the lonely sky, soaring higher and higher against a yellow sunset. I think of the dead man under the juniper on the edge of the world, seeing him as the vulture would have seen him, far below and from a great distance. And I see myself through those cruel eyes.

I feel myself sinking into the landscape, fixed in place like a stone, like a tree, a small motionless shape of vague outline, sand-colored, and with the wings of imagination look down at myself through the eyes of the bird, watching a human figure that becomes smaller, smaller in the receding landscape as the bird rises into the evening—a man at a table near a twinkling campfire, surrounded by a rolling wasteland of stone and dune and sandstone monuments, the wasteland surrounded by dark canyons and the course of rivers and mountain ranges on a vast plateau stretching across Colorado, Utah, New Mexico and Arizona, and beyond this plateau more deserts and greater mountains, the Rockies in dusk, the Sierra Nevadas shining in their late afternoon, and farther and farther yet, the darkened East, the gleaming Pacific, the curving margins of the great earth itself, and beyond earth that ultimate world of sun and stars whose bounds we cannot discover.

Bedrock and Paradox

The tourists have gone home. Most of them. A few still rumble in and ramble around in their sand-pitted dust-choked iron dinosaurs but the great majority, answering a mystical summons, have returned to the smoky jungles and swamps of what we call, in wistful hope, American civilization. I can see them now in all their millions jamming the freeways, glutting the streets, horns bellowing like wounded steers, hunting for a place to park. They have left me alone here in the wilderness, at the center of things, where all that is most significant takes place. (Sunset and moonrise, moaning winds and stillness, cloud transformations in the metamorphosis of sunlight, yellowing leaf and the indolent, soaring vulture. . . .)

Who am I to pity the degradation and misery of my fellow citizens? I, too, must leave the canyon country, if only for a season, and rejoin for the winter that miscegenated mesalliance of human and rodent called the rat race (*Rattus urbanus*). Today is my last day at the Arches; tonight I take a plane for Denver and from there a jet flight to New York. Of course I have my reasons which reason knows nothing about; reason is and ought to be, as Hume said, the slave of the passions. He foresaw the whole thing.

The old pickup truck will stay here. I've already jacked it up on blocks in a friend's backyard, drained the radiator and engine block and covered the hood with a tarp to keep out the rain and dust.

Everything is packed, all my camping gear stored away, even my whiskers shaved off. Bald-faced as a bank clerk, I stood in front of a mirror this morning and tried on my only white shirt, recently starched. Like putting on chain mail. I even knotted a tie around my neck and tightened it in the proper style—adjusting the garrote for fit. A grim business, returning to civilization. But duty calls. Yes, I hate it so much that I'm spending the best part of a paycheck on airplane tickets.

Balance, that's the secret. Moderate extremism. The best of both worlds. Unlike Thoreau who insisted on one world at a time I am attempting to make the best of two. After six months in the desert I am volunteering for a winter of front-line combat duty—caseworker, public warfare department—in the howling streets of Megalomania, U.S.A. Mostly for the sake of private and selfish concerns, truly, but also for reasons of a more general nature. After twenty-six weeks of sunlight and stars, wind and sky and golden sand, I want to hear once more the crackle of clamshells on the floor of the bar in the Clam Broth House in Hoboken. I long for a view of the jolly, rosy faces on 42nd Street and the cheerful throngs on the sidewalks of Atlantic Avenue. Enough of Land's End, Dead Horse Point, Tukuhnikivats and other high resolves; I want to see somebody jump out of a window or off a roof. I grow weary of nobody's company but my own—let me hear the wit and wisdom of the subway crowds again, the cabdriver's shrewd aphorisms, the genial chuckle of a Jersey City cop, the happy laughter of Greater New York's one million illegitimate children.

If I'm serious, and I am, the desert has driven me crazy. Not that I mind. We get some strange ones out here. Last night for example came a fellow in suspenders and short leather britches who spoke English with a Bavarian accent. A toolmaker in a Porsche on vacation from Munich, he carried a case of Lowenbrau under the hood of his car where the motor should have been. He spotted my campfire burning out back of the house-trailer and invited himself over, along with his beer. I was glad enough to see him. He turned out to be a typical comical Nazi, his feelings still wounded by the fact that the United States had fought against instead of with Hitler; Americans, he said, are very much like Germans and should with them the dirty Russians together fight. Courteously I declined the intended honor of the comparison: not yet, I said, not quite. We argued all night long. I defended the Americans—no one else was available—while he explained to me the positive aspects of anti-Semitism. Thus two monologues converged, near dawn, upon a murder. I could have opened his skull with a bottle of his own Lowenbrau, and was powerfully tempted. Maybe I would have done it, too, but fatigue set in, and besides I didn't have the heart—after all he hadn't seen the Arches yet or even the Grand Canyon. When he finally departed my best wishes went with him: may his fan belt snap, his tires develop blisters, his fuel pump succumb to chronic vapor lock—may he never come back.

October. Rabbitbrush in full bloom. The tumbleweeds on the move (that longing to be elsewhere, elsewhere), thousands of them rolling across the plains before the wind. Something like a yellow rash has broken out upon the mountainsides—the aspen forests in their autumn splendor. Sunsets each evening that test a man's credulity—great gory improvisations in scarlet and gold that remind me of nothing so much as God's own celestial pizza pies. Followed inevitably by the night with its razzle-dazzle of stars in silver, emerald and sapphire blue, the same old routine.

For tonight I prophesy a snowstorm. I feel it in the cold stillness of the air, the strange uncertainty of the sun, the unbroken mass of aluminum-gray clouds that hang all day above the north and east, an enormous lid soon to be shoved into place above the canyons and plateaus. The *immanence* of snow.

In the government truck I make a final tour of the park. East past the Balanced Rock to Double Arch and the Windows; back again and north and east to Turnbow Cabin and up the trail to Delicate Arch; back again and northwest beyond the Fiery Furnance into the Devil's Garden, where I walk for the last time this year out the trail past Tunnel Arch, Pine Tree Arch, Landscape Arch, Partition Arch, Navajo Arch, and Wall Arch, all the way out to Double-O Arch at the end of the path. My own, my children, mine by right of possession, possession by right of love, by divine right, I now surrender them all to the winds of winter and the snow and the starving deer and the pinyon jays and the emptiness and the silence unbroken by even a thought.

In deep stillness, in a somber solemn light, these beings stand, these fins of sandstone hollowed out by time, the juniper trees so shaggy, tough and beautiful, the dead or dying pinyon pines, the little shrubs of rabbitbrush and blackbrush, the dried-up stalks of asters and sunflowers gone to seed, the black-rooted silver-blue sage. How difficult to imagine this place without a human presence; how necessary. I am almost prepared to believe that this sweet virginal primitive land will be grateful for my departure and the absence of the tourists, will breathe metaphorically a collective sigh of relief—like a whisper of wind—when we are all and finally gone and the place and its creations can return to their ancient procedures unobserved and undisturbed by the busy, anxious, brooding consciousness of humankind.

Grateful for our departure? One more expression of human vanity. The finest quality of this stone, these plants and animals, this desert landscape is the indifference to our presence, our absence, our coming, our staying or our going. Whether we live or die is a matter of absolutely no concern whatsoever to the desert. Let men in their madness blast every city on earth into black rubble and envelope the entire planet in a cloud of lethal gas—the canyons and hills, the springs and rocks will still be here, the sunlight will filter through, water will form and warmth shall be upon the land and after sufficient time, no matter how long, somewhere, living things will emerge and join and stand once again, this time perhaps to take a different and better course. I have seen the place called Trinity, in New Mexico, where our wise men exploded the first atomic bomb and the heat of the blast fused sand into a greenish glass—already the grass has returned, and the cactus and the mesquite. On this bedrock of animal faith I take my stand, close by the old road that leads eventually out of the valley of paradox.

Yes. Feet on earth. Knock on wood. Touch stone. Good luck to all.

Throughout the afternoon the mountains are wrapped in a storm of clouds, a furious battleground. Tukuhnikivats has gone under, drowning in wild vapors, and a blue light covers the desert. In coat and hat and scarf and gloves and long underwear, freezing, I linger on my terrace near the ramada, which is now being unroofed branch by branch in the winds, the red flag whipped to shreds, the windbells jangling like a Chinese fire alarm. All of my old cedar posts and juniper logs have gone into one last magnificent bonfire, flaring like a transparent rose on the open rock, my signal to the world—unheeded. No matter, it's all one to me and the red dust of Utah. Five hundred and sixty tumbleweeds roll toward the horizon, herded by the wind; may they, too, never come back. All things are in motion, all is in process, nothing abides, nothing will ever change in this eternal moment. I'll be back before I'm fairly out of sight. Time to go.

The trailerhouse is cleaned out, locked up, water lines drained, gas disconnected, windows shut tight, power plant under canvas. My own belongings are packed in the truck. The red bandana, the bells? I'll leave them here in place to wave and jingle all through the winter, unseen and unheard, more power to the both of them.

All is ready for departure and I see by my clock I've already put in ten minutes of free overtime for the government. I had hoped to see the mountains in full glory, all covered with fresh snow, before leaving, but it looks as if the storm will last all night. I had wished also to see the red rock of our 33,000-acre garden, the arches and buttes and pinnacles and balanced boulders, all lit up in evening light but the sun too is buried in clouds.

The fire is dying, the sparks scattering over the sand and stone—there is nothing to do but go. Now that all is finally ready I am overtaken by the insane compulsion to be gone, to be elsewhere, to go, to go. Abruptly I cancel plans for a ceremonial farewell to the hoodoo rocks and the lone juniper with its dead claw snagging the wind—I had planned a frivolous music—and turn away and hurry to the truck, get in, slam the door, drive off.

When I reach park headquarters near Moab I telephone the airport and learn that nobody is flying from here to Denver tonight; the storm has ruled out all flights in the area. A new ranger, Bob Ferris, offers to drive me up to the town of Thompson where I can catch a Western & Rio Grande night train to Denver. I accept and following a good dinner by his gracious wife, we load my baggage into his car and drive to the railway, thirty miles north.

No end of blessings from heaven and earth. As we climb up out of the Moab valley and reach the high tableland stretching northward, traces of snow flying across the road, the sun emerges clear of the overcast, burning free on the very edge of the horizon. For a few minutes the whole region from the canyon of the Colorado to the Book Cliffs—crag, mesa, turret, dome, canyon wall, plain, swale and dune—glows with a vivid amber light against the darkness on the east. At the same time I see a mountain peak rising clear of the clouds, old Tukuhnikivats fierce as the Matterhorn, snowy as Everest, invincible.

"Ferris, stop this car. Let's go back."

But he only steps harder on the gas. "No," he says, "you've got a train to catch." He sees me craning my neck to stare backward. "Don't worry," he adds, "it'll all still be here next spring."

The sun goes down, I face the road again, we light up our after-dinner cigars. Keeping the flame alive. The car races forward through a world dissolving into snow and night.

Yes, I agree, that's a good thought and it better be so. Or by God there might be trouble. The desert will still be here in the spring. And then comes another thought. When I return will it be the same? Will I be the same? Will anything ever be quite the same again? If I return.

Appalachia

COMING HOME

Going back to the Big Smokies always reminds me of coming home. There was the town set in the cup of the green hills. In the Alleghenies. A town of trees, two-story houses, red-brick hardware stores, church steeples, the clock tower on the county courthouse, and over all the thin blue haze—partly dust, partly smoke, but mostly moisture—that veils the Appalachian world most of the time. That diaphanous veil that conceals nothing. And beyond the town were the fields, the zigzag rail fences, the old gray barns and gaunt Gothic farmhouses, the webwork of winding roads, the sulfurous creeks and the black coal mines and—scattered everywhere—the woods.

The trees. Vegetation cradle of North America. All those trees transpiring patiently through the wet and exhilarating winds of spring, through the heavy, sultry, sullen summers into the smoky autumns. Through the seasons, years, millennia. Sensitive and sensible plants, with who knows what aspirations of their own.

The hill country in North Carolina, eastern Kentucky and eastern Tennessee seems today something like Punxsutawney, Pennsylvania fifty years ago. Like Seneca and Powhatan, like Shawnee and Home, Pa., where we grew up. All of it Appalachian, winter or summer, then and now. Land of the breathing trees, the big woods, the rainy forests.

Through town and into the hills, I'd follow a certain road for about seven miles until I came to a church and a graveyard on top of a tall hill. (I worked there once, tending that graveyard and the dead, firing the furnace in the church on winter Sunday

FROM

Appalachian Wilderness

(1970)

mornings, mowing the lawns in spring and summer, me the sexton, best job I ever had, that rich grass, that meditation, those ghosts that haunt the human mind, that deep dark dank earth rich in calcium, those lonely clouds with rosy bottoms drifting pensively on the horizon for a while after sundown, inviting questions, when it was time to go home.)

Time to go home. From the top of the hill you can look down into a long emerald valley where a stream meanders back and forth in lazy loops through overgrazed pastures in which cows drift along as slowly as clouds. All facing in the same direction. Beyond the end of that particular valley, in the woods and sub-marginal cornfields that lay beyond, was my home.

You go down into the valley, an easy, pleasant sort of walk, past the little farms, barns, tile springhouses, pickup trucks, hayrakes and mowing machines, until you come to Crooked Creek, then take a red-dog road under a railroad trestle through a tunnel in the woods. I call it a tunnel because the road is so narrow and winding that the trees on either side interlace their branches overhead, forming a canopy that in winter looks like a network of fine cracks in a plaster ceiling, and in spring and summer like an underwater vision of translucent green, and in the fall, natu-rally, like the scales of a fire dragon. From shady green to dying flame.

At the far end of the living tunnel stood the house. An austere clapboarded farmhouse, taller than wide when seen from the road, it had filigreed porchwork and a steep-pitched roof with lightning rods pointing straight up at the sun or stars. In winter you'd see smoke winding out of the chimney and amber lamps burning behind the curtains of the windows.

Slinking toward me across the damp grass would come a familiar dog, older, more arthritic than before. Too timid to growl, too shy to bark, she still remembered me. Her job was to guard those doors that in nearly thirty years had never been locked. Nobody even knew if there was a key.

Home again.

TREAT YOURSELF TO THE BEST

That's what the sign says on the side of most any barn in these parts, "Chew Mail Pouch, Treat Yourself to the Best." That way a farmer gets at least one wall of his barn painted free, by the tobacco company. Coming down through the extreme southwest corner of Virginia into Tennessee we see that legend many times, as often as "Jesus Saves" and "Get Right with God."

On the way to Gatlinburg, Gateway to the Big Smokies, which is our goal, we drive down a highway with shoulders sprinkled and ditches lined in irredeemable litter. Immortal beer can, immutable chicken basket, eternal plastic picnic spoon. At night the round ends of the cans gleam in your headlights like the glowing eyes of foxes. The hillsides are carpeted with a layer of automobile hulks. This is Trentville, Tennessee, where all old cars come to die, explained a man at a filling station. Poor hillbillies buy them used in Cleveland and Detroit, he explained, get laid off and come home, abandon them when the clutch gives out, the valves burn up, the retreads peel off, the pistons freeze within the worn-out rings.

Orphans. Another thing we notice coming into the South is this: while most of the farmhouses get smaller and flimsier, a few of them get bigger and heavier. Along the road are unpainted frame shacks one story high, but here and there on a hilltop you see a grand brick plantation house with white columns framing its entrance, the house centered in a spacious park of lawn and shrub and tree, approached by a winding asphalt drive.

Comical conical hills appear, like the hills in hillbilly comic strips—Snuffy Smith, Li'l Abner—with sagging gray shacks snagged on their summits. The leafless trees of winter, looking like the bristles on a brush, stand against the skyline. In each yeoman's frontyard there is a great pile of coal. The deadly fumes of coal smoke float on the breeze. Somewhere nearby, somebody's home and farm is being disemboweled by dragline and power shovel to provide such fuel for the family in the shack, for TVA and Oak Ridge, for you and me.

It's all legal. As local boosters point out, strip mining does provide jobs as well as fuel for the turbines. What would you have those men do, weave baskets? fire bricks? bake biscuits?

We drive through fields of dead goldenrod in the gray chill of December. Snow gleams in bald patches on the blue mountains beyond. We pass tawny hills, more ramshackle shacks, then pause for a while at a deserted crossroads to contemplate an abandoned country store.

The store just sits there in the cloud-filtered daylight, its old silvery clapboards warped and sprung, shakes dangling from the edge of the roof, screendoor ajar and hanging by one rusty hinge, the long front porch sagging in the middle, the whole aching creaking vacant structure canted to the east, in line with the prevailing winds.

We read the messages placarded in tin on the walls:

Chesterfields Are Best for You
Drink Dr. Pepper
Drink Coca-Cola
Drink Nesbitt's California Orange
Take Home Kern's Bread
Try W. E. Garrett & Sons' Sweet, Mild Snuff: A Taste Treat
Buy Merita Bread Vitamin-Enriched

Failure. Free enterprise sounds good in theory but look at this old store. Heartbreak and bankruptcy. The metal signs are rusting, they are loose, they flap and rattle in the wind. We pass on.

Past rocky pastures. Beautiful gray-green boulders mottled with lichen rise from the tough winter grass. Cows lounge about in the vicinity, ruminating and thoughtful. Sumac and willow stand with glowing skin along the fencerows. Mighty white oaks grow on the higher ground, their red leathery leaves still clinging to the stems.

Dead trees and dying trees draped in vine come into view on both sides of the road. They are victims of the creeping kudzu, *Pueraria lobata,* a parasitic vine imported from the Orient back in the late 1920's. Entire trees are enmeshed in the smothering stuff, wrapped like flies in a spiderweb. A gift, like karate and kamikaze, from Japan, this fast-growing exotic has spread over much of the Smoky Mountain area.

More trees and different trees appear—hemlock, white pine, pitch pine and other conifers, and rows of planted Scotch pine for the Christmas tree market.

Here's an ancient country church, painted white but faded to gray, with a high cupola on the roof and the bell missing. The New Era Baptist Church—like the store we had passed a mile before, this church looks derelict.

Into the hills we roll, into the past. Far up on the mountainside hangs a log cabin with blue smoke rising from the chimney. Near the road we pass an old barn made of squared-off logs, its roof covered with rusty tin. The barn is wreathed in wisteria.

We enter a little valley. Here we find farms that appear to be actually inhabited and worked. Some of the houses are painted. The barns, while not nearly so grand as Pennsylvania barns, look fairly well kept up; they have gambrel roofs and overhanging eaves at one end to shield the open gable from rain; through the opening under the end of the roof hay is carried by hayfork and pulley into the mow. Above, on a graded, grassy hill, we see another red-brick chateau; it makes a lovely picture from the road below with its white fluted pillars two stories high, the classic pediment, the tall windows flanked by shutters. The landlord's house.

Beyond the valley we enter foothills again. More hillbilly shacks come in sight, chimneys smoking, doorways full of staring children. Why aren't those children in school? I ask, scenting something sociological. Because it's Saturday, says my wife. But the style of poverty is unmistakable.

We see a stand of trees that look like eastern red cedar or *Juniperus virginiana*. There is no true cedar in the Western Hemisphere, the botanists assure us. I think of an old song I once heard, somewhere, long ago:

> You just lay there by the juniper
> When the moon is shining bright,
> And watch them jugs a-fillin'
> In the pale moonlight . . .

Clair de lune, white lightning, lead poisoning and rusty-red radiators. Shine on, harvest moon. We hain't paid no whisky tax since 1792.

We drive through the country, out here where the people used to live, among forgotten general stores and deconsecrated churches. Hysterical hens tear across the path of the car, hogs root in the oak groves, an old horse rests his chin in the crotch of a butternut tree and watches life pass him by. We see hand-built WPA bridges arching polluted but pretty streams where great leprous-skinned sycamores lean above the water. We pass a farmhouse with a somewhat crumpled look, like a worn but comfortable shoe; a swing hangs by chains on the long front porch. We see an antique John Deere tractor, the kind with iron lug wheels, a flatbed Ford with two flat tires. A poor but honest scene.

And then we come round a turn into the Knoxville-Gatlinburg highway and the mainstream of the way things are. By this I mean Sevierville, Tennessee, and the Little Pigeon River, full of acid, and walls of billboards on either side of the pavement drumming up trade:

GOLDRUSH JUNCTION—Cowboys, Indians & Outlaws: Gunfights Every Day
FORT APACHE—Gunfight Hourly—Live Saloon Shows
FRONTIERLAND—See Real Indians—Cherokee, N.C.
Don't Miss the New WAX MUSEUM—See Alan Shepard, Sgt. York real-as-life
See GHOST TOWN, MAGGIE VALLEY, N.C.—Real Life Gun Battles!
FABULOUS FAIRYLAND—Exciting Fun Rides for All Ages
MYSTERY HILL—Amazing Force of Gravity
GHOST TOWN IN THE SKY—Realistic Indian Battles
HILLBILLY VILLAGE—Copter Rides, Flea Market, Souvenirs
CAR MUSEUM & KAMP GROUND
JUNGLE CARGO—Indian Moccasins, Ice Cold Cider, Thick Rich Malts
CHRISTUS GARDENS—Outstanding All-Year All-Weather Attraction
GATLINBURG SKY LIFT—Your Shortcut to Heavenly Delight

Oh well, it's only innocent fun. Like any fungus. No harm in it. We proceed past the motels, filling stations, and Frigid Queen shake-and-burger joints—about ten miles of them—to the bright clean tourist town called Gatlinburg. The Gateway to Great Smoky Mountains National Park. Here we make camp for the night in a pleasant motel room with a wood fire burning in a genuine fireplace. (Small extra charge for use of firewood, says a sneaky notice inside the door.)

Tomorrow we shall conquer Clingman's Dome. By Volkswagen. In the meantime we make a walking tour of Gatlinburg, a town as tidy, efficient, quiet and sanitary as a Swiss ski village.

What's the alternative to this comfortable mediocrity? A grand European-style luxury hotel that most of us would not be able to afford? Or a return to the mode of a century ago, coming into a mountain village on horseback, having a cold supper by lamplight in the cabin-kitchen of some morose mountaineer while savage coon dogs howl and slaver on the other side of the door, then going to sleep in the early dark on a cornshuck mattress, prey to a host of bloodsucking vermin?

Which would I prefer?

You won't believe me but I'll tell you: I fancy the latter, i.e., the horse, cabin, dogs and bugs.

Thus we see the secret failure of American commerce. For all of its obvious successes and benefits, capitalism has failed to capture our hearts. Our souls, yes, but not our hearts. There is something ugly and mean about it which most of us can never accept.

So much for political economy. Walking at night through the quiet streets of Gatlinburg—where have all the tourists gone?—I look up, above the motel-hotel rooftops, and see the dark forms of the mountains bulking beyond, snow gleaming in the starlight.

Real mountains.

A WALK IN THE WOODS TO ALUM CAVE

An inch of virgin snow covers the ground—I am the first to walk this trail today. I cross the West Prong of the Little Pigeon River on a wooden footbridge, pausing in the middle to admire the view upstream. It looks like a picture invented by Eliot Porter: granite-like boulders lodged in the torrent, sheathed in ribbed, rippled layers of ice; spillways and plunge pools, the roil and rush and roar of the complicated waters; giant hemlocks leaning over the stream, fresh snow clinging to their bark; the stones and pebbles of the creekbed gleaming through the clarity of the water; and over all, illuminating the scene and blending with its shadows, the soft gray light of the mountain air.

Across the bridge, I sign my name in the registration book at the trailhead. I'm not only the first tourist today, I'm the first to come this way in a week. Winter time does have advantages. But on the wooden box that shelters the registration book somebody has inscribed Nazi swastikas. The good old boys were here too.

Walking up the snowy trail under snowladen trees, I feel an immense goodwill, despite the swastikas, toward my fellowman. Perhaps because I'm alone. Anthropy, not misanthropy, is what I feel today, and that's unusual for me. I feel a special benevolence toward the national park system and the Federal agency that administers that system. As a one-time employee of the Park Service, I was always impressed by the high esteem which the general public seems to hold for Park Service rangers and naturalists. Impressed and a little puzzled. Most of us most of the time feel toward the uniformed functionaries of the state, especially police and quasi-police like rangers, no more at best than a grudging tolerance, as of a necessary evil. Why should the Park Service enjoy a special privilege in this regard?

Now, today, it seems to me that I have hit upon the answer. Maintaining the national park system is almost the only nice, decent, friendly thing the Federal Government does for ordinary people. Nearly all of its other activities, carried on at our expense, are for the benefit of the rich and powerful, or for the sake of secret, furtive, imperial causes that can inspire feelings only of shame and dread.

But the national parks belong to everyone. To the people. To all of us. The government keeps saying so and maybe, in this one case at least, the government is telling the truth.

A dead tree has fallen across the creek, forming a natural bridge. In the soft fresh snow on this bridge I see the foot-prints—like tiny handprints—of a raccoon going halfway across, turning, coming back. Apparently he lost his nerve midway over the icy current. Or maybe he only changed his mind.

A giant birch looms beside the trail, encrusted with cankers; one of the cankers resembles a tragic mask, scowling horribly. Dead trees stand here and there with stacks of saprophytic fungi, big clamlike shapes, tough and rubbery, clinging to their trunks. Elaborate filigree of ice and crystal decorates the water's edge. The rocks are coated with lichens, moss, frozen slime. I see the tracks of a small animal that has dragged something—its own tail?—across the snow into the brush.

High on the mountainside now, above most of the birch and hemlock, I come to what the mountaineers called a "laurel slick" and the botanists call a "heath bald." Hard to see why one term is more useful than the other. It is a treeless area on an exposed shoulder of the mountain covered with a dense growth of shrub-bery, head high, mostly members of the heath family—mountain laurel, rhododendron, sand myrtle, blueberry. The complete ab-sence of trees in such places as this in the otherwise well-forested Smokies has not been satisfactorily explained. Perhaps eventu-ally the trees will work their way back and resume their climactic place in the natural order here.

Trails like tunnels burrow through the thicket. A man could hardly crawl through there on hands and knees. Far below in the foggy valley crows are yawping. Good hiding place up here, I'm thinking. The thought recalls another old mountain song:

I'm gonna build me a cabin
Up on the mountain so high
That the blackbird can't find me,
Nor hear my sad cry . . .

The sun is a pale white disc behind the flowing clouds, like a holy wafer in the sky. I'll be fogbound pretty soon if I don't get myself down off this smoky mountain. But first— Onward. Upward.

To Alum Cave, which is not a cave but a great overhanging bluff a hundred feet high. The inside is coated with a film of minerals, including alum. The brow of this bluff is festooned with curtains, chandeliers, draperies, fangs and tiers of gigantic icicles, massive sabers of ice ten to twenty feet long. If one of those were to drop on a man it would cleave him from head to toe. I retreat beneath the shelter of the overhang and look out over the valleys, into the clouds, feeling as if I were inside the gaping mouth of Leviathan, peering outward past his teeth.

How strange and wonderful is our home, our earth, with its swirling vaporous atmosphere, its flowing and frozen liquids, its trembling plants, its creeping, crawling, climbing creatures, the croaking things with wings that hang on rocks and soar through fog, the furry grass, the scaly seas. To see our world as a space traveler might see it for the first time, through Venusian eyes or Martian antennae, how utterly rich and wild it would seem, how far beyond the power of the craziest, spaced-out, acid-headed imagination, even a god's, to conjure up from nothing.

Yet some among us have the nerve, the insolence, the brass, the gall to whine about the limitations of our earthbound fate and yearn for some more perfect world beyond the sky. We are none of us good enough for the world we have and yet we dream of Heaven.

Bitter as alum. Lonely laughter in the mountains. I'm close to a mile high, up among the balsam and the spruce, evening and fog are creeping close. I watch the tip of a slowly dripping icicle near my nose. Slower and slower the water oozes down. When that last drop freezes on the point it will form a little bulb, like the button on a fencing foil. Ice daggers, glassy swords and crystal knives crash around me. Time to get out of here.

Out yonder in the purling mist a lank and long-connected bird, dark as a shadow, comes drifting toward me, scarcely moving its black wings.

Time to go.

THE LONG WAY HOME

We check out of the Bearskin Motel. Churlishly I refuse to pay the extra charge for use of firewood, explaining that I think it immoral and unethical for a hotel, even a motel, to advertise as this one does—"YUP, REAL FIREPLACES"—and then penalize the unwary lodger for not bringing his own firewood. The clerk, an insouciant Southerner, smiles graciously and accepts my refusal.

My wife salvages our laundry from the Snow White & Seven Dwarfs Washateria (free Baptist literature on the walls) and we are off, once more up the mountain to Newfound Gap and down the other side into North Carolina and the town of Cherokee, Cherokee Capital of the World.

Here we find more charming and picturesque absurdities: The Wigwam Motel, with wigwams made of reinforced concrete (try dragging one of those down the Platte, Mrs. Crazy Horse); a green stegosaurus made of chicken wire and plaster leering at the passing motorist from the doorway of a curio shop where authentic Indian spears, made in Hong Kong, are offered for sale; The Mystery House, Closed for the Season; Frontierland—20 Rides and Shows, One Price; Deadwood Gulch; Fort Cherokee; Redskin Motel—50 Ultra-Modern Units; Honest Injun Trading Post (behind a gateway of totem poles); and the Twin Tepee Craft Shop.

Exhilarating.

Accelerating, we come next to the town of Sylva where I had lived for one brief term, long ago, while teaching English (I think) at the nearby University of Western Carolina.

Sylva must once have been a lovely place. Small, with a population of 5,000, nestled in the green hills below the Smokies, full of beautiful old houses, bisected by the waters of the Tuckasegee River, enjoying the life of a market center and the dignity of county seat, Sylva may have been beautiful. Now it is something else, for the streets are grimy and noisy, jammed with traffic, the river is a sewer, and the sky a pall of smog. The obvious villain in the picture is the local Mead's Paper Mill, busily pumping its foul garbage into the air and into the river, but general traffic and recent growth must bear the rest of the blame.

When I commented to one of the town's leading citizens, a fine old Southern gentleman, about the perpetual stink in the air, he replied, "Why, sir, that there smells lahk money to me." Smug and smiling all the way to the bank, where—I hope—he drops dead on the doorstep. Pascal said somewhere that in order to grasp the concept of the infinite we need only consider human stupidity.

I don't know. One suffers from hope. Maybe we can learn something from what we have done to this land. Probably not. And in any case is it any better elsewhere? Is it not far worse? No matter in what nation I lived I am certain I would find much to regret. All big social organizations are ugly, brutal, inhuman— prone to criminal acts which no man or community of men, on their own, would even think of. But just the same I despise my own nation most. Because I know it best. Because I love it, suffering from hope.

Enough of these gloomy thoughts. It's time to begin the journey home.

And where might that be? Where is home? That old gray gaunt Gothic farmhouse along a red-dog road in the hills of northern Appalachia? No more; never again. Where then?

A Russian writer named Prishvin said, "Home is where you have found your happiness." I think I know where that may be, at least for myself. I'll reveal this much: it has something to do with those mountains, those forests, those wild, free, lost, full-of-wonder places that rise yet (may they always!) above the squalor of the towns.

Appalachia, we'll be back.

FROM

Black Sun

(1971)

Driving beyond the little beach, which he remembers well, too well, and past the big willow tree where even now he can find, if he wants to search, the blackened stones of a fireplace, he continues for another mile to the end of the road. Where things have changed. There is a ranger station here now, and a commercial marina with store, docks, a launching ramp and boats for rent.

Gatlin chooses a small boat of the type called whaler, double-hulled fiberglass, with a powerful eighty-horsepower outboard engine. Alone, he races up the river at full throttle, through the afternoon, over a waterway that gleams under the sun like polished brass, golden and dazzling, under the red cliffs of the canyon. The wake of his boat flashes in the light, spreading from wall to wall, splashing against the rocky shore and against the white sand of lonely beaches overgrown with young willows and tamarisk. Against the wind blowing in his face, above the roar of the motor, he sings.

> Rejoice, Columbia's sons, rejoice,
> To tyrants never bend the knee,
> But join with heart and mind and voice
> For Jefferson! And Liberty!

In the middle of the channel he twists the boat to the left and works his way around a sandbar into a cove he knows and likes; shutting off the motor, he ties the bow line to a tree growing out over the bank, baits a hook with salmon eggs. The fish are biting; he catches several catfish and a couple of rainbow trout but all too small. Planted fish, hatchery fish. He throws them back into the water.

The heat becomes oppressive. He strips and dives over the side, swims around the boat twice and then to the beach, where he walks up and down for a while, naked and alone. Birds flit darkly through the willow thickets, chattering. A hawk sails overhead in the strip of blue between the cliffs. He lies in the shade, on the warm sand, unable to sleep, dreaming awake.

Late in the afternoon he swims back to the boat, climbs aboard, casts loose and lets it drift with the current down the river. Half in shade, half in sun, he sprawls on the seat and watches through half-closed eyes the slow ponderous movement of the canyon rim a thousand feet above turning against the sky. Carved in that monumental rock he sees alcoves and arches, pillars and buttresses, and on the skyline the profiles of blind, silent, implacable gods, bird gods in stone with the mask of hawks.

A beaver swims by, headed upstream, passing within six feet of the boat. Gatlin watches it go. On shore he sees another, standing, balanced like a tripod on its hind legs and tail, preening its sleek head with the two dexterous forepaws.

The sound of human voices. He is floating past the marina, out of the upper canyon and through an opening in the cliffs toward the lower canyon. Toward the great canyon. Already he can hear, from a mile ahead, the first dull murmur of the rapids. A shout of warning from onshore.

Gatlin starts the engine and turns upriver toward the docks. Hesitates, changes his mind and turns the boat around again. He switches the fuel line from the near-empty tank to the full one, puts on a lifejacket and stands up behind the wheel in order to see more easily what lies directly ahead. Slowing the motor to idling speed, he bears for the smooth shining tongue of the first rapids.

A wave curls before him. He passes around the first rock, a pale slab of limestone dim beneath the green water, and into the rapids. The boat yaws and pitches, shipping water by the bucketful, between two rocks and into a trough in the waves. He guns the motor as a rolling wave crashes into the boat, setting everything loose afloat. His shoes and socks, his rod and tackle box and water jug float around his ankles. Beyond the rapids, in quiet water again, he unscrews the drain plug in the stern and lets the motor pump the boat dry.

Cruising on down the river, between gravel bars and submerged boulders, crashing through more minor rapids like the first, he enters deeper and deeper into the gorge, into deep shadow under a sky charged with evening sunlight, toward the beginning of the wilderness.

Around a bend. Not far ahead he can now see what looks like the end of the river. The water seems to come to a sudden fall or dropping-off place beyond which the river cannot be seen. Along this edge hovers a mist of spray, pale against the darkness beyond, and into the mist, at irregular intervals, writhing waves leap from below.

Down there. Gatlin stares into the chaos before him. Down there, he thinks. Where? How far? Somewhere, down in there, a hundred miles below.

He beaches the boat and walks along the shore toward the rapids, clambering over a delta of boulders washed down from a side canyon. On one of these, surrounded by swirling water, he sits and contemplates the heart of the tumbling river. Fangs of rock split the current as it drops from ledge to ledge, descending twenty feet in a distance shorter than a football field. There are waves in there twelve feet high, holes and explosions in the water, a whirlpool of foam and fury. He might if extremely lucky get the boat down through here; he could never get it back again.

Gatlin is tempted. Why not, he thinks. Go on. Into it. Keep going. All the way into the underworld. Somewhere down in there she may still be alive, waiting for you, hoping for you, dreaming of you as you dream of her. Living on what? On watercress and mesquite beans and the bloom of the sacred datura. On hope and memory.

No. There is no remedy. The river sings, a mad chaotic babble of many voices . . .

Through the twilight he walks slowly back to the boat, deafened by the dull deep roar of the rapids. He almost blunders into a rattlesnake. Stopping suddenly, he is seized for a moment by the primeval fear.

The snake is a diamondback, six feet long and thick as his forearm; agitated, hostile, it lies coiled in the middle of the path, the heavy spade-shaped head aloft and weaving from side to side, ready to strike. The tail vibrates in nervous frenzy, inaudible, however, against the uproar of the river.

Gatlin backs off a step. He crouches low and peers directly into the eyes of the snake. He places his hand on a loose stone.

"Cousin," he cries, "what have you done with her?"

The bleak and dusty eyes stare back at him, the thin black tongue slips in and out as the snake attempts to sense the nature of this unknown danger.

"What have you done with her?" Gatlin cries again. He lifts the stone, advances a step.

On guard, ready to lunge, the big rattlesnake retreats slowly toward the side of the path, toward the shelter of the cactus and tumbled rocks.

Gatlin drops the stone, lifts empty hands palm upward toward the snake.

"Where is she?" he begs. "Where is she?" . . .

The Monkey Wrench Gang

(1975)

SELDOM SEEN AT HOME

Green River, Utah. Susan's house. The watermelon ranch. An easy day's drive from Sheila's place at Bountiful, which was in turn an easy day's drive from Kathy's house near Cedar City. He'd planned it all that way, of course, from the beginning. Seldom Seen Smith hearkened to the prophet Brigham: he was polygamous as a rabbit.

Three o'clock in the morning and the bedroom was full of dreams. Oh pearl of great price! Through the open windows floated the smell of ripening watermelons, the sweet odor of cut alfalfa. (Second cutting of the summer.) Also the smells, poignant and irrevocable, of apple trees, horseshit, and wild asparagus along the irrigation ditches. From the embankment only one field away came the sound of whispering willow, the flat whack! of a beaver's tail slapping the river water.

That river. That river, that golden Green, flowing down from the snows of the Wind River Range, through Flaming Gorge and Echo Park, Split Mountain and The Gates of Lodore, down from the hills of Ow-Wi-Yu-Kuts, from the Yampa, Bitter Creek and Sweetwater, down the canyon called Desolation through the Tavaputs Plateau to emerge from the portal of the Book Cliffs—which John Wesley Powell thought "one of the most wonderful facades in the world"—and there to roll across the Green River Desert into a second world of canyons, where the river gives itself to Labyrinth and Stillwater and the confluence with the Grand, under the rim of The Maze and into the roaring depths of Cataract . . .

Smith lay in his bed beside his third wife and dreamed his troublesome dream. They were after him again. His truck had been identified. His rocks had rolled too far. The Search and Rescue Team was howling mad. A warrant for his arrest had been issued in San Juan County. The Bishop of Blanding raged like a strictured bull over half of Utah. Smith fled down endless corridors of sweating concrete. Under the Dam. Trapped again in the recurring nightmare of That Dam.

Down in the dank bowels of Reclamation. Engineers on skateboards glided past, clipboards in hand. Pneumatic panels opened before him, closed behind him, drawing Smith deeper and deeper into the dynamo heart of The Enemy. Magnetic webs pulled him toward the Inner Office. Where the Director waited, waiting for him. Like Doc and Bonnie and George, also locked up somewhere in here, Smith knew he was going to be punished.

The final door opened. Smith was dragged inside. The door slid shut and sealed itself. He stood again before the ultimate eye. In The Presence.

The Director peered at Smith from the center of an array of metric dials, scintilometers, temblor screens, Visographs and sensorscopes. Tape reels spun, their circuits humming, before the quiet buzz of electronic thought at work.

The Director was monocular. The red beam of its unlidded Cyclops eye played on the face of Seldom Seen, scanning his brain, his nerves, his soul. Paralyzed by that hypnotic ray, Smith waited helpless as a babe.

The Director spoke. Its voice resembled the whine of an electronic violin, pitched in highest register to C-sharp, that same internal note which drove the deaf Smetana insane. "Smith," the voice began, "we know why you are here."

Smith gulped. "Where's George?" he croaked. "What you done to Bonnie?"

"Never mind that." The red beam glanced aside for a moment, shifty-gimbaled in its hooded carapace. The tape reels stopped, reversed, stopped, rolled forward again, recording all. Coded messages flickered in sleek electric flow, transistor-relayed through ten thousand miles of printed circuitry. Beneath the superstructure the dynamo purred on, murmuring the basic message: Power . . . profit . . . prestige . . . pleasure . . . profit . . . prestige . . . pleasure . . . power . . .

"Seldom Seen Smith," the Director said, its voice now tuned to a human intonation (modeled it would seem on the voice of an aging teenybopper balladeer whose scraggly-bearded unisex face has appeared on the cover of *Rolling Stone* seventeen times since 1964), "where are your pants?"

Pants? Smith looked down. Good Gawd Almighty!

The scanning beam returned to Smith's face. "Come closer, fellow," the voice commanded.

Smith hesitated.

"Come closer, Joseph Fielding Smith, known informally as 'Seldom Seen,' born Salt Lake City, Utah, Shithead Capital of the Inter-Mountain West, for behold art thou not he who was foretold in 1 Nephi 2:1–4, The Book of Mormon, wherein it is written, 'The Lord commanded him, even in a dream, that he should take his family and depart into the wilderness'? With ample provision, such as organic peanut butter, and with his family known as one Doc Sarvis, one George W. Hayduke, and one Miz B. Abbzug?"

Some tongue from a higher world answered for Smith, in words he knew not: "Datsa me, Boss."

"Good. But unfortunately for you, fellow, the prophecy cannot be fulfilled. We cannot allow it. We have decreed, Smith, that thou shalt become as one of us."

What?

Four green bulbs winked in the Director's frontal lobes. The voice changed again, becoming clipped and cryptic, clearly Oxonian. "Seize him."

Smith found himself pinioned instantly by rigid, though invisible, bonds. "Hey__?" He struggled feebly.

"Good. Affix the electrodes. Insert the anode into his penis. Quite so. The cathode goes up the rectum. Half a meter. Yes, all the way. Don't be squeamish." The Director issued his orders to invisible assistants, who bustled about Smith's paralyzed body. "Good. Imprint the flip-flop circuits on his semi-circular canal. Below the ear drum. Right. Five thousand volts should be sufficient. Attach sensor wires by strontium suction cup to his coccyx. Firmly. Plug the high-voltage adapter into the frontal sockets of his receptor node. The head, idiots, the head! Yes—right up the nostrils. Be firm. Push hard. Quite so. Very good. Now close circuit breakers. Quickly. Thank you."

Horrified, Smith tried to speak, to protest, But his tongue, like his limbs, seemed gripped in an absolute and infantile paralysis. He gaped in terror at the cables now joining his head and body to the computer bank before him.

"Well now, Smith," the Director said, "—or should we call you (heh heh) Seldom Scanned?—are you ready for your program? What's that? Now now, buck up. That's a good lad. You have nothing to fear if you can pass this simple test we have prepared for you. Nothing to fear but fear itself, so to speak. Call the taper, please. Good. Insert the magnetic tape. No tape slot? Then make one. Between the anode and cathode attachments, of course. Right up through the old perineum. Precisely. Never mind the blood, we'll have George clean that up later. Ready? Insert the tape. All the way. Hold his other foot down. What? Then nail it down! Good. Quite so."

The Director's single eye beamed into Smith's pineal gland. "Now Smith, your instructions. We want you to expand the simple exponential function $y = e^x$ into an infinite series. Proceed as follows: Bn: transfer contents of storage location n to working register; Tn: transfer contents of working register to location n; +n: add contents of location n to contents of working register; xn: multiply contents of working register by contents of location n; ÷n: divide contents of working register by contents of location n; V: make sign of contents of working register positive; Pn: transfer address n to accumulator if contents of working register are positive; Rn: transfer address in location n to accumulator; Z: stop program. Is that clear, Smith?"

Numb as novocaine, Seldom could not speak.

"Good. Get ready. You have 0.000012 milliseconds in which to perform this basic operation. If you fail we will have no choice but to transplant your vital organs into more adapable specimens and to recycle your residue through the thermite crucibles. Are you ready? Good lad. Have fun now. Set the timer, please. On your toes, Smith. Count down from five. Here we go. Five! Four! Three! Two! One! Zero! THROW THE GODDAMNED SWITCH!"

"Aaaaaaaaaaaaaah . . ." Smith rose in his bed, filmed with cold sweat, turned and clutched at his wife like a drowning man. "Sheila," he groaned, struggling toward the surface of consciousness, "great almighty Gawd—!"

"Seldom!" She was awake at once. "Wake up, Seldom!"

"Sheila, Sheila . . ."

"There's nobody here named Sheila. Wake up."

"Oh Lord . . ." He fumbled at her in the dark, feeling a warm hip, a soft belly. "Kathy?"

"You were at Kathy's last night. You have one more guess and it better be right."

He groped higher and fondled her breasts. The right one. The left one. Two of them. "Susan?"

"That's better."

Vision adapting to the starlit darkness, he found her smiling at him, reaching for him with both arms from the warmth of their lawful conjugal bed. Her smile, like her sweet eyes, like her bountiful bosom, was rich with love. He sighed in relief. "Susan . . ."

"Seldom, you are a caution. You are something else. I never."

And she consoled, caressed and loved him, her trembling, stricken man.

While outside in the fields of desert summer the melons ripened at their leisure in the nest of their vines, and a restless rooster, perched on the roof of the hencoop, fired his premature ejaculation at the waning moon, and in the pasture the horses lifted noble Roman heads to stare in the night at something humans cannot see.

Far away in Utah on the farm, by the side of a golden river called the Green.

FROM

The Journey Home

(1977)

The Great American Desert

In my case it was love at first sight. This desert, all deserts, any desert. No matter where my head and feet may go, my heart and my entrails stay behind, here on the clean, true, comfortable rock, under the black sun of God's forsaken country. When I take on my next incarnation, my bones will remain bleaching nicely in a stone gulch under the rim of some faraway plateau, way out there in the back of beyond. An unrequited and excessive love, inhuman no doubt but painful anyhow, especially when I see my desert under attack. "The one death I cannot bear," said the Sonoran-Arizonan poet Richard Shelton. The kind of love that makes a man selfish, possessive, irritable. If you're thinking of a visit, my natural reaction is like a rattlesnake's—to warn you off. What I want to say goes something like this.

Survival Hint #1: Stay out of there. Don't go. Stay home and read a good book, this one for example. The Great American Desert is an awful place. People get hurt, get sick, get lost out there. Even if you survive, which is not certain, you will have a miserable time. The desert is for movies and God-intoxicated mystics, not for family recreation.

Let me enumerate the hazards. First the Walapai tiger, also known as conenose kissing bug. *Triatoma protracta* is a true bug, black as sin, and it flies through the night quiet as an assassin. It does not attack directly like a mosquito or deerfly but alights at a discreet distance, undetected, and creeps upon you, its hairy little feet making not the slightest noise. The kissing bug is fond of warmth and like Dracula requires mammalian blood for sustenance. When it reaches you the bug crawls onto your skin so gently, so softly that unless your senses are hyperacute you feel nothing. Selecting a tender point, the bug slips its conical proboscis into your flesh, injecting a poisonous anesthetic. If you are asleep you will feel nothing. If you happen to be awake you may notice the faintest of pinpricks, hardly more than a brief ticklish sensation, which you will probably disregard. But the bug is already at work. Having numbed the nerves near the point of entry the bug proceeds (with a sigh of satisfaction) to withdraw blood. When its belly is filled, it pulls out, backs off, and waddles away, so drunk and gorged it cannot fly.

At about this time the victim awakes, scratching at a furious itch. If you recognize the symptoms at once, you can sometimes find the bug in your vicinity and destroy it. But revenge will be your only satisfaction. Your night is ruined. If you are of average sensitivity to a kissing bug's poison your entire body breaks out in hives, skin aflame from head to toe. Some people become seriously ill, in many cases requiring hospitalization. Others recover fully after five or six hours except for a hard and itchy swelling which may endure for a week.

After the kissing bug, you should beware of rattlesnakes; we have half a dozen species, all offensive and dangerous, plus centipedes, millipedes, tarantulas, black widows, brown recluses, Gila monsters, the deadly poisonous coral snakes, and giant hairy desert scorpions. Plus an immense variety and near-infinite number of ants, ticks, midges, gnats, bloodsucking flies, and blood-guzzling mosquitoes. (You might think the desert would be spared at least mosquitoes? Not so. Peer in any water hole by day: swarming with mosquito larvae. Venture out on a summer's eve: The air vibrates with their mournful keening.) Finally, where the desert meets the sea, as on the coasts of Sonora and Baja California, we have the usual assortment of obnoxious marine life: sandflies, ghost crabs, stingrays, electric jellyfish, spiny sea urchins, maneating sharks, and other creatures so distasteful one prefers not even to name them.

It has been said, and truly, that everything in the desert either stings, stabs, stinks, or sticks. You will find the flora here as venomous, hooked, barbed, thorny, prickly, needled, saw-toothed, hairy, stickered, mean, bitter, sharp, wiry, and fierce as the animals. Something about the desert inclines all living things to harshness and acerbity. The soft evolve out. Except for sleek and oily growths like the poison ivy—oh yes, indeed—that flourish in sinister profusion on the dank walls above the quicksand down in those corridors of gloom and labyrinthine monotony that men call canyons.

We come now to the third major hazard, which is sunshine. Too much of a good thing can be fatal. Sunstroke, heatstroke, and dehydration are common misfortunes in the bright American Southwest. If you can avoid the insects, reptiles, and arachnids, the cactus and the ivy, the smog of the southwestern cities and the lung fungus of the desert valleys (carried by dust in the air), you cannot escape the desert sun. Too much exposure to it eventually causes, quite literally, not merely sunburn but skin cancer.

Much sun, little rain also means an arid climate. Compared with the high humidity of more hospitable regions, the dry heat of the desert seems at first not terribly uncomfortable—sometimes even pleasant. But that sensation of comfort is false, a deception, and therefore all the more dangerous, for it induces overexertion and an insufficient consumption of water, even when water is available. This leads to various internal complications, some immediate—sunstroke, for example—and some not apparent until much later. Mild but prolonged dehydration, continued over a span of months or years, leads to the crystallization of mineral solutions in the urinary tract, that is, to what urologists call urinary calculi or kidney stones. A disability common in all the world's arid regions. Kidney stones, in case you haven't met one, come in many shapes and sizes, from pellets smooth as BB shot to highly irregular calcifications resembling asteroids, Vietcong shrapnel, and crown-of-thorns starfish. Some of these objects may be "passed" naturally; others can be removed only by means of the Davis stone basket or by surgery. Me—I was lucky; I passed mine with only a groan, my forehead pressed against the wall of a pissoir in the rear of a Tucson bar that I cannot recommend.

You may be getting the impression by now that the desert is not the most suitable of environments for human habitation. Correct. Of all the Earth's climatic zones, excepting only the Antarctic, the deserts are the least inhabited, the least "developed," for reasons that should now be clear.

You may wish to ask, Yes, okay, but among North American deserts which is the *worst*? A good question—and I am happy to attempt an answer.

Geographers generally divide the North American desert— what was once termed "the Great American Desert"—into four distinct regions or subdeserts. These are the Sonoran Desert, which comprises southern Arizona, Baja California, and the state of Sonora in Mexico; the Chihuahuan Desert, which includes west Texas, southern New Mexico, and the states of Chihuahua and Coahuila in Mexico; the Mojave Desert, which includes southeastern California and small portions of Nevada, Utah, and Arizona; and the Great Basin Desert, which includes most of Utah and Nevada, northern Arizona, northwestern New Mexico, and much of Idaho and eastern Oregon.

Privately, I prefer my own categories. Up north in Utah somewhere is the canyon country—places like Zeke's Hole, Death Hollow, Pucker Pass, Buckskin Gulch, Nausea Crick, Wolf Hole, Mollie's Nipple, Dirty Devil River, Horse Canyon, Horseshoe Canyon, Lost Horse Canyon, Horsethief Canyon, and Horseshit Canyon, to name only the more classic places. Down in Arizona and Sonora there's the cactus country; if you have nothing better to do, you might take a look at High Tanks, Salome Creek, Tortilla Flat, Esperero ("Hoper") Canyon, Holy Joe Peak, Depression Canyon, Painted Cave, Hell Hole Canyon, Hell's Half Acre, Iceberg Canyon, Tiburon (Shark) Island, Pinacate Peak, Infernal Valley, Sykes Crater, Montezuma's Head, Gu Oidak, Kuakatch, Pisinimo, and Baboquivari Mountain, for example.

Then there's The Canyon. *The* Canyon. The Grand. That's one world. And North Rim—that's another. And Death Valley, still another, where I lived one winter near Furnace Creek and climbed the Funeral Mountains, tasted Badwater, looked into the Devil's Hole, hollered up Echo Canyon, searched for and never did find Seldom Seen Slim. Looked for *satori* near Vana, Nevada, and found a ghost town named Bonnie Claire. Never made it to Winnemucca. Drove through the Smoke Creek Desert and down through Big Pine and Lone Pine and home across the Panamints to Death Valley again—home sweet home that winter.

And which of these deserts is the worst? I find it hard to judge. They're all bad—not half bad but all bad. In the Sonoran Desert, Phoenix will get you if the sun, snakes, bugs, and arthropods don't. In the Mojave Desert it's Las Vegas, more sickening by far than the Glauber's salt in the Death Valley sinkholes. Go to Chihuahua and you're liable to get busted in El Paso and sandbagged in Ciudad Juárez—where all old whores go to die. Up north in the Great Basin Desert, on the Plateau Province, in the canyon country, your heart will break, seeing the strip mines open up and the power plants rise where only cowboys and Indians and J. Wesley Powell ever roamed before.

Nevertheless, all is not lost; much remains, and I welcome the prospect of an army of lug-soled hiker's boots on the desert trails. To save what wilderness is left in the American Southwest—and in the American Southwest only the wilderness is worth saving—we are going to need all the recruits we can get. All the hands, heads, bodies, time, money, effort we can find. Presumably—and the Sierra Club, the Wilderness Society, the Friends of the Earth, the Audubon Society, the Defenders of Wildlife operate on this theory—those who learn to love what is spare, rough, wild, undeveloped, and unbroken will be willing to fight for it, will help resist the strip miners, highway builders, land developers, weapons testers, power producers, tree chainers, clear cutters, oil drillers, dam beavers, subdividers—the list goes on and on—before that zinc-hearted, termite-brained, squint-eyed, near-sighted, greedy crew succeeds in completely californicating what still survives of the Great American Desert.

So much for the Good Cause. Now what about desert hiking itself, you may ask. I'm glad you asked that question. I firmly believe that one should never—I repeat *never*—go out into that formidable wasteland of cactus, heat, serpents, rock, scrub, and thorn without careful planning, thorough and cautious preparation, and complete—never mind the expense!—*complete* equipment. My motto is: Be Prepared.

That is my belief and that is my motto. My practice, however, is a little different. I tend to go off in a more or less random direction myself, half-baked, half-assed, half-cocked, and half-ripped. Why? Well, because I have an indolent and melancholy nature and don't care to be bothered getting all those *things* together—all that bloody *gear*—maps, compass, binoculars, poncho, pup tent, shoes, first-aid kit, rope, flashlight, inspirational poetry, water, food—and because anyhow I approach nature with a certain surly ill-will, daring Her to make trouble. Later when I'm deep into Natural Bridges Natural Moneymint or Zion National Parkinglot or say General Shithead National Forest Land of Many Abuses why then, of course, when it's a bit late, then I may wish I had packed that something extra: matches perhaps, to mention one useful item, or maybe a spoon to eat my gruel with.

If I hike with another person it's usually the same; most of my friends have indolent and melancholy natures too. A cursed lot, all of them. I think of my comrade John De Puy, for example, sloping along for mile after mile like a goddamned camel—indefatigable—with those J. C. Penny hightops on his feet and that plastic pack on his back he got with five books of Green Stamps and nothing inside it but a sketchbook, some homemade jerky and a few cans of green chiles. Or Douglas Peacock, ex-Green Beret, just the opposite. Built like a buffalo, he hefts a ninety-pound canvas pannier on his back at trailhead, loaded with guns, ammunition, bayonet, pitons and carabiners, cameras, field books, a 150-foot rope, geologist's sledge, rock samples, assay kit, field glasses, two gallons of water in steel canteens, jungle boots, a case of C-rations, rope hammock, pharmaceuticals in a pig-iron box, raincoat, overcoat, two-man mountain tent, Dutch oven, hibachi, shovel, ax, inflatable boat, and near the top of the load and distributed through side and back pockets, easily accessible, a case of beer. Not because he enjoys or needs all that weight—he may never get to the bottom of that cargo on a ten-day outing—but simply because Douglas uses his packbag for general storage both at home and on the trail and prefers not to have to rearrange everything from time to time merely for the purposes of a hike. Thus my friends De Puy and Peacock; you may wish to avoid such extremes.

A few tips on desert etiquette:

1. Carry a cooking stove, if you must cook. Do not burn desert wood, which is rare and beautiful and required ages for its creation (an ironwood tree lives for over 1,000 years and juniper almost as long).
2. If you must, out of need, build a fire, then for God's sake allow it to burn itself out before you leave—do not bury it, as Boy Scouts and Campfire Girls do, under a heap of mud or sand. Scatter the ashes; replace any rocks you may have used in constructing a fireplace; do all you can to obliterate the evidence that you camped here. (The Search & Rescue Team may be looking for you.)
3. Do not bury garbage—the wildlife will only dig it up again. Burn what will burn and pack out the rest. The same goes for toilet paper: Don't bury it, *burn it.*
4. Do not bathe in desert pools, natural tanks, *tinajas,* potholes. Drink what water you need, take what you need, and leave the rest for the next hiker and more important for the bees, birds, and animals—bighorn sheep, coyotes, lions, foxes, badgers, deer, wild pigs, wild horses—whose *lives* depend on that water.
5. Always remove and destroy survey stakes, flagging, advertising signboards, mining claim markers, animal traps, poisoned bait, seismic exploration geophones, and other such artifacts of industrialism. The men who put those things there are up to no good and it is our duty to confound them. Keep America Beautiful. Grow a Beard. Take a Bath. Burn a Billboard.

Anyway—why go into the desert? Really, why do it? That sun, roaring at you all day long. The fetid, tepid, vapid little water holes slowly evaporating under a scum of grease, full of cannibal beetles, spotted toads, horsehair worms, liver flukes, and down at the bottom, inevitably, the pale cadaver of a ten-inch centipede. Those pink rattlesnakes down in The Canyon, those diamondback monsters thick as a truck driver's wrist that lurk in shady places along the trail, those unpleasant solpugids and unnecessary Jerusalem crickets that scurry on dirty claws across your face at night. Why? The rain that comes down like lead shot and wrecks the trail, those sudden rockfalls of obscure origin that crash like thunder ten feet behind you in the heart of a dead-still afternoon. The ubiquitous buzzard, so patient—but only so patient. The sullen and hostile Indians, all on welfare. The ragweed, the tumbleweed, the Jimson weed, the snakeweed. The scorpion in your shoe at dawn. The dreary wind that blows all spring, the psychedelic Joshua trees waving their arms at you on moonlight nights. Sand in the soup du jour. Halazone tablets in your canteen. The barren hills that always go up, which is bad, or down, which is worse. Those canyons like catacombs with quicksand lapping at your crotch. Hollow, mummified horses with forelegs casually crossed, dead for ten years, leaning against the corner of a barbed-wire fence. Packhorses at night, iron-shod, clattering over the slickrock through your camp. The last tin of tuna, two flat tires, not enough water and a forty-mile trek to Tule Well. An osprey on a cardón cactus, snatching the head off a living fish—always the best part first. The hawk sailing by at 200 feet, a squirming snake in its talons. Salt in the drinking water. Salt, selenium, arsenic, radon and radium in the water, in the gravel, in your bones. Water so hard it bends light, drills holes in rock and chokes up your radiator. Why go there? Those places with the hardcase names: Starvation Creek, Poverty Knoll, Hungry Valley, Bitter Springs, Last Chance Canyon, Dungeon Canyon, Whipsaw Flat, Dead Horse Point, Scorpion Flat, Dead Man Draw, Stinking Spring, Camino del Diablo, Jornado del Muerto . . . Death Valley.

Well then, why indeed go walking into the desert, that grim ground, that bleak and lonesome land where, as Genghis Khan said of India, "the heat is bad and the water makes men sick"?

Why the desert, when you could be strolling along the golden beaches of California? Camping by a stream of pure Rocky Mountain spring water in colorful Colorado? Loafing through a laurel slick in the misty hills of North Carolina? Or getting your head mashed in the greasy alley behind the Elysium Bar and Grill in Hoboken, New Jersey? Why the desert, given a world of such splendor and variety?

A friend and I took a walk around the base of a mountain up beyond Coconino County, Arizona. This was a mountain we'd been planning to circumambulate for years. Finally we put on our walking shoes and did it. About halfway around this mountain, on the third or fourth day, we paused for a while—two days—by the side of a stream which the Indians call Nasja because of the amber color of the water. (Caused perhaps by juniper roots—the water seems safe enough to drink.) On our second day there I walked down the stream, alone, to look at the canyon beyond. I entered the canyon and followed it for half the afternoon, for three or four miles, maybe, until it became a gorge so deep, narrow and dark, full of water and the inevitable quagmires of quicksand, that I turned around and looked for a way out. A route other than the way I'd come, which was crooked and uncomfortable and buried—I wanted to see what was up on top of this world. I found a sort of chimney flue on the east wall, which looked plausible, and sweated and cursed my way up through that until I reached a point where I could walk upright, like a human being. Another 300 feet of scrambling brought me to the rim of the canyon. No one, I felt certain, had ever before departed Nasja Canyon by that route.

But someone had. Near the summit I found an arrow sign, three feet long, formed of stones and pointing off into the north toward those same old purple vistas, so grand, immense, and mysterious, of more canyons, more mesas and plateaus, more mountains, more cloud-dappled sunspangled leagues of desert sand and desert rock under the same old wide and aching sky.

The arrow pointed into the north. But what was it pointing *at*? I looked at the sign closely and saw that those dark, desert-varnished stones had been in place for a long, long, time; they rested in compacted dust. They must have been there for a century at least. I followed the direction indicated and came promptly to the rim of another canyon and a drop-off straight down of a good 500 feet. Not that way, surely. Across this canyon was nothing of any unusual interest that I could see—only the familiar sun-blasted sandstone, a few scrubby clumps of black-brush and prickly pear, a few acres of nothing where only a lizard could graze, surrounded by a few square miles of more nothingness interesting chiefly to horned toads. I returned to the arrow and checked again, this time with field glasses, looking away for as far as my aided eyes could see toward the north, for ten, twenty, forty miles into the distance. I studied the scene with care, looking for an ancient Indian ruin, a significant cairn, perhaps an abandoned mine, a hidden treasure of some inconceivable wealth, the mother of all mother lodes. . . .

But there was nothing out there. Nothing at all. Nothing but the desert. Nothing but the silent world.

That's why.

Death Valley

SUMMERTIME. From Daylight Pass at 4,317 feet we descend through Boundary Canyon and Hell's Gate into the inferno at sea level and below. Below, below . . . beneath a sea, not of brine but of heat, of simmering shimmering waves of light and a wind as hot and fierce as a dragon's breath.

The glare is stunning. Yet also exciting, even exhilarating—a world of light. The air seems not clear like glass but colored, a transparent, tinted medium, golden toward the sun, smoke-blue in the shadows. The colors come, it appears, not simply from the background, but are actually present in the air itself—a vigintillion microscopic particles of dust reflecting the sky, the sand, the iron hills.

On a day in June at ten o'clock in the morning the thermometer reads 114 degrees. Later in the day it will become hotter. But with humidity close to zero such heat is not immediately unpleasant or even uncomfortable. Like the dazzling air, the heat is at first somehow intoxicating—one feels that grace and euphoria that come with just the right ration of Old Grandad, with the perfect allowance of music. Sunlight is magic. Later will come. . . . Yes, out of the car and standing hatless under the sun, you begin to feel the menace in this arid atmosphere, the malignancy within that silent hurricane of fire.

We consider the dunes, the sea of sand. Around the edges of the dunes grow clumps of arrowweed tall as corn shocks, scattered creosote shrubs bleached out and still, a few shaggy mesquite trees. These plants can hardly be said to have conquered

the valley, but they have in some way made a truce—or found a point of equilibrium in a ferocious, inaudible struggle between life and entropy. A bitter war indeed: The creosote bush secretes a poison in its roots that kills any other plant, even its own offspring, attempting to secure a place too near; in this way the individual creosote preserves a perimeter of open space and a monopoly of local moisture sufficient for survival.

We drive on to the gas station and store at Stovepipe Wells, where a few humans huddle inside beneath the blast of a cold-air blower. Like other mammals of the valley, the human inhabitants can endure its summer only by burrowing deep or by constructing an artificial environment—not adaptation but insulation, insularity.

Sipping cold drinks, we watch through the window a number of desert sparrows crawl in and out of the grills on the front of the parked automobiles. The birds are eating tourists—bugs and butterflies encountered elsewhere and smashed, baked, annealed to the car radiators. Like the bears of Yellowstone, the Indians of Arizona, and roadside businessmen everywhere, these birds have learned to make a good thing off passing trade. Certainly they provide a useful service; it's a long hot climb out of here in any direction and a clean radiator is essential.

The Indians of Death Valley were cleverest of all. When summer came they left, went up into the mountains, and stayed there until it was reasonable to return—an idea too subtle in its simplicity for the white man of today to grasp. But we too are Indians—gypsies anyhow—and won't be back until September.

FURNACE CREEK, SEPTEMBER 17. Again the alarming descent. It seemed much too hot in the barren hills a mile above this awful sinkhole, this graben (for Death Valley is not, properly understood, a valley at all), this collapsed and superheated trench of mud, salt, gravel, and sand. Much too hot—but we felt obliged to come back once more.

A hard place to love, Death Valley. An ugly place, bitter as alkali and rough, harsh, unyielding as iron. Here they separate the desert rats from the mice, the hard-rock prospectors from the mere rock hounds.

Cactus for example. There is none at all on the floor of the valley. Too dry or too brackish or maybe too hot. Only up on the alluvial fans and in the side canyons 1,000 feet above sea level do we find the first stunted and scrubby specimens of cholla and prickly pear and the pink-thorned cottontop—poor relation of the barrel cactus.

At first glance, speeding by car through this valley that is not a valley, one might think there was scarcely any plant life at all. Between oases you will be impressed chiefly by the vast salt beds and the immense alluvial fans of gravel that look as hostile to life as the fabled seas of the moon.

And yet there is life out there, life of a sparse but varied sort—salt grass and pickleweed on the flats, far-spaced clumps of creosote, saltbush, desert holly, brittlebush, and prickly poppy on the fans. Not much of anything, but a little of each. And in the area as a whole, including the surrounding mountains up to the 11,000-foot summit of Telescope Peak, the botanists count a total of 900 to 1,000 different species, ranging from microscopic forms of algae in the salt pools to limber pine and the ancient bristlecone pine on the peaks.

But the first impression remains a just one. Despite variety, most of the surface of Death Valley is dead. Dead, dead, deathly—a land of jagged salt pillars, crackling and tortured crusts of mud, sunburnt gravel bars the color of rust, rocks and boulders of metallic blue naked even of lichen. Death Valley is Gravel Gulch.

TELESCOPE PEAK, OCTOBER 22. To escape the heat for a while, we spend the weekend up in the Panamints. (Summer still baking the world down below, far below, where swirls of mud, salt, and salt-laden streams lie motionless under a lake of heat, glowing in lovely and poisonous shades of auburn, saffron, crimson, sulfurous yellow, dust-tinged tones of white on white.)

Surely this is the most sterile of North American deserts. No matter how high we climb it seems impossible to leave behind the influence of aridity and anti-life. At 7,000 feet in this latitude we should be entering a forest of yellow pine, with grassy meadows and freshwater brooks. We are farther north than Santa Fe or Flagstaff. Instead there are only the endless barren hills, conventional in form, covered in little but shattered stone. A dull monotonous terrain, duncolored, supporting a few types of shrubs and small, scattered junipers.

From 7,000 to 9,000 feet we pass through a belt of more junipers and a fair growth of pinyon pines. Along the trail to Telescope Peak—at 10,000 feet—appear thin stands of limber pine and the short, massive, all-enduring bristlecone pine, more ancient than the Book of Genesis. Timberline.

There is no forest here. And fifty or sixty airline miles to the west stands the reason why—the Sierra Nevada Range blocking off the sea winds and almost all the moisture. We stand in the rain shadow of that still higher wall.

I walk past three wild burros. Descendants of lost and abandoned prospectors' stock, they range everywhere in the Panamints, multiplying freely, endangering the survival of the native bighorn sheep by trespassing on the latter's forage, befouling their springs. But the feral burros have their charm too. They stand about 100 feet from the trail watching me go by. They are quite unafraid, and merely blink their heavy eyelashes like movie starlets when I halt to stare at them. However they are certainly not tame. Advance toward them and they trot off briskly.

The bray of the donkey is well known. But these little beasts can make another sound even more startling because so unexpected. Hiking up some arid canyon in the Panamints, through what appears to be totally lifeless terrain, you suddenly hear a noise like a huge dry cough behind your shoulder. You spring ten feet forward before daring to look around. And see nothing, nothing at all, until you hear a second cough and scan the hillsides and discover far above a little gray or black burro looking down at you, waiting for you to get the hell out of its territory.

I stand by the cairn on the summit of Telescope Peak, looking out on a cold, windy, and barren world. Rugged peaks fall off southward into the haze of the Mojave Desert; on the west is Panamint Valley, the Argus Range, more mountains, more valleys, and finally the Sierras, crowned with snow; to the north and northwest the Inyo and White mountains; below lies Death Valley—the chemical desert—and east of it the Black Mountains, the Funeral Mountains, the Amargosa Valley and farther mountains, wave after wave of wrinkled ridges standing up from the oceanic desert sea until vision gives out somewhere beyond the curving rim of the world's edge. A smudge hangs on the eastern horizon, suggesting the presence of Death Valley's counterpart and complement, the only city within 100 miles: Las Vegas: Glitter Gulch West.

ECHO CANYON, NOVEMBER 30. A hard place to love. Impossible? No, there were a few—the prospectors, the single-blanket, jackass prospectors who wandered these funeral wastes for a century dreaming of what? Sudden wealth? Not likely. Not Shorty Borden, for example, who invested eight months of his life in building by hand a nine-mile road to his lead and silver diggings in Hanaupah Canyon. Then discovered that even with a road it would still cost him more to transport his ore to the nearest smelter than the ore itself was worth.

Echo Canyon. We are deep into the intricacies of the Funeral Mountains. Named not simply for their proximity to Death Valley, but also for shape and coloration: lifeless escarpments of smoldering red bordered in charcoal, the crags and ridges and defiles edged in black and purple. A primeval chaos of faulted, uplifted, warped, and folded dolomites, limestones, fanglomerates of mud, sand, and gravel. Vulcanism as well: vesiculated andesite, walls embellished with elegant mosaics of rose and yellow quartz. Fool's gold—pyrite—glittering in the black sand, micaceous shales glinting under back light, veins of pegmatite zigzagging and intersecting like an undeciphered script across the face of a cliff: the writing on the wall: "God Was Here."

Shallow caves, holes in the rock, a natural arch, and the canyon floor littered with boulders, deep in coarse gravel.

Nowhere in Echo Canyon can I find the slightest visible trace of water. Nevertheless it must be present under the surface, at least in intermittent or minute amounts, for here and there stand living things. They look dead but are actually dormant, waiting for the resurrection of the rain. I mean the saltbush, the desert fir, the bladderweed, a sprinkling of cottontop cactus, the isolated creosote bush. Waiting.

You may see a few lizards. In sandy places are the hoofprints of bighorn sheep, where they've passed through on their way from the high parts of the range to the springs near Furnace Creek. Sit quite still in one spot for an hour and you might see a small gray bird fly close to look you over. This is the bird that lives in Echo Canyon.

The echoes are good. At certain locations, on a still day, one clear shout will create a series of overlapping echoes that goes on and on toward so fine a diminuendo that the human ear cannot perceive the final vibrations.

Tramp far enough up Echo Canyon and you come to a ghost town, the ruins of a mining camp—one of many in Death Valley. Deep shafts, a tipple, a rolling mill largely intact, several cabins—one with its inside walls papered with pages from the *Literary Digest*. Half buried in drifted sand is a rusted model-T Ford without roof or motor, a child's tricycle, a broken shovel.

Returning through twilight, I descend the narrow gorge between flood-polished walls of bluish andesite—the stem of the wineglass. I walk down the center of an amphitheater of somber cliffs riddled with grottoes, huge eyesockets in a stony skull, where bats hang upside down in the shadows waiting for night.

Through the opening of the canyon I can see the icy heights of Telescope Peak shining under the cloud-reflected light of one more sunset. Scarlet clouds in a green sky. A weird glow pervades the air through which I walk; it vibrates on the canyon walls, revealing to me all at once a vision of the earth's slow agony, the convulsive grinding violence of a hundred million years. Of a billion years. I write metaphorically, out of necessity. And yet it seems impossible to believe that these mountains, old as anything on the surface of the planet, do not partake in some dim way of the sentience of living tissue. Genealogies: From these rocks struck once by lightning gushed springs that turned to blood, flesh, life. Impossible miracle. And *I* am struck once again by the unutterable beauty, terror, and strangeness of everything we think we know.

FURNACE CREEK, DECEMBER 10. The oasis. We stand near the edge of a grove of date palms looking eastward at the soft melting mud hills above Texas Spring. The hills are lemon yellow with dark brown crusts on top, like the frosting on a cake. Beyond the hills rise the elaborate, dark, wine-red mountains. In the foreground, close by, irrigation water plunges into a pool, from which it is diverted into ditches that run between the rows of palms.

The springs of Furnace Creek supply not only the palms but also the water needs of the hotel, the motel (both with swimming pools), Park Service headquarters and visitor center, an Indian village, and two large campgrounds. I do not know the output of these springs as measured in gallons per minute. But I do know that during the Christmas and Easter holidays there is enough water available to serve the needs of 10,000 people. Where does it come from? From a natural reservoir in the base of the bleak, fatally arid Funeral Mountains. A reservoir that may be joined to the larger underground acquifers beneath the Amargosa and Pahrump valleys to the east.

This does not mean that the Furnace Creek portion of Death Valley could support a permanent population of 10,000 drinking, back-scrubbing, hard-flushing suburbanites. For the water used here comes from a supply that may have required 20,000 years to charge; it is not sustained by rainfall—not in a country where precipitation averages two inches per year.

That's the mistake they made in central Arizona—Tucson and Phoenix—and are now making in Las Vegas and Albuquerque. Out of greed and stupidity, but mostly greed, the gentry of those cities overexpanded their investment in development and kept going by mining the underground water supply. Now that the supply is dwindling, they set up an unholy clamor in Congress to have the rest of the nation save them from the consequences of their own folly. Phoenix might rise again from ashes—but not, I think, from the sea of sand that is its likely destiny.

There are about 200 springs, all told, within the boundaries of Death Valley National Monument, counting each and every tiny seep that produces any flow at all. None except those in the northeast corner of the park are comparable to the springs at Furnace Creek. In addition to the springs there are the heavily saline, undrinkable waters of Salt Creek, Badwater, and the valley floor itself.

All this water is found in what meteorologists believe to be the hottest place on earth, year in and year out hotter than the Sahara, the Great Karroo, the Negev, the Atacama, the Rub'-al-Khali ("Empty Quarter") of Arabia, or the far-out-back-of-beyond in central Australia. The world's record is held by Libya, where a temperature of 136 degrees Fahrenheit was once recorded at a weather station called Azizia. Death Valley's high so far is a reading of 134 degrees at Furnace Creek. But Azizia has been unable to come near repeating its record, while temperatures at Furnace Creek consistently exceed the mean maximums for Azizia by ten percent. And Badwater, only twenty miles south of Furnace Creek, is on the average always four degrees hotter. It follows that on the historic day when the thermometer reached 134 at Furnace Creek, it was probably 138 at Badwater. But there was nobody around at Badwater that day (July 10, 1913).

Official weather readings are made from instruments housed in a louvered wooden box set five feet above the ground. In Death Valley the temperature on the surface of the ground is ordinarily fifty percent higher than in the box five feet above. On a normal summer's day in Death Valley, with the thermometer reading 120 degrees Fahrenheit, the temperature at ground surface is 180.

Curiosities: There are fish in the briny pools of Salt Creek, far out on the hottest, bleakest, saltiest part of the valley floor—the inch-long cyprinodon or pupfish. There is a species of soft-bodied snail living in the Epsom salts, Glauber's salt, and rock salts of Badwater. There are fairy shrimp in the *tinajas* or natural cisterns of Butte Valley in the southwest corner of the park; estivating beneath the clay most of the year, they wriggle forth to swim, rejoice, and reproduce after that rarest and most wonderful of Death Valley events, a fall of rain.

More curiosities: Blue herons enter the valley in winter; also trumpeter swans; grebes, coots, and mallards can be seen in the blue ponds of Saratoga Springs; and for a few weeks in the fall of one year (1966) a real flamingo made its home among the reeds that line the shore of the sewage lagoon below Park Village. Where this flamingo came from no one could say; where it went the coyotes most likely could testify. Or perhaps the lion.

A lean and hungry mountain lion was observed several times that year during the Christmas season investigating the garbage cans in the campgrounds. An old lion, no doubt—aging, possibly ill, probably retired. In short, a tourist. But a lion even so.

But these are mere oddities. All the instruments agree that Death Valley remains the hottest place on earth, the driest in North America, the lowest in the Western Hemisphere. Of all deathly places the most deadly—and the most beautiful.

BADWATER, JANUARY 19. Standing among the salt pinnacles of what is called the Devil's Golf Course, I heard a constant tinkling and crackling noise—the salt crust expanding in the morning sun. No sign of life out there. Experimentally I ventured to walk upon, over, among the pinnacles. Difficult, but not impossible. The formations are knee-high, white within but stained yellow by the dusty winds, studded on top with sharp teeth. Like walking on a jumble of broken and refrozen slabs of ice: At every other step part of the salt collapses under foot and you drop into a hole. The jagged edges cut like knives into the leather of my boots. After a few minutes of this I was glad to return to the security of the road. Even in January the sun felt uncomfortably hot, and I was sweating a little.

Where the salt flats come closest to the base of the eastern mountains, at 278 feet below sea level, lies the clear and sparkling pool known as Badwater. A shallow body of water, surrounded by beds of snow-white alkali. According to Death Valley legend the water is poisonous, containing traces of arsenic. I scooped up a handful and sampled it in my mouth, since the testing of desert waterholes has always been one of my chores. I found Badwater lukewarm, salty on the tongue, sickening. I spat it out and rinsed my mouth with fresh water from my canteen.

From here, the lowest point in all the Americas, I gazed across the pale lenses of the valley floor to the brown outwash fan of Hanaupah Canyon opposite, ten miles away, and from the canyon's mouth up and up and up to the crest of Telescope Peak with its cornices of frozen snow 11,049 feet above sea level. One would like to climb or descend that interval someday, the better to comprehend what it means. Whatever it means.

I have been part of the way already, hiking far into Hanaupah Canyon to Shorty Borden's abandoned camp, up to that loveliest of desert graces, a spring-fed stream. Lively, bubbling, with pools big enough and cold enough, it seemed then, for trout. But there are none. Along the stream grow tangles of wild grapevine and willow; the spring is choked with watercress. The stream runs for less than a mile before disappearing into the sand and gravel of the wash. Beyond the spring, up-canyon, all is dry as death again until you reach the place where the canyon forks. Explore either fork and you find water once more—on the right a little waterfall, on the left in a grottolike glen cascades sliding down through chutes in the dark blue andesite. Moss, ferns, and flowers cling to the damp walls—the only life in this arid wilderness. Almost no one ever goes there. It is necessary to walk for many miles.

DEVIL'S HOLE, FEBRUARY 10. A natural opening in the desert floor; a queer deep rocky sinkhole with a pond of dark green water at the bottom. That pond, however, is of the kind called bottomless; it leads down and down through greener darker depths into underwater caverns whose dimensions and limits are not known. It might be an entrance to the subterranean lakes that supposedly lie beneath the Funeral Mountains and the Amargosa Valley.

The Park Service has erected a high steel fence with locked gate around the hole. Not to keep out tourists, who only want to look, but to keep out the aqualung adventurers who wish to dive in and go all the way down. Within the past year several parties of scuba divers have climbed over and under the fence anyway and gone exploring down in that sunless sea. One party returned to the surface one man short. His body has not been found yet, though many have searched. If supposition is correct, the missing man may be found someday wedged in one of the outlets of Furnace Creek springs.

Death Valley has taken five lives this year—one by water, two by ice, and two by fire. A hiker slipped on the glazed snow of the trail to Telescope Peak and tumbled 1,000 feet down a steep pitch of ice and rock. His companion went for help; a member of a professional mountaineering team, climbing down to recover the victim, also fell and was also killed.

Last summer two young soldiers from the Army's nearby Camp Irwin went exploring in the desert off the southwest corner of Death Valley. Their jeep ran out of gas, they tried to walk home to the base. One was found beside the seldom-traveled desert road, dead from exhaustion and dehydration. The body of the other could not be found, though 2,000 soldiers hunted him for a week. No doubt he wandered off the trail into the hills seeking water. Absent without leave. He could possibly be still alive. Maybe in a forgotten cabin up in the Panamints eating lizards, waiting for some war to end.

Ah to be a buzzard now that spring is here.

THE SAND DUNES, MARCH 15. At night I hear tree toads singing in the tamarisk along the water channels of Furnace Creek Ranch. The days are often windy now, much warmer, and rain squalls sail north through the valley, obscuring both sky and sun. The ground squirrels scamper from hole to hole in the mud hills, the Gambel's quail swoop in flocks low over the ground, alight, and run in unison through the brush, calling to one another. Tawny coyotes stand bold as brass close to the road in broad daylight and watch the tourists drive by. And the mesquite thickets, black and lifeless-looking since last fall, have assumed a delicate tinge of spring green.

Death Valley's winter, much too lovely to last, is nearly over.

Between winds and storms I walk far out on the dunes. How hot and implacably hostile this sea of sand appeared last June when we saw it for the first time. Then it seemed to be floating in heat waves, which gathered among the dunes and glistened like pools of water, reflecting the sky.

I bear for the highest of the dunes, following the curving crests of the lesser dunes that lead toward it. On the way I pass a few scraggly mesquite trees, putting out new leaves, and a number of creosote shrubs. No other plants are deep-rooted enough to survive in the sand, and these too become smaller and fewer as I advance and the dunes rise higher. On the last half mile to the topmost point there is no plant life whatsoever, although in the sand I find the prints of ravens, coyotes, mice, lizards. The sand is firm, rippled as the seashore, and virginal of human tracks; nobody has come this far since the last windstorm a few days ago.

Late in the afternoon I reach the summit of the highest dune, 400 feet above the valley floor. Northward the sand drops abruptly away to smaller dunes, mud flats, a scatter of creosote and mesquite—and what looks to be, not a mirage, but a pond of real water encircled by the dunes.

Glissading down the hill of sand, climbing another and down the far side of that, I come to the margin of the pool. The sandy shore is quick, alive, and I sink ankle deep in the mud as I bend to taste the water and find it fresh, cool, with hardly a trace of salt—fit to drink. The water must be left over from the recent rain.

I struggle out of the wet sand onto the dunes. Here I'll make camp for the evening. I scoop a hole in the sand, build a tiny fire of mesquite twigs and sear a piece of meat on the flaming coals. Mesquite makes excellent fuel—burns with a slow hot flame, touching the air with a nut-sweet fragrance, and condenses as it burns to a bed of embers that glow and glimmer like incandescent charcoal. Fire is magic, a purifying and sanctifying magic, and most especially a mesquite fire on a sand dune at evening under desert skies, on the shore of a pool that gleams like polished agate, like garnet, like a tiger's eye.

The sun goes down. A few stray clouds catch fire, burn gold, vermillion, and driftwood blue in the unfathomed sea of space. These surrounding mountains that look during the day like iron—like burnt, mangled, rusted iron—now turn radiant as a dream. Where is their truth? A hard clean edge divides the crescent dunes into black shadow on one side, a phosphorescent light on the other. And above the rim of the darkening west floats the evening star.

Manhattan Twilight, Hoboken Night

Hoboken, New Jersey, is not one of the five boroughs of New York City. But it should be, for it's closer and quicker to the center of Manhattan from Hoboken than from any point in Brooklyn, the Bronx, Queens, or Staten Island. Fifteen minutes by bus, via the Lincoln Tunnel, takes you from Washington Street in Hoboken to the Port Authority Bus Terminal on Forty-First Street; ten minutes by train via the Hudson Tubes takes you from the Erie-Lackawanna Terminal to Ninth Street and Sixth Avenue—the Village. A dash under the river, a roar of iron, and you're there: in Glitter Gulch, U.S.A.—Times Square, the Big Midway, the hanging gardens of electricity. Or down yonder in Green Witch Village. What more could you want? And if New York is not Manhattan, it is nothing. A little worse than nothing. Meanwhile the insane, medieval burgs of New Jersey—Union City, West New York, Jersey City—lie divorced from Hoboken by a wall older than the Great Wall of China. I mean the Palisades, that sill of diabase left over from the Triassic period.

I make this effort to incorporate Hoboken into New York City (where it belongs) rather than allowing it to remain in New Jersey (for which it is much too sweet, pure, romantic) because it is from the Hoboken point of view, the Hoboken mystique, the Hoboken metaphysic, that I must describe what I remember and what I know of New York. Meaning Manhattan. Of the rest I know nothing. The other four boroughs are as remote to my imagination as the Malebolges of the Eighth Circle of Hell. Perhaps only Dante could tell us the truth about them. Perhaps only

Dante—and Dostoyevsky—could tell us the truth about New
York.

For one year I lived in Hoboken, far from my natural habitat.
The bitter bread of exile. Twelve months in the gray light and
the sulfur dioxide and the smell of burning coffee beans from
the Maxwell House plant at the end of Hudson Street. In a dark,
dank, decaying apartment house where the cockroaches—shell-
backed, glossy, insolent *Blatella germanica*—festered and
spawned under the linoleum on the sagging floors, behind the
rippled wallpaper on the sweating walls, among the teacups in
the cupboard. Everywhere. While the rats raced in ferocious
packs, like wolves, inside the walls and up and down the cobble-
stone alleyways that always glistened, night and day, in any kind
of weather, with a thin chill greasy patina of poisonous dew. The
fly ash, ubiquitous, falling softly and perpetually from the pregnant sky. We watched the seasons come and go in a small rectangle of walled-in space we called our yard: in spring and summer
the black grass; in fall and winter the black snow; overhead and
in our hearts a black sun.

Down in the cellar and up in the attic of that fantastic house—
four stories high, brownstone, a stoop, wide polished bannisters,
brass fittings on the street entrance, a half-sunken apartment for
the superintendent, high ceilings, high windows, and a grand
stairway on the main floor, all quite decently lower middle class
and in the better part of town, near the parks, near the Stevens
Institute of Technology—hung draperies of dust and cobweb
that had not been seen in the light of day or touched by the hand
of man since the time of the assassination of President William
McKinley.

In the sunless attic the spiders had long since given up, for all
their prey had turned to dust; but the rats roamed freely. Down
in the basement, built like a dungeon with ceiling too low to
permit a man of normal stature to stand erect, there were more
rats, of course—they loved the heat of the furnace in winter—
and dampish stains on the wall and floor where the great water-
bugs, like cockroaches out of Kafka, crawled sluggishly from

darkness into darkness. One might notice here, at times, the odor of sewer gas.

The infinite richness. The ecology, the natural history of it all. An excellent workshop for the philosopher, for who would venture out into that gray miasma of perpetual smoke and fog that filled the streets if he might remain walled up with books, sipping black coffee, smoking black Russian cigarettes, thinking long, black, inky thoughts? To be sure. But there were the streets. The call of the streets.

We lived one block from the waterfront. The same waterfront where Marlon Brando once played Marlon Brando, where rust-covered tramp steamers, black freighters, derelict Dutchmen, death ships, came to call under Liberian flags to unload their bananas, baled hemp, teakwood, sacks of coffee beans, cowhides, Argentine beef, to take on kegs of nails, Jeep trucks, Cadillacs, and crated machine guns. Abandoned by the Holland-American Line in '65, at least for passenger service, the Hoboken docks—like Hoboken bars and Hoboken tenements—were sinking into an ever deepening state of decay. The longshoremen were lucky to get two days' work a week. Some of the great warehouses had been empty for years; the kids played Mafia in them.

The moment I stepped out the front door I was faced again with Manhattan. There it was, oh splendid ship of concrete and steel, aluminum, glass, and electricity, forging forever up the dark river. (The Hudson—like a river of oil, filthy and rich, gleaming with silver lights.) Manhattan at twilight: floating gardens of tender neon, the lavender towers where each window glittered at sundown with reflected incandescence, where each crosstown street became at evening a gash of golden fire, and the endless flow of the endless traffic on the West Side Highway resembled a luminous necklace strung round the island's shoulders.

Who would believe the city could be so beautiful? On winter evenings when the sun went down early and all the office lights stayed lit, the giant glass buildings across the river glowed like blocks of radium with a cool soft Venusian radiance, magnetic and fatal. And above them all stood the Vampire State Building with its twin beams stroking through the mist and the red spider eyes on the radio mast blinking slowly off and on, off and on, all through the New York night. While deep-sea liners bayed in the roadstead, coming up the Narrows, and tugboats shaped like old shoes and croaking like alligators glided by in the opposite direction, towing freight trains or barges filled with traprock. Once I saw a large dark ship, no visible running lights at all, pass between me and the clustered constellations of the city—a black form moving across a field of stars.

One night Manhattan itself became that dark ship. Under moonlight the city appeared to be deserted, abandoned, empty as a graveyard except for the dim beams of automobiles groping through the blacked-out canyons, fumbling for the way home. From where I stood in Hoboken, on a hill above the waterfront, I could hear not the faintest sound of life, not a heartbeat, from New York. The silence was impressive. But by the next night the power was back and the city shining like a many-colored vision of wealth and glory. From the little park in Weehawken where Aaron Burr shot Alexander Hamilton (good shot!) you could look right down the center line of Forty-Second Street. With glasses powerful enough, you could watch the sports and pastimes of the folk who dwell in the City of Dreadful Night.

If the Lower East Side is now the East Village, Hoboken was (still is, if urban renewal has not yet destroyed it all) the West Village. Down on River Street just past the gothic gables of the Christian Seamen's Home began our own little Bohemia, where the otherwise omnipresent odor of sewer gas, burning coffee beans and the Hudson River was sweetened by the smell of marijuana and smoking joss sticks. Under the vacant eyes of condemned tenements lived the Peace People, the Flower Children, in happy polygamous squalor. Woven god's-eyes dangled from the ceilings; on once blank and dusty storefront windows appeared the American flag, handpainted, with five, six, or seven stripes and anywhere from a dozen to twenty stars, asymmetrical as nebulae. The men wore bands on their heads, beards on their jaws, and their old ladies were as slender, sweet and comely as their tresses were long. My friend Henry the painter was painting nothing but gas stations that year. Esso gas stations. And Rini the sculptor was busy welding and reworking junked auto parts into surreal hobgoblins of iron.

"Look here, Rini," I said to her, "instead of dragging the goddamn junkyard into the art galleries, why don't you throw the goddamn art galleries into the junkyard?"

"That's exactly what we're doing," she replied.

They had a coffeehouse—the Baby Bull—and nocturnal police raids and finally even a murder of their very own. Anything Haight-Ashbury had we had too.

Hoboken may be the only city in America where some of the police were actually caught red-handed in the act of tampering with the voting machines: There was a resolution on the ballot in the election that year which if approved would have authorized a substantial pay increase for the fuzz and the firemen.

Which suggests the role of *power* again: When I lived in Hoboken it was the most densely populated, square-mile city in the United States, inhabited largely by babies; you could not walk down the main drag, Washington Street, at any time during daylight hours without threading your way through traffic jams of loaded baby carriages, many of them containing twins, some triplets, each carriage powered by a pregnant mother with two or three toddlers dragging at her skirts. And who ruled this fecund mass?

The character of the population was mixed, a typical American polyglot boiling pot of Italians, Irish, Puerto Ricans, Poles, Jews, Germans, and Blacks. But there could be little doubt which *ethnos* dominated the structure of authority when you read in the local paper of the latest gathering of dignitaries at the Union Club: "Present were *Mayor Grogan, Councilman Hogan, Bishops Malarkey* and *Moone, Commissioners Hoyle* and *Coyle* and *Boyle.*"

Who were those others we sometimes glimpsed on rare occasions, those heavy short swarthy men with Homburg hats, velvet-collared overcoats, fat cigars, who rode far back in the rear corners of black limousines rolling swiftly, quietly (no sound but the hiss of rubber on asphalt) down the evening streets? Who were the two Mongolian wrestlers in front dressed like FBI operatives, one driving, one scanning the sidewalks with stonefish eyes?

Hoboken. Weehawken. Hohokus. Secaucus. Paramus. Manhattan. And the five boroughs of New York. True, we were separated by a river from the center of the city. But are not the others also cut off by water? The Harlem River. The East River. What is the Brooklyn Bridge for? What is the function of the Staten Island Ferry? New York is a city of waters and islands, like Venice, floating on sewer lagoons, under a sea of fog and smoke and drizzling acid mists. You have to be tough to live there— even the clams on the offshore shelf are full of polluted pride. The chickadees, starlings, sparrows and alley cats of Hoboken were a hardier meaner breed than you find elsewhere. The old trees in the little parks along Boulevard East and Hudson Street seemed lifeless as statuary most of the year; yet in April there came an astonishing outburst of delicate green along the length of those blackened limbs. As if leaves should grow upon gun barrels and—but why not?—bright, fuzzy flowers spring up from the mouths of cannon.

Perhaps I liked best the sunflowers along the railroad tracks and the little purple asters that rose between the ties, out of the cinders. Or the cattails in the ditches and the rank nameless weeds that flourished by the iron wheels of rotting boxcars— *Erie-Lackawanna—The Great White Way—Route of the Phoebe Snow*—forgotten on sidings. Or the feral hollyhocks tall as corn along the walls of the gate tender's shack at the railway crossing, transpiring through July. There was a bitter, forlorn yet stubborn beauty everywhere you looked in Hoboken. Even the smog of heavy summer evenings played a helpful part, enhancing the quality of light and shadow on old brick walls, lending to things only a block away the semblance of magic and mystery.

When I was there I thought New York was dying. Maybe it

really is. I know I was dying to get out. But if it's dying then it's going to be a prolonged, strange, infinitely complex process, a death of terror and grandeur. Imagine a carcinoma 300 miles long, a mile thick, embracing 50 million souls. Whatever else (I tell myself) you may think about New York now, looking back at it from this desert perspective, you've got to admit that Wolf Hole, Arizona, can never have so rich a death.

There are three ways to get from Hoboken to Manhattan. There were four. You can take the Number 6 bus, dive into the Lincoln Tunnel (holding your breath), roar through that tube of tile and light, where the tunnel cops pace forever up and down their cement walkways or stand in glass boxes built into the walls (we used to discuss the question, which is the world's worst job: subway motorman? city bus driver? slaughterhouse worker? switchboard operator? or tunnel cop?), to emerge suddenly into the blue air of the Port Authority Bus Terminal. Or you can take the Hudson Tubes under the river, ride the trains through the sweating tunnels, where little green lights blink dimly beside the rails, and come out in the Village or stay on the train and ride it uptown as far as Macy's, Gimbel's, Herald Square. The third way, if you have a car, is to drive through either the Lincoln Tunnel or the Holland Tunnel and drive back through the other way when you realize finally that there is almost no place on all of God's Manhattan where you can park your machine.

The fourth way was to take the Lackawanna Ferry and although the slowest this was by far the best (A fifth way will be to walk on the water when the Hudson finally coagulates.) Getting to the ferry slips at the railway terminal was part of the pleasure: For whether you went by Washington Street, Hudson Street or River Street, you passed not only such places as the hippie communes and the Christian Seamen's Home but also the most shabby dingy rundown smelly half-lighted dangerous and downright picturesque little Mom and Pop bars in North America.

It was said, on good authority, that Hoboken had more taverns per square block than any other city in the world except

Anchorage, Alaska. I believe it. I never did get into all of them, though for a year I tried. Some I remember: the Old Empire, the Seven Seas, Allie and Jopie's, Anna Lee's, Portview, El Jim's, the Dutch Mill, the Elysian Fields Bar and Grill, the River Street, the Cherokee, the Old Holland House, McSharry's Irish House, the Continental, the Little Dipsy Doodle, the Grand, the Inn, the Idle Hours (how true), Pat's, Pete's, Lou's, Joe's, and Mom's. And the Silver Trail, Hoboken's only genuine western bar, with live western music and authentic cowboy stomp dancing every Saturday night; and Nelson's Marine Bar and Grill, my favorite, where the bartender, Herman Nelson, sole owner and proprietor, is or was the man who *almost* became world welterweight champ in 1931; and the stand-up bar of the Clam Broth House, men only (then), free clam broth, Löwenbrau on tap, the crackle of clamshells underfoot.

Anyway, if you made it past all the bars and the three Chinese laundries—Sam Toy's, Harry Lew's, Gong Lee's—and past the hash peddlers, cops, hippies, Christian seamen, bohemes, bums, panhandlers, whores, winos, shoeshine boys, muggers, rapists, and shiv artists, you arrived at the Erie-Lackawanna building. End of the line. Mouth of the tubes. Home of the ferryboats. The E-L building (is it still there?) looked like a square fruitcake coated with green mold. It was enormous, its cavernous interior capacious enough for a dozen trains plus shops and offices and waiting rooms. Paying our fare at the turnstiles, we stormed up the ramp onto the "Next Boat."

All on board, gangplanks winched up with a rattle of chains, the ferry surged out of the slip and bore east-southeast across the Hudson toward the Barclay Street docks on the far side. Moving partly with the current and partly across it, the ferry left a curving wake as it churned from shore to shore. In winter we glided among drifting ice floes the color of urine; in summer through trails of garbage bobbing in the wake of ships, seagulls screaming as they wheeled and dove for supper. I liked to stand on the open forward deck facing the wind and the solemn monuments of lower Manhattan. For a few minutes at least we were all free, commuters, drifters and students alike, liberated from the confines of lubberly life and at home—so we thought—with sailors and seabirds, the allure of the open sea. It seemed to me I could read on the faces of even the most resigned commuters an emotion the same as mine: exultance.

It was strange, that approach to Manhattan over the open water. No sound but the slap of waves, the wind, the gulls, the distant signals of other boats. The city itself swung slowly toward us silent as a dream. No sign of life but puffs of steam from skyscraper chimneys, the motion of the traffic. The mighty towers stood like tombstones in a graveyard, leaning against the sky and waiting for—for what? Someday we'll know.

And then as we came close we began to hear the murmur of the city's life, the growing and compelling roar, the sound of madness. Newspapers were folded, overcoats buttoned, hat brims tugged—those gray near-brimless little felt hats that all the men wore and which had the peculiar virtue of rendering the wearer invisible. Everyone crowded toward the front of the boat. You could see the tension stealing over each face as 200 full-grown men prepared themselves for the stampede to taxis, buses, the subway trains.

But those were the mornings. Mornings were always absurd and desperate in New York. In the evening, going to the city, the mood was different, only a few of us on the boat, going the wrong way—the right way—against the mainstream of human traffic. In the evening the great glittering ship of Manhattan seemed to promise the fulfillment of every desire, every wish; one sailed toward it through the purple twilight with a heart full of hope. Hope for what? Hard to say—hope for those things a young man desires so much he hesitates to name them: for love; for adventure; for revelation; for triumph. All of it waiting there in that golden city of electric glory. All of it almost within reach.

That was the view from the water, the fantasy of the river crossing. Close to, the scene came into a different focus; we found ourselves back in the profane world of people with problems, embittered cab drivers, Sam Schwartz and his roasted chestnuts, the quiet tragedy of human relationships. No amount of weed or booze or sex or heavy art could permanently alter any of that.

I was a walker. I usually walked from Barclay Street up to the Village, preferring the grim and empty downtown streets to the infernal racket and doomed faces of the subway. Pausing at the White Horse for a drink to the memory of Dylan—the one from Cardigan Bay—the real Dylan, and thence to Dillon's where I *might* meet somebody I knew, and from there to the Cedars, international intersection of all Volkswagen Bohemia where I *always* met somebody I knew, where anybody meets somebody, we threw a few back while deciding whose opening, whose screening, whose party to crash on this wild, full-of-wonder, high-blossoming night.

After a quick trip to the john to read the writing on the wall— Socrates Loves Alcibiades; Joy Shipmates Joy!; Here I Sit Anonymous as Hieronymus Bosch; Caligula Come Back; Mene Mene Tekel—it was out on the jam-packed streets again, through the multitudes, and up a tunnel of stairways into some-body's loft—THIS FLOOR WILL SAFELY SUSTAIN A LOAD OF 70 LB PER SQUARE FOOT—and into The Party.

The Party was permanent, like the revolution, always in swing somewhere, with the same conglutinate crowd, the same faces, the same wilted potato chips, the same sour wine, the same dense atmosphere of smoke and heat and intellection, the same blonde lovely girls down from Boston for the weekend, the same paintings of Esso gas stations on the walls, the same raccoon-eyed lank-haired crepe-clad pale-faced vampire lass hesitating in the doorway, to whom some catty chick would say, "Well do creep in." Somebody like Norman Mailer was always there, a drink in each hand, and Dwight MacDonald, and Joel Oppenheimer, and Joseph Heller, and the man who invented Happenings, I forget his name. Everyone was there but the host, who usually could not be found.

There were other parts of the town I got to know, a little. For a while I had a girl friend who lived on Fourteenth Street, near

Union Square; I worked briefly as a technical writer for General
Electric in an office building on Lower Broadway, editing training manuals for DEW Line soldiers on how to dispose of sewage
in permafrost; we all had to wear white shirts—that was manda-
tory—and I was fired at the end of two weeks for spending too
much time staring out the window. I was invited a few times to
publishers' offices in the midtown region, to an agent's office in
Rockefeller Center, to lunches at Sardi's. My wife had an M.D.
with an office in the East Sixties. Once I went to Wilt Chamber-
lain's nightclub in Harlem. And I worked for a time as a welfare
caseworker in the Atlantic Avenue district of Brooklyn—but that
is another story, that was another world, that was lower Missis-
sippi we were dealing with there; let us now praise famous men.
But I lived in Hoboken.

The Party is over, for me. In the gray light of dawn with the
Sunday *Times,* world's most preposterous newspaper—all those
dead trees!—rolled under my arm, I navigated the deserted
streets. Bleak and God-forsaken Sunday. Down into the subway
entrance, down into the dim calamitous light of the tubes. Into
an empty car. The placards on the walls implored me: GIVE:
multiple sclerosis; muscular dystrophy; heart disease; lung cancer; mental illness; cystic-fibrosis; nephritis; hepatitis; cerebral
palsy; VD; TB; acute leukemia. Buy Bonds: Keep Freedom in
Your *Future!* Good God. The train jolted forward, began to
move; the dripping steam pipes, the little blue lights, the sweating walls slide greasily by. Just a happy little journey through
hell. The train paused at the Christopher Street station. Before
it moved on again I had time to contemplate a pair of rubber
gloves lying in a pool of oil beside the tracks.

We plunged beneath the river. I slept all day. At evening I
walked once more along the waterfront and gazed across the
river at the somber forms of Manhattan, the great towers largely
dark, for on Sunday no one is at work over there but the
janitors. I don't know how New York can survive.

I believe the city is doomed. The air is poisonous, not so much
with filth and disease as with something deadlier—human

hatred. Yes, there's hatred in Arizona, too, but here it is easily dissipated into the nothingness of space: Walk one-half mile away from the town, away from the road, and you find yourself absolutely alone, under the sun, under the moon, under the stars, within the sweet aching loneliness of the desert.

That loneliness is not enough. We must save the city. It is essence and substance of us all—we cannot lose it without diminishing our stature as a nation, without a fatal wound.

My words therefore are dedicated to that city we love, that visionary city of the prophecies, humane and generous, that city of liberty and beauty and joy which will come to be, someday, on American earth, on the shore of the sea.

Telluride Blues—A Hatchet Job

The town of Telluride was actually discovered back in 1957, by me, during a picnic expedition into the San Miguel Mountains of southwestern Colorado. I recognized it at once as something much too good for the general public. For thirteen years I kept the place a secret from all but my closest picnicking cronies. No use: I should have invested everything I had in Telluride real estate.

In 1970 a foreigner from California named Joseph T. Zoline moved in with $5 million and began the corruption of Telluride. Formerly an honest, decayed little mining town of about 300 souls, it is now a bustling whore of a ski resort with a population of 1,500 and many more to come. If all goes badly, as planned.

"We shall develop," announced Zoline, "a ski area bigger than Vail, as large as Ajax, Aspen Highlands, and Buttermilk combined, and twice as big as Mammoth Mountain in California." Two cheers for Zoline. The county Chamber of Commerce was delighted, but those who preferred Telluride as Telluride wept in their beers, prayed in the alleyways. It didn't help. Nothing worked.

Men weep, men pray and barf, but *money talks.* Money walks and talks and gets things done. Four years after his announcement (four years! it took twenty years to get the Wilderness Preservation Act through Congress, forty years to have one tiny remnant of the California redwoods given shabby and inadequate protection as a national park), Zoline has completed five operating double chairlifts, thirty-two miles of trails, and an eighty-seven-cell condominium.

Merely the beginning. Though the town offers only 1,200 beds for hire at present, Zoline's Telluride Company expects 170,000 skiers by 1985. To accommodate such multitudes, Zoline plans to build a village for 8,000 on the mountain meadows at the foot of the lifts; cabin sites or "ski ranches" are already being offered for sale (at $5,000 to $10,000 per acre); and Holiday Inn has begun to make inquiries. The twenty-year plan for Big-T envisions, on paper, a cable monorail system and a total of seventeen lifts with the combined capacity for transporting 17,000 skiers per day up a vertical distance of 4,000 feet; from there dropping them at the head of sixty miles of trail. Bigger than Vail! Better than Aspen!

What—*another* Aspen?

Yes, but different. Telluride's growth will be controlled and orderly, say the company executives, with "full environmental protection." The vague phrase rolls easily from the mouths of all developers these days. "Aspen grew without controls, under inadequate zoning laws," says Zoline. "We shall profit from that lesson here."

Will they? One may hope so; but the ambitious plans make the nature of that profit ambiguous. How can anything so big happen in a place so small as Telluride without changing the town beyond recognition? For those opposing the change the best hope is that Telluride will never make it as a big-time ski resort. There are problems.

Telluride is a hard place to get to. The nearest big town is Denver, 325 miles away on the other side of the Rocky Mountains, an eight-hour auto drive under the best conditions. The nearest primary air access terminal is at Grand Junction, 130 miles to the north. There is no rail line to Telluride, and the buses, at present, arrive only on weekends. If you elect to go by car, during the winter, you must drive the last thirty miles on a two-lane winding mountain road often surfaced with snow and ice, chains advisable. Below the road is the deep canyon of the San Miguel River. Above are the high-pitched mountain walls and thousands of tons of snow, hanging there.

Avalanches have been a problem in Telluride ever since the 1880s. Built in a narrow valley under 14,000-foot peaks, Telluride was hit by death-dealing avalanches in 1902, 1926, and 1927. Smaller ones occur every winter. With an average annual snowfall of 165 inches (Aspen averages 135), the next killer avalanche may come at any time. Even the summertime visitor to Telluride can see on the steep slopes above the town the swaths of destruction cut through the forest by snowslides both old and recent.

Of course this heavy snow cover makes possible good skiing and a long season. Among the runs already open is one called The Plunge. The Plunge drops 3,200 vertical feet in a distance of 2.5 miles—perhaps the longest continuous steep run in North America. Even the experts need time to work their way down that one. The Big-T also offers helicopter transport to areas above and beyond the lifts, providing those skiers who can afford it a chance to play in the deep and virgin powder of the more remote mountain snowbowls.

But the skiing is good everywhere in the Rocky Mountains, and the scenery at Telluride, though magnificent, is merely routine Rocky Mountain magnificence—no grander, for example, than the landscape of Sun Valley, Taos, Vail, Aspen, Alta, Snowbird, Park City, or any of a hundred other crowded, frozen, expensive established ski resorts in the intermountain West. What some of us liked so much about Telluride was not the skiing but that quality of the town which Zoline and his developmental millions must necessarily take away: its rundown, raunchy, redneck, backwoods backwardness. That quality is one you cannot keep in a classy modern ski resort, no matter how much money is spent for preservation, no matter how many town ordinances are passed attempting to protect Telluride's antique Victorian architecture.

Some Telluriders, naturally, the crafty few who got in on the ski boom early, are becoming rich. Do I begrudge these native few their sudden unearned wealth? I sure do. That's normal spite and envy. (Christ, I could have bought the old Senate Bar and Whorehouse for $4,500 in 1962, if I'd had the $4,500. Last year the place was sold for $100,000. Vacant lots that used to sell for five or ten dollars in back taxes now are priced at $10,000. And so on.)

Others among the town's original population, those too slow to speculate, manipulate, scam and scheme are going to have to suffer. A lot of the old folks who have lived in Telluride for many years, sometimes for most of their lives, are going to have to leave. Why? Most of them are pensioners; their fixed and humble incomes will not permit them to pay the runaway property taxes that have multiplied ten times over in the past three years. For instance, a lot formerly assessed at $100 is now appraised at $1,000; a leaning clapboard shack with gingerbread filigree had a valuation of $300 before—now it's $2,500.

You might think it a simple matter to change the rules so that the old folks are taxed for the inflated value of their homes only if they choose to sell out. It would be a simple matter; but that's not the way we do business in this country. Business in this country depends on high volume and fast turnover. That's what keeps the real estate industry operating—displaced human beings. "Our retired people with fixed incomes will have to leave," says Don O'Roarke, the county treasurer. An honest man.

In come the hippies then, the trust funders, the idle rich, the rootless ones, the middle-class proletariat with their beards and unisex ponytails, all of them, male and female, wearing the same bib overalls, Goodwill workshirts and waffle-stomper boots, all trying to look different in the same way. The air is thick with flying Frisbees, the sweet smell of *Cannabis sativa,* the heavy rock electric jungle sound, the industrial beat of hard-core imitation-Negro music. *Rock,* beneath the mountains, where once we heard only the sigh of spindrift from the snowfields and Eddie Arnold on the jukebox. But they have money, these freaks, and want to invest.

All of which poses a serious problem for the natives. A serious psychic bind. On the one hand, the natives want the newcomers' money; on the other hand, they hate their guts. Excruciating inner conflict. What to do? Well, why not take their money first, then call in the cowboys from the outback every Saturday night and have them beat the living shit out of these long-haired weirdos? Such has always been the traditional style of hospitality in the Golden West; still is in Wyoming.

But something has gone wrong with the Colorado cowboys. Although they continue to wear the funny hats and the tight snap-button shirts, they don't seem to like to fight so much anymore, even when they've got the opponent outnumbered by the customary ratio of ten to one. Even on Saturday nights. The bartender at the Sheridan Hotel and Opera House explained it to me: "It's like this. It's that sex revolution. It finally come to San Miguel County about two years ago. Now even cowboys can get laid."

A break for the horses. And the sheep. With the cowboys pacified by sex, the solution to the hippie problem came to rest in the hands of Telluride's former one-man law-enforcement agency, Town Marshal Everett Morrow. Born in Oklahoma, seven years in Telluride, a welder by trade and police officer in his spare time, Morrow wore the classic western lawman's costume: boots, leather vest with tin star, concho-banded Stetson, the quick-draw artist's low-slung .45. Each shady looking newcomer got a personal welcome to Telluride from Marshal Morrow, including identification check with police-record follow-up. His tactics, sometimes rough on the younger generation, made Morrow a focal point of the cultural conflict between Telluride's conservative native establishment and the long-haired newcomers who have swarmed into the town during the recent years.

"The ski area will be the best thing ever happened to this town," says Marshal Morrow, "if we can get it without the goldamn hippies. It ain't the hair bothers me, it's the drugs."

The chief drug being dispensed in Telluride today, however, is the same as it was ninety years ago—alcohol. The town has twelve bars, three package stores, and a special 3.2 beer joint and poolroom for teenagers. With a current population of 1,500, that's one liquor establishment for every 100 citizens—man, woman, child, babe in arms. Contrariwise, there are only three churches and one part-time barbershop. That's the way things go in Telluride: downhill.

One afternoon a few years ago a man named Wayne Webb purchased a bottle of peppermint schnapps in the Belmont Liquor Store, Telluride. (Peppermint schnapps!) From there he went on to every liquor establishment in town, which includes the restaurants, and had a drink or bought a bottle. An hour later he was followed on the same circuit by Town Marshal Morrow, who presented the manager of each place a summons charging him or her with the sale of liquor to a minor. Wayne Webb, who has the looks and manner of a man of thirty, was twenty years old. The legal drinking age in Colorado is twenty-one. Webb, employed by the marshal, was a plant. Every liquor dispenser in Telluride had been entrapped into breaking the law.

That kind of law enforcement does not set well in a town of only 1,500 people. A stormy town meeting promptly followed the citations, during which the bar owners and their partisans (an overwhelming majority of those present, mostly the young long-haired new residents) demanded the resignation or ouster of Marshal Morrow. The town council, consisting largely of old-timers, declined to take action against Morrow but also dropped all charges against the liquor dispensers. This compromise was not sufficient to appease the anger of the crowd, for whom Morrow's entrapment bit was simply a final straw in a long history of alleged abuses. One of the most indignant of those present at the meeting was young Pierre Bartholemy, owner and operator of a restaurant he calls, *naturellement*, Chez Pierre. Around Telluride they call him Chez. He is a newcomer, both to Telluride and to the United States. In the course of his harangue, which was long and passionate, Bartholemy urged the town council to take away the marshal's TV set. "Zis Marshal," he said, "he watch too much zat how you call it? horse *opera?* too much goddamn *Gunsmoke!*"

Marshal Morrow replied by asking for an interpreter, saying,

"Sorry but Ah cain't understand Chez's kinda Anglish. . . ." Someone in the back of the standing-room-only crowd shouted "Fucking bigot!" and crept quickly out of the hall. Another person suggested that it was Chez who needed the interpreter since no new arrival to the American hinterlands could reasonably be expected to understand Oklahoman Morrow's "boll weevil English."

I braced myself for action. Nothing happened. Morrow merely smiled. A stand-down. A draw. The cowboy had the long-hairs outnumbered: There were only 300 of them. He lounged in the swivel chair behind the judge's stand at the head of the hall, listening in scornful silence as the indignation against him ranted on, peaked, leveled off, waned, and petered out. Meeting adjourned. The mob straggled into the night, defeated by the bland inertia of the town council, and dispersed to Telluride's twelve principal establishments of nocturnal worship. Democracy had suffered another crushing setback. Nothing new in that.

I wanted to interview the town marshal and managed to intercept him at his car. "I'm writing a story about Telluride for a magazine," I explained.

Pause.

Morrow considers. He shakes a precise measure of Bull Durham into his ungummed Wheatstraw and checks me over briefly with a pair of the regulation chill blue eyes. "Let's see your ID," he says.

I offer him my old pink *Life* card with the scowling passport photo, plainly stamped "Good Only for March–April 1971." (Issued for a trip to Sinai, called off on account of sloth.)

"So you're from the media," he says.

"That's right. I'm a medium."

He rolls his cigarette with one hand, holding my card in the other, hardly glancing at it. His little cigarette, licked and twisted shut at one end, looks exactly like a joint. That *was* Bull Durham, wasn't it? In the little cotton sack with the black label and the yellow drawstrings?

"I ain't been treated too good by the media," he says. "They take a man like me, they like to make him look like a fool. Like a goddanged hick." (He'd been written up in *Colorado Magazine*.)

"I'm different from the others," I said.

"Yeah?"

"I'll treat you different."

He lights the little cigarette, takes a deep drag down into the delicate lung tissues, holds it for a moment, then blows it out past my nose. It doesn't smell much like tobacco. Smells like a blend of dried cornsilk and half-cured horseshit. That's Bull Durham all right. (And if he tries to draw on me, I thought meantime, I'll grab the tag on his Bull Durham pouch and yank him off balance. That way he'll shoot me in the groin instead of the belly. The groin's nothing but a lot of trouble anyway.)

Marshal Morrow studies me for a few more seconds, his cold steady eyes looking straight into mine, if I'd been standing two feet to the left and about forty miles back.

"I kinda doubt it," he finally says, handing back my obsolete press card.

"Doubt what?"

"What you said."

"You mean the answer is no?"

"Yeah."

That old Morrow, the bartender at the Sheridan explained to me shortly afterward, he's mean but he's fair: He treats *everybody* like shit.

I sulked for a while in a remote corner of the bar, trying to hear myself think against the continuous uproar at ninety decibels from the speakers mounted on the walls. The juvenile voices of what sounded like criminal degenerates united in teeny-bopper song: I believe it was a group called the Almond Brothers. Followed by the Ungrateful Dead. I missed Hank Williams.

Next day I investigated Joe T. Zoline's million-dollar condominium. From the highway it looks like a haphazard arrangement of apple boxes; close up it looks bigger but the same. The roofs are flat. They won't hold up well under 165 inches—about fourteen feet—of snow. The walls seem to be made of plywood. I noticed some of the exterior paneling beginning to peel and warp already, though construction was completed only a year ago. The interiors are cleverly designed: Each of the eighty-seven apartments, whether big or small, has high ceilings, a view of the mountains, and a little private sun deck. Each apartment (priced at $31,000 and up) contains a fireplace, but the fireplaces are miniaturized, more decorative than functional; all heating, as well as all cooking, is by electricity. All-electric homes in the nine-month winters of Telluride, at 8,800 feet above sea level, must be *mighty* expensive. In more ways than one: I thought of the canyon and mesa lands of Utah and northern Arizona—my country—being disemboweled, their skies darkened by gigantic coal-burning power plants, in order to provide juice and heat for frivolous plywood ski hutches like this. Sad? No, not sad— just a bloody criminal outrage, that's all.

I stopped at the office for a few words with Mr. Zoline. Not available, the secretary told me; back in Los Angeles raising more millions. As I walked out of the place I paused for a final look back. The whole condominium rests on a boggy piece of bottomland beside San Miguel Creek. Drainage problems are considerable. May the whole thing sink, I prayed, down into the muck where it belongs.

That afternoon I took the Telluride Company's free bus tour and chairlift ride. Anything to add to the overhead and help hasten the company into its inevitable bankruptcy. The chairlift ride up over the mountain meadows was quite enjoyable. The view of Mount Sneffels and Mount Wilson, two of Colorado's most spectacular 14,000-foot peaks, is certainly a good one. Routine but good. Our tour guide, full of enthusiasm, told us that Mr. Zoline had started his new ski empire by purchasing, for only $150,000, a 900-acre sheep ranch. Sheep ranch? I might have known that a goddamn *sheepman* was at the bottom of all this.

On the way back I asked the guide about the Telluride Company's official symbol, the significance of which escapes me. The official symbol of the Telluride Company is a fried egg with one quarter section cut away.

"That ain't no fried egg," the guide (a local boy) said, "that there's the sun a-comin up behint a mountain with sunshine all around it. What they call a logograph."

"It looks like a fried egg."

"Yessir but it ain't it's a logograph. Ask anybody."

Evasive answer and typical: All you ever get from these company people is doubletalk.

Telluride. To hell you ride. All-year mountain playground. And why not? The people need their playgrounds. We all need a place to escape to, now and then, as the prison of the cities becomes ever more oppressive. But why did they have to pick on my Telluride? One more mountain forest, virgin valley, untainted town sacrificed on the greasy altar of industrial tourism and mechanized recreation. Soon to become, like New York, like L.A., like Denver, like Tucson, like Santa Fe, like Aspen (thus the development proceeds), one more place to escape *from*. Someday soon, if this keeps up, there will be no places left anywhere for anybody to find refuge in. Whereupon, all jammed together in one massive immovable plenum of flesh and machinery, then we may think, at last, in Fullerian-Skinnerian-McLuhanian-Herman Kahnian telepathic unison: Ah! if only! if we had only thought. . . .

Thought what? By that time perhaps even the thought of freedom, even the memory of what (if only) could have been, that too will be lost. Perhaps lost forever.

Forever? Never say *forever*, pardner. Forever is a long time. But say—for a considerable spell of time. For one long long hell of a ride. Until those little voices on the mountain summits, one mile above, calling

don't fret Telluride we're a-coming

have their way, and the huge white walls come down.

P.S.: Since this story was written (many years ago) a few changes have taken place in the Telluride scene. Marshal Morrow's contract was not renewed; he has retired from the law-enforcement business. Mr. Zoline has sold a majority interest in the Telluride Company to Mr. William H. Lewis, a New York investment specialist. The town now has a full-time resident physician. The Idarado Mining Company, a subsidiary of the Newmont Mining Company of New York, which owns the 1,500 acres of prime flat land east and west of Telluride, plans to develop this property for a jet-port, second homes and recreational facilities when skier volume makes it "feasible." The permanent population of Telluride, now about 1,500, could grow to 10,000 or even 20,000 within a decade. (If the ski development does not fail.) The generational conflict within Telluride has largely faded away; many of the old-time residents have sold their homes (at an exponential profit) and moved to places like Sun City and Youngtown in Arizona. The freaks, long-hairs and hippies who have taken their places now own and operate most of the shops, restaurants and other small businesses within the town. They have also taken over the town council and the local Chamber of Commerce and are determined to prevent—somehow—the transformation of Telluride into another Aspen. Two things have not changed: Chez Pierre still offers the best French dinners on the western slope of the Rockies; and Telluride remains this writer's favorite mountain town. I go there every summer and have failed four times now (out of sloth, ineptitude and fear) to climb nearby Mount Wilson, 14,247 feet of rotten rock and ice-glazed snow. I plan to fail to climb it again next year, thereby setting a new world's record.

Abbey's Road

(1979)

Anna Creek

Deep in South Australia, west of Lake Eyre and 700 miles north of Adelaide, lies the Anna Creek cattle station. Big is the word: 11,000 square miles. Running 20,000 cattle, give or take a few thousand, and 700 horses, half of them wild, the mustangs or brumbies of the Australian bush. Plus sixteen domesticated camels, broken to harness, and nobody knows how many wild ones still roaming the open ranges around Lake Eyre.

At the center of this uncaged menagerie stands Dick Nunn, presiding. He is the manager, the boss, the chief among many mates. If I'd thought I'd meet him in an office, dressed like some kind of overseer, I was headed for a surprise. I found him in the main courtyard of the ranch headquarters making beef sausages. Under the bright outback sun of early May, he and old Norm Wood, his chief assistant, stood at the tailgate of a Toyota pickup truck mixing ground beef, ground meal, spices, and preservatives with their hands. In a tub. Flies swarmed over the raw feast. Dick Nunn's handshake was a bit on the greasy side, under the circumstances, but firm.

"Well, Yoink," he said, meaning me, "welcome to Anna Creek. Where the bloody hell've you been?" (I'd written to him from the States months before. He'd invited me to visit.) I tried to explain the delay. Passports and visas. This awkward body of water between San Francisco and Brisbane. The side trip to the barrier reef. Trying to get my bedroll through Australian Customs five minutes before our plane took off for Adelaide.

"Never mind all that," he says. "Give me a hand with this tub."

We carried it into a nearby shed, a kind of butcher shop a century old. Ten thousand flies followed us in random formation. The huge chopping block inside was black with ancient blood, rounded and eroded with years of use. Another man, Bob the Meatax, as he's called, stood at the sausage-packing machine. Bob is from Trieste. Or was, many years ago. Now he works as Anna Creek's chief butcher, almost a full-time job, and sometimes as Dick Nunn's agent in the nearby opal-mining town of Coober Pedy—only 100 miles to the west over a one-lane track of red sand and auburn dust. Out here, that's "nearby." I'm from the American Southwest; I can share the perspective these Aussies have on distance.

I watched Bob the Meatax fit one end of a limp, slimy, translucent casing—part of a cow's intestine—to the nozzle of his machine. He switched the machine on; it pumped the meat into the empty entrail, filling it and extending it like a long, constricted balloon. When the casing was full, Bob shut off the machine and knotted the eight-foot sausage into manageable, natural-looking six-inch links. He hung these chains of pale pink flesh on spikes in the wall and without pausing dumped our tub of sausage meat into the maw of his machine and went on to the next. We talked for a little while of Trieste, of Italy. I'd been there myself once, decades ago, after a certain war. Did he ever get homesick? *"Nunca,"* he said, *"nunca, nunca."* Never! He had a wife and children right here at Anna Creek. Did he ever go back to Italy? About once every two years. When he could afford it. Seeing my smile, he added that his kids would grow up genuine 100 percent bona fide dinkum Aussies.

I returned to my host, Dick Nunn, back at his sausage mixing. The manager of this multi-million-acre, multi-million-dollar cattle operation was wearing nothing but Hong Kong thongs on his feet, faded shorts around the middle, and something that vaguely resembled a cowboy hat on his head—one of the most decayed, grease-stained, sweat-soaked, salt-rimed, degenerate bonnets I've ever seen, anywhere, including the Flagstaff Arizona city jail. "It's the salt holds it together," he explained later. "Till it rains." I thought of the red desert and the huge blazing salt pans—dry lakes—I'd seen when I'd flown from Adelaide to Coober Pedy. When did he expect the next rain?

"Couldn't say," he answered. "Only been here twenty-three years."

And then he offered me a chilled can of Southwark's Bitter Beer, the most popular beer and apparently the only beer anyone drinks between Adelaide and Alice Springs. He opened another for himself. I couldn't help but notice that Nunn carried low over his shorts a formidable belly; like most professional beer drinkers in Australia—and in Australia most of the men are professional beer drinkers; theirs is the national religion—he was proud of his big gut. And what the hell, why not? It was big, but it looked hard. He'd earned it. Dick Nunn is fifty-one years old now, but I wouldn't want to tangle with him. He has blue eyes, a round ruddy face with the inevitable redveined nose, a wide and easy smile, the unselfconscious assurance of a man who knows what he is doing and knows that he is good at it.

Dick Nunn has been resident manager of the Anna Creek station since 1953. The ranch was founded over a century ago, has passed through several ownerships, and now is the property of the Strangways Peake Syndicate, a corporation of one hundred or so stockholders, with offices in Adelaide. Nunn came here from northern Queensland, where he had worked many years—for most of his life—as a stockman and stock drover. A stockman is a cowboy. A drover is one who helps drive a herd of cattle from home range to shipping point. In most of Australia, before the recent improvement and extension of roads made trucking available, it was often necessary to drive cattle on foot for hundreds of miles, in some places a thousand miles (as on the Canning Track in Western Australia) in order to reach a railroad. These great trail drives would take months to complete, for the cattle had to forage off the land as the drive moved slowly forward from day to day.

Nunn was reluctant to talk about himself; but as I would learn later from others, he had been one of the best of the trail bosses,

acquiring a reputation that eventually brought him the man-
agership of the largest cattle station in South Australia and one
of the half dozen largest in the entire nation. Dick is paid a salary
and occasional bonuses, but no share of the net proceeds. "We
ain't had any net proceeds anyway for several years," he said.
"The cattle business is null and void these days." Australia has
not escaped the worldwide recession of recent years, that peculiar combination of unemployment and inflation that so baffles
the economists. The beef-growing industry has been harder hit
than most.

"The frustrating thing," Nunn went on to say, "is that we've
had heavy rains the past three years. Even Lake Eyre is full of
water now. Our range is in better shape than it's ever been before." He glanced around at the rolling plains, covered with
tawny native grasses, that surrounded the homestead. "We could
raise five times the cattle we've got on it now. But there's no
market for them."

I was curious about various aspects of cattle growing in this
part of Australia, which so much resembled my own Southwest
and yet was oddly different. "That grass out there looks short
and dried up," Nunn said, "but it's good sweet feed for stock, the
best there is. Up around Alice Springs you'll see the grass growing up to your waist, but it's sour. Cattle don't do well on it."

What about water? I'd seen a few tanks and windmills around
the place, but Anna Creek itself was bone dry, a broad sandy
wash lined with gum trees. "We have 150 dams and 120 bores on
this station," Nunn said. Bores: drilled wells. Most of the bores
were artesian, he explained, producing water under natural
pressure from the great artesian basin that underlies much of
South Australia. Only fifteen of the wells required windmills to
pump the water to the surface. "But some of that bore water is
very hard," he said, "salty. Stock will drink it, they can get by on
it, but to thrive they need fresh water. That's what the dams are
for. They hold the rainwater."

Dams—in the Southwest we'd call them stock ponds or tanks.
I'd seen many of them from the air as I was flying toward

Adelaide: small rectangles of water flashing under the sunlight, caught by the earthen dams built across drainage channels, scattered out at regular intervals across what otherwise looked, from 5,000 feet above, like an empty wasteland of red and brown. How did they manage before bulldozers were invented?

"Not very well," Nunn admitted. "We used to try to get by with only the bores and the natural springs. And the spring water is usually worse than the bores. It was a chancy business in them days, growing cattle." He grinned at me. "Still is. Gets chancier all the time."

And was there enough rainfall to keep those man-made ponds filled? I knew the precipitation in this area of Australia was said to average two to four inches a year. Not much better than Death Valley. Drier than the canyonlands of southern Utah and northern Arizona. "If the rain comes every year," Nunn replied, "and at the right time of year, we can make it. This station is 100 miles wide and 110 miles long: When it don't rain in one part, it rains in another. We hope. Some years we never get any rain at all. Then we get too much, all at once. Right now there's so much water in Lake Eyre that it's overflowing back down some of the creeks. And that's salt water."

Lake Eyre lies fifty feet below sea level, covering 3,000 square miles. Bigger than our own Great Salt Lake. Ordinarily Lake Eyre is so dry, hard, and smooth that its glittering salt flats are used as a racecourse for land vehicles, like the Bonneville Salt Flats of western Utah.

There was one more thing I had to know about the cattle operation here: Did he raise hay? "Don't need it," Nunn said. "We run our stock on the range all year round. You see, mate, we don't have any real winter here."

How true that statement was, I soon came to realize. May in Australia is Australia's late autumn. And though I'd wake up many a morning with frost on my sleeping bag, the days were always bright, sunny, warm. Thus the ever-present flies. Thus the flocks and swarms and squadrons of always-yammering birds.

I've never seen so many birds in what is supposed to be a

desert region. As Dick Nunn and I talked, the kite hawks soared fifty feet above us, scavengers waiting for leftovers. Flocks of crows flapped about from the trees to the rooftops and back again. They looked like American crows and they squawked like American crows, never stopping, but their cries had a way of falling off at the end. There was something maddening about that incessant yawping and groaning. If I ever came to live in central Australia, I'd keep an automatic shotgun handy and about a carload of twelve-gauge shells.

Nobody else seemed to mind the crows. What the people at Anna Creek did complain about were the cockatoos and their games with the telephone line. I soon saw what the complaint was about. Walking south of the station headquarters one day, I observed parrotlike birds swinging from the telephone line that connected Anna Creek to the exchange at William Creek and points beyond. Taking off, landing again, in well-drilled multitudes, hanging upside down from the wire and swinging back and forth, sometimes flipping clear around, the cockatoos were slowly but surely pulling the line to the ground.

"Goes on all the time," Dick Nunn told me. "God knows how much time we spend restringing that line for them bloody birds to play on."

In the evenings we drive the corrugated dirt road to William Creek. The road is ribbed like a washboard and six inches deep in a reddish flour the outbackers call bulldust. We raise a roostertail of the stuff, a mile-long golden plume that hangs above the road, waiting for a breeze to disperse it, a trace of wind that may or may not come. Penny Tweedie, Sydney photographer, with her cameras and meters and filters and lights, and I with my can of bitter beer, are driving to William Creek, population seven. William Creek is the social center and cultural heart of the world of Anna Creek. Dick Nunn may be the boss of Anna Creek, but William Creek belongs to Connie Nunn. His wife. She runs the William Creek store, post office, petrol station, airport, and hotel.

Penny and I buzz along in our little rented Suzuki, which has a four-cylinder two-stroke engine and sounds like a lawn mower. Like a hornet in a tin can, according to Geoffrey the Road Grader, a man whom we shall soon be seeing again. Must have a few words with him about this traffic artery. We hang a right at the junction with the road to Oodnadatta, drifting around the corner through the soft dust in true Mario Andretti style. Well done, I tell myself. I am driving on the wrong side of the road, of course, but that's the custom here in Australia; they all do it.

A mile ahead in the clear light of evening appears William Creek. It looks like showdown town out of some classic Hollywood western. *High Noon.* A couple of trees. Windmill and water tank. A couple of buildings. One is a depot of the Central Australian Railway, where five of the seven William Creekers live. They work for the railroad. The other building, a single-story structure with tin roof and rambling white wings, is the William Creek Hotel with its pub, the only beer joint and watering hole within 100 miles, in any direction.

This tiny outlier of what is called the modern world sits alone at the center of an enormous flat, red, empty circle of sand, dust, meandering dry streambeds (like that which gives William Creek its name), and open space. No hills, no woods, no chimneys, no towers of any kind break the line of the clean, bleak horizon.

We cross the railroad tracks. There's the gasoline pump with the cardboard sign dangling from its neck: "No Petrol Today." Across the way, beyond a pair of giant athel trees (product of North Africa), are two diesel-powered road graders, a flatbed lorry loaded with fuel drums and other gear, and a small primitive housetrailer—what the Aussies call a "caravan." When not working the highway, Geoffrey Leinart and his mate Butch do some of their living—cooking, sleeping—in that little wheeled box. Not much. I always find them in Connie's pub.

We enter. Geoffrey and Butch are sitting there as usual, on stools at the bar, drinking the bitter beer. Brawny, red-faced blokes. Solid. No one else in sight at the moment. "By God," I say, "good to see some fresh faces in here for a change." They smile, patiently.

"It's the bloody Yoink again," says Butch.

Connie appears, a friendly face behind the bar. Penny orders a Scotch and soda. Connie looks at me.

"I want to buy a beer for every man in the house," I say. "If any."

For just a moment, for the finest split hair of an instant, Geoffrey's smile freezes. I give him my All-American grin to make it clear I'm only kidding. He relaxes. "I mean," I say, "if any beer."

"He's a card, this Yoink," Geoffrey says.

Butch echoes the sentiment. "Yeah, he's a card."

Connie produces three cans of Southwark's finest. We salute one another and drink. There's going to be a party here tonight, a barbecue. Through the ceiling of the pub I can see thin slices of the evening sky. A notice behind the bar: "Spirits 60¢ a Nip." On the end wall is a big drawing, caricatures of Dick Nunn and Norm Wood standing at either end of Connie's bar, with Connie behind it. In lieu of a jukebox, the radio—which outback Aussies still call "the wireless"—is playing American country-western songs, broadcast from Adelaide. The nearest city, 700 miles to the south.

Connie and Dick Nunn have been separated, more or less, for ten years and by the ten miles of dirt road that lie between the Anna Creek homestead and William Creek. But they are still good friends. "Better friends now," Connie would say, "than ever we was when we was bunked down in the same humpy." Hard to doubt: Connie strikes me as being every bit as shrewd, tough, and independent as the boss himself. Independent as a hog on ice. The sparks must fly when these two cross each other. I tried to imagine Gloria Steinem explaining women's rights to Connie Nunn. Connie would laugh and pour Gloria a beer. Connie was born liberated.

Now it's Geoffrey's turn, his "shout." He buys me a beer. He asks me about Ronald Reagan: I tell him what I think, and ask him about Gough Whitlam, the recently deposed Labour Party prime minister. He tells me what he thinks. I see we're not going very far together in politics and change the subject to horses. I had just missed by a couple of weeks the race meeting at William Creek, which was why Dick Nunn had chided me for arriving late. But we're all going up to Oodnadatta this weekend for the next round of outback horse racing. Geoffrey speaks with mixed pride and affected scorn of his son Phillip, "that wiry little runt," who wants to become a professional rider. A small, fierce, handsome boy of seventeen, Phillip works now as one of Nunn's stockmen or "ringers." Everybody calls him Jockey. He'll be here tonight, along with most of the other young Anna Creek cowboys, all coming in from four weeks on the open range. Most of them not even old enough to buy a legal beer at Connie's pub.

Did I say cowboys? Strictly speaking—Aussiewise, in the Strine lingo—there is only one "cowboy" at Anna Creek. He is the old man named Burt Langley whose principal tasks are tending the garden and milking the Guernsey cow back at station headquarters. He seldom gets on a horse anymore.

I slip outside to inspect the brief outback sunset and the railway installations. The sunset is a red glow on the northwest horizon under a huge aquamarine sky untouched by the hint or whisper of a cloud. Three empty boxcars stand at rest on the siding. Farther up the line is a spur with a string of cattle cars parked on it. Dick Nunn will be loading them tonight—after the barbecue. I climb through the open doors of one of the boxcars and discover a hobo jungle beyond.

A dozen Aborigines, men and women, squat on the ground under an athel tree, making tea in a blackened billycan that rests on the coals of a very smoky wood fire. All seem to be talking at once, loudly and rapidly, with many shrieks of laughter from the women and a constant gesturing of thin black arms. They see me and fall silent.

One man wears a condemned sport coat that looks exactly like the one a girl friend of mine stuffed in a garbage can back in Tucson fifteen years ago; the one she called my "wino jacket." The whole mob, men and women both, are dressed in skid row castoffs. They are waiting for the next freight train to Oodnadatta. Like the rest of us, they are going to the races. From

Port Augusta up to Alice Springs, *tout le monde,* anybody who is anybody is bound for Oodnadatta.

They stare at me; I stare at them. No one speaks. Their dark faces with the luminous eyes, with the cast of features made from a genetic mold more ancient than that of any other race on earth, seem to withdraw before me as I look at them, receding into the twilight and darkness under the tree. They are a people hard to perceive, even in the sunlight. The losers in one more among a thousand routine historical tragedies. They are the unwanted guests, the uninvited in their own country. They look at me across a gulf of 20,000 years. I turn away, start back to the pub. As I go I hear their voices begin again, the laughter resume.

"Dole bludgers," one Aussie would tell me later. Welfare parasites. "They won't work. Or they'll work for a month and then go walkabout for six months. The only thing those blacks really want to do is sit under a tree and tell stories. That's about all they *ever* did." Really? Come to think about it, that's what I would like to do. Sit under a coolibah tree, drinking wine with friends and telling funny stories, sad stories, old stories, all the day long. And into the night.

When I return to the pub, it is full of boisterous Aussies. Dick Nunn fills any room the moment he enters. And I don't mean with his girth. Much of his family is there, too: his subteen daughters Anna, Jane, and Margaret; his sons Stewart, Eddie, and Richard; his niece Sue, the homestead cook.

Most of the young stockmen also are here now, a crowd of teenage cowboys, among them Richard, Nunn's youngest boy. Though only sixteen, he works as trail boss of the range crews. He has been out "on camp" for a month, hunting, mustering and branding cattle, breaking horses, sleeping on the ground. He seems a friendly though cocky lad, with bright eyes, freckles, an easy grin. He looks something like Huckleberry Finn, but more like Billy the Kid. He wears high-heeled boots with spurs, dusty jeans, an old faded flannel shirt, and on his head a wide-brimmed, filthy slouch hat ornamented with silvery studs and a tooled leather band. What the Aussies call a "forty-liter" (ten-gallon) sombrero. Like most of the other stockmen, all of whom look like the wildest of desperadoes, Richard is drinking a Coke.

I construct myself a "chuppity-bread" sandwich from the lavish display of makings on the bar—bread, salad, sausages, hamburgers, spareribs, mutton chops, grilled steaks—procure two cold beers and get into talk with one of the few ringers who is old enough to share them with me legally.

His name is Phil, he's twenty-one, and like so many young Australians, he has chosen the life of a drifter. He appears well seasoned: red beard, gap in his front teeth, a rough hulking fellow in black leather jacket with the stars of a brigadier general on the shoulder straps. His cowboy hat looks as weathered as the Kid's: The anchor brand of Anna Creek has been burned into and partly through the front of the brim. Though he resembles a refugee from a motorcycle gang, he turns out to be sociable, if slightly shy. How long's he been working for Dick Nunn? (My guess is maybe four or five years.)

"Two months," he says.

Two months! Then he's done this kind of work before? Phil grins his gap-toothed grin: "Never was on a bloody horse before I came here." So he's learning? "I'm trying." What does the syndicate pay him? "Fifty a week and keep," he says. Since he sleeps on the sand in his own swag, "keep" means he gets all the stewed beef and hamper bread he can eat and all the boiled tea and burnt coffee he can drink. How much time off? "Oh several days every month." Does he like the job? "Reckon I do," he says.

The crowd grows thicker in Connie's pub; the babble of contending voices becomes a steady roar. There must be at least a hundred people in here now—men, women, adolescents, kids, black-skinned and white and various shades in between, sober, half-sober, non-sober, and rotten with the grog. It reminds me of a Saturday night at Eddie Apodaca's Cantina Contenta in Frijoles, New Mexico. Only the hooded Indians are missing, but their place is more than filled by Aborigine stockmen with eyeballs turning red under Neanderthal brows.

I meet a few of the black men, Brian Marks for one, a big cowboy with round and jovial face. Once each year, at the annual William Creek Race Meet and Gymkhana, he spends his entire month's wages at the races, buying at the mock auction for one-day ownership one of Nunn's prize thoroughbreds. (All proceeds from the affair go to the flying doctor service.) What does Brian Marks get out of it? He gets the thrill of sometimes sponsoring a winner, trophy cups, the prestige that goes to a generous man.

Whites and blacks and mixed breeds drink and jabber together in apparent confraternity. Most of them have been working together all year out on the range. Only one discord appears. An Aborigine named George, one of the best of Nunn's stockmen, keeps badgering Connie and her brother Bill for whisky. He is so drunk he can barely stand: his watery, bloodshot eyes are red as gidgee coals. They refuse to sell him whisky. He persists. They sell him a carton of beer (twenty-four cans), and Bill guides him to the door. In a few minutes George is back, angry now, demanding whisky. Fed up, Dick Nunn grabs him by the collar and the seat of the pants and half-carries, half-throws him out the door, across the road, and into the brush by the railway. This time George does not return.

At some time late in the evening, well after dark, the word is passed around to muster all hands at the railroad siding. Time to load the cattle. I follow the crowd. Geoffrey and Butch, each with a carton of beer under an arm, appoint themselves as guides to the bewildered American tourist. "For Godsake," I want to know, "why load the cattle now? We're having a party. And in the dark? Madness."

Geoffrey tries to explain. Train's coming early in the morning; won't be time to do it then. "But half these men are drunk," I say, "ripped out of their minds, and the other half are children who should have been in bed hours ago."

"Now, mate," says Geoffrey, "don't worry your silly Yoink head about it; these boys know what they're doing. These boys are men. Have another beer. Am I right, Butch?"

"That's the bleedin' bloody flippin' truth," Butch says.

They are right. While Geoff and Butch start a blaze with tumbleweeds and railway ties, adding warmth and firelight to the moonlit scene, the Coke-swilling teenagers in their bandit costumes have already begun to move the cattle. The cattle had been assembled earlier that day in the main siding corral, called a "bronc yard" down here. Now the boys drive them into a series of holding pens, breaking the herd up into manageable bunches. The pens lead to a steel chute and ramp and this to the concrete loading dock.

The boys in the yard are pushing the cattle forward from pen to pen. Butch and Geoffrey throw another wooden sleeper on the fire and open more beers. Their big bellies glow in the ruddy light; no true Aussie would allow himself to be seen, after the age of thirty, without a proper beer gut. Dick Nunn leans against his Toyota truck, sipping beer, conferring with Norm Wood, watching everything. The terrified cattle groan, grunt, bellow, pressed hard against one another inside their bars of planking and iron. The chute is full again. I see one cow with its head caught and twisted between the hind legs of another, unable to extricate itself. Two more cars are loaded. The loading goes on by moonlight, by truck headlights, by the sinister, wavering flare of the burning railway ties. The clamor of cattle, men, boys, tractor engine, the clang of steel gates, the rattle of the cattle cars, goes on and on in a confused, violent uproar. Inevitably I think of the use of cattle cars in Nazi Germany, in Stalinist Russia.

"This is a brutal business," I mutter in Penny's ear. "Enough to make a man a bloody vegetarian." She agrees. But sentimental hypocrites both, we know full well that come tomorrow we'll be sinking our fangs in beef again. Pouring the gravy on our potatoes. Pulling on our cowhide boots. Everywhere the smell of blood. Everywhere the brutality and the horror. Nor is it all man-made. Hadn't we seen, only a few days earlier, that cow out on the range, fully alive, with the deformed horn that had curled and grown, somehow, into the cow's right eye?

The loading goes on for half the night. On the last car, door not properly barred, a frenzied bullock kicks it open; four young steers escape, galloping away into the dark.

On another day, a week before the party, we stopped to visit an Aborigine camp near Anna Creek. It looked like a dump. The huts, or "humpies," were made of sheets of corrugated iron propped on sticks. Garbage everywhere: paper, beer cans, wine bottles, plastic junk, gnawed bones, disemboweled mattresses, worn-out shoes, broken glass, puddles of grease, ashes, rags, ropes, dung. A few hungry-looking curs snarled at us as we approached. Smoke rose from smoldering wood fires. The camp appeared deserted.

Then three old women scrambled out of their kennels on hands and knees. They looked like the three witches of *Macbeth*. One was blind. One had, instead of a nose, a wrinkled cavity in the center of her face. The third, though structurally intact, was deaf as a stone and gnarled with arthritis. All looked a century old. They wore long, ragged dresses never washed, nothing else. Their feet were bare, crusty with calluses. They waved their claws, their sticklike arms at us, and chattered like birds. I decided all three were insane, crazy as cockatoos, but Penny, who had met them before, said they were simply glad to see us, eager to talk.

Penny introduced them to me as she squinted through her viewfinder: "This is Jean, the blind one; this is Sheila, missing a nose; this is Lily Billy." Sprawled in the dust and ashes, the witch-ladies gaped at me, including the one without eyes, and jabbered away. They were the most physically hideous human creatures I had ever seen—shrunken, mutilated, gray with filth, pot-bellied, spindle-limbed, crawling with flies to which they appeared supremely indifferent—all of them obviously syphilitic and mad as kookaburras. "My God," I asked Penny, "what keeps them alive?" And Penny, snapping pictures, talking to the three old women as well as to me, said, "Why, the welfare helps. They get about thirty dollars a week. Their old men are off spending it right now, I suppose, down at Connie's pub. But it's not only the welfare. These old girls are still alive, still kicking. They're happy, can't you see?"

I stared at Penny, then again at Jean and Sheila and Lily Billy. The warm autumn sunlight lay on their bodies and faces. The air was clear and fresh. They had nothing important to do and nothing at all to fret over. When the situation is hopeless there is nothing to worry about. I watched their lively hands, their active searching faces, and saw something like gaiety in those irrepressible gestures. Why quit, they were saying. Why quit?

Many miles east of William Creek and Anna Creek we came upon the range crew. Far in advance was the Dogger Man, an old outbacker named Arthur. He drove a Toyota pickup, the front bumper festooned with the scalps and tails of dingoes. This is Arthur's life work, killing the wild dogs. He shoots, traps, poisons them—any way he can get them. The state government pays him a bounty of four dollars for each trophy. He complained that because of the heavy rains there were too many rabbits. Too many rabbits meant that the dingoes were ignoring his traps and poisoned baits.

We drove on, came to a dry lake bed, and stopped. Coming toward us was a herd of horses, fifty or sixty of them, each with a pair of leather hobbles dangling from its neck. Driving the horses were young Richard Nunn, Jockey Leinart and Phil the Drifter. I pulled the Suzuki off the dirt road. We watched them pass. Penny took pictures. We waited. Presently a dog appeared, followed by two pairs of dromedaries harnessed to a rubber-tired wagon. The "bung cart." The camels wore padded collars like horse collars but larger. A small, very dark Abo boy drove the camel team, cracking a whip across the rumps of the near pair from time to time. Huddled under his big hat, within the upturned collars of his coat, his face was nearly invisible. His name was Henry. The bung cart carried the camp's food and cooking gear, bedrolls, two fifty-gallon drums of drinking water, tools, spare ropes, and saddles. What we would call a chuck wagon. Later, when I asked Henry why it was called a bung cart, he grinned shyly and said, "I dunno. 'Cause everything in it gets bunged around, I reckon."

The four camels paced steadily across the flat red lake bed, pulling their wagon. Heads high, they managed to look at the same time both dignified and ridiculous. A fifth camel followed—the spare.

Another gap in the outback caravan, then finally the cattle came in sight. Obscure figures rode back and forth in the dust at the rear of the herd—George the Drunkard, sober now, in charge, and two other Aborigine stockmen.

Penny and I drove south along the railroad and that evening camped with a different crew mustering cattle in a different paddock. On the Anna Creek station, a "paddock" may be twenty by thirty miles wide and long. The "muster" is the round-up, and at Anna Creek these musterings are taking place, somewhere, all year around.

The camp was made near a clump of finish, or finnis, trees, a type of slow-growing desert scrub. Like the mesquite of the American Southwest, the finish makes excellent firewood. On a fire of this fuel the boys were stewing their beef in a pot and heating water for tea. They used the lowered tailgate of their bung cart for a counter, cutting up chunks of salted beef, slicing their camp-baked "hamper" bread. I ate some. Enclosing a slab of stewed beef, it made a substantial sandwich.

A young man named Darrell was the head stockman here. With him were Rodney, and Willie (the son of Norm Wood and his Aborigine wife Jean), and a boy called Froggie (about sixteen), and a little Aborigine boy named Jonesy. Jonesy looked like a child, hardly big enough to climb onto a horse; I would have guessed he was ten years old, but he insisted he was a full-grown fifteen, and the others backed him up. As I would see the next day, Jonesy did a man's work. They all had been out on the range for five weeks.

Willie, at twenty-one, was the oldest. He was also, among other duties, the camp cook. I asked him what he fed the crew. He pointed to the pot on the fire. "Stewed beef." To the wagon gate. "Hamper and jam. Coffee and tea."

"Right," I said, "that's dinner, and what about breakfast?"

"Same thing."

"And lunch?"

"Same thing."

Two more Abo boys came into the firelight, carrying their saddles. They had been hobbling the horses. There was much talk of horses around the fire as the crew ate dinner. Some of the boys asked me questions about America, especially about cowboys, Indians, the Wild West. I told them a little of ranch life in the Southwest, explained the differences in technical terminology. They seemed pleased to hear that our West was no longer quite so wild as the Red Centre of Australia. As we talked the battery radio on the wagon played country-western music, most of it manufactured in a city called Nashville. Every hour on the hour came the five-minute news bulletin, exactly as trivial and superficial as the best of NBC, CBS, and ABC.

We were awakened at four-thirty the next morning by that same radio, playing the same music. Fire blazing, water boiling. The Aborigine boys—the best trackers—were out in the dark hunting the horses. When the first faint glow of dawn appeared, the dingoes began to howl, far off in the bush. Arthur the Dogger Man had not got them all. Like coyotes in America, the dingoes seem to thrive under persecution, breeding smarter all the time.

I borrowed a horse and rode out to where the camels were browsing, hull-down on the skyline. Where the land is so flat the horizon, as at sea, must be generally no more than twelve miles away from the viewpoint of a man on the ground. The camels were not nearly so far away as that. I found them behind a sand ridge, munching on the clumps of short tough dried grass.

Hobbled by the forelegs, they made only a half-hearted attempt to escape my approach. I rode close. This was the first time I'd ever seen camels outside a zoo. They raised their heads to stare at me, the loose jaws moving with a sideways, rotary motion as they chewed their feed. Strange beasts out here in central Australia. "You fellas are a long way from home," I said. They blinked, nodded, lowered their heads again. Anna Creek is a long way from Afghanistan, their ancestral stomping grounds. But the camels have been here a long time, nearly a century and a half. Their breed has adapted well to the unbelievable emptiness of Australia. As have, come to think of it, a number of other exotic creatures. Rabbits, for example. Donkeys, horses, sheep, cattle. Pigeons and house cats. Englishmen.

Englishmen? Exotics? I stood up in the stirrups and gazed around. A mile east a cloud of dust rose from the bronco yard, where dark figures moved back and forth. Somewhere beyond was the Central Australian Railway, invisible among the sand dunes. In all directions extended the rolling savannahs of the world of Anna Creek—red earth, scattered green trees, golden grass. Far to the northwest, in a cloudless sky, hung the autumn sun. There wasn't an Englishman in sight.

I thought of Dick Nunn and his proud belly, ruddy face, stubborn and independent mind. He is no more an Englishman than I am. I'm a bloody Yoink. He's a bleeding Aussie barstid. I thought of Connie Nunn, every bit as tough and generous as her old man, and of their sons—Stewart, master mechanic, tamer of wild camels; Eddie the horseman; and Billy the Kid. They had come a long way from that little green and sceptered isle anchored in the North Sea on the other side of the globe. And never would return. Dick Nunn and his wife and his boys had created an island of their own out here in the great sea of the desert. They could, if they ever felt like it, tell the whole world to go to hell. And probably get away with it. I am all for them. If I ever have to, I thought, I could live here myself. It's my kind of bloody country.

But I was pledged to another. The camels lifted their heads again as I turned my horse. Come to think of it, I was a long way from home myself.

The Outback

Oodnadatta, central Australia.

The name of the town, so I am told, comes from an Aborigine word meaning "no water." One can easily believe it; everyone here drinks from fliptop tin cans—the children soda pop, the adults Southwark's Bitter Beer. A vile brew with the color of horse piss and the flavor of detergent, but strong, twice as strong as any commercial American beer. The barmaid draws mine from a tap and slides the head off with the side of a table knife. I am reminded of the home brew a neighbor of mine once made back in New Mexico. One quart of that massive potion would rattle the brain cells of a bull. But these outback Aussies are a hardy—as well as hearty—lot.

We're in the bar of the Transcontinental Hotel, Oodnadatta's only pub. Oodnadatta's only hotel. The place is jammed with Aussie stockmen on one side, Aborigines on the other. The babble of voices speaking Anglo-Australian, or Strine, blends with the excited, high-pitched gabble of the Aborigines to form a continuous, clamorous uproar. A jukebox rumbles in the background: Johnny Cash singing "Ring of Fire." (A big hit in America ten years ago.) The decibel level is so high that men lean into one another, foreheads nearly touching, to converse. Though "to converse" is not the right infinitive; "to wrangle opinions" would be more nearly correct.

A few years ago this scene, this uneasy commingling of the races, white and black and interbred, would have been impossible. Liberated by recent federal and state advances in civil rights, the Abos are as free as anyone else to bloat their guts and corrode their livers with beer and alcohol in public places. They have taken advantage of their new privileges with gusto. Every country town in Australia now has a bar or pub that has been largely taken over by the blacks. Where voluntary segregation is not possible, as in Oodnadatta with its solitary pub, the races must share. The Aborigines, both men and women, are violently attracted to alcohol and, as the whites are always pointing out, "they can't hold their liquor." Whether this is really any more true of the blacks than of the whites is a tricky question. It is certainly true, however, that drunkenness among the Abos is much more *visible*. When a white man begins to sag at the bar, his friends lug him out, roll him into a car, and pack him home. The drunken Abo, however, most likely has no home, at least not in town; his home is his "swag"—a pile of filthy blankets under a gum tree down by the riverbank in a migrants' camp, a hobo jungle. The drunken Abo, therefore, usually ends up sick on the sidewalk, stretched out in alleyways with his mates, male and female. The scene is not unlike that of downtown Flagstaff, Arizona, or Gallup, New Mexico, on a Saturday night—comatose bodies everywhere. But the American Indians are old hands at this game; the Australian Aborigines are just getting started.

"We ruined the barstids when we give them equal rights," said one middle-aged Aussie to me, well into his third or fourth bitter beer. His face was flushed, his blue eyes slightly out of focus, but the expression and tone of voice were perfectly straight; I could detect no hint of irony. "We should've killed them all when it was still ly-gel." Peering into my face, he must have seen there something like shocked disbelief. He gave me a ponderous wink. But he probably really meant it. At any rate down in some secret recess of his simple, honest Aussie heart he really meant it. And why not? How many of us are absolutely free of any taint of racism? Who among us has not at one time or another entertained the furtive thought that our social problems would be much simpler if that other race—*them*—would only conveniently cease to exist? A famous American writer has been quoted as saying that he is "bored with the Negroes and their problems." *Their* problems. Ah yes, I know exactly what he means.

I didn't come to Australia to argue with Australians about their racial difficulties. (Trivial compared with ours.) Hardly. But I was now into my second cannister of Southwark's detergent and could not suppress one innocent observation. "They must be a clever people," I said, "to have survived for so long—with so little."

My ad hoc drinking partner gave the statement full consideration. He said, "They *are* bloody good trackers." But quickly amended his concession. "Or they was till they all got on the welfare."

This was an ordinary complaint. I heard it often in the outback towns. The aborigines won't work because they're all on the dole; usually accompanied by the not quite logical corollary that "they'll work for a few months then go walkabout for six months and not come back till they're broke and hungry." Well, I don't know. That attitude makes sense to me; I work best under duress myself. In fact, I work only under duress. And it did seem odd to hear it from Aussies, who are noted for their easygoing approach to hard work. When the Australians have some big project on their minds, they usually import an American firm to do the job. An admirable quality, it seems to me, so long as they take care not to let the Americans—and the Japanese— buy up their country. Most of the Aussies I met seemed more interested in enjoying life than in hustling their way through it to ulcerdom, cancer, and an early grave.

For instance. Even the humblest Australian working bloke—a janitor, a shop clerk, a stenographer—gets at least a four-week vacation his or her first year on the job. With longer vacations later. The American custom of chaining working people to their jobs for fifty weeks out of every year seems to Australians barbarous, even cruel. As indeed it is.

Another instance. There are no paved highways through the Australian interior. The only road from the city of Adelaide in the south through Alice Springs in the center to the city of Darwin in the north is an abominable, dusty, corrugated dirt highway that was constructed—by the insane Americans, of course—during World War II. Ever since V-J Day the Australians have been talking about surfacing that road with asphalt, making it a genuine highway in the American sense of the word. By 1976 they had paved the road from Darwin down to Alice Springs and a little beyond, and from Adelaide up to Port Augusta. A 1,000-mile gap of washboard remains in the middle. East by west through central Australia there is not even the pretense of a highway; merely a few meandering tracks of the type that in the western U.S. we call jeep trails. Unlike America, Australia is still a young, healthy country; its maps are free of that tangle of red lines, symbol of varicose decay, characteristic of an overdeveloped, hypertensive economy, which we call the national highway system.

What's the hurry? say the Aussies.

What am I doing in Oodnadatta? I don't belong here. I'm on my way elsewhere—to Alice Springs—by railway. Maybe. It's taken me about forty hours to get here, by rail, from Adelaide, which is 800 miles to the south. Twenty miles per hour—not bad. I've stopped in Oodnadatta to replenish my food and drink supplies—neither available on the train. My train is a "slow mixed goods." That is, a freight ("goods") train with one ancient, derelict, condemned passenger car hitched to the rear. Thus "mixed." And "slow" because it's slow—shunted off to a siding for every other train that passes.

I think of my train with emotions that are also mixed. Pleasure in my slow progress across the red heartland of Australia; exasperation at the many and mysterious delays.

The ants, for example. We were making one of our many inexplicable halts in the middle of nowhere—and in central Australia everywhere looks like nowhere—with nothing visible in any direction but the flat and largely treeless plain. The landscape looked something like that of eastern New Mexico. There was nothing human in sight, no town, no siding, not even a corral or windmill. Reading a book, I'd been vaguely aware of the train's coming to a slow, shuddering stop, followed by repeated efforts at forward motion. Much clatter of couplings, the crash of passengers' baggage tumbling from a rack. Then another stop, hesitation, further strain and groan of mechanical effort, and what appeared to be a final stop. Heavy silence. An hour or two passed in the calm autumnal sunshine of May. As usual during these meaningless halts, the train crew seemed to have disappeared. The engine was a half mile ahead, out of sight on a slight upgrade. I could barely hear the sound of its distant panting. A few passengers leaned out the open windows; most were sleeping. Perhaps the crew was doing the same thing, taking a siesta, or maybe off in the bush hunting rabbits, dingoes, lizards.

Another hour of stillness. Finally a brakeman came in view, trudging down the roadbed, bucket in hand. He looked bored and weary. One of the passengers with his head out a window asked about the delay. The brakeman said, "Ants," and walked on by us. He climbed into the crew's car (not a caboose) at the tail of the train. Shortly afterward we heard, coming toward us, the rumble of couplings under stress, one after another in swift succession. I braced myself; there was a clang of iron. The passenger car lurched forward with a violent jerk. Bags fell again. The train began to roll; beneath us the wooden sleepers rose and sank under the weight of the advancing wheels. The sleepers were laid on sand. They creaked and groaned. Looking back, I could see the rails recede toward the southern horizon. They lacked geometric precision; the perspective was that of an informal, cartoonlike sinuosity, the rails rising and dipping in congruence to the rolling profile of the desert. I thought naturally of the Toonerville Trolley; I thought of the Little Engine That Could.

Ours could not. Not always. Later, we would come to another grade that was too much for the most heroic efforts of our little engine. Here the train was divided in two. The engine hauled the forward half ten miles up the line, parked it on a siding, and came back for the rest of us. That operation helped pass the time, some four or five hours. Nobody, least of all the crew, seemed concerned about schedules.

When Oodnadatta finally appeared on the horizon, we were glad to disembark for a while. The station master (we had no conductor) said there would be an indefinite delay. We knew what that meant. Catching him alone for a moment, I inquired about the ants. He stared at me. "The ants," I explained, "they stopped our train." Were we likely to run into more ants on the way to Alice Springs? He stared at me a moment longer. "I think me phone is ringing," he said, and disappeared into a back office. I didn't hear any phone.

No matter. We had arrived in Oodnadatta, stopping point for many a weary traveler on the epic journey from Adelaide to the Centre (as they call it here). What is there to say about Oodnadatta? Not much, and of that little, nothing good. A bleak town, with a permanent population of some 60 whites and anywhere from 150 to 500 blacks, depending on what, if anything, is happening on a given weekend. When I arrived, the streets were swarming with Aborigines—men, women, and children—hundreds of them, all come to town for the annual race meet. The Transcontinental Bar was the focus of prerace activity, and the talk centered on horses and horse racing. Radiating outward from the jammed entrance to the pub were clusters of the black fellows with their wives and progeny, most squatting in the dust in the meager shade of a few mulga trees. Even as I watched, a battered half-ton Toyota pickup truck pulled in, stopped, and unloaded (I counted carefully) seven adult Abos from the cab and about five times that number from the open bed in back. They piled into the lefthand entrance to the pub, trying with vigor to force their way in. Bottles of sweet wine and cartons of bitter beer passed out over the heads of the crowd, carried along by willing hands. Taking a closer look at the individuals on the outside, I discovered that most were on the way toward a smashing weekend. Beer cans, pop cans, empty wine bottles lay scattered everywhere.

The main street of Oodnadatta is broad and unpaved. Each

passing motor vehicle stirred up lingering clouds of fine, floury, auburn-colored soil—the bulldust. On one side of the main street is the railway station and yards; on the other, the hotel and pub, a general store and petrol station, the town hall, a church-supported medical clinic, and a row of bungalows. The houses are built mostly of corrugated steel or sheet iron, lumber being a scarce commodity in these arid parts. Most of the houses have screened-in verandahs running along two, sometimes all four, sides. Many stand off the ground on blocks or low piers for easier cooling. Although Oodnadatta has its own power plant, there is no air conditioning, nor did I notice any of the evaporative "swamp coolers" common in the American Southwest. The people here rely on cross ventilation and ceiling fans for relief from the heat.

Except for windmills and water tanks looming against the sky, Oodnadatta does not much resemble what we think of as a Western town. What it does look like is a shantytown, one of those squalid settlements typical of back road areas in our own Deep South. The flies of Alabama would be at home here.

Did I say something about flies? Have I mentioned the Australian national bird? The subject is unavoidable. The flies are a fact of life here, at all seasons, a basic datum. Outbackers joke about the Australian salute: the right hand brushed repeatedly across the face. In summertime white residents wear fly veils or a row of corks dangling by threads from the brim of the hat. These outback flies are persistent, sticky, maddening; they cling to your skin. Only the Aborigines are indifferent to them.

A strange people, these Abos, supposedly the most primitive on earth. Scarcely human, according to some Aussies I met. Yet they have, or had, as is now well known, a culture more complex and to me more interesting than anything the white Australians have so far been able to invent on their own. The traditional Aborigines wandered this continent nearly naked, following the game and the weather up and down the transient watercourses, from lake to ephemeral lake. They carried nothing but weapons like the boomerang and the spear, and a leverlike instrument, the *woomera*, with which to hurl the spear with great velocity and accuracy. They had fire sticks, water skins, and stone tools to grub in the earth with. Nothing more, not even the bow and arrow. No domestic animals but the dog. All they possessed in worldly goods they carried in their hands. Their culture was not material and technological but intellectual, spiritual, esthetic. They carried the world in their minds, with an elaborate mythology as subtle in its way as our own. Our mythology we call history and science—knowledge; so did the Aborigines. They could explain to their children everything in their world as well as we can explain our world to ourselves. Each rock, tree, hill, and stream, each living thing had its history, function, meaning. They invented languages—many languages. They invented their own painting, sculpture, music, dance, ritual, religion, the psychology of dreams and literature. They studied and memorized their land, its climate and weathers, the finest details of the flora and fauna. Without knowledge, there could be no survival. The wisest among them, the old men and old women, knew not only where to find water and game even in the hardest years, but also the whole story of the creation of the human race—the Dream Time.

Few of us would be willing to exchange our place in European industrial culture for a place in that ancient and primitive society. We feel our world is more open, vast, and free than that of primitive man. Perhaps it is. But what we have gained in depth and breadth we may have lost in immediacy and intensity. For the savage hunter, every day and every night must have been an adventure on the edge of exaltation or despair. We don't know. How can we know? We do know what life has become most of the time for most Europeans-Aussies-Americans. It has become soap opera. Tragic but tedious.

But the Aborigine world was destroyed long ago. Except for remnant bands rumored still to be wandering the western deserts, the Abos of today are a sick and sorry lot. They hang about the white man's towns surviving on federal charity. They buy their suits and dresses at the Good Will store. They drink too much and breed too much—every tribe is stricken with alcoholism, poverty, syphilis, multiplying hordes of unwanted children. Their lands reduced, their mythic culture lost, they exist in the limbo between a vanished past and a new world in which there is no place for them. "Poor fellow, my country," says the black man.

A group of them sat in the dust under a tree, drinking wine, telling stories. As I shuffled past one of the men called to me, inviting me to have a drink. I paused. The bloodshot eyes in the black faces stared at me. I stared at them.

Some of the men had faces like Socrates, others like Darwin and Tolstoy. Prognathous jaws, wide mouths, broad flat noses, the eyes sunk deep beneath primeval brows. The skin not so much black or brown as gray, the color of dust and wood ashes. Some of the children had blond, curly hair, characteristic of certain tribes. The old men had white hair, white beards, a certain dignity and beauty. But the women were poor misshapen creatures with no waists, swollen abdomens, limbs like sticks— like a child's drawing of a human. Caricatures, deformed by a lifetime of child-bearing and welfare nutrition. Their voices, as they cackled at one another, sounded like the cawing of crows. The flies crawled unheeded over their syphilitic, ravaged faces. One of these scarecrows squawked at me, lifting her skirts to show me the filthiest pair of knickers I'd ever seen south of Soho. The other ladies shrieked with laughter. I blew the old girl a kiss, but squatted down with the men.

The youngest, a middle-aged chap in a cowboy hat, offered me the wine jug, almost empty. I sensed a trap closing, but took a swallow anyhow and passed it on. "Where you from?" he asked. I told him. "Amedica," he said, "Amedica." The accent Oxonian. No doubt he'd had an immigrant teacher. "There are many black fellows in Amedica?" he asked. "About 22 million," I said. "At last count. Plus the one who lives in Tuba City, Arizona." He whistled in surprise, then translated my words for our circle of listeners. The old men nodded solemnly. The man in the cowboy hat said, "I am going to Amedica. I am going to marry a blonde Amedican gel and live in Hollywood, New York. But she must be rich. She must have . . ." He made the appropriate gesture with both hands and spoke a few words to his mates. The old men laughed and nodded. "You will introduce me to the rich blonde Amedican gel?"

Of course; I pulled out my notebook and scribbled the names, addresses, and telephone numbers of some lady friends in California and New York; tore off the sheet; and gave it to him. He studied it, folded it with care, and stuck it in his shirt pocket.

The old men watched us eagerly. The one who looked like Leo Tolstoy handed me the wine jug, upside down, tapping on it and smiling. He said something. My friend in the cowboy hat translated. "He says the bottle is empty."

I nodded, and waited for further explanation. The old man spoke again; all the old men stared at me, smiling. "He says there is a grog shop across the street." I turned my head and read the sign above the doorway of a sheet-iron bungalow: Transcontinental Hotel. My friend in the hat winked, grinning at me. The circle of old men grinned at me. I counted eight grins and twelve teeth. Trapped. I bought the wine.

Our train was scheduled to depart at two in the afternoon, but when I checked in at the station I found departure time adjusted to six-thirty. I spent the afternoon at the races. I won four Australian dollars on a long-legged filly named Morning Star and lost eight on a camel named Stormy Red. Oh they said it was a horse, but it rather resembled a camel, especially when it went down on its knees in the back stretch. Nobody hurt, not even the horse, I regret to say. I bought a huge beefsteak sandwich for fifty cents. Beef is the one thing in Australia that's still cheap.

Back at the station at six, I learned that departure time was now postponed till ten. Apparently the ants were winning. With four more hours to wait I went off to see the walk-in movie. The swift autumn night had already settled in. The walk-in movie was a vacant lot with screen, projector, a few benches, and space for a row of cars at the rear. Most of the patrons brought their own chairs or sat on the ground. The film was an Italian Western starring a Mr. C. Eastwood. Once the moviegoers were hooked on the action, the projectionist walked through the crowd collecting a dollar per head. I left.

Strolling down the unlighted street, I discovered preparations for a dance under way in the one-room town hall. The front door was open, lights on, bunting on the walls; clusters of balloons, filled with gas, clung to the high ceiling. The one-man orchestra, a man in cowboy costume who looked remarkably like America's own beloved Buck Owens, was already warming up with his electric guitar and what he called a rhythm box, an amplifying machine that filled the hall with booming vibrations.

Those Aborigines who could not afford a dollar for the movie were gathering around the doorway, peering in. Folding chairs lined the walls; the wooden floor glistened with a fresh wax job. I took a seat near the musician, out of line of the direct blast from the twin speakers. The musician called himself Dusty Slim. When he paused for a beer, I asked him if he knew any Kristofferson or Willie Nelson. Never heard of them, he said, but he knew the entire repertoire of Johnny Cash, Charlie Pride, and John Denver.

The hall quickly filled, with most of the girls on one side, boys on the other. Chatting nervously among themselves, each sex stole furtive glances at the other. All were whites, scrubbed, brushed and rosy, blond and beautiful, dressed for Oodnadatta's big annual Saturday night; many of the girls wore floor-length party dresses, the boys clean cowboy shirts, jackets, pressed jeans. Dusty Slim played a few numbers and gradually the dancing began, led by a handsome couple who turned out later to be Americans, schoolteachers on vacation.

The Abos crowded outside the door were filtering in now, one by one, first little barefoot kids with wide eyes, staring awestruck at the dancers; then some shoeless teenage girls with bulging pregnant bellies, wearing miniskirts. One of these black girls started to sing along with Dusty Slim in a harsh voice that carried well, despite the mighty rhythm box. The Abo men remained outside, drinking. Two witches crept in, dark shriveled little women with wild woolly electric hair, claws, broomstick legs, splayed and dusty feet. They wore Mother Hubbards that hadn't been washed since the Year One, so greasy that—as an Aussie would say—your eyes slid off 'em. The first witch crouched in a corner, among the black children. The second staggered onto the dance floor, drunk as a wallaby, and tottered round and round in dreamy parody of the dancers, eyes shut, arms making rotary motions.

A big red-haired girl dropped into the chair beside me. "Hi," she says. "Hi yourself," I says. "Where you from?" she says. "Winnebago, Wisconsin; how about you?" "I'm from Homer City, Pennsylvania." After a moment she added, "This is the funniest dance I ever saw in my life."

Funny? I thought it the most tragic dance I had ever seen in my life. La Danse Macabre, that's what I thought it was. The Aborigine lady with the nest of vipers in her hair had now attached herself to one particular couple, mimicking each movement. They whirled, she whirled. They bumped, she bumped, though her timing was off, and some kind of torn gray rag had fallen to her left ankle.

The young man, red-cheeked as an apple, pretended to ignore the shadow at his side, but his girl friend was exasperated. She kept shouting at the witch, waving her away. What she said was lost in the uproar. It made no difference. The old woman floated high in private ecstasy, looking as if at any moment she would crumple to the floor. A big, beef-fed Aussie rancher emerged from the mob and guided her, gently but firmly, through the mass of jiggling whites and out the door.

The teenage black girl, still singing along with Dusty, raised a fist and screamed, "Black Power!" The big man threw her out. The second witch began to howl; he threw her out too.

The dance went on. The floor rocked, the hall shook as outback Aussie cattle growers stamped and stomped to the big beat of the rhythm box, the thin whine of Dusty Slim singing John Denver's "Country Road."

Time for me to check on my train again, though I had little real hope it would leave as promised. As I crossed the street I saw a writhing mass of drunken Abos pushing a Ford Falcon (made in Australia) toward the south edge of town. The car was full of more Abos, laughing and shouting, arms and legs sticking out the windows.

A white boy stood by watching. I asked him what was going on. He said they were pushing the car out of town to burn it. Why burn it? "Because it won't run," he said. He explained the history and evolution of the Aborigines' understanding of the white man's proudest toy. When the Abos first began to buy automobiles (he said), nobody bothered to tell them that it was necessary to refuel the things from time to time. The happy new owner would go roaring off into the desert in his first car, keep going until it ran out of gas, and abandon it. The used-car dealer sent somebody out with a can of petrol to recover the car, had it brought back to town, and sold it over again to the next Abo to come along with a pocketful of wages.

But after a while the Abos caught on to this scam; they learned about gasoline. Then they would buy a car and drive it until something functional went wrong and it refused to run. Again the car was abandoned; again it was recovered, repaired, resold. The Abos were not deceived for long. Now, said my informant, when their cars break down they burn them. "Give them ten more years," the boy said, "and the bloody blacks will be selling *us* cars."

I found my train actually ready to go. The rust-colored engine stood by the station house, panting. Two phlegmatic engineers stared at me, without interest, from the cab. The station master was not around but a crewman leaning against the wall pointed out the passenger car, about a half mile down the track, still joined to the rear of the train.

I took my duffel bag and my box of food and beer and my old leather trunk that I use for intercontinental travels out of the waiting room, where I had cached them for the day. Burdened with this awkward load, I struggled down the side of the roadbed—there was no walkway—toward my car. I had nearly reached it when the train gave a grunt, a jolt, and pulled away. I watched it trundle slowly up the tracks and stop again, the passenger car now aligned with the station house, as per regulations. The engineers stared back at me, their faces blank. I struggled up the roadbed and managed to get gear and myself aboard just as the train began pulling out. I found a compartment, filthy but empty, and settled down for a long journey.

First, I would kill one of the engine crewmen, chosen by lot; second I would sleep; later, I would open my trunk and begin my study of the selected works of a Mr. H. James. I knew we had 200 miles to go before reaching Alice Springs, the dead epicenter of Australia and my primary destination. I reckoned it would take a day, maybe two or three days, probably no more, to arrive there. Providing, of course, that the bleeding ants gave us no more bloody trouble.

A Desert Isle

Isla de la Sombra is a small island off the coast of Mexico. Twenty miles long, five to ten miles wide, with 4,200 feet of vertical relief, it has no human inhabitants whatsoever. Not one. And this for the very good reason that la Sombra, so far as is known, lacks any trace of spring, seep, or surface stream. Except for a few natural stone basins—*tinajas*—high in the canyons, which may hold water for a time after the rare winter rains, la Sombra is absolutely waterless. It is a true desert isle.

Naturally we had to go there. Me and Clair Quist, a friend from Green River, Utah. Clair is a professional river guide by trade, a jack-Mormon by religion. He doesn't talk much, but says a lot when he does. I like that.

To get us to the island we hired Ike Russell, a veteran bush pilot out of Tucson. There are no recognized landing fields on the island but Ike had landed there a couple of times earlier anyway and thought he could do it again if conditions were favorable. Loaded with twenty gallons of drinking water and other baggage, we took off one morning from Tucson in Ike's old Cessna 185, a refurbished aircraft fitted with oversize tires, reinforced landing-gear struts, and other special equipment. We rose about thirty feet in the air and dropped back to the runway. Power failure.

Half an hour later, with twelve new spark plugs installed, we tried again. Made it. On the way south, Ike landed and took off twice from a small dirt strip in the desert, for practice. The plane carried a heavy load: 160 pounds of water, food for ten days, and two passengers weighing nearly 200 pounds each. We landed again at Nogales, Sonora, to be cleared through Mexican Customs. Easy enough—Ike paid the customary bite, *la mordida,* about five dollars to each official lounging around the office—but it made me nervous all the same. I always get scared when I enter Mexico. Something about those short, heavy, mestizo police with their primitive sullen eyes—the way they look at you—and the bandits loafing along the highways with stolen assault rifles, picking their teeth with lizard bones. I don't know which I fear most, the cops or the bandits. In fact, except for the uniform, I can't tell one from the other.

But we were flying 6,000 feet above it all, across the cowburnt wastelands of Sonora, toward the blue Pacific and a remote, uninhabited island. Nothing to worry about.

We reached the coast and flew across some fifty miles of choppy open sea. The island came in sight, dark and craggy through the haze—la Sombra. We circled over the south half of the island, close above the rugged mountains. They looked like the mountains of Death Valley—barren, volcanic, with the color and form of rusty, mangled iron. Down in the narrow canyons we could see wild palms and other small trees, but no sign of water.

Ike made a pass over one possible landing place, a 700-foot strip near the beach and the mouth of the palm canyons. He had landed there before, but not with such a big load. He flew five miles farther to a dry lake and put us down. The lake was a little muddy beneath its dried crust, and we made a very short stop. We got out, glad to be on land again. From beyond the waves of gravel and pebbles, piled like a dike along the shore, we could hear the surge and uproar of the sea. The wind was blowing hard.

We agreed that the area near the first landing strip would make a nicer base camp. To lighten the load, we removed five gallons of water from the airplane and decided that Clair and I would walk back to the first strip. Ike took off with most of our food, the rest of our water, and the camping gear. Clair and I cached the water jug and started walking.

Late afternoon: The sun stood low over the western hills. Though the distance was short, we had to climb three coastal ridges and find our way by starlight through a cactus jungle before Ike's bonfire guided us to his airplane and our camp. As we arrived, a huge full moon—a little late—rose out of the sea, looking ruddy as an orange through the eastern mists. Happy to find our pilot alive and his plane right side up, we celebrated with Ronrico 151 and three mighty steaks grilled on an iron-wood fire.

Early next morning Ike took off, promising to return in ten days to take us home. Clair and I were alone on the island.

On our island. We could hear the seagulls shrieking and cackling by the shore. We saw a file of brown pelicans sail by, sedate, dignified, skimming low above the waves in graceful and perfect unison. Far above, a hawk patrolled the lonely sky.

Clair wanted to go look for lobster. He has this dream of lobster unlimited, fresh from the boiling pot (a quick death, they assure us; I hope so), of sinking his fangs in that tender sweet meat from claw and tail. But I was thinking of water. Fresh water. We had fifteen gallons with us. Enough for ten days, probably. If we were careful with it. If nothing went wrong. If Ike returned on schedule. I suggested, therefore, that for our peace of mind—my peace of mind—we might take a little walk up into the canyons before doing anything else. To look for water.

Clair knows a paranoid when he sees one. He takes a hundred of them down through the Grand Canyon every summer. So off we went, into the desert, toward the mountains. I carried a day-pack over my shoulders, with cheese, nuts, oranges, and a gallon of water. We trudged up the sand and gravel of a dry wash, into the mountains, following what we thought was the main drainage. Though early February, the heat seemed intense—and the seaside humidity even more unpleasant. We found ourselves sweating heavily as we climbed, mile after mile, through the sand, around and over the boulders, higher and higher into the narrowing canyon. We paused several times to drink from my canteen. Despite the grandeur of these desert mountains, the strangeness of the desert plant life, we thought of water rather often. We weren't finding any. One likely pothole after another turned out on inspection to be full of nothing but dry sand. Cheap, leaky, volcanic rock, full of fissures and vesicles: the winter rains had apparently percolated right on through into the substrata.

We passed a few small fan palms but found no trace of water on the surface. Palm trees suggest oasis, but this boulder-choked gulch we were ascending was hot, arid, and waterless. It would seem that the wild fan palm, like the cactus, the mesquite, the ironwood, has adapted to a situation where water is available only intermittently.

Halfway up the mountain, sitting in the shade of an overhanging cliff, Clair and I ate our lunch, drank the last of our canteen water, and contemplated the bright blue sea 2,500 feet below and four or five miles away. A long dry march back to camp. We had about given up hope of finding water and were feeling a bit discouraged. Then I thought I heard a dove calling, farther up in the canyon.

"Dove," I said.

"You're crazy," Clair said.

But we heard it again. The soft, sad coo of a mourning dove; *hey . . . hoo . . . hoo . . . hoo.*

Dove means water. We scrambled farther up through the rocks and about fifty yards higher, deep in a grotto under the shade of a palm, we found a beautiful basin in the bedrock half-filled with the precious and lovely stuff. Good water—clear, cool, fresh—left there, no doubt, by the last rain. Filling the canteen, I slipped and fell in, not ungracefully. The pool was knee-deep, about three feet wide by four feet long. Fifty gallons at least; enough for a month of survival, if necessary. If the damned doves didn't drink it all first. Several of them sat about on nearby rocks and trees, staring at us reproachfully.

"Wish I had my shotgun," said Clair.

"Such ingratitude." But I knew what he meant.

Refreshed and reassured, we climbed on to the saddle of the mountain. We were now about 3,000 feet above the sea, up among the century plants and ocotillos. We descended into the canyon beyond, scrambling down bluffs and scarps of the rottenest rock I've encountered anywhere. We didn't care. We were pleased with ourselves and our island. We reached the sandy floor of the canyon and checked out a narrow gorge beyond. The rock here was solid and monolithic, some kind of consolidated volcanic tuff, pale yellow with red and brown nuggets of jasper embedded in the matrix.

We walked into a corridor carved through the stone over centuries by rare but violent desert floods, and made our best discovery of the day: a pool of drinkable water, ten feet wide, twenty feet long, of unknown depth. There were probably more tanks beyond, around the bend of the gorge, but we would have had to swim the pool to find out. The walls on either side were smooth, polished, overhanging. Deep in the shade, the water was too cold for a swim. And besides, as everyone knows, it is not good manners to swim in a desert pool. Well-brought-up desert rats such as ourselves, sweaty and greasy, do not go paddling about in what may be the next man's drinking water. This pond might last for several months, before evaporation took it all.

Canteen full and bellies gurgling with water, Clair and I made tracks for camp. At an easy pace; we knew the moon would be up, sooner or later, to light our way. No longer concerned about water, we paid more attention to the novelty of the plant forms along the route. On the hillsides grew stands of the elephant tree—a short, thick, grotesque plant no more than ten to fifteen feet tall, with bright green waxy leaves and peeling white bark. We named it the leprosy tree. An unfair name, maybe; in their way, these things are beautiful, particularly in contrast to the rust-red cliffs behind them. We saw many more of the palms, some of them up to forty feet tall. Their high fronds, rustling in the sea breeze, sounded like running water. Some were bare-trunked; most were clothed in thick skirts of dead fronds reaching from near the top to the ground. A kind of fruit, grapelike bunches of green berries the size of cherries, dangled within reach on the females. I bit into one: bitter, hard, almost all seed.

We thought of food, now that our water supply was assured. So far we had seen no sign of any possible game except the doves—and there *is* something about the piteous bleating of those little chickens, as they flee before you, that makes a man want to reach for a shotgun. I understand and sympathize with that reaction. But the doves were few, and we were unarmed. We had not seen the tracks or scat of any mammals larger than mice—no trace of deer, bighorn sheep, rabbit, hare, coyote, fox. This, more than anything else, convinced us that la Sombra truly is a barren isle. The doves, when the potholes dried up, would fly back to the mainland; but mammals, all but a few species of desert rodents that manufacture their own water metabolically, must have a reliable, permanent supply of surface water. Furthermore, if springs or seeps had ever been found here, the Indians and then the Mexicans would have moved in, together with their goats, pigs, cattle, and burros.

We saw plenty of chuckwallas, a big, fat, ugly, remarkably stupid lizard. A vegetarian, it grazes on the leaves of such desert plants as brittlebush and creosote. Dozens scurried out from perfectly good hiding places, rushing across our path and trying to hide again between or under rocks, digging in frantically. The animal's only defense seems to be the heavy tail, which it switches back and forth like a whip. Wedged in a crevice it puffs itself up, hoping to become inextricable. The Indians, so I've heard, would deflate them with a sharp-pointed stick, pull them out, take them home alive. Adequate, if not good, eating. How are they cooked? The same way you cook a lobster. I suppose, if starving, I could do it.

Into twilight. We stumbled home through the dark—moon late again—over the rocks and among the cholla, passing a forest of the giant cardón cactus on our right. Monstrous forms of bronze and thorn, twenty, thirty, forty feet high, they are the biggest cactus in the world. When swollen with moisture, as these were, each must weigh many tons.

We heard and then smelled the sea. Dark ridges loomed

against the 2,800 visible stars in the sky. Where the hell were we? Wait for moonlight or go on? We guessed the correct direction and went on. Another fifty feet and we walked right into the ashes of our morning campfire.

The moon rose. We built a little fire. Clair set two cans of beans, unopened, in the flames. I lit my cigar, backed off a bit, and waited for the explosion. The cans went *bleep! . . . bleep! . . . bleep!* At the third bleep Clair pulled them out, opened them. The beans were ready, pressure cooked. Neither of us thought of cooking anything more. We don't go into the wilderness to cook fancy meals, for chrissake. We ate our beans and smoked our smokes and drank some more Ronrico and were content.

Next morning Clair took his snorkeling outfit and a pair of leather gloves and went lobster hunting down where the surf was pounding against the slimy rocks. I walked for miles down the rocky, pebbled shore, naked except for sandals and a hat. The seabirds hollered at me, and once a big bull sea lion came wallowing up out of the waves, staring at me with huge eyes like those of a basset hound. I tried to coax him ashore; nothing doing. He lay on his back among the billows, loafing; then dived and vanished. Cormorants, frigate birds, pelicans, and gulls sailed by. I found a small sandy beach in a sheltered cove, took a swim, stretched out on the warm sand, hat over my face, and let the sun blaze down on my body. The sun, the sand, the clamoring sea, my naked skin. Close to peace for the first time in weeks, I began to think of women. Of this one, that one, all the lovely girls I've found and known and lost and hope to find again. That girl in Tucson, for example: her light brown hair, her docile eyes, the glow of her healthy flesh.

"Take me to Mexico," she had said.

"I'd rather take you tonight," I said.

God damn it. Really a mistake to come to a perfect place like la Sombra without a good woman. God damn it all. I committed adultery with my fist and went back to see how Clair was doing.

Powerful, shaggy, and dripping, he looked like Triton emerging from the waves. But no lobster in his grip. I borrowed his mask and cruised the surface for a while, admiring the schools of green-gold coral fish streaming over the underwater rocks. I saw a small stingray rise from the pale sand and dart away, terrified. Both of us. And starfish. And one dark somber creature hovering in place below me, not more than three feet long but with the unmistakable outline of a shark.

The tide went out. We crawled upon the damp rocks, searching the tidal pools, pursuing long-legged crabs. Never got near them. Thousands of primitive looking bugs, with long antennae, many short legs, and the forked tails of earwigs swarmed over the rocks before us, hustling out of our way, making suicidal leaps. I suppose they were feeding on microorganisms left behind by the receding water.

We played all day in the Sea of Cortez and walked home near sundown to our camp. That camp consisted of two flat stones with a pile of ashes between; of two bigger stones for sitting on; of a skillet, coffeepot, and two tin cups nearby; of a cloth sack of food off the ground in a limber bush (*sangre de dragón* in Mexican); of three water jugs under the bush; of Clair's bedroll over there and mine down yonder and Ike Russell's "airport" in between.

We thought now, in the cool of the day, that we might do a little work on the airport. Ike had thoughtfully left behind, as a hint, one shovel, one hatchet, and a pinch bar. He had marked out a 1,000-foot runway he hoped we would clear, but—all rocks and shrubs—it looked like a week's work to us. Instead, we pried loose a few boulders at the head of the old strip, chopped down some limber bushes at the lower end (those bushes with their bright red sap—blood of the dragon!) and made it ninety feet longer. We agreed that we preferred a possible death by airplane smashup to certain death by hard labor under a desert sun—an easy choice.

"What's for supper?" said Clair a half-hour later.

"Whose turn to cook?" I said.

"Yours."

"Beans."

* * *

Days passed; nothing happened.

No boat appeared on the sea.

One morning we found a dead sea lion on the beach, rapidly decaying amid the wrecked turtle shells, driftwood, lost cordage, sun-blued rum bottles, pelican skulls, broken clam shells, spiny blowfish, limestone starfish, and other castoff wrack from the ocean. Not the same sea lion I had seen before, this one looked smaller, younger. The big eyes were already gone, pecked out by the shore birds.

I sat down on a log and thought about sea lions. Those remote cousins of ours, returned to the beginning. I thought of the big one I had seen a few days earlier, staring at me from the waves, and wondered if these ocean-going mammals ever felt a twinge of nostalgia for the land world they had left behind, long ago. (At night I often heard forlorn cries coming up from the shore.) The whales, the dolphins—do they feel a sense of loss, of longing, exiled forever from the land, the open air, sunlight? Or—the obvious counterthought—do they feel pity for *us*? After all, theirs is the larger world, perhaps the more rich and strange.

Useless speculations. The melancholy of the sea—the "bitter, salt, estranging sea"—was getting into my nervous system. Clair had vanished somewhere around the headlands, still exploring the underwater realm. I went for a walk into the place we had named Paradise Valley. (And in fact we were privileged to name every place on this forgotten, enchanted isle.) Paradise Valley was full of flowers—purple lupine, glowing like candelabra, the coral-colored globe mallow, yellow brittlebush, many others I could not identify. Light green vines—the type known as dodder—briefly resurrected by the winter rains, crawled upon the giant cardóns and wreathed themselves about the walnut brown shapes of old-time, long-dead, rugose ironwood trees. Smokethorn floated on the heat waves in the sandy wash. The fishhook cactus sported its delicate lavender blossoms; some were already bearing fruit. I ate a few of the red morsels, their flavor like wild strawberries. Butterflies and hummingbirds also explored this wild, perfumed garden. Under a man-high shrub spangled with blue flowers, I found a rattlesnake coiled in striking position, observing me. It looked fat, fresh, and dangerous: scales a coppery pink, coon-tailed rattles whirring vigorously. I teased it for a minute or two with a long stick, then left it in peace. Ravens croaked on the crags. High above, a red-tailed hawk screamed, the sound of its cry—as the *koan* says—exactly like the form of its fatal beak.

Death Valley by the sea. Salmon-colored clouds float over the water. Reflecting that light, those images, the sea, now still, looks like molten copper. The iron, wrinkled, savage mountains take on, briefly, a soft and beguiling radiance, as if illuminated from within. Canyons we have yet to look at—deep, narrow, blue black with shadow—wind into the rocky depths. Sitting on a hill above our camp, listening to the doves calling far out there, I feel again the old sick romantic urge to fade away into those mountains, to disappear, to merge and meld with the ultimate, the unnameable, the bedrock of being. Face to face with the absolute—whatever it is. Sweet oblivion, final revelation. Easy now. What's the hurry? I light a cigar instead.

Old moon in the morning, worn and pale as a beggar's last peso, hangs above the western skyline. Last day before departure—if the plane gets here. Coffee and oranges for breakfast. Clair and I sit in silence on our rocks by the fire of ironwood coals and contemplate the conflict in our heads. Regret to be leaving—the longing to be gone. We resolve the conflict by making plans for a return next winter by boat, with loads of water and food and, of course, women. What women? Our women. Good women, what else? What other kind is there?

Time for one more walk up into the canyons. Clair has other notions. I go alone, across the wash, chuckwallas crawling out of my way, past tiny pink flowers shining in the sand, through the cardón forest over a field of tough, tawny grass. Unspeakable beauty, unbearable seasick loneliness. Murmur of the shore, distant cries. I climb a long ridge and find, at the end of it, on a good lookout point, a circle of flat stones set on edge in the ground. The circle is five feet in diameter, big enough for several small human bodies. For Indians. By the look of the stones, the growth around them, they've been here for centuries.

Silence.

The day seems very hot. I notice that my heart is beating rapidly, that I feel slightly giddy, as if veering toward heatstroke. I sit down in the shade of a giant elephant tree and drink some water, eat some lunch. A hummingbird comes close to inspect the red bandana around my neck. Feeling better, I get up, go on, tramp into the dry stillness of a new canyon.

I enter a thick grove of wild palms. A dozen ladies in thick grass skirts, their green living fronds hang thirty feet above my head. Birds are poking about up in there. The loose stones clatter under my feet like broken glass. I walk through a funnel of solid rock, like the stem of a wineglass, like the passageway to birth, into the womb of the mountain.

Sunlight again and the oppressive heat. More palms line the route, many of them, both dead and living. Some appear to have been struck by lightning, burned alive. I clamber over boulders polished by floods, inlaid with mosaics of garnet and obsidian. I sit again in the shade of a palm, drink the last of my water, and listen to what sounds like a mockingbird singing nearby, concealed in the top of another palm tree. It moves. I see it—the white wing patches, the long tail and slender bill. It is a mockingbird: What is a mockingbird doing here? What am I doing here? Indifferent to my presence—or is it performing for my benefit?—the bird sings on and on, a sweet clear song with subtle variations. This bird and I, companions in the wilderness, are going gently insane. Far away and far below, beyond the deep notch of the canyon, the blue rim of the sea glitters under the sun.

The bird flickers away. I wait. What *am* I doing here? Who cares? I can't think of any other place I'd rather be, despite the sensation in my heart of panic and dread. Of fear. Fear of what? I don't know.

Going on, thinking of water now. There should be water up in here somewhere, and the search for it gives a purpose to my meaningless wandering. At the head of a second stony corridor in the canyon I come to the end, a wall of rock fifty feet high that, at first glance, seems to block any further advance. I tramp across the sandy basin under this dry waterfall and look up at the smooth polished chute of the pour-off. Above, in that basic bedrock, there will be, almost certainly, a series of natural tanks, some of them containing water. The pattern is obvious. At the side of the chute, where the stone has not been worn so sheer, I find, on closer examination, a number of possible handholds and toeholds. The pitch is climbable. Clair, a good climber, would go snaking up there with little hesitation. But he is not here. A dim memory from my past, from long ago, tells me to turn around. Instead, I reach for the rock.

I start climbing, putting my fingertips into little holes in the vesiculated rock that would make ideal scorpion dens. Halfway up or more, about thirty feet above the base, I pause to survey the route beyond. Still looks like it will go, but already I am dreading the necessary return and descent, which will be much scarier than the climb. I look down; always a mistake. A long way down. Not a fatal fall, perhaps, but worse—crippling. Should go on up before I lose the rest of my nerve. Instead, I stand there on a tiny ledge a couple of inches wide, embracing with both arms the column of stone in front of my chest. The taste of fear on my tongue—a green and sour flavor. The blue-green corrosion of an old battery terminal. Catastrophe theory: the quantitative description of discontinuous functions, as of a heavy body falling from point to point. Of course, Clair will come looking for me, tomorrow. Should have told him where I was going.

The mind whimpers on, tormenting itself. What a lonely place to die. But death is always a lonely business. Let's go on. Maybe we can find some other way down. Climb the ridge into the next canyon, maybe.

Resolving to climb, I reach for a higher handhold and discover that the rock I've been clinging to is loose, attached by gravity and nothing more to the pedestal on which it rests. That settles the matter. I abandon any notion of going higher on this murderous, rotten, decaying rock. Instead, I descend. How? Very carefully. Back down to the relative safety of the canyon floor. Back down the gorge, back down through the canyon, back down to the sea and the shore and the long walk homeward through the dark, guided by the screeching laughter of seabirds on my right and Clair's towering signal fire against the stars.

Last day. We cleaned up camp, cached what was left of our food (coming back someday), cleared a few more boulders from the landing strip, and waited for Ike and his airplane. Clair stood on the knoll nearby, surveying our island one last time. A curious osprey circled several times above his head, nearly close enough to touch. I went down to the beach and gathered some pretty shells for my daughter. The dead sea lion was still there, still recognizable, but leaving us cell by cell, atom by atom. I took one last tumble in the roaring surf and went back to the airport.

Between the wild clamor of the sea and the hot mystic stillness of the desert, we waited for the return of the aluminum bird of the north. The bird came, precisely on time, and carried us aloft and away. Our bright lonely island with its red mountains and golden fields, encircled by blue, became smaller and smaller behind us until it was lost in the vastness of the sea.

Sierra Madre

Our pilot is Ike Russell. Again. We're flying in his old wrinkled Cessna from Tucson and Nogales south-southeast to a little logging town known as Creel in the state of Chihuahua. Named for the Mexican entrepreneur and politician who helped establish the Ferrocarril de Chihuahua al Pacífico—that fabulous railway which runs from Chihuahua City across the western Sierra Madre to Los Mochis and Topolobampo (perfect name) on the west coast of Sonora.

The sky is extremely hazy this afternoon in spring, full of windblown dust and the smoke from forest fires to the east. Northwest Mexico, like the American Southwest, has been suffering a prolonged drought. Below, I see the barren desert hills rising gradually toward the crest of the Sierra Madre Occidental. Brown, burnt, sere, denuded hills, stripped of grass and largely waterless. Somewhere down in there, in the slight shade of cactus and mesquite, the cattle are dying by the thousands from thirst and starvation. The Sonora newspapers call it, appropriately, a disaster area.

The hills become bigger, rougher, with deep vertical escarpments facing the west. We fly over the trenchlike canyons of the Rio Moctezuma, the Rio Papagochic, the Rio Yaqui, mere threads of water winding among the foothills. Somewhere up around the headwaters of the Rio Yaqui there may be—maybe—a surviving remnant of the once-numerous Mexican grizzly population. No one seems to know for sure. The great bear survives mostly on rumor.

Although the approaches are rugged, the range ahead of us lacks any prominent peaks. Some points rise 10,000 feet above sea level, but from the air this part of the Sierra Madre ("Mother Mountains") presents only long ridges and high plateaus with a rolling surface, all trending in a northwesterly-southeasterly direction. There are no snowy summits here or any snow in sight at all. Arid, arid country. The scenic grandeur of the region lies not in the mountains but in the canyons or *barrancas* carved by the rivers, where the vertical relief may often exceed 5,000 feet. According to unverified report. Northwest Mexico has never been mapped in a thorough and scientific manner. Stories of canyons deeper than Arizona's Grand Canyon must be regarded with suspended judgment.

We fly over the forests now, thin but extensive growths of jack pine, scrub oak, yellow pine. Everything I can see appears to be well logged; the land is overlaid with an intricate network of dirt roads. According to Russell, who has been flying over, exploring, and prospecting the Sierra Madre for twenty years, there is almost no virgin forest remaining.

Fires are burning in many places, apparently unattended. As an old-time fire lookout, my instinctive reaction is to grab the radio mike and sound the alarm to all points—but down here, who knows? Maybe nobody cares. Let them burn. In any case, we are beyond my jurisdiction. Furthermore, Ike tells me, while some of the fires below were probably lightning-caused, the majority are deliberate, started by the Indians to clear the ground for the planting of their corn and beans, the slash-and-burn economy.

That forested range below is plainly not uninhabited. Everywhere I look I see not only the logging roads and fires but also the milpas of the Tarahumara Indians, small clearings of one to two acres scattered about on every bench and swale of land with a slope of less than fifty degrees off the perpendicular. You might call it wild or primitive country, but as in most of Mexico the land is occupied to the limit of its carrying capacity by human beings—and by their cattle, burros, goats, dogs, chickens, pigs. To the limit and then some.

Ike flies on, holding his course steady. We pass above the tracks of the Chihuahua al Pacífico, and suddenly more great breaks appear—the barrancas. Hard to make much of them through the smoke, the dust, the glare of the midday sun. I see craggy drop-offs, the serrated edge of rimrock, brushy slopes descending at precipitous angles into obscure depths, out of which a few buttes and pinnacles rise into the light. Water glints far below. The cornfields, the corrals and granaries, the little stone huts of the Indians are perched on the edge of the barranca and on the open slopes far down within it. Barranca del Cobre, Ike tells me; "Copper Canyon." That faint hint of water down in the shadows must be the Rio Urique.

To call it a canyon is not quite exact. There is a distinction of meaning between *barranca* and *canyon,* both of them, of course, Spanish words. The term "canyon" refers to a long and narrow defile, well defined, walled in by cliffs, usually though not necessarily with a stream running through it. "Barranca" means, literally, a "break"; in Spanish landform terminology the word functions as a broader, more inclusive term than canyon, denoting any area where the land falls off steeply from one level to the next in an irregular, very rough, highly eroded fashion. For example, Santa Elena in Big Bend is clearly a canyon; Bryce Canyon in Utah is not a canyon at all, but something that better exemplifies the word break (like Cedar Breaks, also in Utah) or barranca.

The Barranca del Cobre, as I can see from the air, huge as it is in itself, is only one barranca among several in the area. Easy to see why this portion of the Sierra Madre has been for so long a formidable barrier to east-west traffic. Even today, from the Arizona line down to the Durango-Mazatlán highway, a distance of 700 miles, there are no paved roads across the range. The railroad is still the only reliable transportation from one side to the other.

We make a pass over the right-angled bend of the Rio Urique, then turn north past the town of Creel for a quick aerial look at the Cascada de Basochiachic on the little river called Chinipas. Basochiachic is a waterfall with a straight pour-off a thousand feet down, making it one of the highest single-jump falls in North America. But it's been a dry winter in the Sierra Madre, and the waterfall, as we approach it, is not in good form. The volume of water that pours from the brink of the falls is not sufficient to reach the plunge pool below; blown sideways by the wind, the veil of falling water dissolves into vapor halfway down.

Banking east and south again, we return to Creel. Ike buzzes the Hotel Nuevo twice, hoping to rouse the management to the advent of gringo tourists without reservations, then drops us off at the airstrip five miles south of town.

There is nothing here but the strip itself, a limp windsock, a few Indian huts, a few gaunt cattle munching weeds. The Indians stare. The dogs bark. Ike takes off and disappears. My wife Renée and I shoulder our packs, climb the hillside to the road, and start marching toward town. We've walked a mile when a flatbed truck comes grinding along, headed our way. I stick out a thumb and we've got a ride. There are five adults in the cab of the truck, and as many more plus children in the back. We join the crowd on the bed.

One of the passengers is an old man, a Tarahumara, with a big gray Zapatista mustache. His handsome, leather-skinned face looks as if it has faced the mountain sun and mountain winds for a century. He wears the conventional Tarahumara dress: straw hat, white shirt, red bandana around the neck, and a loose white baggy sort of dhoti around the loins. His lean brown legs are bare; on his feet he wears homemade thong sandals, the soles cut from discarded auto tires. Huaraches.

I am fascinated by his feet. The old man owns the most beaten-up, stone-battered, cactus-cured, fire-hardened pair of feet I have ever seen on a human being—so cracked, splayed, and toughened they almost suggest hoofs. No doubt he has gone barefoot most of his life, the sandals being for dress-up occasions, for Saturday night in the big town: Creel, population 2500.

The Tarahumara are famed for their long-distance running. Their races are said to go on for fifty miles, sometimes 200 miles.

This old man whose feet I am gaping at may be, in his world, a once-great racer.

Though it's rude to stare, I cannot help but look again at his weathered face, the map of his soul. The expression there is attractive and appealing—serene, far-seeing eyes; a calm and easeful smile. Where have I seen that kind of face before? And I remember: yes, among old folk in Appalachia, in west Texas, in Norway, in Calabria. The sign of honor, an interior victory of some kind that cannot be won in less than seventy years—the Biblical threescore and ten. The faces of beautiful old men and women around the world.

We enter Creel, a little mountain logging town 7,000 feet above sea level. We pass the mill, its conical sawdust burners belching woodsmoke, while little boys stack boards, dragging slab lumber out of the sheds as spinning buzzsaws bite with a snarl into fat logs of ponderosa.

Into the town. Rutted dirt streets. Stone cabins, slabwood shacks, log huts. Children swarming everywhere—filthy, ragged, snot-nosed *mucositos*, shouting, screaming, laughing and happy. Despite the food shortages, the alarming rise in the price of such staples as corn and beans, these children seem to be adequately fed, active, irrepressible. What does it take to sober a child? I don't want to know.

Renée and I check in at the Hotel Nuevo, opposite the rail-road station. Despite the name, it is the oldest hostelry in town, definitely second class. The rooms are small, dank, dingy; the beds sag like hammocks; the lighting is erratic; and the hotel food (American plan) perturbs the imagination. Peculiar looking vegetables, unidentifiable. Stringy bits of flesh, obscure in origin, wrapped in limp and greasy folds of dough. Everything disguised, the flavor—if any—buried beneath a mucous membrane of melted cheese and last week's tomato sauce. You can always count on the tomato sauce: Every dish comes immersed in it.

I am glad we've brought with us a week's supply of dehydrated All-American ersatz. Once we get out in the woods we'll *eat*. But there was a better reason for that than mere gringo caution. By bringing in our own food we will not be competing with the natives for something to eat, will not be helping to force up the price of local foods. The *rico* tourist may think, when he pays the extravagant bill at a Mexican restaurant, that he is at least contributing to the welfare of the workers in the local economy. False. A few will benefit, but the majority, deriving no income whatsoever from the tourist racket, find they are paying higher prices for their daily tortillas.

Next morning we are joined by old friends. Bill Hoy and his Argentine wife Marina arrive by train from Ciudad Chihuahua. The four of us plan a walk together down into the Big Barranca—el Cobre—by a new and unknown route. We spend the day packing our packs, inspecting Creel, eating the Hotel Nuevo dinner, recovering, going to bed. Next morning, early, we are off in the hotel jeep for a ride to the head of a side canyon—unnamed on our map—that leads to the Rio Urique and Barranca del Cobre. Our intention is to hike down this canyon to the river, follow the river upstream to the next tributary canyon, and walk out to the Creel-La Bufa road, completing the loop. We carry food for five days.

The trek begins down a Tarahumara footpath along a pretty stream. On either side of the stream lie the corn patches and bean fields of the Indians—tiny, cultivated plots that don't look big enough to support a flock of chickens, let alone a human family. Early May: The corn is a foot high, green and fragile. There is no attempt at irrigation; all depends on the summer rains. Each miniature field is fenced in with brush, rocks, or logs, presumably to keep out the animals—the burros, pigs, cattle, and flocks of voracious goats that swarm like hooved locusts across the hillsides. Subsistence agriculture, close to the margin of survival: One must credit the courage and faith of these peasant Indians. Each year they gamble their lives on a few acres of sand and dust, a rocky hillside for their beasts, the rainclouds. An earnest and serious wager, for there is no public welfare system in the Republic of Mexico. The losers simply—disappear.

We tramp in single file between their fields, four big gringos with grotesque packs on our backs, while the Indians near their huts review our parade, shyly, furtively, from a safe distance. Quite likely they have never seen such a procession before. We are shy ourselves, fully aware of the incongruity of our presence here (Vietnam!), the pounds of luxury foods in our backpacks, the goosedown sleeping bags, our big solid boots, the Vibram tracks we leave on the trail. The Indians squatting around small fires, cooking their pinole, or cornmeal mush, in handmade clay pots, watch without a word as we go by. But their yellow curs bark vigorously enough, vicious yet prudent.

What the hell *are* we doing here? Sightseeing? Not very dignified. Call it exploration. Science, that's the word. We are exploring a canyon that, according to the manager of the Hotel Nuevo, no gringo has ever trod before. Certainly no self-respecting Mexican would come down here. And even the Indians' trail will peter out long before we come in sight of the Rio Urique.

Onward, over the goat dung, through the dust, over the shelves of smooth volcanic rock that skirt the stream. I notice that the fields are protected from floods by flimsy barricades of brush. I think of the heavy logging now taking place in the upland forests, of the vast excavations for a new truck and tourist highway, of the hordes of hungry cattle scouring the clearings and hillsides for a blade of grass, a bite of browse. What will happen when the dry spell breaks and the rains finally do come? When all that runoff water and all that grazed-off soil come pouring down these narrow canyons in a flood of muck and mud? The 35,000 Tarahumara have survived in this rough, beautiful "undeveloped" land for centuries, with their hard and heroic way of life; but things are happening to their country now that they have never had to deal with before.

Indians, Indians, the goddamned Indians. As if we don't have enough to worry about without them on our hands, and hearts and minds as well. The one thing we could do for these people, I am thinking as I trudge along at the rear of the column, the one and only decent thing we could do for them (and by "we" I mean mainly the Mexicans and the Mexican "authorities," but include gringo Americans and Europeans, too), is leave them alone. Throw out the teachers, the missionaries, the government doctors and public health technicians; close off the roads and stop the road building; stop the logging; shut down the mines; burn down the hotels; tear up the airstrips; throw out the totalitarian fanatics from so-called Third World politics; ban all tourists, including us; and let these people alone. *Leave them alone.*

But leaving them alone is the one thing we will not do. So the Indians are doomed. The Tarahumara, unless saved by a quick collapse of the world industrial megamachine now moving in on them, haven't a chance. Like the Tupi of the Amazon, like the Kurds of Iran and Iraq, like the herdsmen of Tibet, like the Hopi of Arizona, like a hundred other small and once-independent tribes around the globe, these Indians are going to be . . . incorporated. Assimilated. Extinguished.

Well, it's not my problem. I've got my own problems. Like trying to overcome my white liberal guilt-neurosis. I am not responsible, I tell myself, for what the Mexicans are doing to their own land and their own people. I am not responsible for the coming revolution—though I wish it well. We march steadily on and soon leave the Indians and their milpas and their tedious troubles far behind, out of sight, out of mind. The goat paths continue on for a few more miles, but the huts become fewer and fewer, and the few we see appear to be unoccupied. We have a final glimpse of a goatherd—a woman—trying to hide from us in the brush; she is the last Indian or other human being of any variety that we shall see for days.

The stream descends, growing bigger, augmented by springs, seeps, and tributary runs, through a canyon walled by ragged, brush-covered formations of volcanic origin—consolidated tuff interbedded with thin conglomerates. Dark, broken, craggy rock reaching far above us, perhaps 1,500 to 2,000 feet high. I am reminded of the canyons in the Gila Wilderness of New Mexico. Every slope short of bare-rock vertical cliff is terraced by animal paths. Domestic animals. Not surprisingly, we find little wildlife except lizards, a few minnows in the pools, and birds.

Many birds. A multitude of birds. Some of them, like the coppery-tailed or elegant trogon and the solitary eagle (their proper names), I have never seen before, anywhere. Marina Hoy, the most able birdwatcher among us, will identify sixty-three different species before this walk is done.

The trogon, as its full name implies, is a striking and colorful bird. But shy: We catch only glimpses of it flitting among the trees. A pair of nesting solitary eagles (for even the solitary must sometimes mate—and these, like other eagles, mate for life) give us a much better show. We lie on our backs at the side of the path for half an hour, watching them soar and circle over the cliffs, alighting on trees and taking off again, screaming from time to time, no doubt disturbed by our presence, even though we are hundreds of feet below the focus of their domestic operations. We apologize for the intrusion but they are beautiful birds in their black-and-white regalia, hard to give up watching.

Finally we go on, leaving the eagles in peace. Our bird list continues to grow. Even I spot a few I can recognize: a robin, a common flicker (all flickers are now classfied as one species by the avian authorities), some kind of hummingbird, and a buzzard. Marina helps me find some of the more special, unusual, or beautiful: a caracara, a Cassin's kingbird, a crested flycatcher, a Townsend's solitaire, a painted redstart, a blackheaded grosbeak, a red crossbill. But those rarest and most spectacular of Sierra Madre birds—the thick-billed parrot and the imperial woodpecker—are nowhere to be seen. It is possible that the imperial woodpecker is now extinct and the thick-billed parrot close to extinction.

Despite decades of heavy overgrazing and overbrowsing, a great variety of plant life still survives in this nameless side canyon of Barranca del Cobre. There is yellow pine *(Pinus ponderosa)*, Arizona cypress, manzanita, alligator juniper, tamarisk, willow and bamboo along the creek, silverleaf oak, a fig tree (introduced) growing by an ancient stone hut, Apache pine, the wine-colored madroña, Emory oak, palmetto, a few small aspen on the slopes (this surely must be near the southernmost extension of the aspen's range), some type of maple, some species of locust. And on the lower, south-facing, hotter and drier slopes we find a mixture of typical desert flora: prickly pear, hedgehog cactus, aloe, sotol, flowering agave, and yucca. We see a woody shrub blooming with what look exactly like sunflowers. Impossible but true. And air plants, orchids, flourishing on the pines. And many other plants, the identity of which we can hardly even guess at.

"What is it?" we ask, meaning what is its name? This odd quirk of the human mind: Unless we can name things, they remain for us only half-real. Or less than half-real: nonexistent. A man without a name is nobody. A man's name can become more important than his person. A plant, an animal, a thing without a name is no thing—nothing. No wonder we humans like to think that in the beginning was—the Word. What word? Any word. Any word at all, anything rather than the silence and terror of the nameless.

We don't get far this first day. We spend more time ogling birds or bushes or the rocky walls upstairs, or talking and eating and resting, mainly resting, than in serious businesslike hiking. Compatibly indolent, we call a halt in midafternoon and make our first camp on a nice, pebbly beach with sand pockets, sleeping-bag size, by the side of the stream.

After our supper of reconstituted freeze-dried glop, we lie about the evening fire sipping rum, listen to the poorwills and whippoorwills (both), and watch the little lights that float through the dusk around us. *Molto misterioso.*

The first light I saw, from the corner of my eye, startled me. Unimagined and quite unanticipated, a small globe of furry luminescence drifts unblinking toward my face. For a moment I think I'm seeing one of Carlos Castaneda's Don Juan magic-button spooks: a spirit from some separate reality incarnated for my very own spiritual benefit in the form of a low-wattage bug. No, not so; the bug blinks, and I recognize our old friend the firefly. The lightning bug.

Alas, occult visions seem to come only to those who believe in them beforehand. First the faith, then the hairy little miracle. First the pill, the tab, the wafer, the space capsule—then come the ruby-eyed six-legged alligators swimming through your psychedelic dome.

To hell with mysticism.

Next day we push on at a comfortable pace downward and deeper into this jungle-brush, jumbled-rock side canyon. Where is the Rio Urique? There is no longer any trail, only a welter of animal paths following the contours of the terrain and winding among the boulders that choke the stream bed. No easy way. We follow the rock shelves, we climb over and around the boulders, we scramble up and down the brushy slopes, our hands clutching tree trunks for support. At one point, far beyond the last of the Indian fields, we discover a long-legged boar wallowing in the water, enjoying himself. Half-wild or maybe wholly wild, he scuttles off like a javelina when he finally sees us. I dislodge a stone; a red scorpion scurries under the leaves. Four piebald burros high on the slope watch us pass; they have long dark eyelashes, like cocktail waitresses; they do not bray but *cough* at us.

We are not making much progress, I suspect, and God only knows where the Rio Urique and the Big Barranca are; but it doesn't seem to matter. There's plenty to look at and feel, plenty of time to think about where we are. The growing consensus among the four of us is, "If we get there we get there and if we don't we don't." To hell with science too. Thus the ambience of Mexico infects our nervous systems: Montezuma's revenge in its subtler form.

In late afternoon we come to the loveliest scene yet: a series of pools big enough for swimming, joined to one another by noisy cascades pouring through sculptured grooves and polished chutes in the rose-colored bedrock. Tall willow trees shade the sand and stone at the water's side. Thickets of oak on the slope higher up promise good fuel for cooking. Against the blue, on either side of us, behind and ahead, rises a metropolitan skyline of towers, blocks, pinnacles, and spires of unknown height, though the pine trees on the rim suggest by their scale that the distance must be at least 3,000 feet.

A good, clean, well-furnished campsite with a view. Here we

shall camp tonight, and the next night and yet another. Too fine a place for only an overnight stop. We unload the packs from our backs, strip, and plunge into the clear green pools, then sit in the sun on the smooth andesite and study our creased, coffee-stained topographic map, trying to determine where we are. The map is a Xerox copy of a copy, printed in Mexico on recycled tortilla paper with iguana piss for ink. Hard to read. We end up guessing we may be halfway to the Urique. We build a fire of oakwood in a cove in the stone, cook supper, uncap the Ron Bacardi, contemplate the coagulation of twilight and the organic lanterns afloat on the currents of evening—the fireflies, the lightning bugs. I remember from childhood that a firefly stays luminous even when ducked under water—it should lure trout? But there are no trout in the tepid waters of this creek; nothing but chub, carp, dace, mudsuckers. The biggest fish we've seen so far was six inches long.

Morning. We have decided to make this stopping place a base camp. Hoy and I, leaving our packs in camp, plan a fast reconnoiter down-canyon to see if the river and main barranca are within reach; Renée chooses to spend the day at home; Marina accompanies us part way, then drops back for photography. Bill and I go on alone.

We find that the canyon gets rougher the farther we descend. A few miles beyond base camp it becomes a narrow gorge, walled in by rotten-rock cliffs a couple of hundred feet high. Above the cliffs are benches and talus slopes covered with brush and forest, then the higher cliffs. The complexity of the landscape, with its lavish growth of vegetation, reminds me of scenes depicted on Chinese tapestries. Hoy the shutterbug cannot resist pausing for more picture taking. Click, click—we hasten on.

Fallen rocks big as boxcars lie tumbled and heaped across the creek, jamming the gorge from wall to wall. We climb over between and under them. The gradient becomes steeper, which may or may not mean we are getting close to the Urique. Waterfalls tumble ten, fifteen, twenty feet down to emerald basins. We belay one another off the vertical pitches, climb down trees, in one place descend, chimney-style, between a giant slab and the canyon wall.

We realize that we are not going to crawl down through here with full field packs on our backs plus a pair of girls not too keen on bouldering. Our proposed loop expedition is hereby canceled for this year. Bill and I go further, but by two in the afternoon, after rounding several more bends without seeing any hint of the main canyon through the hazy vistas beyond, we admit defeat. We are not going to reach Barranca del Cobre by this particular side canyon. That much is clear.

In cheerful ignominy we stop, rest, eat some gorp and jerky, then turn back without regrets, retracing the route up rocks and trees and chimneys, boulder hopping back to camp. Taking our time. We don't talk about it, but I'm sure Bill is as conscious as I am of the trouble we'd be in if one of us bent a bone or tore a cartilage in here. You couldn't get even a burro down into this shattered maze.

We spend two more days and nights in Little Eden Camp before starting the long walk back to the Indian farms, the dusty road to Creel. On our return, we pause to examine more closely a Tarahumara plow left leaning against the wall of an unoccupied stone hut. The plow has been carved—whittled, rather—from a single big chunk of oak, with one root still attached serving as the handle, much like the one-handled plow that Hesiod tells us the ancient Greek farmers used. The plowshare is simply the frontal tip of the oak, chipped to a point and hardened in fire. In the center of the beam a square hole has been cut or burnt (somehow); inserted in this hole is a square peg by which, apparently, the implement is drawn when hitched to an ox. Primitive? From the Indians' point of view, quite up to date: The plow was introduced into Mexico by the Spanish only 470 years ago.

A day later we're riding the *ferrocarril*, the iron road from Creel to the west coast of Mexico. But we stop for two days at a point on the rim of Barranca del Cobre called Divisadero, mean-

214

ing "overlook." Before hiking off into the woods we check out the local facilities. Divisadero is the Grand Canyon Village of Mexico and that is bad, but not the worst thing I can say about it. Perched on the extreme rim of the barranca, just like Bright Angel Lodge, is a brand-new hotel built Holiday-Inn style for the accommodation of tourists. A fat black sewer hose, leading from the hotel, dangles over the cliff in full view of the principal lookout point, dripping its contents onto the next terrace down, about a hundred feet below.

The air is filled with the roar of a diesel generator nearby, busy making electricity for the lodge, bellowing continuously night and day. The building is surrounded by a barbed-wire fence seven strands high—obviously a people fence meant to keep out the Indians who have gravitated here in hopes of selling their clay pots and wooden fiddles and other trinkets to the passing trade. Against this fence the wind has piled a solid layer of papers, trash, junk.

We go into the hotel restaurant for cold beer. The Cerveza Bohemia is good—Mexican beer is better than most American commercial beer—but we foolishly make the mistake of ordering sandwiches to go with the beer. Half an hour later, after long whispered consultations back in the kitchen, the *mozo* in his red monkey jacket brings us each what is meant to be a gringo sandwich: two slices of pale Kleenex balloon bread, exact imitations of our own back-home unspeakable Holsum, Wonder, and Rainbo, between which are concealed a transparent sliver of tomato, a film of mayonnaise, and a token wisp of cheese; with each sandwich we get one green olive impaled on a toothpick.

The tab for this affront (including the beer) comes to the equivalent of about $12.00. Adding injury to insult. Got to learn Mexican for "rip-off." Walking out I inquire, from curiosity only, how much the rooms are; the desk clerk says fifty dollars a night for two. Fred Harvey would love this place.

We clear out, evading the temptation to provoke an international incident, hoist backpacks, and walk several miles along the rim until we are well beyond sight, sound, smell, and taste of

Divisadero. We set up camp on a slab of rock cantilevered over the edge of a 500-foot drop-off. There we relax, perusing from above the impressive depths of the Barranca del Cobre.

How deep is it anyway? As I mentioned before, no exact surveys have been made in this part of Mexico. Boosters of the barranca claim it is 6,500 feet deep in the Divisadero area; Arizona's Grand Canyon is a mile deep, if measured from the South Rim, 6,000 feet deep if measured from the North Rim. The trail from near Divisadero to the Rio Urique in the bottom of the barranca is eighteen miles long, according to Michael Jenkinson in his book *Wild Rivers of North America*—making it comparable to the walk down to the Colorado River from the North Rim.

To me the barranca does not look as deep as the Grand Canyon. But Bill Hoy thinks it does. Subjective, chauvinistic prejudices play a role here: The Grand Canyon, for me, is part of my backyard, home.

Which is bigger? The Grand Canyon is 285 miles long from Lee's Ferry to the Grand Wash cliffs; the Barranca del Cobre is approximately 150 miles long. If its length is added to that of the neighboring barrancas, however, we get a combined barranca system that may be four times the length of the Grand Canyon.

Which is more impressive? They are different. The Grand Canyon descends steeply and dramatically to its inner gorge, revealing more varied and colorful rock strata than the barranca, which is wider, generally brushy, and formed mostly of dark, broken volcanic rock.

Which is wilder? Once again such comparisons are difficult and maybe useless. The Grand Canyon, except for Phantom Ranch, is uninhabited. The Barranca del Cobre and the other barrancas are settled in every tillable nook and cranny by the Tarahumara Indians. But the barrancas of the Sierra Madre make up a vaster area, mostly roadless (except for logging and mining roads); most of the interior is far, far from any town, telephone, or Park Service comfort station.

We spend the evening with our feet hanging over the edge of

the abyss, spying on the Indians down below. How slowly they seem to move among their huts and fields and stone corrals, along the winding threadlike paths that lead from one tiny settlement to the next. A life in slow motion. The Tarahumara live deliberately, wasting no movements; and when they run, they run all day, all day and half the night. We hear roosters crowing, dogs yapping, the tinkle of goat bells, the sound of somebody playing a tune on a wooden flute. I think of southern Italy, Crete, North Africa.

The Rio Urique, studied through field glasses, looks from our perch on the rim like a trickling steam hardly larger than the one we'd followed down the side canyon a few days earlier. It has indeed been a dry winter. The barranca floor is full of rocks, boulders, fallen debris, through and under which the water moves. A river of rocks. Parts of the Urique have been run by boaters with kayaks in early spring after a winter of normal precipitation in the mountains, but the feat looks impossible now.

As the evening settles in, we become more aware of the fires burning around us, miles away in all directions, on hillside and ridgetop. Smoke and haze overlie the barranca and the rolling high country beyond. Tangerine-colored flames creep through the brush and jack pine: all that potential forest going up in gaseous waste. My lookout's reflexes are agitated by the spectacle. Useless to remind myself that fires are perfectly natural phenomena, good and necessary for the long-term health of the forests. But these are not natural fires; these are man-made, the intentional extermination of the plant cover of an entire region.

The demographers tell us that the population of Mexico has risen from 15 million in 1900 to 60 million today—a fourfold increase in three generations—and that it continues to increase at a rate of 3.5 percent per year, compounded annually. Machismo! Half the present population of Mexico is under the age of seventeen. A nation of babies, kids, and horny adolescents. Youthful vigor! Dare one mention—would it be impolite and impolitic?—the name of the real and true specter haunting this glamorous land, a dilemma that no amount of *turismo* and no amount of *industrialismo* is going to solve? May one?

No. One may not. We are guests here and the reply, if one were reckless enough to provoke it, can easily be anticipated: *No, gringo, mind your own focking beez-ness and geev me ten billion dollar debt service loan or I cut your focking gringo throat.*

There is another India aborning on our southern borders: Laredo, Juarez, Nogales, Tijuana will be the cactus Calcuttas of the year 1999. No wonder a million desperate wetbacks, a million hungry aliens infiltrate each year our southern defense lines. Living bodies hanging on the coils of concertina wire, hands clutching at the barbs—someday soon.

Nightmares. Impossible. The violet green cliff swallows whizz past our rock, flaunting their aerial supremacy. Little do they care what happens to humankind, the little feathered bastards.

The red sun goes down in smoke and flame. Great balls of fire!

The red sun rises through the smoky dawn. Lying in my sack I hear trogons barking from the oak thickets under the rimrock. Yes, they bark, the elegant trogons. Then I hear the Tarahumara roosters crowing from the hamlets far below. Now there's a barbaric yawp if I ever heard one. The call of the male chicken, if not so familiar, would seem to us like the wildest, most thrilling cry in all of nature. (Shocking and depressing to think that now, these days, most Americans have probably never heard a rooster crow—except on television.)

We cook breakfast during the smoky sunrise while a little yellow dog sniffs around camp, watching us with beggar's eyes, the same wretched, mangy, starved cur—abject and unwelcome, vicious and pathetic—we see everywhere south of the border. He must have followed Hoy all the way from Ciudad Juarez. The magical dog, with who knows what supernatural powers? Don Juan's dog. Mescalito, or Son of Mescalito, or Mescalito's dog. Throw him a tropical Hershey bar, somebody, or a salami rind, a pair of peanuts, a bag of Crunchy Granola, something, anything, quick! Got to appease them gods. This here's Mexico, you know, not Georgetown. Not Shaker Heights. Home of the taco bender, the bloody sacrifice, the gay *pistolero*. Give him a stick of jerky and take no chances. Then let's get the hell out of here.

And so we bid farewell to carefree, colorful, romantic Mexico. *Adiós, amigos*—and keep your flies with you.

We hang around the rim for another day, tramp back to the railway station, and ride the rails down through the tunnels, down through the terrific chasms of the western Sierra Madre to Los Mochis ("The Flies"), north to Nogales ("Walnuts") on the night train, cross through the Berlin Wall, and ride a bus back to Tucson and the Great Big Cafeteria of the North, counting our money.

I don't know. Take your choice. For my own part I regard all of these American nations with extremely moderate love. Best to stay in Wolf Hole, behind the Virgin Mountains, near Dutchman Draw and Pakoon Springs, the kind of place where an anarchist belongs.

The world is wide and beautiful. But almost everywhere, everywhere, the children are dying.

Down There in the Rocks

We're driving these two little boats down Lake Powell in Utah, Clair Quist and his girl friend Pamela Davis in one, me and Mark Davis in the other. Mark, Pam, and Clair are professional river guides, boatmen, characters, honest folk. They work for an outfit called Moki-Mac (or Murky Muck) Expeditions out of Green River, Utah. Work for it? Hell, Clair and his two brothers own the damn thing. Whatever it is. What it is is one of the three or four best river-running outfits in the West.

Nobody's working today. This is a holiday outing for the four of us. Our goal is Escalante Canyon and its arboreal system of branch canyons. We're going by way of the so-called lake because we plan to explore a few side canyons, the mouths of which are now under water. Starting at Bullfrog Marina, our course takes us south-southwest past old familiar landmarks—Halls Creek Canyon, the south end of the Waterpocket Fold, the Rincon, the mouth of Long Canyon. Around that next bend will be the opening to the Escalante.

Bright blue above, the golden sun at high noon. On either side the red walls of what once had been—and will again be—Glen Canyon. No use fretting about it anymore. We throw our orange peels overboard to feed the fish. These hatchery fish will eat anything. Clair and Mark amuse themselves by steering as close as they can, without quite ramming them, to the buoys marking the channel. There's nothing much else to do out here on this smooth expanse of flat and stagnant water. Pam reads a book; I stare at the cliffs, and at the domes, plateaus, and mountains beyond, remembering what I sometimes wish I could forget: Glen Canyon as it was, the wild river, the beaches, the secret passages and music temples and hidden cathedrals of stone, the wilderness alive and sweet and charged with mystery, miracle, magic.

No use fretting. I throw my torn beer can into the lake, where it sinks and disappears. We clear the corner and plane upcanyon into the broad Escalante. Sheer, slick vertical walls of Navajo sandstone rising on either side, one wall in blue shadow, the other in radiant light. But nothing lives along those stone barriers; all that was living and beautiful lies many fathoms below, drowned in dead water and buried under slime. No matter. Forget it. Write it off.

Cabin cruisers roar past; we wallow across their wakes. A houseboat like a floating boxcar comes toward us, passes. The people on board stare, then wave tentatively, unsure whether or not we, in our little open boats, deserve the dignity of recognition. That doesn't matter either. We wave back.

A few miles up the canyon we go ashore in a cove without a name. Others have been here before, as the human dung and toilet paper, the tinfoil, plastic plates, abandoned underwear, rusty fishhooks, tangled lines, discarded socks, empty Coors cans, and broken glass clearly attest. But on the shores of Lake Powell, Jewel of the Colorado and National Recreational Slum, you have no choice. All possible campsites look like this one. There is no lower form of life known to zoological science than the reservoir fisherman, the speedboat sightseer.

We have stopped here because we want to climb an old stockman's trail that leads to the rim from this vicinity. We tie the boats to a rock, load our packs, and ascend the humps of bare slickrock toward the skyline 800 feet above. Halfway up we find traces of the long-abandoned trail—wide, shallow steps chiseled in the sandstone, sufficient to enable a horse to climb or descend.

Over the rim, out of sight of the lake and its traffic, we make camp for the night. In the morning we march north and west

over a petrified sea of stone waves, across sandy flats studded
with juniper, yucca, single-leaf ash, scrubby Gambel oak, and up
monolithic ridges that seem to lead right into the sky. Far beyond
are the salmon pink walls of upper Stevens Canyon, the Circle
Cliffs, and the incomprehensible stone forms, pale rose and
mystical, of the great monocline known as Waterpocket Fold.
We'll never get there; this is merely a reconnoiter, a scouting
trip, and we're not even sure we want to get there. Perhaps a few
places are best left unexplored, seen from a distance but never
entered, never walked upon. Let them be, for now and for always.

At some point out there, among a circle of sandstone mam-
maries hundreds of feet high, we find a deep groove in the
endless rock. Down in the groove stands a single cottonwood
tree, alive and golden with its October leaves. Alone in all these
square miles of desolate grandeur, this dry Elysium, it is the tree
of life. We find a way down to it, and sure enough, as we had
hoped, we discover a series of deep potholes, some of them half-
filled with sand but others with water. Old rainwater but clear
and cool and heartening. We fill our jugs and bottles and camp
nearby for a couple of days.

Campfire of juniper and scrub oak. The smell of coffee, the
incense of burning wood. Vast, lurid sunsets flare across the sky,
east as well as west, portending storm and winter, but we don't
care. Showers of meteors streak across the field of the stars,
trailing languid flames. An old, worn moon goes down as the
rising sun comes out. In the chill mornings we make a breakfast
and track off again in another direction. What direction? Any
direction.

One afternoon we sit by a pool on the lip of stone that over-
hangs the head of one of the Escalante's many side canyons. The
drop-off must be 1,000 feet straight down. Down . . . and . . .
down and . . . down, your mind falls to the green pool in a sandy
basin far below. Perennial springs flow there, under this overhanging spout we lie upon; we can see the glaze and glitter of a

stream snaking through jungles of willow, box elder, redbud, and Frémont poplar toward the Escalante River somewhere beyond, hidden in its profound meanders.

We see a natural stone arch below, under the west wall, and balanced rocks, free-standing pillars, pinnacles, alcoves, grottos, half-dome amphitheaters. The pathways of many deer curve with the contours of the talus slopes. A redtail hawk rides the air, soaring *beneath* us. Ravens clack and croak and flap around, quarreling over nothing. Over anything. Over nothing.

In the shallow pond at our side are dozens of tadpole shrimp, the grotesque, helmet-headed *Apus longicaudatus,* swimming back and forth, pursuing one another, the large capturing and devouring the small. They look like tiny horseshoe crabs—or like miniature trilobites from the earliest seas of all, come back to haunt us with the memory of the earth's long, strange, splendid, and meaningless history. The spiral of time. The circle of life. The vanity of death. The black hole of space.

The hot radiance of the sun, pouring on our prone bodies, suffusing our flesh, melting our bones, lulls us toward sleep. Over the desert and the canyons, down there in the rocks, a huge vibration of light and stillness and solitude shapes itself into the form of hovering wings spread out across the sky from the world's rim to the world's end. Not God—the term seems insufficient—but something unnameable, and more beautiful, and far greater, and more terrible.

My friends and I touch one another, smiling, and roll a few boulders into the canyon, only for fun, meaning no harm. We listen, and when the bedrock stops trembling, and after the last far-off echoes of our thunder die away, we shoulder our packs and start the long tramp back to where we came from, wherever that was. It makes no difference. Willing or not, ready or not, we'll get there.

Behind us, back at the canyon's head, the sun blazes down on the shallow pool. The hooded grope-things swim writhing through the water. One thousand feet beneath, the spring continues to flow and the little stream to snake its shining way through canyon jungle toward the hidden river. The hawk soars, the ravens quarrel. And no man sees. No woman hears. No one is there. Everything is there.

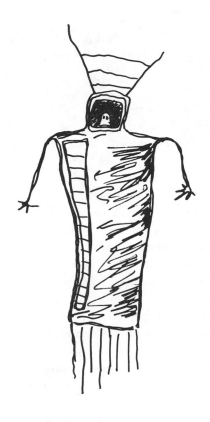

Science with a Human Face

Science with a human face—is such a thing possible anymore? We live in a time when technology and technologists seem determined to make the earth unfit to live upon. According to C. P. Snow, scientists are happy in their work, especially when contrasted with poets, novelists, artists, philosophers, all those customarily lumped together in the category of the "humanities." The humanitarians? The term connotes self-mocking futility, reflecting accurately the trend and tempo of the age. But I want to ask Mr. Snow this question: "Sir Charles, sir, if the scientists, technicians, researchers, whatever you wish to call them, are so happy in their work and so pleased with the world they are creating, why are they also and at the same time so earnestly devising ever more efficient ways to blow it all to hell?"

The mad scientist, once only a comic figure in a specialized branch of fiction, has now come luridly to life in a hundred thousand forms. Together with his co-workers in big government, big industry, and the military, he dominates our lives. United, they will tyrannize the planet. H. G. Wells, prophet and visionary, described the type exactly when he wrote: "Intelligences vast and cool and unsympathetic watched our world with envious eyes . . . and made their plans."

Wells called them Martians; we know today they are our own, sons of our fathers, the busy men with white smocks and clipboards who are planning our future. *For* us. "The World of Tomorrow—and You." And *you,* of course, are never consulted on the matter. Like the imaginary Martians in Wells's novel, the

engineers and technicians have no interest in our personal pref-
erences except as data to be tabulated and attitudes to be
manipulated. They love us no more than we love them; and they
certainly have no love for the earth. What is perhaps most sinister of all is the fact that in this worldwide drive to reduce life,
human and otherwise, to the limits of a technetronic system,
there is not even a mind at work. Many brains, but no mind. Nor
heart nor soul. There is no intelligence directing this enormous
and enormously complex process; merely the cumulative efforts
of thousands of specialists, experts, each sequestered in his tiny
niche in the technological apparatus, each unaware of or indifferent to the investigation of all but his closest colleagues, each
man in his way an innocent. How can we think of a man who
spends years studying the behavior of hamsters in an electrified
maze as anything but a harmless idiot? Yet the results of his
study, combined with the studies of many other similar harmless
idiots, may result in knowledge useful, let us say, to a central
police agency concerned with the problem of controlling an urban populace in revolt.

And in the evening, after a good day in the nausea-gas lab, the
innocent scientist goes home to the arms of his wife and children
and after supper plays with his model railroad in the rumpus
room. As Hannah Arendt has pointed out, the most destructive
men of our time are distinguished chiefly by the banality of their
characters and private lives. Harry S. Truman liked to boast that
he had never lost a night's sleep over Hiroshima and Nagasaki;
Lyndon Johnson and General Westmoreland, with the blood of
hundreds of thousands of Vietnamese peasants and American
adolescents on their hands, were perfectly capable of getting
down on their knees every Sunday morning and praying to what
they guilelessly believed is the God of Love. And Adolf Eich-
mann, as he correctly pointed out, was only following orders, as
millions of other men have done for their respective "authorities"; the Nazi leaders were punished because they had the
misfortune of ending up on the losing side. Political and military
leaders win the publicity, but the fantastic crimes they have com-

mitted against humanity in this century were made possible for them by the achievements of our scientists and technologists.

What I have written so far will seem to sober-minded professors of the scientific method (the type I remember from my own student days) as an irrational and hysterical outburst of misapplied indignation. They will scarcely credit my insistence now that I am, despite the horrors of the twentieth century, fully in sympathy with the basic and traditional aim of science, which I define as the pursuit of knowledge. Knowledge—not power. That I think of men like Democritus, Galileo, Copernicus, Kepler, Newton, Lyell, Darwin, and Einstein as liberators of the human consciousness, intellectual workers whose insight and intelligence have expanded our awareness of existence infinitely more than all the pronouncements of all the shamans, gurus, seers, and mystics of the earth, East and West, combined. The simple telescope, for instance, has given us visions of a world far greater, lovelier, more awesome and full of wonder than that contained in an entire shipload of magic mushrooms, LSD capsules, and yoga textbooks.

But having made this disclaimer, I can only repeat the charge, itself a banality but no less true for being so, that science in our time is the whore of industry and the slut of war, and that scientific technology has become the instrument of a potential planetary slavery, the most powerful weapon ever placed in the hands of despots. Nothing new in this discovery, of course; the poets, with their fine sensitivity to changes in the human weather, have been aware of the danger from the outset, for 200 years. It may even be the case that the situation has so far deteriorated that the only appropriate question now is whether or not technology will succeed in totally enslaving mankind before it succeeds in its corollary aim of destroying life.

In this general condemnation of the prostitution of science we must allow exceptions. Many will assert that science, *true* science, cannot be held responsible for the aberrations of uncontrolled technology. Others will point out that some men of science, such as Linus Pauling, Leo Szilard, Karl Morgan, Otto Hahn, Norbert

Wiener, and many of their younger students in the universities have been among the first to attempt to organize resistance to the technological culture, both in America and in the Soviet Union. The latter statement is unquestionably true but, so to speak, not true enough; the defenders of freedom and sanity among professional scientists have been far outnumbered by the Herman Kahns, Glenn Seaborgs, Hans Bethes, Edward Tellers, and Dr. Barnards ("the operation was a success although—sorry—the patient died") of the scientific world.

Is science responsible for the perversions of technology? To what extent can science and technology be separated and distinguished from one another? Can either exist independently of the other? These are intricate questions of history, method, and practice that I am not competent to answer with more than this diffident opinion, humbly offered: Pure science is a myth; both mathematical theoreticians like Albert Einstein and practical crackpots like Henry Ford dealt with different aspects of the same world; theory and practice, invention and speculation, calculus and metallurgy have always functioned closely together, feeding upon and reinforcing each other; the only difference between the scientist and the lab technician is one of degree (or degrees)—neither has contributed much to our understanding of life on earth except knowledge of the means to destroy both. Einstein is reputed to have said, near the end of his career, that he would rather have been a good shoemaker than what he was, a great mathematician. We may take this statement as his confession of participatory guilt in the making of the modern nightmare.

The denunciation of science-technology that I have outlined here, simple-minded and oversimplified though it may undoubtedly be, should be taken seriously at least as an expression of the fear millions now feel for the plastic-aluminum-electronic-computerized technocracy forming around us, constricting our lives to the dimensions of the machine, divorcing our bodies and souls from the earth, harassing us constantly with its petty and haywire demands. What most humans really desire is something quite different: liberty, community, spontaneity, nakedness, mystery, wildness, and wilderness.

In such a climate of thought and emotion it is not surprising that a large-scale revolt against not only science but even reason itself is under way in Europe and the United States. Because of the filth, ugliness, slavery, and mass murder it has engendered, the scientific-technological establishment faces a deep-seated reaction against the whole Western tradition of rational thought which is (or was) the foundation of science. The addicts of the occult and the Eastern religions have always been among us, but probably never before have so many abandoned realism and naturalism and rushed to embrace the fantasies of spiritualism, the life weariness of Buddhism, the world negation of Hinduism, the doper's heaven of institutional Christianity. As an antidote to a poisonous overdose of technology and crazy rationality I can understand why so many of the spiritually sick have switched to Zen, *om,* I Ching, and tarot. As an approach to effective resistance against the on-coming tyranny of the machine, however, these worn-out doctrines and obscure little magics will prove as futile as the machine can prove fatal. In fact, there is no reason why psychedelics and occultists, for example, and the most sophisticated technetronic system cannot comfortably coexist—the former inside the latter. They do; and they will. I find it ironic to see the enthusiasm with which hairy little gurus from the sickliest nation on earth (India) are welcomed by the technological idiots of all-electric California. Computerology, futurology, "high" technology and astrology—basic superstitions of our time—are comfortably compatible.

In this embrace of easily reconcilable opposites I wish to stand apart, alone if need be, and hold up the ragged flag of reason. Reason with a capital *R*—Sweet Reason, the newest and rarest thing in human life, the most delicate child of human history. Reason without technology, if that seems best; reason without science, if that seems necessary. By "reason" I mean intelligence informed by sympathy, knowledge in the arms of love. (For knowledge without conscience is the ruin of the soul, sayeth the

Proverb—and the oldest wisdom is usually most reliable.) By "reason" I mean fidelity to what alone we really know and really must love—this one life, this one earth on which we live. I find myself equally opposed to the technological mania of the West and the occult morbidity of the East: Both are the enemies of reason, and of life, and of the earth.

The orthodox scientific view reduces the world to measurable and predictable units, to that which can be charted, graphed, statistically analyzed; the traditional religious or mystical view reduces the world to a reflection of human, anthropomorphic desires and intuitions. Both have in common the psychological compulsion to scale the world down to humanly comprehensible limits, and both have in common, also, at their most profound level, the tendency to think of the world as essentially (and only) a *process* that lies beyond direct sensory perception. At this point the Yogi and the physicist come close together, and both, I would like to suggest, are mistaken, guilty of the most obvious reductionism, insofar as either insists on the fallacy that existence, nature, the world, is *nothing but* the flow of process, and that the beings of this life whom we know and love—a woman, a child, a place, a tree, a rock, a cloud, a bird, the great sun itself—are mere ephemera, illusory shadows, nothing.

They are wrong. Even a rock is a being, a thing with character and a kind of spirit, an existence worthy of our love. To disparage the world we know for the sake of grand abstractions, whether they are called mesons and electrons or the vibrations of an endlessly slumbering and reawakening Brahma, is to be false to the mother who sustains us. The highest treason, the meanest treason, is to disavow and deny this lone but gracious planet on which we voyage through the cold void of space. Only a fool, milking his cow, denies the cow's reality. Be true to the earth, said Nietzsche.

For what do we really know? I think of a lightning-blasted but still living shagbark hickory in the pasture back home on my father's farm in Pennsylvania; I think of a twisted juniper on a ledge of sandstone at Cape Solitude, far above the Colorado

River; I think of the pelicans that sail along the shores of the Sea of Cortez; I think of a thousand other places I have known and loved, east and west, in North America and Australia and Europe, and all the creatures great and small that live there— each a part of a greater whole but each an individual as well, one and unique, never to be known again, here or anywhere, each as precious as the vivid moment in which it first appeared on earth.

Don't talk to me about other worlds, separate realities, lost continents, or invisible realms—I know where I belong. Heaven is home. Utopia is here. Nirvana is now.

Walking up the trail to my lookout tower last night, I saw the new moon emerge from a shoal of clouds and hang for a time beyond the black silhouette of a shaggy, giant Douglas fir. I stopped to look. And what I saw was the moon—the moon itself, nothing else; and the tree, alive and conscious in its own spiral of time; and my hands, palms upward, raised toward the sky. We were there. We *are*. That is what we know. This is all we can know. And each such moment holds all that we could possibly need—if only we can see.

In Defense of the Redneck

Oh I got plenty of money
And money's plenty for me . . .
—M. Proust

There's a town in Arizona called Glob. Named for a nugget. It's a mining town, specializing formerly in gold and silver, now devoted to copper. The smog produced daily by the local smelter poisons the air for fifty miles downwind. The smell is like that of a decomposing jellyfish. Nobody here seems to mind. The Glob businessmen have built their golf course and country club at the foot of the 300-foot-high tailings dump. They are proud of the dump. When the wind blows the air is filled with fine white powder. The golfers inhale the powder and the gases and swell with pleasure. Mention pollution and they say, "Son, that smells like money to me." Aha!—where did I hear that line before?

Of course they're right. I like Glob myself. You get used to the stink. I drop in there every other week to pick up my mail, buy some groceries, and have a drink or two before heading back to my job in the mountains. For instance:

I had a late lunch at the U-Et-Yet? Café, then parked my '68 VW Fastback in front of the Broad Street Social Club. Closed. The only hippie bar in town—closed. Probably because of my friend Greenspan, who played here last week. Bob Greenspan and the Monkey Wrench Gang. His new song, "Big Tits, Braces and Zits," a ballad of adolescent passion, had been a hit. But as usual he overdosed on ego and bourbon and insulted first the management, then the audience, then the Glob law enforcement people. Not a wise thing to do. Now, I suppose, he was back in Boulder.

I drove on up the street, following the parade of gleaming

231

new welfare-financed pickup trucks. Every Chicano, Navajo, and redneck Anglo in the state drives a pickup. They can't afford condoms, diaphragms, or birth control pills—but they all seem to find the financing for a $10,000 Ford Ranger or Chev Apache or Dodge Power Wagon. Wish I could do it. My poor old Nazi folk's wagon is burning oil, has a slipping clutch, no shocks, squealing brakes, the floor corroded by battery acid, and a sprung hood that I have to tie down with rope.

The bumper sticker in front of me reads: Ass, Gas, or Grass—Nobody Rides for Free. I liked that sentiment better than what I saw when I pulled into a slot close to the Ruins Bar. The sticker on the rear of a tractorlike pickup truck—gun rack in the cab—said: Did the Coyotes Get Your Deer? Being an old-time coyote lover, I resented the bigotry and yokel ignorance of that remark. There was a broad-tipped marking pen in my car. With heavy strokes of indelible black ink I wrote across the windshield of the truck: Did the Rednecks Get Your Coyote? Like Nietzsche says, Live Dangerous. He was a mountain man too.

I straightened the yellow nylon carnation on the hood of my VW (every sporty car should wear a boutonniere) and felt my way into the bar. Out of the dazzling desert sun into the darkness of the cave. I ordered a tall double gin screwdriver with lots of orange juice. A healthy drink. A man should take care of himself. The body is the temple of the soul. I braced my foot on the rail, steadied my right hand with my left, and drank. Feeling better, I ordered a second and smiled at the half dozen gloomy, mean, hostile, ravaged faces ranged around the bar, staring at me. "Why do they call this place the Ruins?" I said.

Nobody answered. None of them even laughed. I'm not going to get out of here alive, I thought. Unless I crawl out on my hands and knees, feeling along the wall for the door. Maybe not then. Silently, the bartender served me another screwdriver, took my money, leaned back with folded arms. A baseball bat stood in the corner. Ignoring me now, the regulars resumed their mumbling conversation. Two hardhats, two cowboy hats, and two crew cuts. The bartender was bald—a tough egg. He

smoked an economical cigar, which had at least this virtue: It
neutralized the all-pervasive stench of the copper smelter. But
not the smell of hatred. I rubbed my hairy jaws, then sidled off
to the jukebox to check out the musical values of this here metal-
lurgical community.

As I'd suspected, there was no Gustav Mahler available. No
Purcell. No Palestrina. Not even filthy Mozart. Nothing but the
standard country-western stuff from a big city in the East called
Nashville. Music to hammer out fenders by at the Shade Tree
Body Shop. Music to vomit by after a shift in the copper pits.
Take this job and shove it. I picked out a couple of Johnny
Paycheck numbers and retired for a minute to the men's pissoir.
I read the writing on the wall. The voice of the people:

> Will trade three blind crabs
> For two with no teeth

Suggests the political situation in these southwestern states. But
what about this one?

> If you ain't a cowboy
> You ain't shit

Grub for thought there. I looked at myself—quickly—in the
cracked fragment of mirror screwed to the wall. Found consola-
tion in the fact that I still didn't look as bad as I felt. Or feel as
bad as I looked. I returned to my friends at the bar. None of
them spoke or looked at me. I studied the placards tacked to the
wall above the ranks of bottles:

> This is a high-class place
> Act respectable

> Helen Waite is our credit manager
> If you want credit go to Helen Waite

Finishing my second health drink, it occurred to me that more
and more we communicate with one another as indirectly as

possible. Through wall placards. Through graffiti. Through bumper stickers, headgear, lapel buttons, T-shirts . . . anything but face-to-face exchange. Perhaps this has been obvious to everyone else for a long time. Perhaps I've been living too long in the mountains. Perhaps I should rejoin what they call civilization. If there is one. I'm willing to listen to reason. If I hear any.

Direct communication. I turned to the morose face on my right, a new arrival. He was wearing a baseball cap with the legend BEEF stitched on the forepeak. His mate's cap said CAT. Mr. Beef and Mr. Cat.

"Where you fellas from?" I asked politely.

Mr. Beef stared at me for a while. "Flat Rock," he finally said.

"Where's that?"

The long stare. "East of here."

"Why do they call it Flat Rock?" Careful, I thought; you're not getting out of here alive if you're not careful. Receiving no immediate answer, I repeated the question. "Why Flat Rock?" Live dangerous.

Mr. Beef exchanged a glance with this taciturn friend. Mr. Cat nodded. Mr. Beef said, "Because of the rain."

"Because of the *rain?*" I paused for a moment. "What do you mean, because of the rain?" I pushed my empty glass toward the bartender.

"The way it comes down."

"The way it comes down?"

"Yeah." Mr. Beef toyed with his can of Coors, scowling at his thumbs. "Like a cow."

The bartender brought me my third drink. The turning of the screw. I had a momentary feeling of vertigo. But I plunged recklessly ahead. "The rain comes down like a cow?"

"That's right." Mr. Cat raised his head. The two men stared at me solemnly. "Like a cow pissing on a flat rock," Mr. Beef said.

I paid for the next round and recorded the story, for posterity, in my cerebral files. What do I have against rednecks? Nothing. I am here to defend them. My father has been a sidehill farmer, a logger, a schoolbus driver most of his life. My little brother is a construction worker and truck driver. Another is now a cop in L.A. I am a redneck myself, born and bred on a submarginal farm in Appalachia, descended from an endless line of dark-complected, lug-eared, beetle-browed, insolent barbarian peasants, a line reaching back to the dark forests of central Europe and the alpine caves of my Neanderthal primogenitors. Like my neighbor Marvin Bundy says (he lives on the other side of Wolf Hole Mountain), like Marvin says, "Us poor folks got to stick together."

A few words about my neighbor. Marvin Bundy is a poet and female liberationist. "Wummin?" says Marvin. "I liberate a wummin ever' chanct I git. Wummin's place is in mah arms. The destiny of her anatomy is in mah hands." True enough, Marvin; us nature mystics got to stick together. However it is with Mr. Bundy's poetry that I am here primarily concerned. The other day he came over the gap and asked me to read his "latest masterpiece."

"Well, Marvin," I said, "I have yet to see your first."

"Read this," he said, "and I don't need no smart-aleck criticism."

Invictus

Did the coyotes git your deer?
40,000 shitkickers caint be wrong.
Did the screwworms git your cow?
Yeah! thass mah song.

Them goldam Sahara Clubbers
Them candy-ass Defenders of Fur Bearers
Them sombitchin' FOES of the Earth
I say shoot 'em all full of arrers.

Googly-eyed bleeding hearts
Cryptic Communist pointy-heads
Little ole ladies in inner tubes
All need brain retreads.

Mining is Ever' Body's Future.
Sahara Go Home. Exxon Come Along.
Save Oil, Burn Conservationists.
Thass mah song.

Now entering Utah. (Set watches back 50 years.)
Golden goddam Beehive State.
Full of busy buzzin' bees.
Latter Day Shitheads. Cottonwood trees. Jaycees.

95,000 us deerslayers. 95 deer.
Got 92 last year.
There's one left on Blue Mountain,
One down in Slickhorn Gulch,
And the other one's a queer.

Don't care what them Bambi-lovers say,
Like I tell my wife,
Ever' time you shoot a deer
You're savin' some cow's life.

Outa work? Hungry?
Eat a environmentalist.
They taste like jungle boots
But sure wont be missed.

Puttin' on weight and losin' mah hair
But gotta new boat.
Gotta new pickup so I don't care
And them as caint swim better learn to float.

Got mah CB radio.
Got mah *Hook & Bullet News,*
Got mah old wummin and eleventeen kids,
And they never wear shoes.

So long.
Thass mah song.

Marvin is a special case, a coy and crafty yeoman, not a stand-
ardized rustic. More common, perhaps, is a young fellow I once
worked with in the Coronado National Forest, down along the
Mexican border in Arizona. I'll call him Calvin. We patrolled the
woods and collected garbage from the public campgrounds.
Dumping our load one afternoon at the forest landfill site, we
saw a large chulu, or coatimundí, picking its way across a mound
of garbage looking for something to eat. The chulu is a rare

animal on the American side of the border; it looks like a hybrid mix of bear, anteater, and raccoon. A strange and interesting creature. Calvin's immediate reaction when we spotted the animal was, "Gee, I wish I had my gun."

I argued with him but it was a waste of time. Like most rednecks, rural or urban, he could see nothing of interest in the world of nature unless he was trying to shoot it or set a hook in its throat or trap it and skin it. Same with humans. After work that evening, I suggested to Calvin that we go into Nogales and pick up a couple of women. Calvin shrugged. "Ah haint too interested in girls," he mumbled. Then he gave me a shy, sly, sidelong look: "But you oughta see mah gun collection."

Not that I'm against guns. As I've said elsewhere, I keep a few myself. The freeborn American's right to own and bear firearms must remain inviolate. Nor am I against hunting and fishing when the prey is abundant and the primary object of the pursuit is to put meat on the table—or in the skillet. I do think we should take it easy, out here in the West, on our dwindling deer population: The mountain lions need those deer more than we do.

This thought leads me to that contemporary phenomenon, the instant redneck. The natural redneck comes from the country, from small towns, and is generally too dumb or too stubborn to leave. The instant redneck comes from the city or the affluent suburbs, where his father has made a lot of money. Cushioned by a nice trust fund or comfortable inheritance, the instant redneck migrates west, buys himself a little hobby ranch, a pair of tight jeans, a snap-button shirt, one of those comical hats with the rolled brim like the male models wear in Marlboro ads, and a ninety-dollar pair of tooled leather boots with undershot heels and pointy toes (for kicking snakes in the ass) like those you see on the feet of pretty young men walking their toy poodles in Greenwich Village. Now in full cowboy costume, he buys his first pickup truck, a huge lumbering four-by-four tractorlike gas hog of a *deus machina* loaded with roll bars, mag rims, lug tires, KC road lights, gun rack, spotlight, AM-FM cassette player, Kleenex dispenser, gyroscopic beer can holder, CB (Cretin Broadcasting) radio, and Tampax slot. He buys a gun for the gun rack, pops the top from his first can of Coors (a sweet, green provincial brew mass-produced from reprocessed sewage water near Denver), and roars off in all directions to tear up the back country and blast away at the wildlife. The instant redneck. A real man at last.

But not interesting. Much too familiar a type. More problematic were those chaps surrounding me (on all sides) at the Ruins Bar in Glob, Arizona, on a hot summer afternoon in 1981. Two more cowboys had come in, accompanied by their heifers. All wearing the funny hats, the tight pants, the flowered shirts. You could tell the cowboys from the cowgirls by the wider hips. On the cowboys. The girls looked like they couldn't calve a salamander.

And then a cool young woman, elegant as a sylph, golden-haired, walked in and sat down at the bar one stool away from me. She wore oversize black sunglasses, opaque, inscrutable, and a T-shirt printed with the image of a life-size owl. Two great protruding eyes confronted me. Like an oaf, I stared; the lady gave me a slight smile.

I was about to move onto her adjoining stool when a burly fellow came between us, taking the seat, putting an arm about the girl and a large hairy elbow on the bar in front of my face. The bartender was silent as he poured my fourth double-shot screwdriver. I was getting tired of the orange juice but figured I'd best stick to the regimen. Strict self-discipline, that's the secret of a full, healthy, productive life. I stared at the blonde, aware of the owl.

"You like my girl?" the large fellow said. He was a Mexican, a Chicano, with round, brown, solemn face, dark eyes, the shoulders of a fullback. A Mexican but a *big* Mexican.

"Now, Primo . . ." the woman began.

"You like her, eh?" The dark eyes were aimed at me—not at the wall, not at the mirror, not at the other guy.

I knew he probably carried a knife, a switchblade. All *cholos* carry switchblades, everybody knows that. The trouble was he was so big, and ugly, and mean, he wouldn't need a knife. My sole weapon was my superior WASP intelligence. Which only functions, however, in retrospection. "I'm never getting out of here alive," I said, to myself but aloud.

Primo smiled, laughed, gripped my shoulder in his enormous paw, and said, "You're right, man. You're not. Better buy us a drink."

Under the volcano. I was glad to buy time by buying Primo and his Blondie each a drink. Bar buddies. He called me Grizzly Adams; I called him Pachuco. We discussed his occupation. He was an operating engineer, he said with pride—a Cat-skinner, a bulldozer driver. I asked him the best way to disable a D-9. "You mad at the company?" he asked. "That's right," I said. Primo recommended pure shellac, about two quarts, in the fuel tank, and a few handfuls of fine sand in the crankcase. But don't touch *my* machine, he added with a slow, smiling flash of teeth, gripping my shoulder again. I could hear the gristle squeak.

We spoke of my trade. Fire-tower lookout. Lightning on the tin roof. The sound of trees breathing. Ten days of solitaire, two days of Glob. "That'd drive me crazy," Primo said. "Watcha do for love? Screw chipmunks? You must be crazy as a bedbug, Griz." To the bartender, he said, "Bring old Grizzly here another double OJ. Before I have to cut him up."

"Why not?" I said. Never argue with the man who's buying the drinks. Growing more reckless, foolish, even suicidal, I kept leering at his woman. "Take off them big shades, honey," I said. "Lemme see the light of your eyes. *La luz de mi vida.*"

She smiled but shook her head. Probably had a black eye, thanks to her pet gorilla here. Maybe two. He looked like the type that would do it. "I like your owl," I said. "Both of them." I was seeing double. Better get out of here. Fairly soon. For the first time I noticed the four young thugs in a nearby booth, watching me. *Compadres.* But not *my* compadres. *La raza* here and everywhere. *"Viva la causa!"* I heard myself shouting. Not a friendly face anywhere—except Primo himself, my Primero, sitting here beside me.

He whacked me on the back. "What cause you talkin' about, Griz?" His eyes were glowing now, reflecting perhaps the blood in my own; his grin looked bigger, more fierce than a scowl.

His slap made me spill part of my drink. I muttered three Spanish words, five little syllables that one should never utter, aloud, in the border states, unless one is prepared to die. I could see the words floating on the smoke before us.

The chatter came to a stop. The cowboys looked at me with pity. But not much pity. Drunken hippie, they were thinking. A dog's death. Kicked to pieces in a dusty ditch. And I was thinking (I think), well, what the hell. This is it. Never apologize, never explain.

Primo turned his glass in his big hands, looking solemn and serious. "Griz," he said, "we better step outside for a few minutes."

"Right," I agreed. Really. The happy hour. I got up and looked for the front door.

"No," he said, "this way." One arm around my shoulders, he guided me out the back door and into a sun-bleached alley, among the crumpled garbage cans.

Blinking and swaying, I turned to face him. The sunlight dazzled my eyes. Primo looked for a moment like my brother Howard, the dark one, the truck driver, the high steel man.

"Griz," he said, "you know what you said in there?" I said nothing. "You must be crazy." I was silent. Primo said, "I'm not going to kill you, Griz. You're too drunk and ugly and stupid. But don't come back in there. If I was you I'd go out in the desert for a while and crawl under a bush and get some sleep. But before you pass out, try to think about some things. If you got any brains left." He watched me; I watched the hard edge of a silver cloud move above the skyline of the backside of the Dominion Hotel.

A door slammed. "Primo," I said—or meant to say. But he was gone. Never apologize. Never explain. I stepped carefully down the alley, leaned around the corner, and felt my way brick by brick back to my car. Some son of a bitch had snatched the flower off the hood. I got in and drove out of town, through the shining miasma of my drunkenness, turned off the highway, and went up a steep dirt road that led to a pass between a pair of cactus-studded hills. I stopped there and shut off the motor.

I could hear the insane singing of the cicada in the desert heat. About 102 degrees in the shade. But there was no shade. Not a mesquite tree in sight. I thought of Hemingway—Lieutenant Henry—walking through the rain. Catherine has just died in childbirth. Much to the hero's relief—no, that's not it. It's the screaming of the locusts defying the sun, which sounds in a way like rain.

Towering clouds hung on the far horizon, shot with a flickering incandescence, twenty miles to the east. Thunder rumbled. God growling at me again. I don't care, I ain't afeard of Him. Not with that big .357 magnum in the glove compartment. Under the gloves. Ain't gettin' outa here alive? Ain't none of us gettin' outa here alive. That's the way it is, boys, and that's the way it's meant to be. It's hard but it's fair. Is that gun loaded? Of course it's loaded. What good is a gun that ain't loaded? Guns don't kill people; people kill people. Sure, people with guns kill *more* people. But that's only natural. It's hard. But it's fair. My God but this car is hot.

I stumbled out, opened the flowerless hood. The engine was gone. Damned Nazi automobile. I took out my canvas cot, unfolded it, set it up on the shady side of the car. Why sleep on the ground if you don't have to? Only an idiot sleeps on the ground from choice. Little bugs crawl in your ears. A panicked pissant, scrambling over your eardrum, sounds like a horse marching through cornflakes. Horrible, undesirable, unnecessary sensation.

Miles below the tough little town of Glob wavered under heat waves. Went to the town library once, asked the librarian for a book—*Philosophy of William James.* The librarian, a middle-aged lady with mustache, began rummaging through her card index under the letter *F.*

I lay down on the cot, placing my hat over my eyes. Who built this old road? Why? Who knows? Who cares? Who found that big nugget down there? Forgotten now. I thought of my brother. I thought of Mr. Bundy hunting his cactus-fed cows along the Utah line. Seventy years in the sun. Forgotten. Fear no more. Primo? Somewhere in Missouri a truck driver named Hinton pulls into an all-night truck stop. Kidneys aching. Forget him. I thought of my father at seventy-eight, still going out to the woods every day to cut locust posts for the coal mines. Pit props for the miners, down there in the dark. Forget them too. I thought of those who do the world's work and are never paid enough and never will be, and they rise and are beaten down, and rise again and are beaten down again, and always lose.

The clouds grumbled on the east. God crept closer, mumbling. I raised the right fist, shook it at the old Bastard, and passed out.

To wake in the dark, hours later. There were no stars. A soft and misty rain was falling on my face.

Fire Lookout

Men go mad in this line of work. Read a book called *The Dharma Bums* by Jack Kerouac and you'll see what I mean. He spent a summer as fire lookout in a shack on Sourdough Mountain in the Cascades, a lookout haunted by the spirit of Gary "Japhy Ryder" Snyder who had also worked there. Kerouac never recovered. A few years later the Forest Service offered me the same job at the same place. Trying to maintain their literary reputation. Prudently I turned it down.

Women too go mad in the solitary confinement of a mountain peak, though not so readily as men, being stronger more stable creatures with a lower center of gravity. Perhaps the severest test of a marriage is to assign a man and wife to a fire lookout; any couple who survive three or four months with no human company but each other are destined for a long, permanent relationship. They deserve it.

My career as a fire lookout began by chance. Having injured my knee during the Vietnam War (skiing in Colorado), I was unable to resume my usual summer job as patrol ranger in a certain notorious Southwestern national park. I requested a desk job. The Chief Ranger thought I lacked the competence to handle government paper work. He offered me instead the only job in the Park which required less brains, he said, than janitor, garbage collector or Park Superintendent. He made me fire lookout on what is called the North Rim, a post so remote that there was little likelihood I'd either see or be seen by the traveling American public. An important consideration, he felt.

The lookout tower on North Rim was sixty feet tall, surmounted by a little tin box six feet by six by seven. One entered through a trapdoor in the bottom. Inside was the fire finder—an azimuth and sighting device—fixed to a cabinet bolted to the floor. There was a high swivel chair with glass insulators, like those on a telephone line, mounted on the lower tips of the chair's four legs. In case of lightning. It was known as the electric chair. The actual operations of a fire lookout, quite simple, I have described elsewhere.

My home after working hours was an old cabin near the foot of the tower. The cabin was equipped with a double bed and a couple of folding steel cots, a wood-burning stove, table, shelves, cupboard, two chairs. It made a pleasant home, there under the pines and aspen, deep in the forest, serenaded by distant coyote cries, by poorwills, and sometimes by the song of the hermit thrush, loveliest of bird calls in the American West.

My father came to visit one day and stayed for the season. He was given the job of relief lookout on my days off. In the evenings after supper we played horseshoes. Whenever I hear the jangle of horseshoes now I think of North Rim, of that forest, that cabin, that summer. My father has powerful hands, hard, gnarled, a logger's hands, very large. In his hand a playing horseshoe looks like a quoit; a horse's shoe can hardly be seen at all. His pitch is low and accurate, the shoe—open end forward— sliding with a soft *chunk* full upon the upright, rigid peg. A firm connection. Top that ringer, son, he'd say. We walked the Grand Canyon from rim to rim that summer, and once again a few years ago. The second time he was seventy-two years old.

The first sensible thing I did at North Rim, before my father appeared, was fall in love with the ranger. Not the Chief Ranger but the one who manned the park entrance station a few miles down the road. Park Ranger Hendrickson (GS-4) was one of those golden Californians from the San Diego area. She wore her sea-bleached hair in a heavy ponytail that fell below her clavicles. Like most girl swimmers she had a well-developed pair of lungs, much admired by the boys. Pretty as a Winesap in

September, she looked especially fetching in her ranger suit: broad-brimmed straw hat, white blouse with Park Service pin, the snug skirt of forest green twill that ended, as was the fashion then, a good six inches above her knees. Like most sexual perverts I've always suffered from a fatal weakness for women in uniform—for cheerleaders, majorettes, waitresses, meter maids, prison matrons, etc. On my first meeting with Bonnie Hendrickson (as we shall here name the young woman) I said to her, frankly, "You know—I've always wanted to lift a ranger's skirt."

"You'll need a hiking permit," she replied. A quick-witted girl—with a B.A. in French. We soon became good friends. On my days off I sometimes helped her get through the tedious hours at the entrance station. While she leaned out her little window collecting entrance fees from the tourists, answering questions, chatting about Smokey the Bore and the fire danger, I was kneeling at her feet, unseen from outside, gently rolling down the ranger's pantyhose. We played various such experiments in self control. I experimented, she displayed the self control. An innocent game, like horseshoes, with similar principles. Top that ringer . . .

On her days off she would visit me in the lookout tower, assisting me in *my* duties. As I'd be reporting a fire over the Park Service radio system she was unbuttoning my Levi's. "Fire Dispatch," I said into the microphone, "this is North Rim Lookout."

"Yeah?" The Fire Dispatcher had the weary, cynical voice of a police desk sergeant. "What's your problem now, Abbey?"

"Reporting a smoke, sir."

"Yeah? And where do you think this one is, Abbey?"

"Well sir, I've got a reading of zero-four-two degrees and thirty—oooh, watch those fingernails!—thirty minutes. Near Fredonia."

"Yeah . . ." A long pause. Then the weary voice. "I hate to tell you this, Abbey, but that's the same fire you reported last week. Like I told you then, that's the Fredonia sawmill and it's been smoking away in that same spot for fifty years. Ten four?"

"Yes sir, ten four. Oh Christ . . . oh *yes* . . . !"

"No swearing on the airwaves. These here transmissions are monitored by the Federal Communications Commission."

One cold rainy afternoon Bonnie and I were down in the cabin on the bed, a fire crackling in the stove, when our experiments were interrupted by a banging on the door. Bonnie ducked beneath the covers, I yanked on my pants and cracked the door open. Two Park Service fire fighters stood there grinning at me through the drizzle, their truck snuggled against the plump round rear of Bonnie's little car. "Hey Ed," says one, "we got a report of a hot fire in this area."

"Get out of here." I slammed and barred the door.

But I don't want to give the impression that a fire lookout's life is all work. There was time for play. One night a week we'd drive to the village on the Canyon rim and visit the bar. My Hopi friend would be there, old Sam Banyaca the shaman, and the veteran mule wrangler known only as Walapai, a leathery runt of a half-Indian cowboy who always squatted on top of his barstool, having never learned to sit anything but a horse. Behind the bar was Robert the intellectual bartender, smug smirk on his fat face, about to recite a new limerick. He claimed to be the only living composer of original limericks in America. I still remember two of them. I wish I could forget.

A modest young fellow named Morgan
Had an awesome sexual organ;
    It resembled a log
    Dredged up from a bog,
With a head on it fierce as a Gorgon.

And the other:

An old Mormon bishop named Bundy
Used to wed a new wife every Sunday;
    But his multiple matehood
    Was ruined by statehood—
Sic transit gloria Monday.

"Mundi!"

"Monday!"

"It's Friday, f'crush sake," says old Walapai, turning his bleary eyes toward us and swaying on his stool. "You honkies drunk already?" He crashed to the floor.

I spent four sweet summers on that sublime North Rim, not always alone in my tower. During the third summer a thing happened which caused me the deepest grief of my life. So far. The pain of my loss seemed unendurable. I called an old friend, Ann Woodin of Tucson, for comfort. She came to my part of the forest bearing apples, a flagon, black caviar and a magnum of Mumm's. We sat on a log under the trees at evening, by a fire, and listened to the birds, and talked, and ate the caviar and drank the champagne and talked some more. She helped me very much. A lady with class, that Ann. A lady *of* class. The same who once rescued me at two in the morning from the Phoenix City Jail down in Goldwater country, where the police had locked me up for what they called "negligent driving." Joseph Wood Krutch, another Tucsonan, dedicated one of his books to Ann Woodin. She is, he wrote, "an ever-present help in time of trouble."

Four summers. Sweet and bitter, bittersweet hilarious seasons in the forest of ponderosa and spruce and fir and trembling aspen trees. The clang of horseshoes in the twilight. The smell of woodsmoke from the cabin. Deep in the darkling pines the flutesong of a hermit thrush. Lightning, distant thunder, and clouds that towered into evening. Rain on the roof in the night.

One day somebody in Park headquarters down on the South Rim of the Canyon, the bad rim, the grim rim, said to somebody else, "Do we really need a fire lookout on North Rim?"

And the other man said, "I didn't know we had one."

The lookout was closed at the end of my fourth season and has never been used since. My father had long before returned to his own woods in Pennsylvania where he still lives and works. He is now eighty-three. And Ranger Hendrickson—sweet witty lovely daring Bonnie—she had gone back to California where,

I've heard, she married well, to a man with a steady job, property, money, prospects, a head on his shoulders. Not a fire lookout. Not by a long shot.

The Sorrows of Travel

When I think of travel I think of certain women I have known. So many of my own journeys have been made in pursuit of love. In pursuit of pain. And in flight from both.

Landscape and women. Whenever I discover a natural scene that pleases me, that I find beautiful, my first thought is: What a place to bring a girl! And our world is so rich in both—beautiful places, lovely women. We should all be as happy as birds. How clever of the inventor of this scheme to create from such abundant, glorious materials so tangled a web of confusion and misery. The medieval Schoolmen in proving God's existence overlooked this potent variation on the argument from design: The world's disorder, cruelty, and desperation could not possibly have resulted from chance alone.

Scene One: On the northbound bus from Fort McClellan, Alabama. During the war. My first furlough after completing basic training. In the fertile darkness of the crowded bus I find myself seated beside a young woman, a stranger, a Southerner. I am eighteen, a virgin, shy as a doe; she is perhaps five years older, married, lonely. Her husband, she tells me, is in Italy, has survived Sicily, the disastrous landing at Salerno, the battle of Monte Cassino. She prays for his safety and longs for his return. As she tells me about him her hand comes to rest on mine; she takes my hand and places it on her silken knee. She asks me to tell her about myself.

What have I to tell her? My life is nothing. All I know is my own homesickness. I am sick for home. I think of the hills of

Appalachia—the red-dog dirt road that winds beside the crooked creek, under the massed transpiring greenness of the trees, toward a gray farmhouse where a kerosene lamp glows behind the curtains of the windows that face the road. But I cannot tell her what that scene means to me. She leans close and kisses me and lifts that inert, ignorant hand of mine to her breasts. Kiss me back, she whispers. Touch me. Touch me! And we fumble at each other's bodies in the constrained plush gloom of the rumbling bus, make love with our hands, in a fashion, through the awkward obstacles of buttons, snaps, garters (this was long ago).

The bus enters the outskirts of a city. Clasping my left hand between her thighs, trapping it where she wants it, she whispers in my ear: "Stay with me tonight. I have a place here." And when I make no reply, she repeats: "Please. Stay with me. Just to-night."

That was some time ago. Writing these funny sentences, I pause now and then to perform other duties. I get up from this small table, step out the door, and pace the catwalk that forms a complete balcony around the four glass walls of my one-room house. My house stands fifty feet above the ground on a skeletal tower of steel, and it belongs to the United States Forest Service. Unlike most writers I work for my living. I watch for forest fires and when I see one I do something about it.

This tower is 8,000 feet above sea level and the view is good. When the air is clear I can see the San Francisco Peaks near Flagstaff and the desert ranges south to the border of Mexico. There are many black bear in the wilderness that surrounds me; also whitetail deer, coyotes, a few mountain lions, vultures, hawks, falcons, and odd creatures like the javelina and black rattlesnakes with yellow lateral bands. Right now the black-berries are ripe; the clownish bears shamble through the forest with stains of red juice streaking their muzzles, paws, summer fur. A bear does not pick berries with a little tin pail; instead, the bear grasps an entire blackberry branch between its paws, bends it down and into the mouth, and strips it clean of berries, thorns, leaves, bugs, spiders, everything. The bear rolls this mix around for a while in its mouth, looking thoughtful, like a wine lover sampling a new wine, makes distinctions, spits out the leaves and thorns, and grabs another branch.

And the woman on the bus? I did a cruel thing. As cruel as it was stupid. I declined the lady's invitation. I let her leave that bus, in that midnight southern city, without me. I rode on into the cold North alone, simple and single-minded, bound for home. For that sin I shall pay, all my life, in the cheap coin of regret. It has not escaped my reflections on the incident that the young woman may have been a prostitute, or part-time prostitute, conning a country boy—an easy trick. I don't think she was; I believed in her then and I believe in her now. What she wanted, I imagine, was to hold me in her arms while thinking of her husband. It makes no difference. My rejection of her remains, in my eyes, unforgivable.

At present I am alone here. In the evening I descend from my tower and walk through the forest. Nearby is an escarpment of sandstone, a kind of natural promontory projecting above the canyons, nearly flat but tilted slightly, like the deck of a listing ship. A few yellow pines have taken root in the fissures of the stone, along with some stunted, twisted Arizona white oaks, and a few mescal or century plants—that odd member of the amaryllis family that resembles a rosette of bowie knives planted hilt-first in the ground. Like a girl the mescal blossoms splendidly but only once, and much more briefly, in its lifetime.

On the rim of the scarp sits a weathered figure of rock, semihuman in form; you might think some Druid priest had seated himself there 5,000 years ago, resolving never to move again, and allowed himself to petrify, cell by cell, through the centuries. Each time I approach this sacred grove with its white rock and quiet, listening trees, I am reminded of the Mediterranean. I think of Delphi and half expect that stone figure to rise

at last and confront me, prepared—after appropriate sacrifice—
to answer the question I have been seeking, all my life, to learn
how to ask.

But the figure does not stir. Not yet. I gaze across its shoulders, through the trees, at the vast sea beyond. Not the blue sea
of the Mediterranean but the rust red sea, the lilac purple sea,
the wave-wrinkled but static sea of the desert. On that
motionless immensity ride enchanted ships: Table Mountain,
Four Peaks, Haystack Butte, Aztec Peak, Battle Mountain,
Heliograph Peak, the Superstition Mountains. And others,
many others, floating on waves of haze at distances we measure
but do not comprehend. Contemplating this picture (but picture
of what?), I feel again the vague but poignant urge to grasp it,
embrace it, *know* it all at once and all in all; but the harder I strive
for such a consummation the more elusive and mysterious that *it*
becomes, slipping like a dream through my arms. Can this desire
be satisfied only in death? Something in our human consciousness seems to make us forever spectators of the world we live in.
Maybe some of my crackpot, occultist friends are right; maybe
we really are aliens here on earth, our spirits born on some
other, simpler, more human planet. But why then were we sent
here? What is our mission, comrades, and when do we get paid?

A writer's epitaph: He fell in love with the planet earth but the
affair was never consummated.

Edinburgh. The Firth of Forth. The dank, dark, medieval
walls of the university, inside the old quad. In midwinter I escape the miasmal shades of Hume, Reid, Boswell, Scott, Burns
by fleeing to the Arlberg, Saint Anton in the Tyrol, Austria. In a
company of British students—ruddy young folk but very
proper—I take a room in a pension or hostel, here in this fairy-
tale village high in the magic mountains. I don't waste much
time in the pension among those severe Scots and stern *Anglais;*
the Austrians seem livelier and the Germans more romantic, in
their usual sinister but comic way—stock villains from a Nazi
melodrama. One of them, a sturdy young fellow named Kurt or

Wolfgang or Helmut, I forget which, becomes my daily skiing companion. We like each other; or at least we interest each other. Like me, he is a university student, a would-be intellectual, and very competitive. We ski all day; he is the better skier; we eat and play chess in the cafés in the evening—he always wins—and drink together and dance with the girls until closing time. We talk about the war, of course, and agree that it was a most regrettable affair; like me, he was too young to have taken any direct part in it. But the war is not over, never over, when two young males discover the same likely female.

Her name was Penelope Duval-Holmes; she came not from England, however, but from South Africa, a smart, witty, liberal South African of the Nadine Gordimer variety (one could talk with her). She was traveling Europe alone and she was very beautiful. *Very* beautiful? Well, a bit short in the leg—her tragic flaw—but beautiful all the same. Long, soft, light brown hair; great violet eyes with coal black lashes; breasts like two fawn at play in a garden of roses; a superior assembly of delectable parts. Wolfgang and I spotted her our third day together and bore down like twin schussboomers grooved for collision.

She seemed to like us both. Too wise and too amused to accept one and cast off the other, Penelope kept the three of us playing together. We skied as a threesome, picnicked together high on the snowfields under the alpine crags, dined and talked and drank and danced together every evening. Wolfgang proved each time, in his droll Continental manner, that he could out-ski me, out-drink me, was the better dancer, knew more songs and sang better, knew more languages, had read more books, and knew more about music than I ever would. Defeated, all I could do was make surly jokes about Ludwig van B. and His Viennese Jug Band, Amadeus and the Wolfgang, Tony Bruckner and The Tyroleans.

Getting nowhere. Each night Penelope said goodnight to the two of us, but her eyes seemed always to linger last on my charming rival; I knew that I was losing and that one night soon she was going to invite Wolfgang—not me—to her hotel room. That room on the second floor, with balcony, above the frozen snow-banks of a narrow sidestreet. Yes, I knew well enough where her room was; I'd spent several chilly interludes between closing time at the bar and my cold bed at the pension standing in the street watching Penelope's light go on, the blinds come down, the light, after a time, go out again. My futile and hungry love.

A week passed in concealed but intense competition for the favor of a girl—an aristocrat—much too good for either of us. In another week I would have to return to Edinburgh. I made overtures to other women, even to one of those clean, bright, prim English girls in the tour group, but my heart was not with it. I thought of cutting my vacation short; back to the bloody books, the charcoal fire in my cold tiny digs on Prince's Street, bloodsausages for breakfast, scones and cakes at teatime.

One night I prepared to give up. Sitting at a little table in the bar of Penelope's hotel, sipping my fifth or sixth double schnapps, I watched Wolfgang and my sweetheart embraced in dance, some lush slow romantic Viennese number, the last dance—as the bandleader had announced—of the night. Wolf-gang whispered in her ear; she was smiling. She nodded in assent to his obvious question. One possible gesture remained; a graceful surrender on my part. I slipped out before the dance was over, so drunk I could hardly see; or was I weeping? Or both?

Once in the street, however, I was overcome by the agony of jealousy. I could not suppress the self-torturing need to watch my defeat made plain before my eyes. I leaned on a corner wall below her room and waited and watched. I was freezing, no doubt, and drunk, but despair kept me warm.

Finally her light went on. I could see, through gauzy curtains, Penelope enter her room. My heart jumped. She was alone. She closed and locked her door, began to undress. Then remem-bered to lower the blinds. As she came to the French windows of her balcony, peering, it seemed to me, down into the street, I shrank back into the shadows. She lowered the blinds. A mo-ment later the light went out.

I stared at the darkened room. The balcony. The high-piled bank of hardened snow, reaching to within two or three feet of the balcony's supporting members. Yes. Why not? Remember—Siegfried! I scrambled up the frozen snow, found a hold on the balcony supports, pulled myself up, got a leg over the railing, fell inside, scrabbled on my knees to the French windows, tried the handles—locked. "Penny," I groaned.

"Who is it?"

"It's me, me."

She opened the doors. "Edward, what are you *doing* out there? *Idiot*. Get in here before you freeze." I staggered into the warm room, into her even warmer arms—she was wearing, I remember, some kind of slippery little nightie. She guided me to the billowy luxury of an Austrian feather bed, tucked me under the quilt, crawled in beside me. I reached for her—and passed out.

But all turned out well next morning. Then we rested. "My God, Penny," I said, "I've been wanting to do this—since the first moment I saw you. For a week!"

She replied, "Why didn't you ask?"

Later I said, "Did Wolfgang . . . did he ask?"

"Oh yes, the very first night. And every night since. He's been very persistent. Of course he is a gentleman and so sweet about it but—oh dear, he is so *very* persistent. So awfully—*tenacious*. Let's go to Vienna."

"And you turned him down?"

"Of course. Shall we go to Vienna?"

I could not refrain from probing further. Savoring my victory. "But why?"

"Why go to Vienna?"

"Why did you turn him down?"

"I don't like Nazis."

"Nazi! Wolfgang? But he's a Christian Democrat—whatever that is. And a gentleman. You said so yourself."

"He would have been a Nazi."

I thought that over. A Nazi and a gentleman? Both? After a moment I said, "Guess I'm lucky."

"Yes," she said, "you are. But you deserve it."

"Maybe I'd rather be a goddamned gentleman."

She laughed. "Dear Edward, that you'll never be. And be-sides—we've seen so *many* of *those.*"

1400 hours (forest time) on the lookout tower. 2 P.M. I sit here chuffing on a cheap cigar, watching the cumulo-nimbi gather above. Rumbles of discontent—shattered molecules of air—sound from overhead. Penelope Duval-Holmes, where are you now? I was a happy man that week. We went to Vienna, where I fell asleep during a performance of the Saint Matthew Passion. We said goodby in Paris. I never saw her again. Oh lovely and patient Penelope, how are you now? Back in Johannesburg, no doubt. Married, I suppose, with two or three babies. What is your husband like? Does he keep a shotgun in the bedroom? What will become of your children when the Zulus and Bantus overrun your beloved country? *Whose* beloved country? Dear Penelope, how are you now?

A rattle of hail on the tin roof. A jagged bolt of lightning plunges into the forest below, where I have counted eleven different shades of green. A puff of pine dust and a twist of blue smoke rise in the air and drift away. I disconnect the short-wave radio. Incommunicado now. Through a mist of rain to the north, less than a mile away, I see pink lightning vibrate, an illuminated nerve, between cloud and mountain. Five seconds later comes the crash, the sound like toppling masonry. I shut the windows, close the door—lightning follows air currents.

The storm clouds hover close above me, dark as death ships. From the steel legs and struts of this tower rises a curious singing, the thin, high, metallic tremolo of billions of agitated electrons. I sit inside a little cabin mounted on the negative pole of a high-voltage open circuit; at any moment, unpredictable but certain, a gigantic spark—lightning—is going to leap the gap. As long as I stay inside I'm safe; the tower is completely grounded, with a resistance, say the electrical engineers, of ten ohms. It doesn't sound sufficient but it is.

This tower has been struck several times with me inside it, and so far as I can tell I'm no crazier now than before taking up this lonely trade. In any case there is no escape; I can only wait while the screaming of electrons in distress builds gradually in intensity toward the unendurable climax. Another bolt strikes below, through the rain, a fireball dangling at its tip. My turn. Here. Now. The *crack!* of a whip above my head, the flash of blue light, a smell of ozone followed by waves of thunder reverberating outward—the noise suggests the sound of something rugged, immense, and rigid being ripped apart by hands of unimaginable force. A huge limb wrenched from a giant oak.

After the storm, in the twilight of a misty rain, work day over, I walk again through the forest. A pint of Foster's Aussie lager settles in my gut. A buzz in my brain. Out on the prow of my listing sandstone ship, beyond the sacred grove, the stone priest still sits in contemplation, rain dripping from his weathered head and eroded shoulders. No sign. I walk down the trail deep into the woods, under the ponderosa pine, the spruce, the white fir, the Douglas fir, the aspen, and smell the fragrance of wet weeds, pine needles, rotting logs, the soaked and respiring earth. Glowworms shine in the rich corruption, like foxfire in Appalachia.

Other girls, other places. Sandy and Death Valley, our camp at Texas Springs—she betrayed me by running off with a cheap movie actor. Bonnie Claire and our idyll on the rim of the Grand Canyon—*she* betrayed me by running off with her husband. And Ingrid in Berlin. Rita and Provincetown. Judy in New York, her little room in the hospital—Mount Sinai!—and the two of us listening to Mozart on the radio while firecrackers sputtered like frying grease in the streets below; my God, it was the Fourth of July; and I betrayed her by letting her die. By letting it happen. By finding no way—no way—to stop the thing that was destroying her. I loved and still love all of them.

I stumble over a rock in the trail. Sun down and gone, not a star in the clouded sky. The woods are deep, and very dark, and not lovely. I stop and stare at the dim silhouettes of the trees against the fainter dark of the sky. Sound of crickets down below; it must be August one more time. An autumnal month here in the mountains. And I'm alone again. Once more I ask myself the simple, obvious question: Why not die? Why keep hanging around, stumbling over rocks, bending beer cans, hurting people with your stupidity, losing your children here and there? What are you waiting for, you drunken clown?

But I'm grinning in the dark, not about to give up yet. I find it comfortable here in the cool damp womb of the forest, alone in the velvet night. I think I could stand here all night long and if it doesn't rain too hard, be content. Even happy. Me and the crickets and the oafish bears (they'll never make it as gentlemen), snuffling about through the brush, grubbing for something good to eat. At this moment I think: If he'd let me I'd get down on all-fours and shuffle along side by side with Cousin Bear, rooting for slugs, smearing my hairy face with crushed blackerries, tearing at roots.

Aliens on this planet? Us? Who said so? Not me. And if I did, that was yesterday. Tonight I know better. We are not foreigners; we were born and we belong here. We are not aliens but rather like children, barely beginning here and now in the childhood of the race to discover the marvel, the magic, the mystery of this sweet planet that is our inheritance.

Fools talk of leaving the earth, launching themselves by space shuttle and revolving cannisters of aluminum into permanent orbit somewhere between here and the moon. God speed them. While others plan the transformation of the earth through technology into a global food factory, fusion-powered, computer-controlled, supporting a close-packed semihuman population of 10 billion—twice the number already stifling themselves in the mushroom cities of today. R. Buckminster Fuller thinks it can be done. Herman Kahn thinks it can be done. The Pope thinks it can be done. All good Marxists think it can be done. Their counterparts in Europe, Brazil, China, Japan, Uganda, Mexico, everywhere, think it can be done. And if it *can* be done, therefore, by their logic it *must* be done. But Kahn and Fuller and their look-alikes are in for many a surprise before that Golden Age of Technocracy encloses us. (It never will.) As with all fools, their lives shall consist of a constant succession of surprises, mostly unpleasant, as surprises tend to be.

The Devil take them.

The Devil take them!

Brimming with malice and glee, I trudge up the trail, up the ridge, back to the tower. Only one thing is lacking to complete my happiness. I want to wake at dawn with a woman in my arms. I want to share the day's beginning with her, while woodpeckers drum on hollow snags of yellow pine and the sun rises into the crimson clouds of morning. I want to share an orange, a pot of black cowboy coffee, the calm and commonsense of breakfast talk, the smiles, the touch of fingertips, the yearning of the flesh, the comradeship of man and woman, of one uncertain human for another.

No need for doubt. She will appear. She has always come before and she will come again. At least once more.

FROM

Good News

(1980)

On the roof of the Tower, on the terrace of his penthouse suite, the Chief stands alone, looking up at the stars. The great constellation Scorpio sprawls across the southern sky; far in the north, over the mountains, a scribble of lightning races among banked clouds.

The Chief is dressed in his slate-blue uniform, trim and immaculate; his black riding boots, adorned with the brass spurs, without rowels, of a cavalry soldier, shine like mirrors. As usual he wears no insignia of rank and no decorations but the simple ribbon of the Medal of Honor. Hands clasped behind his back, he gazes up at the crown of Heaven—Corona Borealis—directly overhead. Those inaccessible realms. Inaccessible? he thinks. We shall see.

He paces to the parapet and looks down into the dark streets, the whispering city, fifteen stories below. A few lights move about down there, not many—vehicular lights, electric torches, a few small campfires on the sidewalks. Three blocks south a building burns, unattended; the glow illuminates a vacant street, a glass wall opposite, the metal shells, like dead insects, of a mass of abandoned automobiles. One company of soldiers, commanded by an officer on horseback, approaches the broad esplanade of the headquarters building, marching through the floodlit emptiness of Unity Square. Three dark bodies dangle on the gallows. From the bowels of the Tower, discernible from this height only as a steady, comforting, feline purr, rises the sound of the diesel generators.

The Chief returns to a small table on the terrace. He pours himself a dash of cognac (Three Stars), tastes it. Clasping his

262

hands again behind his back, boots set well apart at parade rest, he opens his mouth and speaks, his firm, resonant tenor pitched toward the stars:

"Gentlemen: The Army is ready. Are you ready?" He pauses, hearing from the sky a chorus of manly cheers. "Good. Tomorrow we march. Motorized column in the lead, cavalry following, labor battalion marching in the rear—under escort. We shall keep parade formation until we reach the outskirts of the city, at which time motorized units will proceed at optimum speed to first designated base camp, there to await arrival of cavalry. Eventually, of course, we hope to find motor vehicles and fuel sufficient to motorize the entire Army. Until that time we shall advance in leapfrog fashion, with first the motorized column and then the cavalry taking the lead. Radio communication will be maintained at all times. The logistics of the entire operation, which as you know we have designated *Coronado,* will be under the immediate command of Colonel Barnes, until and unless we encounter organized opposition, at which time I will assume personal command of military and political operations. Are there any questions?"

The Chief pauses, tilting his head. "No, Captain Fannin, we are not going to abandon this city. We are leaving it under the able command of my trusted friend, adviser, and aide, Major Roland, assisted by Captain Myers and his military police company, and by you, Captain Fannin, with your detachment of R&R specialists." Pause; the Chief smiles. "Don't laugh, gentlemen, don't laugh."

"No, no, no, that won't do," the Chief goes on, pacing forward and looking down. "Delete that passage." He looks up again at the stars, seeking nobler inspiration. "*Ad astra, ad astra . . .* Yes, indeed. Gentlemen, the first objective is a modest one: the city of Santa Fe. From there, augmenting our forces, we continue eastward to Amarillo, Oklahoma City, and St. Louis, overcoming whatever obstacles may appear. Since we have had no communications with any of those cities, we assume that conditions there are similar to conditions prevailing in this city—before I relinquished my studies, to establish order."

Pause. The Chief waits, smiling at the applause, then raises a hand. Instant silence. "At St. Louis we shall consolidate our position, multiply our forces many times over (I have no doubt), and prepare for the final push eastward. The goal, of course, is Washington, D.C., which we shall re-establish as the nation's capital. The overall plan, gentlemen, quite simply, is to rebuild America, to make her once again the world's foremost industrial, military, and—if I may say so—spiritual power, an example to mankind of what human beings, properly organized and disciplined, can accomplish."

Another pause, for applause. "As for New York City"—the Chief's thin lips form a condescending smile—"as for New York, if that wretched hive of moral degeneracy and ethnic pollution still exists, we shall erect around it a radioactive wall a mile high!"

Silent applause. "Thank you. Thank you, gentlemen. Now as to the grand design of our new American society, let me say this. This is not the time or place for a blueprint but let me say this: The new America will be organized along sound military lines. Not an oligarchy as before, hiding behind a façade of democracy, but a hierarchy of power based on merit and ability. Meritocracy. Government of the people, yes. Government for the people, yes. But government *by* the people? Never again. We want a strong, centralized State, capable of dealing quickly and mercilessly with enemies, whether foreign or domestic. It will also be, out of necessity, a thoroughly technological State. The conquest of Nature, once far advanced, now temporarily interrupted, will be resumed and completed. Not a single square foot of soil, nor a single living creature, will ever again be allowed to escape the service of humankind, society, and the State."

The Chief clears his throat, pacing back and forth more rapidly as he becomes excited by his own oration. "A harsh doctrine, you say. Indeed, gentlemen, it is a harsh doctrine—but a necessary one. What is the function of Nature? The function of Nature is to serve the needs of humanity. And what is the purpose of humanity? The purpose of humanity is to serve the aims of society as a whole. As a whole, gentlemen, as a unified, living organism. You say that humanity as presently constituted is any-thing *but* a unified, organic whole. Quite so. It is our purpose, our duty, as leading and organizing element, to bestow that unity upon mankind. To impose it, if necessary."

The Chief strays near the table for another sip of cognac. He sighs thoughtfully, staring up at the stars. "The people, gentle-men, the people are like children. We must guide them. Lead them. Use them. Help them fulfill their inner purpose, whether or not they are aware of that purpose. It is not in fact necessary that they be aware of purpose. Even better if they are not—such awareness might stimulate the tiresome conflict of opinions familiar to us from our recent past. No, they—the people—must be instructed only in their duty, each individual assigned his proper place. Thus the need for hierarchy, central authority, unified command. Consider, gentlemen, the most enduring ar-chitectural structure that human ingenuity has so far devised. What is the oldest and best-preserved type of manmade building on earth, gentlemen?" Pause. "The pyramid. Yes, the power of the pyramid. Think about it, gentlemen. . . ."

They think about it. Allowing time for reflection, the Chief continues. "And what, you may ask, can be the purpose of this great social pyramid, this living, pulsating, integrated pyramid of human flesh, animal flesh, plant flesh? What is the point of a pyramid? The apex, the summit, of course. And to what does the great summit direct our attention? Think, gentlemen. Think carefully. . . ."

Again the Chief looks up at the sky, giving his invisible audi-ence a broad hint. He waits for a few more seconds, accumulat-ing intellectual suspense, then smiles richly—that fair, fine-featured face, those intense and interesting eyes transformed, transfigured by the radiance of his soul—and reveals the secret.

"To the stars, gentlemen. *Ad astra. Ad astra per aspera.* This earth, this gross material planet, this so-called Nature, this animal and human populace, these squirming masses of sweat-ing, striving, copulating, ignorant, and self-obsessed bodies, all will be welded into one great pyramidal footstool—for our leap to the stars. The greatest adventure. The adventure for which all history to date has been merely a preamble, a groping, fumbling, confused, and semiconscious search. And when I say that our purpose is to sail among the stars I do not mean to limit our adventure at that point. No, gentlemen, not at all, not at all."

The Chief's voice rises to a new level of inspiration. "To the stars, gentlemen—and beyond. *Beyond!* For I speak no longer of the merely physical journey, the technological voyage—glorious as that will be—but of a spiritual voyage. I speak of transcendence. The transcendence of the physical. The transcendence of the flesh. I speak of the disembodied spirit of humankind, united in one indivisible and ultradimensional entity, rising like a wave to converge upon—the Absolute. Upon—Godhead Itself. That is what I am speaking of now, gentlemen: union with God. Think about it. Think about it. . . ."

The Chief smiles, pacing about, hands clasped behind his back. "Oh I've lost them now," he mutters, shaking his head with pity, "I've lost them now. Too far. No matter—they'll believe whether they understand or not. The less they understand the more eagerly they will believe." He chuckles. "As always. God, I love them." He returns to the table for one more sip of cognac.

Young Corporal Buckley appears and raps gently, timidly, on the penthouse door. The Chief ignores him. A pause. Corporal Buckley raps again, more gently, more timidly. The Chief ignores him. Corporal Buckley waits for the prescribed thirty seconds and raps once more, even more timidly, even more gently.

"Buckley!" the Chief snaps.

"Yes sir!" Buckley snaps to attention.

"Come here, Buckley." Buckley advances toward the Chief in a semi-goosestep. "Halt." Buckley halts. "Buckley, do you consider yourself a loyal follower of your Chief?"

Buckley blinks. "Beg pardon, sir?"

The Chief repeats his question.

"Yes sir. Absolutely sir, begging the Chief's pardon."

"Will you obey any order I give you, Buckley?"

"Absolutely, sir."

"Good." The Chief swirls the cognac in his glass. He points to the waist-high parapet along the edge of the roof. "Buckley—I want you to go and stand on that wall."

Corporal Buckley turns pale. "Oh sir . . . sir, begging the Chief's pardon, but I can't, sir, I can't."

The Chief looks stern. "That's an order, Corporal Buckley."

"But sir . . . I have this awful fear. I can't bear heights, sir."

The Chief looks very stern. "I know that, Corporal Buckley." He places a hand on the sheathed dagger at his waist. "But I gave you an order."

"Yes sir." Buckley walks slowly to the parapet. He puts one hand and one foot upon it, looking over and down into the streets, the beguiling yawn of the awful fall. The parapet, built of brick, is one foot wide on top. Buckley begins to tremble.

"Mount the parapet, Buckley."

"Sir, I can't."

"You're a soldier, Buckley. Mount the parapet."

Buckley whimpers, a doglike mewling of fear. He makes blind, pawing gestures at the wall, brings down the first foot and tries the other, then goes back to the first.

"Buckley!"

Buckley crouches, one foot on the wall. "Yes sir?"

"Come here, Buckley."

"Yes sir." Still shaking and pale, but immensely relieved, Corporal Buckley approaches his Chief.

"Do you love me, Corporal Buckley?"

"Oh yes sir. Very much sir."

"Come closer, Buckley."

"Yes sir."

"Kneel down, Buckley."

"Yes sir." The corporal kneels, his eyes on the Chief's boots.

The Chief strokes the corporal's pale, thin hair. "Good boy." The Chief smiles sweetly, thoughtfully, at the corporal's lowered and waiting head. "Are you a homosexual, Corporal Buckley?"

"No sir."

"That's good. Homosexuals produce no soldiers. Are you a heterosexual, Corporal Buckley?"

"No sir."

"What is a heterosexual, Buckley?"

The young man hesitates. "I don't know, sir. Begging the Chief's pardon, sir."

"That's all right, Buckley. Innocence is a virtue. Chastity is an admirable virtue." The Chief pauses. "Kiss my boot."

"Sir?"

"Kiss my boot."

Again the corporal hesitates. "Which one, sir?"

The Chief considers. "You choose, Buckley."

The corporal bends low and, after a moment of indecision, kisses the Chief's right boot.

"Thank you, Corporal Buckley. I commend your sense of fitness. Your initiative. Someday you'll be a sergeant, Corporal Buckley."

"Thank you, sir."

The dull glaze of boredom appears on the Chief's eyes. "You may go now, Buckley." The corporal shuffles backward on his knees, rises, turns to leave. "By the way, Buckley—"

"Yes sir?"

"What did you have to tell me?"

The corporal has forgotten, but immediately remembers. "The woman is ready, sir."

"Which one?"

"Her name is Valerie, sir."

"Has she been up here before?"

"Ah—yes sir, I believe so."

"Haven't we got any new ones?"

"Not tonight, sir. Begging the Chief's pardon, sir."

"Very well. Now go, Buckley. Quickly."

"Yes sir." The corporal vanishes.

The Chief retires to his dressing room and removes his boots and uniform. Completely nude, he contemplates with justified pride the image of himself in the floor-length mirror on the wall. Though over fifty, the Chief has the figure of an athlete. His white body is shapely, well-muscled, sparsely haired, the shoulders wide, the hips narrow, the buttocks firm and small as a boy's; there is only the faintest classical roll of excess flesh around his waist. Although short, he looks (he thinks) like a god. (A short god.) (Greek.)

The Chief opens a wardrobe, puts on a blue woolen robe that sets off nicely the marble tone of his skin. He opens another door and enters the next room, the transcendence chapel.

The Muzak system, forever operational in the Tower, is playing, at the moment, a melody from an ancient musical—"Some Enchanted Evening." Dim rose-colored lights, recessed in the walls, cast an erotic ambience upon the furniture of the room: a straight-backed chair, a fireplace, the Chief-size bed draped in black velvet, and the woman.

She smiles but does not speak as the Chief enters and takes his place on the chair, facing the bed. Letting his robe fall open, saying nothing, he looks at her.

She is young, beautiful, as required, fulfilling the simple needs of male fantasy: She looks like a virgin and moves like a dancer. Reclining on the bed, wearing a translucent gown that reveals the glow but not the details of her pink body, she smiles and makes a few subtle movements. The Chief watches and says nothing. She lifts one leg toward the ceiling, letting the gold-trimmed hem of her gown slip to the knee. The Chief watches but does not stir. The girl performs a simple dance, not rising from the bed.

When she stops for a moment the Chief says, "Come here, my child."

She slides from the bed and undulates toward him, sinking to her knees between his outspread legs. He lifts her lovely face in both hands.

"Your name is Valerie?"

"Yes sir."

"You are very beautiful."

"Thank you, sir."

"You were here before?"

"Once, sir. About a month ago."

"Are you afraid of me, Valerie?" He strokes her long hair.

"Yes sir. A little."

The Chief smiles. "Don't be afraid, Valerie. As you can see, I am quite harmless."

She glances down, murmuring, "I can change that, sir."

"Do your duty, my child."

The girl goes at once to her work, skillfully, eagerly, employing her lips and her fingertips, her mouth, her hands, her breasts, stopping now and then to whisper words of encouragement, of admiration, of provocative and extravagant invitation. But the Chief is not stirred. Is not moved.

Tiring of the game, he gently pushes her head back and turns up her face. "That's enough. You may go now."

"I'm very sorry, sir." She looks fearful. "I tried, sir."

The Chief smiles. "My dear, you are perfect. You are beautiful and sweet and perfect. My officers must love you. Don't be afraid, I won't harm you. But before you go I want to show you something." He turns the girl's face down toward his genitals again. "The secret of love, my dear Valerie, is not the flesh, but—the will. The *will,* my dear. Observe."

The Chief looks down at his penis. Limp, sluggard a moment before, it now begins to redden and stiffen and rise, as a cock should for a comely woman; the pale worm becomes the scimitar of manhood. Not a great cock, perhaps, a little less than average size, but clearly ready, hard, potent with power. Small, but—small is beautiful.

The girl moans with exaggerated admiration. She cups both hands around the Chief's tumescent organ, as if it were a delicate candle flame she would shield from the wind. Moistening her lips, she again leans forward.

"No." He pushes her back. "I don't need that. You can go now." Feigning reluctance, she murmurs a protest; he commands. "Go!" He points to the outer door. "Out!"

She rises and glides away, glancing back once with a coquettish pout on her lips. Useless: The Chief still sits on his chair, gazing with satisfaction at the rigid, superfluous, supernumerary digit rising from his groin. . . .

Down the River

(1982)

Down the River
with Henry Thoreau

November 4, 1980

Our river is the Green River in southeast Utah. We load our boats at a place called Mineral Bottom, where prospectors once searched for gold, later for copper, still later for uranium. With little luck. With me are five friends plus the ghost of a sixth: in my ammo can—the river runner's handbag—I carry a worn and greasy paperback copy of a book called *Walden, or Life in the Woods.* Not for thirty years have I looked inside this book; now for the first time since my school days I shall. Thoreau's mind has been haunting mine for most of my life. It seems proper now to reread him. What better place than on this golden river called the Green? In the clear tranquillity of November? Through the red rock canyons known as Labyrinth, Stillwater, and Cataract in one of the sweetest, brightest, grandest, and loneliest of primitive regions still remaining in our America?

Questions. Every statement raises more and newer questions. We shall never be done with questioning, so long as men and women remain human. QUESTION AUTHORITY reads a bumper sticker I saw the other day in Moab, Utah. Thoreau would doubtless have amended that to read "Always Question Authority." I would add only the word "All" before the word "Authority." Including, of course, the authority of Henry David himself.

Here we are, slipping away in the early afternoon of another Election Day. A couple of us did vote this morning but we are not, really, good citizens. Voting for the lesser evil on the grounds that otherwise we'd be stuck with the greater evil. Poor grounds for choice, certainly. Losing grounds.

We will not see other humans or learn of the election results for ten days to come. And so we prefer it. We like it that way. What could be older than the news? We shall treasure the bliss of our ignorance for as long as we can. "The man who goes each day to the village to hear the latest news has not heard from himself in a long time." Who said that? Henry, naturally. The arrogant, insolent village crank.

I think of another bumper sticker, one I've seen several times in several places this year: NOBODY FOR PRESIDENT. Amen. The word is getting around. Henry would have approved. Heartily. For he also said, "That government is best which governs not at all."

Year by year the institutions that dominate our lives grow ever bigger, more complicated, massive, impersonal, and powerful. Whether governmental, corporate, military, or technological— and how can any one of these be disentangled from the others?—they weigh on society as the pyramids of Egypt weighed on the backs of those who were conscripted to build them. The pyramids of power. Five thousand years later the people of Egypt still have not recovered. They remain a passive, debased mass of subjects. Mere fellahin, expendable and inter-changeable units in a social megamachine. As if the pride and spirit had been crushed from them forever.

In many a clear conclusion we find ourselves anticipated by the hoer of beans on the shores of Walden Pond. "As for the Pyramids," wrote Henry, "there is nothing to wonder at in them so much as the fact that so many men could be found degraded enough to spend their lives constructing a tomb for some ambitious booby, whom it would have been wiser and manlier to have drowned in the Nile. . . ."

Some critic has endeavored to answer this observation by claiming that the pyramid projects provided winter employment for swarms of peasants who might otherwise have been forced to endure long seasons of idleness and hunger. But where did the funds come from, the surplus grain, to support and feed these hundreds of thousands of two-legged pismires? Why, from the taxes levied on the produce of their *useful* work in the rice fields of the Nile Delta. The slaves were twice exploited. Every year. Just as the moon rides, concrete monuments, and industrial war machines of contemporary empire-states, whether called capitalist or socialist, are funded by compulsory taxation, erected and maintained by what is in effect compulsory labor.

The river flows. The river will not wait. Let's get these boats on the current. Loaded with food, bedrolls, cooking gear—four gourmet cooks in a party of six (plus ghost)—they ride on the water, tethered to shore. Two boats, one an eighteen-foot rubber raft, the other an aluminum dory. Oar-powered. We scramble on board, the swampers untie the lines, the oarsmen heave at their oars. Rennie Russell (author of *On the Loose*) operates the raft; a long-connected, lean fellow named Dusty Teal rows the dory.

We glide down the golden waters of Labyrinth Canyon. The water here is smooth as oil, the current slow. The sandstone walls rise fifteen hundred feet above us, radiant with sunlight, manganese and iron oxides, stained with old tapestries of organic residues left on the rock faces by occasional waterfalls. On shore, wheeling away from us, the stands of willow glow in autumn copper; beyond the willow are the green-gold cottonwoods. Two ravens fly along the rim, talking about us. Henry would like it here.

November 5, 1980

We did not go far yesterday. We rowed and drifted two miles down the river and then made camp for the night on a silt bank at the water's edge. There had been nobody but ourselves at Mineral Bottom but the purpose, nonetheless, was to "get away from the crowd," as Rennie Russell explained. We understood. We cooked our supper by firelight and flashlight, ate beneath the stars. Somebody uncorked a bottle of wine. Rennie played his guitar, his friend Ted Seeley played the fiddle, and Dusty Teal played the mandolin. We all sang. Our music ascended to the sky, echoing softly from the cliffs. The river poured quietly seaward, making no sound but here and there, now and then, a gurgle of bubbles, a trilling of ripples off the hulls of our half-beached boats.

Sometime during the night a deer stalks nervously past our camp. I hear the noise and, when I get up before daybreak, I see the dainty heart-shaped tracks. I kindle the fire and build the morning's first pot of black, rich, cowboy coffee, and drink in solitude the first cupful, warming my hands around the hot cup. The last stars fade, the sky becomes brighter, passing through the green glow of dawn into the fiery splendor of sunrise.

The others straggle up, one by one, and join me around the fire. We stare at the shining sky, the shining river, the high canyon walls, mostly in silence, until one among us volunteers to begin breakfast. Yes indeed we are a lucky little group. Privileged, no doubt. At ease out here on the edge of nowhere, loafing into the day, enjoying the very best of the luckiest of nations, while around the world billions of other humans are sweating, fighting, striving, procreating, starving. As always, I try hard to feel guilty. Once again I fail.

"If I knew for a certainty that some man was coming to my house with the conscious intention of doing me good," writes our Henry, "I would run for my life."

We Americans cannot save the world. Even Christ failed at that. We Americans have our hands full in trying to save ourselves. And we've barely tried. The Peace Corps was a lovely idea—for idle and idealistic young Americans. Gave them a chance to see a bit of the world, learn something. But as an effort to "improve" the lives of other peoples, the inhabitants of the so-called underdeveloped nations (our nation is overdeveloped), it was an act of cultural arrogance. A piece of insolence. The one thing we could do for a country like Mexico, for example, is to stop every illegal immigrant at the border, give him a good rifle and a case of ammunition, and send him home. Let the Mexicans solve their customary problems in their customary manner.

If this seems a cruel and sneering suggestion, consider the

current working alternative: leaving our borders open to unlimited immigration until—and it won't take long—the social, political, economic life of the United States is reduced to the level of life in Juarez. Guadalajara. Mexico City. San Salvador. Haiti. India. To a common peneplain of overcrowding, squalor, misery, oppression, torture, and hate.

What could Henry have said to this supposition? He lived in a relatively spacious America of only 24 million people, of whom one-sixth were slaves. A mere 140 years later we have grown to a population ten times larger, and we are nearly all slaves. We are slaves in the sense that we depend for our daily survival upon an expand-or-expire agro-industrial empire—a crackpot machine—that the specialists cannot comprehend and the managers cannot manage. We are, most of us, dependent and helpless employees.

What would Henry have said? He said, "In wildness is the preservation of the world." He said, somewhere deep in his thirty-nine-volume *Journal,* "I go to my solitary woodland walks as the homesick return to their homes." He said, "It would be better if there were but one inhabitant to a square mile, as where I live." Perhaps he did sense what was coming. His last words, whispered from the deathbed, are reported to us as being "moose . . . Indians . . ."

Looking upriver toward Tidwell Bottom, a half mile away, I see a lone horse grazing on the bunch grass, rice grass, saltbush and sand sage of the river's old floodplain. One horse, unhobbled and untended, thirty miles from the nearest ranch or human habitation, it forages on its own. That horse, I'm thinking, may be the one that got away from me years ago, in another desert place not far from here. Leave it alone. That particular horse has found at least a temporary solution to the question of survival. Survival with honor, I mean, for what other form of survival is worth the trouble? That horse has chosen, or stumbled into, solitude and independence. Let it be. Thoreau defined happiness as "simplicity, independence, magnanimity and trust."

But solitude? Horses are gregarious beasts, like us. This lone horse on Tidwell Bottom may be paying a high price for its freedom, perhaps in some form of equine madness. A desolation of the soul corresponding to the grand desolation of the landscape that lies beyond these canyon walls.

"I never found the companion that was so companionable as solitude," writes Henry. "To be in company, even with the best, is soon wearisome and dissipating."

Perhaps his ghost will forgive us if we suspect an element of *extra-vagance* in the above statement. Thoreau had a merry time in the writing of *Walden;* it is an exuberant book, crackling with humor, good humor, gaiety, with joy in the power of words and phrases, in ideas and emotions so powerful they tend constantly toward the outermost limit of communicable thought.

"The sun is but a morning star." Ah yes, but what exactly does this mean? There's a great day a-coming? Could be. But maybe the sun is also an evening star. Maybe the phrase had no exact meaning even in Thoreau's mind. He was, at times, what we today might call a put-on artist. He loved to shock and exasperate; Emerson complains of Henry's "contrariness." The power of Thoreau's assertion lies not in its meaning but in its exhilarating suggestiveness. Like poetry and music, the words imply more than words can make explicit.

Henry was no hermit. Hardly even a recluse. His celebrated cabin at Walden Pond—some of his neighbors called it a "shanty"—was two miles from Concord Common. A half-hour walk from pond to post office. Henry lived in it for only two years and two months. He had frequent human visitors, sometimes too many, he complained, and admitted that his daily rambles took him almost every day into Concord. When he tired of his own cooking and his own companionship he was always welcome at the Emersons' for a free dinner. Although it seems that he earned his keep there. He worked on and off for years as Emerson's household handyman, repairing and maintaining things that the great Ralph Waldo was too busy or too incompetent to attend to himself. "Emerson," noted Thoreau in a letter, "is too much the gentleman to push a wheelbarrow." When Mrs. Emerson complained that the chickens were scratching up her flower beds, Henry attached little cloth booties to the chickens' feet. A witty fellow. Better and easier than keeping them fenced in. When Emerson was off on his European lecture tours, Thoreau would look after not only Emerson's house but also Emerson's children and wife.

We shall now discuss the sexual life of Henry David Thoreau.

November 6, 1980

Awaking as usual sometime before the dawn, frost on my beard and sleeping bag, I see four powerful lights standing in a vertical row on the eastern sky. They are Saturn, Jupiter, Mars and, pale crescent on a darkened disc, the old moon. The three great planets seem to be rising from the cusps of the moon. I stare for a long time at this strange, startling apparition, a spectacle I have never before seen in all my years on planet Earth. What does it mean? If ever I've seen a portent in the sky this must be it. Spirit both forms and informs the universe, thought the New England transcendentalists, of whom Thoreau was one; all Nature, they believed, is but symbolic of a greater spiritual reality beyond. And within.

Watching the planets, I stumble about last night's campfire, breaking twigs, filling the coffeepot. I dip waterbuckets in the river; the water chills my hands. I stare long at the beautiful, dimming lights in the sky but can find no meaning there other than the lights' intrinsic beauty. As far as I can perceive, the planets signify nothing but themselves. "Such suchness," as my Zen friends say. And that is all. And that is enough. And that is more than we can make head or tail of.

"Reality is fabulous," said Henry; "be it life or death, we crave nothing but reality." And goes on to describe in precise, accurate, glittering detail the most subtle and minute aspects of life in and about his Walden Pond; the "pulse" of water skaters, for instance, advancing from shore across the surface of the lake. Appearance *is* reality, Thoreau implies; or so it appears to me. I begin to think he outgrew transcendentalism rather early in his career, at about the same time that he was overcoming the influence of his onetime mentor Emerson; Thoreau and the transcendentalists had little in common—in the long run—but their long noses, as a friend of mine has pointed out.

Scrambled eggs, bacon, green chiles for breakfast, with hot *salsa*, toasted tortillas, and leftover baked potatoes sliced and fried. A gallon or two of coffee, tea and—for me—the usual breakfast beer. Henry would not have approved of this gourmandising. To hell with him. I do not approve of his fastidious puritanism. For one who claims to crave nothing but reality, he frets too much about *purity*. Purity, purity, he preaches, in the most unctuous of his many sermons, a chapter of *Walden* called "Higher Laws."

"The wonder is how they, how you and I," he writes, "can live this slimy, beastly life, eating and drinking. . . ." Like Dick Gregory, Thoreau recommends a diet of raw fruits and vegetables; like a Pythagorean, he finds even beans impure, since the flatulence that beans induce disturbs his more ethereal meditations. (He would not agree with most men that "farting is such sweet sorrow.") But confesses at one point to a sudden violent lust for wild woodchuck, devoured raw. No wonder; Henry was probably anemic.

He raised beans not to eat but to sell—his only cash crop. During his lifetime his beans sold better than his books. When a publisher shipped back to Thoreau 706 unsellable copies of his *A Week on the Concord and Merrimack Rivers* (the author had himself paid for the printing of the book), Henry noted in his *Journal*, "I now have a library of 900 volumes, over 700 of which I wrote myself."

Although professing disdain for do-gooders, Thoreau once lectured a poor Irish immigrant, a neighbor, on the advisability of changing his ways. "I tried to help him with my experience . . ." but the Irishman, John Field, was only bewildered by Thoreau's earnest preaching. "Poor John Field!" Thoreau concludes; "I trust he does not read this, unless he will improve by it. . . ."

Nathaniel Hawthorne, who lived in Concord for a time and knew Thoreau, called him "an intolerable bore."

On the subject of sex, as we would expect, Henry betrays a

considerable nervous agitation. "The generative energy, which when we are loose, dissipates and makes us unclean, when we are continent invigorates and inspires us. Chastity is the flowering of man. . . ." (But not of flowers.) "We are conscious of an animal in us, which awakens in proportion as our higher nature slumbers. It is reptile and sensual. . . ." "He is blessed who is assured that the animal is dying out in him day by day. . . ." In a letter to his friend Harrison Blake, Henry writes: "What the essential difference between man and woman is, that they should be thus attracted to one another, no one has satisfactorily answered."

Poor Henry. We are reminded of that line in Whitman (another great American oddball), in which our good gray poet said of women, "They attract with a fierce, undeniable attraction," while the context of the poem makes it clear that Whitman himself found young men and boys much more undeniable.

Poor Thoreau. But he could also write, in the late essay "Walking," "The wildness of the savage is but a faint symbol of the awful ferity with which good men and lovers meet." Ferity—now there's a word. What could it have meant to Thoreau? Our greatest nature lover did not have a loving nature. A woman acquaintance of Henry's said she'd sooner take the arm of an elm tree than that of Thoreau.

Poor Henry David Thoreau. His short (forty-five years), quiet, passionate life apparently held little passion for the opposite sex. His relationship with Emerson's wife Lidian was no more than a long brother-sisterly friendship. Thoreau never married. There is no evidence that he ever enjoyed a mutual love affair with any human, female or otherwise. He once fell in love with and proposed marriage to a young woman by the name of Ellen Sewall; she rejected him, bluntly and coldly. He tried once more with a girl named Mary Russell; she turned him down. For a young man of Thoreau's hypersensitive character, these must have been cruel, perhaps disabling blows to what little male ego and confidence he possessed to begin with. It left him shattered, we may assume, on that side of life; he never again approached a woman with romantic intentions on his mind. He became a professional bachelor, scornful of wives and marriage. He lived and probably died a virgin, pure as shriven snow. Except for those sensual reptiles coiling and uncoiling down in the root cellar of his being. Ah, purity!

But we make too much of this kind of thing nowadays. Modern men and women are obsessed with the sexual; it is the only realm of primordial adventure still left to most of us. Like apes in a zoo, we spend our energies on the one field of play remaining; human lives otherwise are pretty well caged in by the walls, bars, chains, and iron gridwork of our industrial culture. In the relatively wild, free America of Henry's time there was plenty of opportunity for every kind of adventure, although Henry himself did not, it seems to me, take advantage of those opportunities. (He could have toured the Western plains with George Catlin!) He led an unnecessarily constrained existence, and not only in the "generative" region.

Thoreau the spinster-poet. In the year 1850, when Henry reached the age of thirty-three, Emily Dickinson in nearby Amherst became twenty. Somebody should have brought the two together. They might have hit it off. I imagine this scene, however, immediately following the honeymoon:

EMILY (raising her pen)
Henry, you haven't taken out the garbage.
HENRY (raising his flute)
Take it out yourself.

What tunes did Thoreau play on that flute of his? He never tells us; we would like to know. And what difference would a marriage—with a woman—have made in Henry's life? In his work? In that message to the world by which he challenges us, as do all the greatest writers, to change our lives? He taunts, he sermonizes, he condemns, he propounds conundrums, he orates and exhorts us:

"Wherever a man goes, men will pursue and paw him with their dirty institutions. . . ."

"I found that by working six weeks a year I could meet all the expenses of living."

"Tell those who worry about their health that they may be already dead."

"When thousands are thrown out of employment, it suggests they were not well-employed."

"If you stand right fronting and face to face with a fact, you will see the sun glimmer on both its surfaces, as if it were a scimitar, and feel its sweet edge dividing you through the heart and marrow, and so you will happily conclude your mortal career."

". . . The hero is commonly the simplest and obscurest of men."

"Little is to be expected of a nation when the vegetable mould is exhausted, and it is compelled to make manure of the bones of its fathers."

"Genius is a light which makes the darkness visible, like the lightning's flash, which perchance shatters the temple of knowledge itself. . . ."

"When, in the course of ages, American liberty has become a fiction of the past—as it is to some extent a fiction of the present—the poets of the world will be inspired by American mythology."

"We should go forth on the shortest walk . . . in the spirit of undying adventure, never to return."

". . . If I repent of anything, it is very likely to be my good behavior. What demon possessed me that I behaved so well?"

"No man is so poor that he need sit on a pumpkin; that is shiftlessness."

"I would rather sit on a pumpkin and have it all to myself than be crowded on a velvet cushion."

"A man is rich in proportion to the number of things which he can afford to let alone."

"We live meanly, like ants, though the fable tells us that we were long ago changed into men. . . ."

"A living dog is better than a dead lion. Shall a man go and hang himself because he belongs to the race of pygmies, and not be the biggest pygmy that he can?"

"I will endeavor to speak a good word for the truth."

"Rather than love, than money, than fame, give me truth."

"Any truth is better than make-believe."

And so forth.

November 7, 1980

On down this here Greenish river. We cast off, row south past Woodruff, Point, and Saddlehorse bottoms, past Upheaval Bottom and Hardscrabble Bottom. Wherever the river makes a bend—and this river comes near, in places, to bowknots—there is another flat area, a bottom, covered with silt, sand, gravel, grown up with grass and brush and cactus and, near shore, trees: willow, cottonwood, box elder, and jungles of tamarisk.

The tamarisk does not belong here, has become a pest, a water-loving exotic engaged in the process of driving out the cottonwoods and willows. A native of arid North Africa, the tamarisk was imported to the American Southwest fifty years ago by conservation *experts*—dirt management specialists—in hopes that it would help prevent streambank erosion. The cause of the erosion was flooding, and the primary cause of the flooding, then as now, was livestock grazing.

Oars at rest, we drift for a while. The Riverine String Band take up their instruments and play. The antique, rowdy, vibrant music from England and Ireland by way of Appalachia and the Rocky Mountains floats on the air, rises like smoke toward the high rimrock of the canyon walls, fades by infinitesimal gradations into the stillness of eternity. Where else could it go?

Ted Seeley prolongs the pause, then fills the silence with a solo on the fiddle, a Canadian invention called "Screechin' Old Woman and Growlin' Old Man." This dialogue continues for some time, concluding with a triumphant outburst from the Old Woman.

We miss the landing off the inside channel at Wild Horse Bench and have to fight our way through thickets of tamarisk and cane to the open ground of Fort Bottom. We make lunch on crackers, canned tuna, and chopped black olives in the shade of a cottonwood by the side of a long-abandoned log cabin. A trapper, prospector, or cow thief might have lived here—or all three of them—a century ago. Names and initials adorn the lintel of the doorway. The roof is open to the sky.

We climb a hill of clay and shale and limestone ledges to inspect at close hand an ancient ruin of stone on the summit. An Anasazi structure, probably seven or eight hundred years old, it commands a broad view of river and canyon for many miles both up and downstream, and offers a glimpse of the higher lands beyond. We can see the great Buttes of the Cross, Candlestick Tower, Junction Butte (where the Green River meets the Colorado River), Ekker Butte, Grandview Point, North Point, and parts of the White Rim. Nobody human lives at those places, or in the leagues of monolithic stone between them. We find pleasure in that knowledge. From this vantage point everything looks about the same as it did when Major John Wesley Powell and his mates first saw it in 1869. Photographs made by members of his party demonstrate that nothing much has changed except the vegetation types along the river, as in the case of tamarisk replacing willow.

We return to our river. A magisterial magpie sails before us across the barren fields. Two ravens and a hawk watch our lazy procession downstream past the long straightaway of Potato Bottom. We make camp before sundown on an island of white sand in the middle of the river. A driftwood fire under an iron pot cooks our vegetable stew. Russell mixes a batch of heavy-duty cornbread in the Dutch oven, sets the oven on the hot coals, and piles more coals on the rimmed lid. The cornbread bakes. We drink our beer, sip our rum, and listen to a pack of coyotes yammering like idiots away off in the twilight.

"I wonder who won the election," says one member of our party—our boatwoman Lorna Corson.

"The coyotes can explain everything," says Rennie Russell.

It's going to be a cold and frosty night. We add wood to the fire and put on sweaters and coats. The nights are long in November; darkness by six. The challenge is to keep the fire going and conversation and music alive until a decent bedtime arrives. Ten hours is too long to spend curled in a sleeping bag. The body knows this if the brain does not. That must be why I wake up every morning long before the sun appears. And why I remain sitting here, alone on my log, after the others have crept away, one by one, to their scattered beds.

Henry gazes at me through the flames of the campfire. From beyond the veil. Edward, he says, what are you doing here? Henry, I reply, what are you doing out there?

How easy for Thoreau to preach simplicity, asceticism and voluntary poverty when, as some think, he had none but himself to care for during his forty-five years. How easy to work part-time for a living when you have neither wife nor children to support. (When you have no payments to meet on house, car, pickup truck, cabin cruiser, life insurance, medical insurance, summer place, college educations, dinette set, color TVs, athletic club, real estate investments, holidays in Europe and the Caribbean. . . .)

Why Henry never took a wife has probably more to do with his own eccentric personality than with his doctrine of independence-through-simplicity. But if he had *wanted* a partner, and had been able to find one willing to share his doctrine, then it seems reasonable to suppose that the two of them—with their little Thoreaus—could have managed to live a family life on Thoreauvian principles. Henry might have been compelled to make pencils, survey woodlots, and give public lectures for twenty-four weeks, rather than only six each year, but his integrity as a free man would still have been preserved. There is no reason—other than the comic incongruity of imagining Henry Thoreau as husband and father—to suppose that his bachelorhood invalidates his arguments. If there was tragedy in the life of Thoreau, that tragedy lies not in any theoretical contradiction between what Henry advocated and how he lived but in his basic loneliness. He was a psychic loner all his life.

But a family man nevertheless. Except for his two years and two months at Walden Pond, his student years at Harvard, and occasional excursions to Canada, Cape Cod, and Maine, Thoreau lived most of his life in and upon the bosom of family—Emerson's family, part of the time, and the Thoreau family—mother, sister, uncles, and aunts—during the remainder.

When his father died Henry took over the management of the family's pencil-making business, a cottage industry carried on in the family home. Always a clever fellow with his hands, Henry developed a better way of manufacturing pencils and a better product. Some think that the onset of his tuberculosis, which eventually killed him, was hastened by the atmosphere of fine powdered graphite in which he earned a part of his keep.

A part of it: Thoreau had no wish to become a businessman—"Trade curses everything it handles"—and never gave to pencils more than a small part of his time.

He was considered an excellent surveyor by his townsmen and his services were much in demand. His work still serves as the basis of many property lines in and around the city of Concord. There is a document in the Morgan Library in New York, a map of Walden Pond, signed "H. D. Thoreau, Civil Engineer."

But as with pencil-making, so with surveying—Thoreau would not allow it to become a full-time career. Whatever he did, he did well; he was an expert craftsman in everything to which he put his hand. But to no wage-earning occupation would he give his life. He had, he said, "other business." And this other business awaited him out in the woods, where, as he wrote, "I was better known."

What was this other business? It is the subject of *Walden*, of his further books and essays, and of the thirty-nine volumes of his *Journal*, from which, to a considerable extent, the books were quarried. Thoreau's subject is the greatest available to any writer, thinker and human being, one which I cannot summarize in any but the most banal of phrases: "meaning," or "the meaning of life" (meaning *all* life, of course, not human life only), or in the technical usage preferred by professional philosophers, "the significance of existence."

It is this attempt to encircle with words the essence of being itself—with or without a capital *B*—which gives to Henry's prose-poetry the disturbing, haunting, heart-opening quality that some call mysticism. Like the most ambitious poets and artists, he was trying to get it all into his work, whatever "it" may signify, whatever "all" may include. Living a life full of wonder—wonderful—Henry tries to impart that wonder to his readers.

"There is nothing inorganic. . . . The earth is not a mere fragment of dead history, stratum upon stratum, like the leaves of a book, to be studied by geologists and antiquaries chiefly, but living poetry like the leaves of a tree, which precede flowers and fruit; not a fossil earth but a living earth. . . ."

That the earth, considered whole, is a kind of living being, might well seem like nonsense to the hardheaded among us. Worse than nonsense—mystical nonsense. But let us remember that a hard head, like any dense-hulled and thick-shelled nut, can enclose, out of necessity, only a tiny kernel of meat. Thinking meat, in this case. The hard head reveals, therefore, while attempting to conceal and shelter, its tiny, soft, delicate, and suspicious mind.

The statement about earth is clear enough. And probably true. To some, self-evident, though not empirically verifiable within the present limitations of scientific method. Such verification requires a more sophisticated science than we possess at present. It requires a science with room for more than data and information, a science that includes sympathy for the object under study, and more than sympathy, love. A love based on prolonged contact and interaction. Intercourse, if possible. Observation informed by sympathy, love, intuition. Numbers, charts, diagrams, and formulas are not in themselves sufficient. The face of science as currently construed is a face that only a mathematician could love. The root meaning of "science" is "knowledge"; to see and to see truly, a qualitative, not merely quantitative, understanding.

For an example of science in the whole and wholesome sense read Thoreau's description of an owl's behavior in "Winter Visitors." Thoreau observes the living animal in its native habitat, and watches it for weeks. For an example of science in its debased sense take this: According to the L.A. *Times,* a psychologist in Los Angeles defends laboratory experimentation on captive dogs with the assertion that "little is known about the psychology of dogs." Anyone who has ever kept a dog knows more about dogs than that psychologist—who doubtless considers himself a legitimate scientist—will learn in a year of Sundays.

Or this: Researchers in San Francisco have confined chimpanzees in airtight glass cubicles (gas chambers) in order to study the effect of various dosages of chemically polluted air on these "manlike organisms." As if there were not already available five million human inhabitants of the Los Angeles basin, and a hundred other places, ready, willing, and eager to supply personally informed testimony on the subject under scrutiny. Leaving aside any consideration of ethics, morality, and justice, there are more intelligent ways to study living creatures. Or nonliving creations: rocks have rights too.

That which today calls itself science gives us more and more information, an indigestible glut of information, and less and less understanding. Thoreau was well aware of this tendency and foresaw its fatal consequences. He could see the tendency in himself, even as he partially succumbed to it. Many of the later *Journals* are filled with little but the enumeration of statistical data concerning such local Concord phenomena as the rise and fall of lake levels, or the thickness of the ice on Flint's Pond on a January morning. Tedious reading—pages and pages of "factoids," as Norman Mailer would call them—attached to no coherent theory, illuminated by neither insight nor outlook nor speculation.

Henry may have had a long-range purpose in mind but he did not live long enough to fulfill it. Kneeling in the snow on a winter's day to count the tree rings in a stump, he caught the cold that led to his death on May 6, 1862. He succumbed not partially but finally to facticity.

Why'd you do it, Henry? I ask him through the flames.

The bearded face with the large, soft, dark eyes, mournful

and thoughtful as the face of Lincoln, smiles back at me but offers no answer. He evades the question by suggesting other questions in his better-known "mystical" vein:

"There was a dead horse in the hollow by the path to my house, which compelled me sometimes to go out of my way, especially in the night when the air was heavy, but the assurance it gave me of the strong appetite and inviolable health of Nature was my compensation for this. I love to see that Nature is so rife with life that myriads can be afforded to be sacrificed and suffered to prey on one another. . . . The impression made on a wise man is that of universal innocence. Compassion is a very untenable ground. It must be expeditious. Its pleadings will not bear to be stereotyped."

Henry, I say, what the devil do you mean? You sound like Darwin.

He smiles again and says, "I observed a very small and graceful hawk, like a nighthawk, alternately soaring like a ripple and tumbling a rod or two over and over, showing the underside of its wings, which gleamed like a satin ribbon in the sun. . . . The merlin it seemed to me it might be called; but I care not for its name. It was the most ethereal flight I have ever witnessed. It did not simply flutter like a butterfly, nor soar like the larger hawks, but it sported with proud reliance in the fields of the air. . . . It appeared to have no companion in the universe . . . and to need none but the morning and the ether with which it played. It was not lonely, but made all the earth lonely beneath it."

Very pretty, Henry. Are you speaking for yourself? I watch his lined, gentle face, the face of his middle age (though he had no later) as recorded in photographs, and cannot help but read there the expression, engraved, of a patient, melancholy resignation. All babies look identical; boys and adolescents resemble one another, in their bewildered hopefulness, more than they differ. But eventually the inner nature of the man appears on his outer surface. Character begins to shine through. Year by year a man reveals himself, while those with nothing to show, show it.

Differentiation becomes individuation. By the age of forty, if not before, a man is responsible for his face. The same is true of women too, certainly, although women, obeying the biological imperative, strive harder than men to preserve an appearance of youthfulness—the reproductive look—and lose it sooner. Appearance *is* reality.

Henry replies not to my question but, as befits a ghostly seer, to my thought: "Nothing can rightly compel a simple and brave man to a vulgar sadness."

We'll go along with that, Henry; you've been accused of many things but no one, to my knowledge, has yet accused you of vulgarity. Though Emerson, reacting to your night in jail for refusing to pay the poll tax, called the gesture "mean and skulking and in bad taste." In bad taste! How typically Emersonian. Robert Louis Stevenson too called you a "skulker" on the grounds that you preached more strongly than you practiced, later recanting when he learned of your activity in the antislavery movement. The contemporary author Alan Harrington, in his book *The Immortalist,* accuses you of writing, at times, like "an accountant of the spirit." That charge he bases on your vague remarks concerning immorality, and on such lines as "Goodness is the only investment that never fails."

Still other current critics, taking their cue from those whom Nabokov specified as "the Viennese quacks," would deflect the force of your attacks on custom, organized religion, and the state by suggesting that you suffered from a complex of complexes, naturally including the castration complex and the Oedipus complex. Your defiance of authority, they maintain, was in reality no more than the rebelliousness of an adolescent rejecting his father—in this case the meek and mousy John Thoreau.

Whatever grain of truth may be in this diagnosis, such criticism betrays the paternalistic condescension of these critics toward human beings in general. The good citizen, they seem to be saying, is like the obedient child; the rebellious man is a bad boy. "The people are like children," said our own beloved, gone but not forgotten, Richard Nixon. The psychiatric approach to dissidence has been most logically applied in the Soviet Union, where opposition to the state is regarded and treated as a form of mental illness.

In any case, Henry cannot be compelled to confess to a vulgar sadness. The vulgarity resides in the tactics of literary Freudianism. Of the opposition. Psychoanalysis is the neurosis of the psychoanalyst—and of the psychoanalytic critic. Why should we bother any more with this garbage? I thought we stopped talking about Freud back in 1952. Sometime near the end of the Studebaker era.

Fading beyond the last flames of the fire, Henry lulls me to sleep with one of his more soporific homilies:

"The light which puts out our eyes is darkness to us. Only that day dawns to which we are awake. There is more day to dawn. The sun . . ."

Yes, yes, Henry, we know. How true. Whatever it means. How late it is. Whatever the hour.

I rise from my log, heap the coals of the fire together, and by their glimmering light and the cold light of the stars fumble my way back and into the luxury of my goosedown nest. Staring up at mighty Orion, trying to count six of the seven Pleiades, a solemn thought comes to me: We Are Not Alone.

I nuzzle my companion's cold nose, the only part of her not burrowed deep in her sleeping bag. She stirs and half opens her eyes. We're not alone, I whisper in her ear. I know, she says; shut up and go to sleep. Smiling, I face the black sky and the sapphire stars. Mark Twain was right. Better the savage wasteland with Eve than Paradise without her. Where she is, there is Paradise.

Poor Henry.

And then I hear that voice again, far off but clear: "All Nature is my bride."

November 8, 1980

Who won the election? What election? Mere vapors on the gelid air, like the breath from my lungs. I rebuild the fire on the embers of last night's fire. I construct the coffee, adding fresh grounds to yesterday's. One by one, five human forms reassemble themselves about me, repeating themselves, with minor variations, for another golden day. The two vegetarians in our group—Rennie and Lorna—prepare their breakfast oatmeal, a viscous gray slime. I dump two pounds of Buck-sliced bacon into the expedition's wok, to the horror of the vegetarians, and stir it roughly about with a fork. Stir-cooking. The four carnivores looking on with hungry eyes. The vegetarians smile in pity. "Pig meat," says Lorna, "for the four fat pork faces." "Eat your pussy food," says Dusty Teal, "and be quiet."

The melody of morning. Black-throated desert sparrows chatter in the willows: *chirr . . . chirr . . . chit chit chit.* The sun comes up, a glaring cymbal, over yonder canyon rim. Quickly the temperature rises five, ten, twenty degrees, at the rate of a degree a minute, from freezing to fifty-two. Or so it feels. We peel off parkas, sweaters, shirts, thermal underwear. Ravens croak, a rock falls, the river flows.

The fluvial life. The alluvial shore. "A river is superior to a lake," writes Henry in his *Journal,* "in its liberating influence. It has motion and indefinite length. . . . With its rapid current it is a slightly fluttering wing. River towns are winged towns."

Down the river. Lorna rows the dory, I row the raft. We are entertained by water music from our string trio, a rich enchanting tune out of Peru called "Urubamba." The song goes on and on and never long enough. The Indians must have composed it for a journey down the Amazon.

Fresh slides appear on the mud banks; a beaver plops into the water ahead of us, disappears. The beaver are making a comeback on the Green. Time for D. Julien, Jim Bridger, Joe Meek, Jed Smith, and Jim Beckwourth to reappear. Eternal recurrence, announced Nietzsche. Time for the mountain men to return. The American West has not given us, so far, sufficient men to match our mountains. Or not since the death of Crazy Horse, Sitting Bull, Dull Knife, Red Cloud, Chief Joseph, Little Wolf, Red Shirt, Gall, Geronimo, Cochise, Tenaya (to name but a few), and their comrades. With their defeat died a bold, brave, heroic way of life, one as fine as anything recorded history has to show us. Speaking for myself, I'd sooner have been a liver-eating, savage horseman riding with Red Cloud than a slave-owning sophist sipping tempered wine in Periclean Athens. For example. Even Attila the Hun, known locally as the Scourge of God, brought more fresh air and freedom into Europe than the crowd who gave us the syllogism and geometry, Aristotle and his *Categories,* Plato and his *Laws.*

Instead of mountain men we are cursed with a plague of diggers, drillers, borers, grubbers; of asphalt-spreaders, dam-builders, overgrazers, clear-cutters, and strip-miners whose object seems to be to make our mountains match our men—making molehills out of mountains for a race of rodents—for the rat race.

Oh well . . . revenge is on the way. We see it in those high thin clouds far on the northern sky. We feel it in those rumbles of discontent deep in the cupboards of the earth: tectonic crockery trembling on the continental shelves. We hear it down the slip-face of the dunes, a blue wind moaning out of nowhere. We smell it on the air: the smell of danger. Death before dishonor? That's right. What else? Liberty or death? Naturally.

When no one else would do it, it was Thoreau, Henry Thoreau the intolerable bore, the mean skulker, the "quaint stump figure of a man," as William Dean Howells saw him, who rang the Concord firebell to summon the villagers to a speech by Emerson attacking slavery. And when John Brown stood on trial for his life, when all America, even the most ardent abolitionists, was denouncing him, it was himself—Henry—who delivered a public address first in Concord, then in Boston, not only defending but praising, even eulogizing, the "madman" of Harpers Ferry.

We go on. Sheer rock—the White Rim—rises from the river's left shore. We pause at noon to fill our water jugs from a series of potholes half filled with last week's rainwater. We drink, and sitting in the sunlight on the pale sandstone, make our lunch—slabs of dark bread, quite authentic, from a bohemian bakery in

Moab; a serious hard-core hippie peanut butter, heavy as wet concrete, from some beatnik food co-op in Durango, Colorado (where Teal and Corson live); raspberry jam; and wild honey, thick as axle grease, for esophageal lubrication.

"What is your favorite dish?" another guest asked Thoreau as they sat down to a sumptuous Emersonian dinner.

"The nearest," Henry replied.

"At Harvard they teach all branches of learning," said Ralph Waldo.

"But none of the roots," said Henry.

Refusing to pay a dollar for his Harvard diploma, he said, "Let every sheep keep its own skin." When objections were raised to his habit of exaggeration, Henry said, "You must speak loud to those who are hard of hearing." Asked to write for the *Ladies' Companion,* he declined on the grounds that he "could not write anything companionable." He defines a pearl as "the hardened tear of a diseased clam, murdered in its old age." Describing the flavor of a certain wild apple, he wrote that it was "sour enough to set a squirrel's teeth on edge, or make a jay scream." On the art of writing he said to a correspondent, "You must work very long to write short sentences." And added that "the one great rule of composition . . . is to speak the truth."

And so on. The man composed wisecracks and epigrams even on his deathbed. "Henry, have you made your peace with God?" asked a relative. "I am not aware that we had ever quarreled, Aunt," said Henry. To another visitor, attempting to arouse in him a decent Christian concern with the next world, Henry said, "One world at a time."

One could make a book of Henry's sayings. And call it *Essais. Areopagitica. Walden.*

Many of his friends, neighbors, relatives, and relative friends must have sighed in relief when Henry finally croaked his last, mumbling "moose . . . Indians . . ." and was safely buried under Concord sod. Peace, they thought, at long last. But, to paraphrase the corpse, they had *somewhat hastily* concluded that he was dead.

His passing did not go unnoticed outside of Concord. Thoreau had achieved regional notoriety by 1862. But at the time when the giants of New England literature were thought to be Emerson, Hawthorne, Alcott, Channing, Irving, Longfellow, Dr. Lowell and Dr. Holmes, Thoreau was but a minor writer. Not even a major minor writer.

Today we see it differently. In the ultimate democracy of time, Henry has outlived his contemporaries. Hawthorne and Emerson are still read, at least in university English departments, and it may be that in a few elementary schools up in Maine and Minnesota children are being compelled to read Longfellow's *Hiawatha* (I doubt it; doubt that they can, even under compulsion), but as for the others they are forgotten by everyone but specialists in American literature. Thoreau, however, becomes more significant with each passing decade. The deeper our United States sinks into industrialism, urbanism, militarism— with the rest of the world doing its best to emulate America—the more poignant, strong, and appealing becomes Thoreau's demand for the right of every man, every woman, every child, every dog, every tree, every snail darter, every lousewort, every living thing, to live its own life in its own way at its own pace in its own square mile of home. Or in its own stretch of river.

Looking at my water-soaked, beer-stained, grease-spotted cheap paperback copy of *Walden,* I see that mine was from the thirty-third printing. And this is only one of at least a dozen current American editions of the book. *Walden* has been published abroad in every country where English can be read, as in India—God knows they need it there—or can be translated, as in Russia, where they need it even more. The Kremlin's commissars of literature have classified Thoreau as a nineteenth-century social reformer, proving once again that censors can read but seldom understand.

The village crank becomes a world figure. As his own Johnny Appleseed, he sows the seeds of liberty around the planet, even on what looks like the most unpromising soil. Out of Concord, apples of discord. Truth is the enemy of power, now and always.

We walk up a small side canyon toward an area called Soda Springs Basin; the canyon branches and branches again, forming more canyons. The floor of each is flood-leveled sand, the walls perpendicular sandstone. Each canyon resembles a winding corridor in a labyrinth. We listen for the breathing of the Minotaur but find only cottonwoods glowing green and gold against the red rock, rabbitbrush with its mustard-yellow bloom, mule-ear sunflowers facing the sunlight, their coarse petals the color of butter, and the skull and curled horns of a desert bighorn ram, half buried in the auburn sand.

The canyons go on and on, twisting for miles into the plateau beyond. We turn back without reaching Soda Springs. On our return Dusty Teal takes up the bighorn trophy, carries it back to the dory and mounts it on the bow, giving his boat dignity, class, a Nordic and warlike glamour.

We camp today at Anderson Bottom, across the river from Unknown Bottom. We find pictographs and petroglyphs here, pictures of deer, bighorns, warriors, and spectral figures representing—who knows—gods, spirits, demons. They do not trouble us. We cook our dinner and sing our songs and go to sleep.

November 9, 1980

Early in the morning I hear coyotes singing again, calling up the sun. There's something about the coyotes that reminds me of Henry. What is it? After a moment the answer comes.

Down near Tucson, Arizona, where I sometimes live—a grim and grimy little-big town, swarming with nervous policemen, dope dealers, resolute rapists, and geriatric bank robbers, but let this pass for the moment—the suburban parts of the city are infested with pet dogs. Every home owner in these precincts believes that he needs whatever burglar protection he can get; and he is correct. Most evenings at twilight the wild coyotes come stealing in from the desert to penetrate the suburbs, raid garbage cans, catch and eat a few cats, dogs, and other domesticated beasts. When this occurs the dogs raise a grim clamor, roaring like maniacs, and launch themselves in hot but tentative pursuit of the coyotes. The coyotes retreat into the brush and cactus, where they stop, facing the town, to wait and sit and laugh at the dogs. They yip, yap, yelp, howl and holler, teasing the dogs, taunting them, enticing them with the old-time call of the wild. And the dogs stand and tremble, shaking with indecision, furious, hating themselves, tempted to join the coyotes, run off with them into the hills, but—afraid. Afraid to give up the comfort, security, and safety of their housebound existence. Afraid of the unknown and dangerous.

Thoreau was our suburban coyote. Town dwellers have always found him exasperating.

"I have traveled a good deal in Concord; and everywhere, in shops and offices and fields, the inhabitants have appeared to me to be doing penance in a thousand remarkable ways. . . . By a seeming fate, commonly called necessity, they are employed, as it says in an old book, laying up treasures which moth and rust will corrupt and thieves break through and steal. It is a fool's life, as they will find when they get to the end of it, if not before. . . . I sometimes wonder that we can be so frivolous. . . . As if you could kill time without injuring eternity."

Oh, come now, Henry, stop yapping at us. Go make love to a pine tree (all Nature being your bride). Lay off. Leave us alone. But he will not stop.

"The mass of men lead lives of quiet desperation. What is called resignation is confirmed desperation. . . . A stereotyped but unconscious despair is concealed even under what are called the games and amusements of mankind. There is no play in them."

But is it *true* that the mass of men lead lives of quiet desperation? And if so, did Henry escape such desperation himself? And who, if anyone, can answer these questions?

As many have noted, the mass of men—and women—lead lives today of *un*quiet desperation. A frantic busyness ("business") pervades our society wherever we look—in city and coun-

try, among young and old and middle-aged, married and un-
married, all races, classes, sexes, in work and play, in religion,
the arts, the sciences, and perhaps most conspicuously in the
self-conscious cult of meditation, retreat, withdrawal. The symptoms of universal unease and dis-ease are apparent on every
side. We hear the demand by conventional economists for in-
creased "productivity," for example. Productivity of what? for
whose benefit? to what end? by what means and at what cost?
Those questions are not considered. We are belabored by the
insistence on the part of our politicians, businessmen and military leaders, and the claque of scriveners who serve them, that
"growth" and "power" are intrinsic goods, of which we can never
have enough, or even too much. As if gigantism were an end in
itself. As if a commendable rat were a rat twelve hands high at
the shoulders—and still growing. As if we could never have
peace on this planet until one state dominates all others.

The secondary symptoms show up in the lives of individuals,
the banalities of everyday soap opera: crime, divorce, runaway
children, loneliness, alcoholism, mental breakdown. We live in a
society where suicide (in its many forms) appears to more and
more as a sensible solution; as a viable alternative; as a workable
option.

Yes, there are many who seem to be happy in their lives and
work. But strange lives, queer work. Space technicians, for example, busily refining a new type of inertial guidance system for
an intercontinental ballistic missile bearing hydrogen bombs.
Laboratory biologists testing the ability of mice, dogs, and chimpanzees to cultivate cancer on a diet of cigarettes and Holsum
bread, to propel a treadmill under electric stimuli, to survive
zero gravity in a centrifuge. And the absurd R. Buckminster
Fuller hurtling himself around the globe by supersonic jet with
six wristwatches strapped to each forearm, each watch set to a
different time zone. "The world is big," says Fuller, "but it is
comprehensible." Why indeed so it is, when you take myopia for
utopia, travel in a tin tube, and think the Astrodome is home.

And also, to be fair, young dancers in a classroom; an old

sculptor hacking in fury at a block of apple wood; a pinto bean farmer in Cortez, Colorado surveying his fields with satisfaction on a rainy day in July (those rare farmers, whom Thoreau dismissed with such contempt, we now regard with envy); a solitary fly fisherman unzipping his fly on the banks of the Madison River; wet children playing on a shining, sun-dazzled beach.

Compared with ours, Thoreau's was an open, quiet, agrarian society, relatively clean and uncluttered. The factory system was only getting under way in his time, though he took note of it when he remarked that "the shop girls have no privacy, even in their thoughts." In his day England, not America, was "the workhouse of the world." (America now in the process of being succeeded by Japan.) What would Henry think of New England, of the United States, of the Western world, in the year 1980? 1984? 2001? Would he not assert, confidently as before, that the mass of humans continue to lead lives of quiet desperation?

Quiet desperation. The bite of the phrase comes from the unexpected, incongruous juxtaposition of ordinarily antithetical words. The power of it comes from our sense of its illuminating force—"a light which makes the darkness visible." Henry's shocking pronouncement continues to resonate in our minds, with deeper vibrations, 130 years after he made it. He allows for exceptions, indicating the "mass of men," not all men, but as for the truth of his observation no Gallup Poll can tell us; each must look into his own heart and mind and then deny it if he can.

And what about Henry himself? When one of his friends, William Ellery Channing, declared morosely that no man could be happy "under present conditions," Thoreau replied without hesitation, "But I am." He spent nearly a year at his dying and near the end, too weak to write any more, he dictated the following, in answer to a letter from his friend Blake:

"You ask particularly after my health. I *suppose* that I have not many months to live; but of course I know nothing about it. I may add that I am enjoying existence as much as ever, and regret nothing."

When the town jailer, Sam Staples, the same who had locked

Thoreau up for a night many years before, and had also become a friend, paid a visit to the dying man, he reported to Emerson: "Never spent an hour with more satisfaction. Never saw a man dying with so much pleasure and peace." A trifle lugubrious, but revealing. Henry's sister Sophia wrote, near his end, "It is not possible to be sad in his presence. No shadow attaches to anything connected with my precious brother. His whole life impresses me as a grand miracle. . . ."

A cheerful stoic all the way, Thoreau refused any drugs to ease the pain or let him sleep; he rejected opiates, according to Channing, "on the ground that he preferred to endure the worst sufferings with a clear mind rather than sink into a narcotic dream." As he would never admit to a vulgar sadness, so he would not allow himself to surrender to mere physical pain.

It must have seemed to Henry during his last year that his life as an author had been a failure. Only two of his books were published during his lifetime and neither received much recognition. His contemporaries without exception—Emerson included—had consigned him to oblivion, and Henry could not have been unaware of the general opinion. But even in this he refused to acknowledge defeat. Noting the dismal sales of his books, he wrote in his *Journal:* "I believe that the result is more inspiring and better for me than if thousands had bought my wares. It affects my privacy less and leaves me freer."

Emerson declared that Thoreau was a coldly unemotional man, stoical but never cheerful; Emerson had so convinced himself of this that when, in editing some of Thoreau's letters for publication, he came across passages that indicated otherwise, he deleted them. But Ralph Waldo's son Edward, in his book *Henry Thoreau as Remembered by a Young Friend,* wrote that Henry loved to sing and dance, and was always popular with the children of Concord, whom he often led on berry-picking parties into the woods. ("Oh I got my thrill . . . on Blueberry Hill. . . .")

In her *Memories of Hawthorne,* Hawthorne's daughter Rose gives us this picture of Thoreau ice skating, with Emerson and Hawthorne, on the frozen Concord River: "Hawthorne," she writes, "moved like a self-impelled Greek statue, stately and grave" (the marble faun); Emerson "closed the line, evidently too weary to hold himself erect, pitching headforemost . . ."; while Thoreau, circling around them, "performed dithyrambic dances and Bacchic leaps."

But what of the photographs of Henry referred to earlier, the daguerreotype in his thirty-ninth year by B. W. Maxham, made in 1856, and the ambrotype by E. S. Dunshee, made in 1861? Trying to get some sense of the man himself, in himself, which I do not get from his words alone, or from the accounts of Thoreau by others, I find myself looking again and again at these old pictures. Yes, the eyes are unusually large, very sensitive and thoughtful, as is the expression of the whole face. The nose is too long, the chin too small, neither an ornament; the face deeply lined, the brow high, the hair and beard luxuriant. A passable face, if not a handsome one. And it still seems to me that I read in his eyes, in his look, an elemental melancholy. A resigned sadness. But the man was ailing with tuberculosis when the former picture was made, within a year of his death when the second was made. These facts should explain the thoughtful look, justify a certain weariness. In neither picture can we see what might be considered a trace of self-pity—the *vulgar* sadness. And in neither can we perceive the faintest hint of any kind of desperation. Henry may have been lonely; he was never a desperate man.

What does it matter? For us it is Henry's words and ideas that count, or more exactly, the symbiotic and synergistic mutually reinforcing logic of word and idea, and his successful efforts to embody both in symbolic acts. If it were true that he never had a happy moment (I doubt this) in his entire life, he surely had an intense empathy with the sensations of happiness:

". . . I have penetrated to those meadows on the morning of many a first spring day, jumping from hummock to hummock, from willow root to willow root, when the wild river valley and the woods were bathed in so pure and bright a light as would have waked the dead, if they had been slumbering in their graves, as some suppose. There needs no stronger proof of immortality."

The paragraph is from the springtime of Henry's life. *Walden* is a young man's book, most of it written before his thirtieth year. But the infatuation with the sun and sunlight carries on into the premature autumn of his years as well; he never gave them up, never surrendered. Near the end of his life he wrote:

"We walked [jumping has become walking, but the spirit—and some of the phrasing—remains the same] in so pure and bright a light, gilding the withered grass and leaves, so softly and serenely bright, I thought I had never bathed in such a golden flood, without a ripple or a murmur to it. The west side of every wood and rising ground gleamed like the boundary of Elysium, and the sun on our backs seemed like a gentle herdsman driving us home at evening."

And concluding: "So we saunter toward the Holy Land, till one day the sun shall shine more brightly than ever he has done, shall perchance shine into our minds and hearts, and light up our whole lives with a great awakening light, as warm and serene and golden as on a bankside in autumn."

November 10, 1980

Onward, into Stillwater Canyon. We have left Labyrinth behind, though how Major Powell distinguished the two is hard to determine. The current is slow but no slower than before, the canyons as serpentine as ever. In the few straight stretches of water we gain a view of Candlestick Tower, now behind us, and off to the southwest, ahead, the great sandstone monadnock three hundred feet high known as Cleopatra's Chair, "bathed," as Henry would say, "in a golden flood of sunlight."

We row around an anvil-shaped butte called Turk's Head. Hard to see any reason for the name. Is there any reason, out here, for any name? These huge walls and giant towers and vast mazy avenues of stone resist attempts at verbal reduction. The historical view, the geological view, the esthetical view, the rock climber's view, give us only aspects of a massive *presence* that remains fundamentally unknowable. The world is big and it is incomprehensible.

A hot still morning in Stillwater Canyon. We row and rest and glide, at two miles per hour, between riparian jungles of rusty willow, coppery tamarisk, brown cane and gold-leaf cotton-woods. On the shaded side the crickets sing their dirgelike monotone. They know, if we don't, that winter is coming.

But today is very warm for mid-November. An Indian-summer day. Looking at the rich brown river, jungle on both banks, I think how splendid it would be, and apposite, to see the rugose snout of an alligator come sliding through the water toward us. We need alligators here. Crocodiles, also. A few brontosauri, pteranodons, and rocs with twenty-five-foot wingspan would not be amiss. How tragic that we humans arrived too late, to the best of our conscious recollection, to have witnessed the fun and frolic of the giant thunder lizards in their time of glory. Why was that great chapter ripped too soon from the Book of Life? I would give ten years off the beginning of my life to see, only once, *Tyrannosaurus rex* come rearing up from the elms of Central Park, a Morgan police horse screaming in its jaws. We can never have enough of nature.

We explore a couple of unnamed side canyons on the right, searching for a natural stone arch I found ten years ago on a previous river journey. Hallucination Arch we named it then, a lovely span of two-tone rosy sandstone—not shown on any map—somewhere high in the northern fringes of the Maze. We do not find it this time. We pass without investigating a third unknown canyon; that must have been the right one.

We camp for two nights at the mouth of Jasper Canyon, spend the day between the nights exploring Jasper's higher ramifications, toward the heart of the Maze. If the Maze has a heart. We go on the following day, down the river, and come sailing out one fine afternoon into the confluence of the two great desert streams. The Green meets the Colorado. They do not immediately merge, however, but flow along side by side like traffic lanes on a freeway, the greenish Colorado, the brownish Green, with a thin line of flotsam serving as median.

Henry never was a joiner either.

"Know all men by these presents that I, Henry Thoreau, do not wish to be considered a member of any incorporated body which I have not joined."

A crusty character, Thoreau. An unpeeled man. A man with the bark on him.

We camp today at Spanish Bottom, near the first rapids of Cataract Canyon. Sitting around our fire at sundown, four of us gnawing on spareribs, the other two picking at their pussy food—tofu and spinach leaves and stewed kelp (it looks like the testicles of a sick octopus)—we hear the roar of tons of silty water plunging among the limestone molars of Brown Betty Rapid: teeth set on edge. The thunderous vibrations rise and fall, come and go, with the shifting evening winds.

We spend the next day wandering about the top of the Maze, under the shadows of Lizard Rock, Standing Rock, the Chimney, looking down into five-hundred-foot-deep canyons, into the stems, branches, and limbs of an arboreal system of part-time drainages. It took a liberal allowance of time, indeed, for the rare storms of the desert to carve out of solid rock these intricate canyons, each with its unscalable walls, boxlike heads, stomach-turning dropoffs. A man—aye and a woman too—could spend the better part of a life exploring this one area, getting to know, so far as possible, its broad outline and its intimate details. You could make your summer camp on Pete's Mesa, your winter camp down in Ernie's Country, and use Candlestick Spire all year round for a personalized private sundial. And die, when you're ready, with the secret center of the Maze clutched to your bosom. Or, more likely, never found.

Henry spent his life—or earned his life—exploring little more than the area surrounding his hometown of Concord. His jaunts beyond his own territory do not amount to much. He traveled once to Minnesota, seeking health, but that was a failure. He never came west although, as he says, he preferred walking in a westerly direction. He never saw our Rocky Mountains or the Grand Canyon or the Maze. He never reached the Amazon, Alaska, Antarctica, the Upper Nile or the Mountains of the Moon. He journeyed once to Staten Island but was not impressed.

Instead he made a world out of Walden Pond, Concord, and their environs. He walked, he explored, every day and many nights, he learned to know his world as few ever know any world. Once as he walked in the woods with a friend (Thoreau had many friends, we come to realize, if not one in his lifetime with whom he could truly, deeply share his life; it is we his readers, over a century later, who must be and are his true companions), the friend expressed his long-felt wish to find an Indian arrowhead. At once Henry stopped, bent down and picked one up.

November 14, 1980

Today will be our last day on the river. We plan to run the rapids of Cataract Canyon this morning, camp on Lake Powell this afternoon, go on to Hite Marina and back to civilization, such as it is, tomorrow.

I rise early, as usual, and before breakfast go for a walk into the fields of Spanish Bottom. I see two sharp-shinned hawks roosting in a cottonwood. A tree of trembling leaves, pale gold and acid green. The hawks rise at my approach, circle, return to the tree as I go on. Out in the field, one hundred yards away, I see an erect neck, a rodentian head, a pair of muley ears displayed in sharp silhouette against the redrock cliffs. I stop, we stare at each other—the transient human, the ephemeral desert mule deer. Then I notice other deer scattered beyond the first: one, two, three, four, five—nine all told. Two with antlers.

My first thought is *meat*. Unworthy thought—but there they are, waiting, half of them standing broadside to me, their dear beating hearts on level with the top of the sand sage, saltbush, rice grass. Two of them within a hundred yards—easy range for a thirty-thirty. Meat means survival. Survival, by Christ, with honor. With *honor!* When the cities lie at the monster's feet we shall come here, my few friends and I, my sons and my daughters and we will survive. We shall live.

My second thought is more fitting, for the moment. Leave them in peace. Let them be. Efface yourself for a change and let the wild things be.

What would Henry say? Henry said, "There is a period in the history of the individual, as of the race, when the hunters are the 'best men,' as the Algonquins called them. We cannot but pity the boy who has never fired a gun; he is no more humane, while his education has been sadly neglected." But then he goes on to say: "No humane being, past the thoughtless age of boyhood, will wantonly murder any creature which holds its life by the same tenure that he does. The hare in its extremity cries like a child. I warn you, mothers, that my sympathies do not make the usual *philanthropic* distinctions." Is that his last word on the subject? Hardly. Henry had many words for every subject and no last word for any. He also writes, "But I see that if I were to live in a wilderness, I should become . . . a fisher and hunter in earnest."

So let them be for now. I turn back toward camp, making one step. The deer take alarm, finally, and move off at a walk. I watch. Their fear becomes contagious. One begins to run, they all run, bounding away toward the talus slopes of the canyon wall. I watch them leap upward into the rocks, expending energy with optimum ease, going farther and rising higher until they disappear, one by one, somewhere among the boulders and junipers at the foot of the vertical wall.

Back to camp and breakfast. We load the boats, secure the hatches, lash down baggage, strap on life jackets, face the river and the sun, the growing roar of the rapids. First Brown Betty, then Ben Hur and Capsize Rapids, then the Big Drop and Satan's Gut. Delightful names, and fitting. We feel the familiar rush of adrenaline as it courses through our blood. We've been here before, however, and know that we'll get through. Most likely. The odds are good. Our brave boatman and boatwoman, Dusty and Lorna, ply the oars and steer our fragile craft into the glassy tongue of the first rapid. The brawling waters roar below, rainbows of broken sunlight dance in the spray. We descend.

Henry thou should be with us now.

I look for his name in the water, his face in the airy foam. He must be here. Wherever there are deer and hawks, wherever there is liberty and danger, wherever there is wilderness, wherever there is a living river, Henry Thoreau will find his eternal home.

Watching the Birds:
The Windhover

We used to live, my wife and I, in a glassy cabin on a mountain peak, surrounded by a national forest. Our job was to watch. Watch what? Well, watch just about everything. To us it seemed like the center of the world. When clouds gathered, we watched for lightning, where it struck. After the lightning we'd watch for smoke in the trees and when and if it appeared, a few hours later or a couple of days later, we'd locate the smoke with our precision fire-finder and radio the news to forest headquarters. The report generally went like this: "Phoenix, this is Aztec Peak, ten-seventy-three." (10-73 is forest radio code for fire.)

"Go ahead, Aztec."

"We've got a little smoke for you at eight-four-two degrees and thirty minutes, southwest side of Two Bar Ridge. It's a single snag, blue-gray smoke, small volume, intermittent puffs. Light wind from the west. Heavy fuel but not spreading."

"Ten-four, Aztec. Let us know if it grows."

While fire crews were dispatched to find and put out the fire, my wife and I returned to our job of watching. We watched the clouds again and the weather, and approaching and departing storms. We watched the sun go down behind Four Peaks and the Superstition Mountains, that sundown legend retold and recurring every evening, day after day after day. We saw the planet Venus bright as radium floating close to the shoulder of the new moon. We watched the stars, and meteor showers, and the snaky ripple of cloud-to-cloud lightning coursing across the sky at night.

We watched the birds. One day a little nuthatch flew into our cabin through an open window, banged its silly head against the closed window opposite, and dropped to the floor. I picked up the tiny bird, holding it in my palm. I could feel the beating of its furious heart. I set it down on the catwalk outside, in the sunlight. After a while the nuthatch came to, shook its head, lofted its wings, and fluttered off. What can you think of a bird that crashes into glass and creeps headfirst down the trunk of a pine?

The forest spread below us in summer in a dozen different hues of green, from olive drab to aquamarine. There were yellow pine and piñon pine, blue spruce and Engelmann spruce, white fir and Douglas fir, quaking aspen, New Mexico locust, alligator juniper, and four kinds of oak. Along the rimrock of the escarpment, where warm air rose from the canyons beneath, grew manzanita, agave, sotol, and several species of cactus— prickly pear, pincushion, fishhook. Far down in the canyons, where water flowed, though not always on the surface, we could see sycamore, alder, box elder, cottonwood, walnut, hackberry, wild cherry, and wild grape. And a hundred other kinds of tree, shrub, and vine that I would probably never learn to identify by name.

The naming of things is a useful mnemonic device, enabling us to distinguish and utilize and remember what otherwise might remain an undifferentiated sensory blur, but I don't think names tell us much of character, essence or meaning. Einstein thought that the most mysterious aspect of the universe (if it is, indeed, a *uni*-verse, not a pluri-verse) is what he called its "rationality." Being primarily a mathematician and only secondarily a violinist, Einstein saw the world as rational because so many of its properties and so much of its behavior can be described through mathematical formulas. The atomic bomb and Hiroshima made a convincing argument for his point of view. As does the ignition of juniper twigs, by the agency of friction, into heat, smoke, and flame. Mass is transformed into energy, emitting light. Employing fire lookouts.

Even so, I find something narrow and too specialized in Einstein's summary of the situation. The specialist's viewpoint may go deep but it cannot go all the way through. How could it if the world, though finite, is unbounded? Nor does its practical utility—nuclear bombs—make up for its lack of breadth. All special theories suffer from this defect. The lizard sunning itself on a stone would no doubt tell us that time, space, sun, and earth exist to serve the lizard's interests; the lizard, too, must see the world as reducible to a rational formula. Relative to the context, the lizard's metaphysical system seems as complete as Einstein's.

But to me the most mysterious thing about the universe is not its rationality but the fact that it exists. And the same mystery attaches to everything within it. The world is permeated through and through by mystery. By the incomprehensible. By creatures like you and me and Einstein and the lizards.

Modern science and technology have given us the engineering techniques to measure, analyze, and take apart the immediate neighborhood, including the neighbors. But this knowledge adds not much to our understanding of things. "Knowledge is power," said Francis Bacon, great-great-grandfather of the nuclear age. Power, exactly—that's been the point of the game all along. But power does not lead to wisdom, even less to understanding. Sympathy, love, physical contact—touching—are better means to so fine an end.

Vague talk, I agree. This blather about mystery is probably no more than a confession of intellectual laziness. Let's have no more metaphysical apologetics. Throw metaphysic to the dogs, I say, and watch the birds. I'd rather contemplate the noble turkey vulture soaring on the air, contemplating me, than speculate further on Einstein's theories, astrophysics, or the significance of the latest computer printouts from Kitt Peak Observatory and NASA. The computer tapers (tapirs?) have a word for it: GIGO. Garbage In, Garbage Out. Output equals Input. Numbers in, numbers out—nothing more. NINO, a double negation. Anything reduced to numbers and algebra is not very interesting. Useful, of course, for the processing of data, physical relations, human beings—but not interesting.

The vultures are interesting. In the morning they would rise, one by one, from their communal roost a quarter-mile below our lookout, and disperse themselves to the four quarters of the firmament. Each patrols its chosen—or allocated—territory, rising so high and sailing so far it soon becomes invisible to human eyes, even when our human eyes are aided by Bausch & Lomb 7×50 binoculars. But although we cannot always see them, the buzzards keep an eye on one another as well as on the panorama of life and death below, and when one bird descends for an actual or potential lunch its mates notice and come from miles away to join the feast. This is the principle of evolutionary success: mutual aid.

At evening, near sundown, the vultures would return. Friendly, tolerant, gregarious birds, they liked to roost each night on the same dead pine below. One by one they spiraled downward, weaving transparent figures in the air while others maintained a holding pattern, sinking slowly, gradually—as if reluctant to leave the heights—toward the lime-spattered branches of the snag. They might even have had nests down in there somewhere, although I could never see one, with little buzzard chicks waiting for supper. Try to imagine a baby vulture.

Gathered on their favorite dead tree, heads nodding together, the vultures resembled from our vantage point a convocation of bald, politic funeral directors discussing business prospects—always good. Dependable. The mature birds have red, wrinkled, featherless heads; the heads of the young are a bluish color and also naked. The heads are bald because it's neater, safer, more sanitary, given the line of work. If you made your living by thrusting your beak and eyes and neck deep into the rotting entrails, say, of a dead cow, you too would prefer to be bald as a buzzard. Feathers on the head would impede a hasty withdrawal, when necessary, and might provide lodging for maggots, beetles, worms, and bacteria. Best for the trade to keep sleek and tidy.

I respect vultures myself, even like them, I guess, in a way, and fully expect someday to join them, internally at least. One should plan one's reincarnation with care. I like especially the idea of floating among the clouds all day, seldom stirring a feather, meditating on whatever it is that vultures meditate about. It looks like a good life, from down here.

We had some golden eagles in the area too, but seldom got a look at them. Uncommon and elitist birds, aloof as warlords, they generally hang out as far as possible from human habitat. Who could blame them? Sheepmen and others shoot them on sight, on general principles. Our hero Ernest Hemingway could not resist the temptation to bag an eagle now and then, though he hated himself afterward. Not an easy job to be, or to have been, Ernest Hemingway. Elinor Wylie advised emulation:

> Avoid the reeking herd,
> Shun the polluted flock,
> Live like that stoic bird
> The eagle of the rock.

But she spent most of her time in New York City. Can't blame her either. Every bird in its proper place.

The redtail hawk is a handsome character. I enjoyed watching the local hunter come planing through the pass between our mountaintop and the adjoining peak, there to catch the wind and hover in place for a while, head twitching back and forth as it scans the forest below. When he—or she—spots something live and edible, down she goes at an angle of forty-five degrees, feet first, talons extended, wings uplifted, feathers all aflutter, looking like a Victorian lady in skirts and ruffled pantaloons jumping off a bridge.

The hawk disappears into the woods. I watch, binoculars ready. She rises seconds later from the trees with something wriggling, alive, in her right foot. A field mouse. The hawk sails high in the air. The mouse is fighting, bites the hawk on the shank (I can see these details without difficulty), and the startled redtail drops her prey. The mouse falls down and away, also at an angle of forty-five degrees, carried eastward by the wind. The hawk stoops, swoops, and recaptures the mouse a hundred feet above the treetops, carries it to the broken-off top of a pine, perches there, still holding the struggling mouse in her claws, and makes one quick stab of beak to the mouse's head. I see a spurt of red. The mouse is still. The hawk gulps down her lunch raw and whole, in one piece, as an owl does. *Hors rodentine.* Later, after craw and gizzard have done their work, the hawk will regurgitate a tiny ball of fur and toenails.

We watched the storms of late afternoon. Sun descending in a welter of brawling purple clouds. Spokes of gold wheel across the sky, jags and jets of lightning flicker from cloud to cloud and from cloud to earth. Mighty kettledrums thunder in the distance. My wind gauge reads thirty-five knots. The trees sway, the wind booms through the forest.

Watching the vultures gather below, I noticed a disturbance. A small gray-backed falcon was diving among the vultures, harrying the laggards. It was a peregrine falcon—rare but not extinct. Watching through the glasses, I saw one vulture actually flapping its wings to escape the falcon—unusual exertion for a vulture. The falcon strikes, their bodies collide in what appears to me as a glancing blow. A few vulture feathers float off on the wind. The vulture flaps into the shelter of the trees, swearing quietly, apparently unharmed. Tiring of this sport, the falcon skims upward in a sweeping arc, shooting through the circling vultures, winging higher and higher into the sky, and stops at the apex of its parabola to hover there, still as a star, facing the wind, the lightning, the advancing storm.

The falcon hangs in space for second after second, motionless, as if suspended on a thread, its wings, body, and spirit in perfect equilibrium with the streaming torrents of the air. Give your heart to the hawks, urged Robinson Jeffers. Okay, I thought, I'll do that. For this one splendid moment. Until the falcon sheers off on the wind and vanishes in storm and light.

Appealing as I find the idea of reincarnation, I must confess that it has a flaw: to wit, there is not a shred of evidence suggesting it might be true. The idea has nothing going for it but desire, the restless aspiration of the human mind. But when was aspiration ever intimidated by fact? Given a choice, I plan to be a long-winged fantailed bird next time around.

Which one? Vulture, eagle, hawk, falcon, crane, heron, wood ibis? Well, I believe I was a wood ibis once, back in the good old days of the Pleistocene epoch. And from what I already know of passion, violence, the intensity of the blood, I think I'll pass on eagle, hawk, or falcon this time. For a lifetime or two, or maybe three, I think I'll settle for the sedate career, serene and soaring, of the humble turkey buzzard. And if any falcon comes around making trouble I'll spit in his eye. Or hers. And contemplate this world we love from a silent and considerable height.

Of Protest

Rocky Flats, Colorado; November 1978

A canvas tepee straddled the railroad tracks, clearly obstructing passage. The railway—a spur—curved across a field of tawny grass and basaltic rocks toward a distant complex of buildings, towers and lights enclosed within a high-security fence topped with barbed wire, patrolled by armed guards. Occasional wisps of steam rose from the short stacks within the plant, fading out in the chilly blue as they drifted toward the rich brown haze of Denver, sixteen miles to the southeast. West of the railroad and the highway nearby stood the foothills of the Front Range of the Rocky Mountains.

A steady stream of truck and auto traffic moved on the highway, but few of the drivers of these vehicles paused to wonder at the strange sight of a wigwam erected across a railroad track. Mostly local people, they had grown accustomed to this oddity; the archaic tent had been standing here for most of the last six months.

Two flags and two young men attended this structure and the scatter of camping equipment around and within it. One flag was the blue, red and white of the United States; the other bore a golden sun on a field of green, representing—what? Some adventurous new nation in the human community? A nation within a nation? A gesture toward another form of independence? Aspen poles twenty feet tall carried the flags well above the peak of the tepee; the cool November breeze rolling down

316

from the mountains stirred both flags with separate but equal nonchalance.

One of the young fellows was a student at Denver University. He wore a wool shirt, a light blond beard, a shy but friendly smile—I failed to catch his name. The other looked like a pirate: bandana for a headband, gold earrings, black beard, skin darkened by sun and wind. He wore a green sweat shirt, baggy gray sweat pants, the canvas sneakers of a jogger, the fingerless wool gloves of a rock climber—or of a golfer. He admitted with a grin to a touch of Irish in his genes; his name was Patrick Malone.

Patrick Malone had been here, like the wigwam, for most of the previous six months. He said he planned to stay through the winter—blizzards, ice, subzero temperatures notwithstanding— until that quiet but industrial-looking installation at the end of the railway spur was shut down forever, or converted perhaps to the manufacture of something different—of solar heating devices, let us say, or skis, or mopeds, bicycles, plowshares.

An electric power line on wooden poles paralleled the railway and led into the factory. Wooden poles: it occurred to me that one resolute man with a chainsaw could put that place out of business for a short while, easily and quickly. Such a suggestion would not be welcome here; Malone and his friend were opposed both in principle and in practice to violence in any form. Even to moderate violence, technically restrained, tactically precise, against mere inanimate property.

They did not consider their wigwam on the tracks, barring the right-of-way near a sign that read U.S. PROPERTY NO TRESPASSING, to be a form of violence. Once a week, when the train came, the short train of specially designed armored cars marked FISSILE MATERIAL—RADIOACTIVE, Malone and helpers dismantled the tent and carried it out of the way (saving it from confiscation and the security forces from unnecessary paperwork). Then he and friends, a series of them totaling about two hundred so far, returned to the railway and sat on the tracks, offering only their bodies to the advancing engine. The train always halted, or had so far, and the people on the rails were taken away by the police, booked for trespass and obstruction of traffic, and jailed or released on their own recognizance.

This scene had been repeated more than twenty times since April 29, 1978, when some four thousand people, mostly from the cities of Denver and Boulder (nine miles to the north), gathered in a well-organized and peaceful assembly at the gates of the Rocky Flats nuclear weapons plant to make their feelings known to whoever, or whatever, might be in charge. There had been so far no fights, no bodily injuries of any kind on either side. Demonstrators, protestors, security guards, and the Jefferson County sheriff's deputies who made the actual arrests had all been on their best behavior. The world was not watching, but a small part of it had been here, including the local press.

After saying goodbye to Malone and his mate—they were now being visited, interviewed, and photographed by a German professor of American literature from the University of Hamburg—we attempted to enter the plant itself. We were turned back at the gate. The guards were polite but firm: No entry, they said, without a pass from Rockwell International Corporation, which manages the plant under contract with the U.S. Department of Energy and the Pentagon. What Rockwell makes here is no longer a secret, if it ever was, though it was only gradually revealed to the public after 1952, when the plant was established. Rockwell is making an essential component—the plutonium "trigger"—of what the government calls thermonuclear devices. Hydrogen bombs. The trigger, which itself is an atomic detonating device equivalent in explosive power to the atomic bombs dropped on Japan, is shipped from here to another factory near Amarillo, Texas, where the actual H-bombs are assembled.

Our government has been in this business, operating through various private corporations (Rockwell was preceded by Dow Chemical here at Rocky Flats), for thirty years. The total number of atomic and hydrogen bombs now available for use is a state secret; but everything leaks, eventually. Careful students of the matter, such as Daniel Ellsberg, estimate the size of the

American stockpile at something between eleven thousand and thirty thousand nuclear bombs. Since a few dozen of these weapons could obliterate most mammalian life from Dublin to Vladivostok, that should be, from a layman's point of view, a sufficient number. But production continues, a $1.7 billion annual business.

The government justifies continued production on the grounds that bombs made ten, twenty, and thirty years ago are no longer reliable or adequate, and that ever more sophisticated refinements in design and delivery make regular model changes desirable. Furthermore the Russians are doing the same thing. And the Chinese. And the English, and the French. And maybe the Israelis, the Indians, the South Africans, the Brazilians. All governments need enemies.

We have lived for so long under the umbrella of Mutual Assured Destruction (MAD) that perhaps we would feel uncomfortable, even defenseless, without it. It is certainly arguable that the threat of nuclear devastation has helped prevent a major war. When presidents and premiers, commissars and commissioners, generals and admirals are compelled to share the dangers of war with ordinary citizens and common soldiers, then we are all a little safer. We hope.

We drove on to the town of Golden, seat of Jefferson County, State of Colorado, where the trial of the railway trespassers was taking place. An arch across the main street proclaimed WELCOME TO GOLDEN—WHERE THE WEST BEGINS. (If so, this must also be where the East begins.) We found the courtroom packed, the proceedings under way, with thirty-one-year-old Judge Kim Goldberger presiding over his first criminal case.

Several days had already been spent in selecting the six-member jury, a touchy and difficult process, and in the presentation of its case by the prosecution, a much simpler affair. The defendants freely confessed to being present on the tracks at the time alleged, freely admitted their attempt to block rail traffic into the weapons plant. But they did not plead guilty; they pleaded not guilty, using as their defense an old Colorado "choice-of-evils" statute that allows the intentional commission of an illegal act when the purpose of such act is to prevent a greater harm or a greater crime. For example, the law allows you to violate speed limits when your purpose is to save a life, or to escape imminent danger.

Unfortunately for the defendants and their lawyers, the judge had ruled that only he, and not the jury, had the right to determine if the choice-of-evils defense was "applicable" in this instance. The defendants were obliged, therefore, to present their case without being heard by a jury of their peers; the jury had been excused, forbidden to hear the defense, read about it, or talk about it. Since trial by jury in criminal cases is supposed to be a constitutional right, the judge had already given the defense firm grounds for appeal to a higher court. Which *might* have been his purpose, since he had been quoted earlier as saying that the issues involved were too important to be settled in a county court. But as will be seen, Judge Goldberger would make no secret of his prejudgment of the defendants.

The defense went ahead with its case, jury or no jury, calling a number of experts to the stand to testify to the reality of radiation hazards imposed on the residents of Boulder, Denver, and environs by the Rocky Flats installation. One witness came from England, another from Georgia, another from California; the remainder were recruited locally. All traveled at their own expense and gave their testimony without monetary compensation.

The seven Denver attorneys working for the defense were doing the same thing; they had volunteered their time out of sympathy. The defendants, though presumed innocent until proved guilty, are not allowed under our system of justice any form of reimbursement for their loss of income or livelihood, even if they should finally be acquitted. The judge, meanwhile, and the prosecuting attorneys (including a couple of lawyers on loan from the U.S. Department of Energy) continued to receive their pay without interruption. Since the trial dragged on for eleven days, the defendants and their counsel were effectively punished even before the judge pronounced sentence. But nobody questions this way of doing things. Perhaps, in a rationalized society like ours, there is no better way. As Hegel concluded in his 457-page *Philosophy of History,* stealing a line from Leibniz, Whatever is—is right.

The defendants and their legal counsel did not appear to share my sense of the injustice already imposed on them. They were busily and happily engaged not so much in defending themselves as in prosecuting the adversary, putting on trial the Rocky Flats weapons plant itself, and by implication the Department of Energy, the Department of Defense, the U.S. government, the Russian government, the nuclear arms race, the freight train of history, the complacency and cowardice of us all in meekly accepting, like mice in a laboratory, the miserable nightmare that statesmen and scientists, industrialists and technologists have laid upon our lives, without our consent, and upon the lives of our descendants (if any) for thousands of years to come.

The first witness that I heard was Karl Z. Morgan, a professor at Georgia Tech of what is called "health physics." Dr. Morgan, age seventy-two, is an old-timer in the nuclear enterprise; he took part in the origins of the Manhattan Project, when the first atomic reactor was built under the stadium at the University of Chicago during World War II; he served for twenty years as director of safety operations at the nuclear laboratories at Oak Ridge, Tennessee, before returning to teaching. He has published many books and papers on the subject of radiation-induced illness and is considered to be one of the world's authorities on the subject.

In a soft, gentle voice, with a slight Southern accent, Dr. Morgan reviewed for us what should be familiar stuff by now: the invisible and insidious effects of low-level radiation, intangible to the senses, measurable only by instruments, but potentially fatal all the same, given sufficient exposure, to any organism unlucky enough to inhale or ingest even the most minute particles of plutonium or its derivative, americium. There is no such thing, he maintained, as a safe or "permissible" dose of internal radiation; the slightest quantity can be enough, in a susceptible human, to cause some form of cancer.

He is not, said Dr. Morgan, against nuclear power, nor would he support unilateral nuclear disarmament; but he thinks present safety standards are dangerously inadequate. Accidents are inevitable, he said, given human fallibility, and he mentioned (over objections from the county attorney) the three deaths at Los Alamos and the three at Idaho Falls that resulted from nuclear mishaps. People living near or downwind of Rocky Flats are subject to a 3 to 6 percent greater risk than those in other areas; he accused the Environmental Protection Agency of failure to enforce uniformly even its present inadequate safety standards; the Rocky Flats installation should never have been built so close to a city, and should be shut down or relocated as soon as possible, "preferably deep inside a mountain."

Did he think the dangers posed by Rocky Flats justified the demonstrations, protests, and railway sit-ins staged by the defendants? Since ordinary political means have so far failed to produce the needed changes (Colorado's governor and Congressional delegation have been advocating removal of the Rocky Flats plant for years), Dr. Morgan thought that yes, any nonviolent action that served to publicize the problem was justified—even though, he added, the railway trespass would not "miraculously" decontaminate the estimated eleven thousand acres stretching from the plant grounds toward Denver that were already poisoned by plutonium leakage from waste-storage barrels.

Dr. Morgan's testimony required three hours for its detailed elaboration. Two more days of similar testimony by other defense witnesses followed. Dr. Alice Stewart from Oxford University, an epidemiologist by trade, and Dr. John W. Gofman of the University of California at Berkeley, a specialist in physical chemistry and, like Dr. Stewart, an M.D., reinforced Dr. Morgan's fears of the long-range effects of nuclear contamination in the Denver area. "Protest is always justified," said Gofman, "when it is the only means to make a deaf government listen."

Local scientists from the University of Colorado, the Colorado Department of Health, and the Atmospheric Research Center appeared on the stand to back up Drs. Morgan, Stewart, and Gofman. Dr. Anthony Robbins testified that he had "serious concerns as to whether one could believe or trust the statements of the Department of Energy" about radioactive emissions at the plant. Dr. Edward Martell, a nuclear chemist, said that Rocky Flats officials had "resisted suggestions" that they make tests for nuclear contamination in the soil beyond the plant boundaries. Therefore Dr. Martell made the tests himself and found, in Jefferson County and the Denver area, concentrations of plutonium—"hot spots"—more than 250 times greater than normal background levels of radiation.

Dr. John Cobb, a member of a governor's task force appointed to investigate the safety of the plant, said that he had made sixteen recommendations for improving safety operations, but that none, so far as he had been able to find out, were put into effect. As for nuclear power in general, Dr. Cobb said that he was in favor of it but only if reactors were confined to a safe distance from human habitation, "about 93 million miles away . . . on the sun."

Like the other witnesses and most of the defendants, Cobb opposed unilateral nuclear disarmament, given the present state of international affairs, but did think it would be worthwhile, from the point of view of human survival, for the U.S. government to take a significant initial step toward such disarmament; world opinion, he felt, as well as its own best interests, would compel the Russian government to follow. The present course, he said, is one of premeditated suicide.

The trial was adjourned for four days of official Thanksgiving. After the recess some of the defendants were allowed, through a constant barrage of united objections by the judge and prosecution, to make their statements directly to the three men and three women of the jury. Said Roy Young, age thirty, a Boulder geologist: "I was on those tracks not to commit trespass but to prevent random murder on the population of metropolitan Denver." [Objection, your honor! Objection sustained.] "And if I thought," continued Young, "that by staying on those tracks . . . I could close that plant tomorrow, I would be willing to stay there for the rest of my life." [Objection! Sustained.]

Said Nancy Doub, age forty, housewife and child-care worker from Boulder, who with her seventeen-year-old daughter had been arrested on the night of May 8: "It was a pretty far-out thing. I'm not accustomed to going out at night in two feet of snow to stop a railroad train." They waited two hours for the train to emerge from the plant. "When we saw the light we walked up the tracks together . . . singing 'We Shall Not Be Moved.'" [Objection! Sustained.]

Skye Kerr, age twenty-three, a registered nurse and student at the University of Colorado, said that she had received her training at Boston Children's Hospital and was familiar with the effects of radiation-caused cancer and leukemia. She said, "There were three-year-old children with their hair falling out. They were getting sick from the medicine they were taking and didn't understand." [Objection! Sustained.] She said, "The children keel over and die. They gush out blood from all over." [Objection! Objection! Inciting sympathy in the jury, Your Honor! Sustained.] "It happens years later. You can't see or feel or touch radiation, but it's as real as a gun." [Objection! Sustained.] "I felt the only thing I could do . . . was to bodily put myself on the tracks. I knew that laws much, much higher [than trespass] were being broken." [Objection! Sustained.] What kind of laws? she was asked. "Laws of human—of life. You know—violations of rights you have as a human being." [Objection! Objection sustained.]

The defense rested its case a day later, after a summation by chief defense attorney Edward H. Sherman that appealed to the jury as "the conscience of the community." (The ancient and traditional role, in Anglo-Saxon law, of any jury.) The prosecuting attorney, Steve Cantrell, summed up his argument by saying that this was "a case of simple trespass. We are not here to change the policy of the U.S. government. . . ."

The judge read his instructions to the jury. It took him twenty minutes to guide—or delimit—their deliberations. He reminded the jury that he had ruled as irrelevant the choice-of-evils defense, as well as a defense based on the First Amendment right to assemble peacefully for redress of grievances. The members of the jury were to disregard "emotional appeals" and consider only, and nothing but, the formal charges of obstruction of traffic on a public right-of-way and trespass against U.S. government property.

The jury went into deep seclusion. It emerged five hours later to confess inability to reach a decision. The judge excused the jury for the night but put it back to work next morning. After another five hours, the jury announced its verdict: All defendants guilty of trespass, innocent of obstructing traffic.

The jurors explained that though in sympathy with the defendants, they could not, under the judge's instructions, acquit them of the trespassing charge. One juror wrote a note to the defendants: "My support and prayers are with you all." Another, Diana Holman, said to defendant Jack Joppa, "We support you and your cause." Another juror tried to explain her decision to reporters, faltered in midsentence, left the courtroom weeping.

The judge looked glum and a little bored. The defense attorneys looked weary, sad, disappointed, the prosecuting attorneys tired and exasperated.

Both sides claimed a moral victory but the divided verdict satisfied no one. No one, that is, but the defendants and their supporters; they alone seemed pleased by the results of the trial—not jubilant, but serenely happy. Linking hands and arms they sang "We Shall Overcome," about seventy of them there in the crowded little courtroom, while the flashbulbs flashed, the high-intensity video lights glared, the cameras clicked and clashed.

The judge set a later date for sentencing; penalties up to six months in jail and/or a fine of $500 were possible. The defense attorneys announced, as expected, their plans for appeal to a higher court.

I spoke briefly with a few of the defendants, including Daniel

Ellsberg, who now lives in San Francisco and makes his living, he told me, as a writer and lecturer, devoting most of his efforts to the antinuclear crusade. I met Steve Sterns and Ellen Klaver, both students at the University of Colorado; the latter supports herself by working as a seasonal ranger with the National Park Service. I met Peter Ediger, about age fifty I would guess, who is the minister of the Mennonite Church in nearby Arvada, another Denver suburb.

The defendants impressed me not so much with what they had to say as with their manner. They are happy people, these crusaders, at ease with themselves and with others, radiant with conviction, liberated by their own volition from the tedious routine and passive acquiescence in which most of us endure our brief, half-lived, half-lives. One single act of defiance against power, against the State that seems omnipotent but is not, transforms and transfigures the human personality. At least for a time. For a while. Perhaps that is enough.

I had come to the Rocky Flats affair in a state of mind vaguely sympathetic with the protesters, but basically skeptical, burdened by the resigned cynicism that passes for wisdom in contemporary America. Like some people I know, I could sometimes settle for the belief that our most serious problems are finding a place to park the car, the ever-rising costs of gasoline and beefsteak, and the nagging demands of the poor, the old, the disinherited.

Now I felt a guilty envy of the protesters, of those who actually act, and a little faint glow of hope—perhaps something fundamental might yet be changed in the nature of our lives. Crusaders for virtue are an awkward embarrassment to any society; they force us to make choices; either side with them, which is difficult and dangerous, or condemn them, which leads to self-betrayal.

While the glow lasted, one of the defendants—Robert Godfrey, transplanted Englishman, mountaineer, filmmaker, writer—and I walked down the streets of Golden (golden Colorado!) to the Coors Brewery where visitors are always welcome for the free beer. We had been denied entrance to the Rocky

Flats nuclear-weapons plant; here we were admitted by cheerful ladies wearing red-and-white uniforms and genuine simulated Disneyland smiles. Which was gracious of the Coors Corporation, I thought; people like Godfrey and myself have never felt or said anything nice about Adolph Coors and Company—a highly influential right-wing force in Rocky Mountain and now national politics.

We took the official "short" tour of the plant, direct from front door to free-beer dispensary, and sampled the product, generously offered, liberally taken. If we could not celebrate exactly a victory, then—as César Chavez has said—we would celebrate our defeat. The beer tasted fine, I am happy to report, despite what seemed to me a strange Day-Glo phosphorescence in the foaming head.

Yes, I had come by now to imagine particles of plutonium 239 and americium 241 everywhere I looked, floating on the air, settling on my shoulders like microscopic flecks of dandruff, lodging in my lungs, where they—the particles—could carry on, undisturbed, their peculiar half-life of twenty-four thousand years. Nevertheless we drank the beer.

Drank the beer and carried on. Driving home to Boulder that evening, Godfrey and I were happy to see Patrick Malone and his wigwam, flags flying, still firmly and symbolically obstructing traffic on the nuclear railroad. Can one man derail a train with nothing but his will? Can a few thousand human beings armed with nothing but audacity and purpose bring to a halt the mighty freight train of government, industry, power, war, that overwhelming vision of a future charged by pride and ambition?

The only answer we know is the most comforting and terrifying of answers: anything is possible.

Author's Note: The defendants received six-month suspended sentences. Patrick Malone maintained his stand, violating probation, and served three months of a six-month jail sentence before friends paid his fine. In April of the following year fifteen thousand people took part in the protest at Rocky Flats. The nuclear-weapons plant remains in operation.

My Friend Debris

We met one evening in the streets of Santa Fe (Holy Faith!), New Mexico, in the springtime of 1959. A good year that one, excelled—at least in my experience—only by 1960 and each succeeding year. My friend Debris was staggering down Palace Avenue, supported on the arms of an artistic woman named Rini Templeton, whom I had met a short time previously in the editorial offices of a Taos newspaper called *El Crepúsculo de la Libertad.* I had not yet learned how that name was translated into American but I did know that I was supposed to be the paper's editor-in-chief. As proof of my newfound dignity I carried in an inside pocket of my 1952 Sears Roebuck wino jacket (burgundy corduroy—threads of the king) a bona fide paycheck for *one hundred dollars.* A powerful sum of money in those subbohemian, underground-beatnik days. And all for only one week's work.

How this came about is a complicated story of confusion, misunderstanding, mistaken identity, extravagant hopes, exaggerated credentials, and general good will. One day I was a student of classical philosophy subsisting on Cheez-Its in a basement pad in the undergrad ghettos of Albuquerque; a week later I was dining on rack of lamb *bouquetierre* and rice pilaf and Châteauneuf-du-Pape or something at a five-star restaurant in Taos—I forget the name of the joint—where I paid the tab by scribbling my signature on a chit and walking out with a fat flaming cigar. It's quite true, what I'd always heard: when you're rich and important you don't need money. You never touch it.

One hundred dollars a week!

I sang, as I walked along, to the tune of "Red Flag" and "O Tannenbaum," an old song of the revolution, *viz.*,

> The working class
> Can kiss my ass,
> I've got the fore-
> man's job at last!

As for Taos, New Mexico, there is little that need be added to the volumes already available on the subject. Nabokov described the town adequately in a letter to Edmund Wilson: ". . . a dismal place inhabited by third-rate artists and old faded pansies." Nabokov was thinking of painters, not writers, but Taos and New Mexico as a whole suffered then and suffer still, despite pretensions, from a conspicuous lack of first-rate literary artists. D. H. Lawrence had died and been cremated nearly three decades earlier, and not in New Mexico; the gaseous essence of his mortal envelope had now become mere traces in the smog nuisance over southern France. John Nichols was a boy in New York City. William Eastlake, hidden from the world on his rancho near the village of Cuba, was more a part of Indian Country than of the "Land of Enchantment." And he would not stay. Robert Creeley was another transient. Judson Crews would soon depart for Africa. Willa Cather was in Heaven, where she had always wanted to be. And so—who was left? Only Frank Waters, the Hopi transcendentalist.

Anyway, this is the story of my friend Debris. He was staggering, as I've said, marching to a drummer all his own, down the avenue and into the Plaza, propped up none too steadily by our mutual friend Rini Templeton. He seemed to be singing, a song of which I caught only the refrain, repeated with dogmatic insistence:

> *Nous allons, nous allons,*
> *Nous allons sur la motif . . .*

If I heard aright. Rini introduced us. "This is John De Puy," she said, pronouncing his name *duh-pwee* in the correct French manner.

"Debris?"

"De *Puy*," she repeated. "Of the well."

The tall thin fragile-looking fellow glared at me, his eyes enormous, intense, half demented, behind the thick lenses of his spectacles. His hair was bushy, curly, black, his mustache full and drooping in the style of Emiliano Zapata. Or of Bartolomeo Vanzetti. He could have passed for an anarchistic organ-grinder. Only the monkey was lacking, and the tin cup. Perhaps the monkey was on his back; I suspected more than alcohol at work here. But the drug, as I would eventually understand, was not chemical but alchemical: the alkaloids of genius.

"My name is Del Poggio," he said in deep and somber tones, "and my people come from the mountains."

"From the cistern," said Rini, hugging him tightly around his lean waist. "They crawled out of a cistern."

I held out my hand. He considered for a moment, then allowed me to shake his hand. "I've heard of you," I said. "You're the artist, right?"

"The man, the artist, the failure," he corrected.

"He calls himself an artist," Rini said, "but right now he couldn't draw a sober breath."

"It is true that I am drunk," De Puy said, "but it is not true that I am always drunk. We will meet again, Abbey. Beware."

I watched them wobble past the Palace of the Governors, arm in arm, mutually supportive, bound for another bar en route to an Odetta concert. That Rini Templeton was a fine figure of a woman—still is—but De Puy looked too thin, almost emaciated; inside his stiff new Levi Strauss blue jeans there appeared to be no hams at all. No buttocks. The man would never be popular in Santa Fe. Nor get far in the art world. I assumed that I would never see him again.

But I encountered them both once more, that very evening, at the concert. I too was in love with Odetta—beautiful and magnificent black goddess, planted solid as a tree on stage, belting out her freedom songs with a power that made the house rock. I found De Puy backstage afterwards, on hands and knees among the crowd that pressed upon the singer. Like me he desired only to kiss the hem of Odetta's garment, maybe lift it a little.

In the twenty-two years that have since lapsed, relapsed, prolapsed and collapsed between us, Debris and I have shared many adventures and some misadventures, helping each other through the anxieties of fatherhood, the joys of marriage, the despair of separation and divorce, the deep purple funk of creative inertia. And survived. And thrived. We have both been very lucky. But we earned it.

We have hiked through the Maze together. The little maze and the big maze. We have circumambulated Navajo Mountain—navel of the universe—and camped together under its slickrock buttresses. We have climbed to the shoulders of Wilson Peak, leaving the summit untouched, out of natural piety. We have blundered through the cactus forests of Arizona and penetrated to the secret heart of the canyonlands. We have dropped off North Rim down to Thunder River, lain in the shade of limestone ledges while the sun roared like a lion three feet away, and discussed the mystery of the death of a father, of a wife—that inexplicable *disappearance.*

We have staggered together, like him and Rini, down the icy winter streets of Santa Fe, of Telluride, of Hoboken and Manhattan—yes, Manhattan, where Debris hammered on the locked doors of Saint Patrick's Cathedral at two in the morning, demanding admittance. God would not let us in. Can't blame Him. Two kindly policemen led us away, commandeered a taxi, sent us home. Home to Moab, Utah. To Oracle, Arizona. To Ojo Caliente (Hot Eye), and Jemez Springs, New Mexico.

I saw my friend Debris, enraged, overturn a punchbowl in the Seligman Galleries, New York, and smash it against the wall, and once I saw him dip a survey pole in gasoline and hurl it like a spear, flaming, from the verge of Dead Horse Point above the

Colorado River, down into darkness a thousand feet below. As a matter of course, like good sagebrush patriots, we have burned or leveled innumerable billboards together, and sanded and sugared a goodly number of earthmovers, ore trucks, front-end loaders and Caterpillar bulldozers. Naturally.

And we have quarreled, and lied, and thieved from each other when necessary: he sold my best deer rifle for an airline ticket to Zurich, whence his wife had fled; in retaliation, when I discovered the loss, I sold his bedroom furniture to a dealer in Distressed Freight, turning a fair profit. Those were dark days in Santa Fe, and long ago, never to return.

I have touched upon certain high points, making our long friendship seem, perhaps, more bright and merry than it actually was. In truth when we are together now we spend half our time semisodden with cheap American beer, reviewing the past and previewing the future in ever more flattering light, and the other half engaged in our plodding, furtive, solitary labors, Debris at his sketchbook or easel, me at my last where I am cobbling a shoe of wood *(le sabotage)* that will kick down all doors from all jambs forever.

My friend Debris looks today more like a sheepherder than an organ-grinder, more like Einstein than Zapata. He is and appears part Basque, part Cretan, part stargazer, wholly a mystic. The rich curly dark hair has turned gray (like my beard) and his face is the lined, browned, wind-burned face of a man who has spent at least half of his fifty-odd years in the out-of-doors. Where we are happiest. Blessed with a hyperactive metabolism, Debris has never put on weight, despite the fact that he drinks beer from morning to night, every day, a continuous "transfusion" as he calls it, and eats with the gusto of a hungry wolf, moaning and groaning over his feed like a man in the throes of love. He remains as skinny and scrawny, as wiry and fibrous and hard as he was in the days of our youth.

He loves to eat. He loves to drink. He loves to cook. An insomniac, he rises always before the dawn, lights his Coleman lantern, starts the fire, brews a powerful Earl Grey tea loaded with honey and milk. He stumbles about camp in the dark, mumbling and chanting, comes presently to me and my lady with a hot steaming mug in each fist, a grin full of teeth below the Zapatista mustache. Salmon-colored clouds float on the east. Stars all over the west. We sit up naked in our ziplock sleeping-together bag.

"Drink," says the grin; "hot tea."

"It's early, Debris."

"Drink!" He thrusts the mugs into our hands, then weaves back to the campfire, there to prepare the breakfast omelets—huge mucoid globs of chicken embryo quivering with potency denied, browned and folded over the slime of melted cheese, the hot viscous kelplike green chiles, the sliced and sautéed onions, the reek of garlic and garlic salt. . . .

"My God, Debris, too much garlic."

"There can never be too much garlic."

"I hate garlic, you goddamned Frog."

"Don't whine and snivel at me, you puking Presbyterian. Eat!"

De Puy's cooking, like his art, reminds me of Poe at his most Byronic: "Of the glory that was Greece/ And the garlic that was Rome."

His wife Tina Johnson emerges from the back of their pickup camper, approaches us through *el crepúsculo,* the twilight, of our mountain morning. She is a plump and pretty woman, brown and fair and Scandinavian, feisty but sweet, a total female, and about twenty years younger than Debris. She is his fifth wife. His fifth and *final* wife, says Tina, and hopefully John agrees.

She had come to him several years before as a student and apprentice from Evergreen College in Washington, and stayed, graduating into matrimony with honors and distinction. She is a crafty artisan, a maker of jewelry that she sells from New York to Scottsdale. She is dressed this morning like a gypsy in full skirt, flowered blouse, a scarlet kerchief on her head and golden hoops dangling from her pierced ears. She wears sandals. She plays the guitar. She smokes a pipe, farts when she feels like it, and swears like a man. A good honest woman.

I like her, and I usually don't approve of my friend's wives. His others had been too political, constantly getting poor John

into trouble with their Red Brigades, Fidelismo, Maoist Mau
Mau, Socialist Workers and Socialist Labor and Weathermen
Underground. Distracting him from his duty, which is to paint
pictures, Tina is not like that. She is a natural anarchist like us,
like all genteel, sensible, petit-bourgeois people in these days of
total institutions and global power. (Our highest criminal ambition is to rob the World Bank. Give the money to the deserving
poor, to you and me and Muzzie Schwartz down there on the
street peddling his roasted chestnuts. Let's hear no more of this.)

Not only does Debris's wife look gypsylike, so does his summer
home. He owns twenty acres on a wooded mesa in southeast
Utah. From the center of his place you can see mountains and
marvels in all directions: the Blue Mountains close by on the
northwest, the San Juans to the east in Colorado, Sleeping Ute
Mountain, Shiprock and the Chuskas and Monument Valley in
the Navajo Nation, Comb Ridge and Cedar Mesa and the Bear's
Ear Buttes to the west and southwest. On a clear day you can see
all the way to Navajo Mountain, a hundred miles by line of sight.

For five years De Puy has been planning to build a cabin here,
an A-frame on stilts, but so far he has built nothing substantial.
The kitchen is a large juniper tree with ramadalike shelter attached, from the struts and spars and limbs of which hang skil-
lets, pots, towels, rags, mirror, waterbags, canteens, shovel, ax,
bucksaw, and other tools. We eat breakfast on a government-
surplus picnic table. John and Tina sleep in their camper-truck,
a veteran GMC. The guesthouse is a tent. When in residence
here they do their work in a battered housetrailer that Debris
had hauled in a couple of years previously.

This housetrailer—an immobile home—is old and drafty, infested with mice, hooked up to nothing; there is no plumbing or
electricity. Not needed. The trailer is jacked up on cinderblocks
but not properly leveled. It sags to the east. To walk inside is like
entering on the deck of a listing boat.

Here in this listing trailerhouse, during the summer months,
Tina manufactures her jewelry and my friend Du Puy paints his
paintings. His studio is small but well lighted, well ventilated. He
has room for a stack of stretched canvases, a shelf of books, a

worktable, the easel and the work-in-progress. There are post-
ers, drawings, and photographs tacked to the wall—photos of
friends, of natural scenes, and one of the artist himself posed
dramatically, with pipe and walking stick and slouch hat, before
a sunset sky. The only concession to vanity.

And what do we see on the easel? A window. An opening
through a wall. In a moment I will explain.

Most of the year, eight or nine months, Debris and his wife
spend in their adobe home near Jemez Springs in the high country of New Mexico. Harsh country—too hot in summer, cold in
winter. Debris hauls and cuts a lot of firewood. And every morning, all year around, he brews his black, bitter tea. He smokes a
pipe continuously, makes his own jerky, and cooks about half the
time over an open fire. He drinks too much—not only beer but
whatever's available with an appreciable alcoholic content.
Blackberry brandy for chilly nights.

The effect of these incontinent habits has been, through the
decades and so far, to keep my friend well preserved, pickled in
alcohol, tobacco, woodsmoke, tannic acid, vitamin C, and old
underwear, inside and out. He walks with a long and loping
stride, uphill and downhill, through brush and over rocks, like a
man accustomed to exploring, prospecting, searching. He expects to live for about 140 years—"indefinitely."

What he is seeking and what he has found appears in the
powerful, brooding and mystical art that has been his lifework.
His graphics and oil paintings represent clearly, recognizably,
the landscape of the American Southwest—mountains, mesas,
volcanoes, abysmal gorges and gleaming rivers, the stillness of
the desert under vast moons and domineering suns. But De
Puy's landscape is not the landscape we see with routine eyes or
can record by camera. He paints a hallucinated, magical, sometimes fearsome world—not the world that we think we see but
the one, he declares, that is really there. A world of terror as well
as beauty—the beauty that lies beyond the ordinary limits of
human experience, that forms the basis of experience, the
ground of being.

Obscure, pompous, pretentious words. I'm not sure what they

mean. One would prefer to be precise and clear. But there is something in the art of John De Puy, as there is in a mountain or butte or canyon itself, that defies the precision and clarity of simple descriptive language. Whatever we can find to say about a desert mountain or a De Puy painting, there is always something more, dim but ominously *present,* which cannot be said.

It will not suffice to dismiss this essential mystery as mere romanticism. The Romantics, after all, in art, music, poetry, philosophy, in action and in life, were onto something. Something real. Something as real as rock and sun and the human mind. Thus they were and they remain—necessary. There is no "mere" about it.

Bloated rhetoric, I agree. A breezy effort at explanation. "Let Being be," said Martin Heidegger, *das Denker Kraut,* in a mere seventeen volumes. Exactly. "Whereof one cannot speak, thereof one must be silent," said Ludwig Wittgenstein in one sentence. Precisely. When Beethoven was asked to explain the meaning of one of his sonatas, he simply sat down at the piano and played it through again.

The facts in the case of J. Debris, as Poe would put it, are as follows:

Born in New Jersey during the Coolidge-Hoover era, he studied anthropology with Ruth Benedict at Columbia University; these studies brought him to the Southwest and into contact with the landforms and ancient cultures of our region. The Korean War interrupted this phase of his development. De Puy is a Navy veteran of World War II and had been enlisted (by mistake, he says) in the naval reserve. When he was called up for service in Korea he went over the hill—Absent Without Leave. At the time he believed he was Thoreau, and lived on the Navajo reservation, working at a trading post. When he was caught and tried, his military lawyer pleaded temporary insanity for him. The Navy locked him up in a psychiatric prison.

Debris spent six months rattling bars and chanting "More guns. Less butter. Man is made for war, woman for procreation." The Navy gave him a medical discharge and turned him loose; the government was glad to get off so easy. Debris took advantage of his new freedom to study art and philosophy for a year at Oxford, then returned to New York for a year of Action Painting with Hans Hofmann and the push and pull school. When he'd had enough of that he came home to the West for good.

Except for journeys to France, Switzerland, Greece and Crete, he has lived and worked ever since in the highlands of New Mexico and Utah. God's country—and the artist's. Thirty years of hectic marriages, four children, two deaths in the family, troubles and accidents, have not diminished his appetite for love, nature, life. Nor has the relative obscurity of his professional career—he makes little effort to show or promote his work—dimmed his enthusiasm for the craft and the passion of his art. He continues to paint as steadily, earnestly, furiously as before, with an ever-growing boldness and simplicity. Not so much for the glory of it—glory is fleeting—as for the joy in the act itself and for the satisfaction in the object created.

How would I place De Puy in the contemporary art scene? He belongs, I suppose, to the school called Expressionism, or to what I would call romantic naturalism, in the tradition of El Greco, Goya, Van Gogh, Nolde, Dove, Clyfford Still, Georgia O'Keeffe. And no doubt others. But in my opinion John De Puy belongs to no school but his own. In my opinion he is the best landscape painter now at work in these United States. I never tire of looking at his pictures. They have a liberating quality. They make a window in the wall of our modern techno-industrial workhouse, a window that leads the eye and the heart and the mind through the wall and far out into the freedom of the old and original world. They take us back to where we came from long ago. Back to where we took the wrong fork in the road.

My friend is not only a great painter of romantic landscapes but also a maker of superior jerky. In return for my recipes for Voluntary Poverty Pinto Bean Sludge and R. K. Stew, he gives me his for *Jerky Supreme à la Debris®:*

Take five pounds frozen round steak or brisket, slice into thin (⅛-inch) strips. Marinate for 12 hours in a mixture of wine vinegar, Worcestershire sauce, olive oil, red chili powder, salt, garlic salt *(mais oui!)* and beer. (Heineken's will do.) (Or Black Swan.) Pin to a line in hot sun, if in an arid climate, for about twenty-four hours or until done, or dry in an oven for eight to twelve hours 200°F.; leave the oven door open about one inch to allow circulation of air. Remove. Cool. Place in pack. Place pack on back. March twenty miles into wilderness. Open pack. *Mangez!*

For the discriminating gourmet, Debris offers his jerky stew:

In pot or Dutch oven, dump onions, green peppers, potatoes (I prefer turnips myself—I like that iron and earthy flavor), carrots, chopped celery, chili, garlic, a pound or two or three of Jerky Supreme à la Debris,® a bottle or two of red wine, and basil, oregano, more garlic, more chili, more wine, and more what have you, what the hell, I've forgotten the exact amounts or what ingredients, it all comes out fine in the end, cook until ready, eat. Will feed five hungry storm troopers or two starving artists.

Debris is willing to grant the authenticity of my concern with eating, but has somehow gotten the impression that I am not seriously interested in the art of cookery. He listens, therefore, with feigned attention at best, with impatience, with visible disinterest, as I sketch out my culinary inventions. To wit:

Voluntary Poverty Hardcase Survival Pinto Bean Sludge®

1. Take one fifty-lb sack Dipstick County pinto beans. Remove cockleburs, stones, horseshit, ants, lizards, etc. Wash in cold clear crick water. Soak twenty-four hours in cast-iron kettle or earthenware pot. (DO NOT USE TEFLON, ALUMININUM, OR PYREX. THIS WARNING CANNOT BE OVERSTRESSED.)

2. Place kettle or pot with beans on low fire, simmer for twenty-four hours. (DO NOT POUR OFF WATER IN WHICH BEANS HAVE SOAKED. VERY IMPORTANT.) Fire must be of juniper, piñon pine, scrub oak, mesquite, or ironwood. Other fuels may tend to modify or denigrate the subtle flavor and delicate bouquet of Pinto Bean Sludge.

3. DO NOT BOIL. Add water when necessary.

4. Stir gently from time to time with wooden spoon.

5. After simmering, add one gallon green chiles. Stir gently. Avoid bruising beans. Add one-half quart pure natural sea salt. During following twelve hours stir frequently and add additional flavoring as desired, such as, for example, ham hocks. Or bacon rinds. Or saltpork, corncobs, kidney stones, jungle boots, tennis shoes, jockstraps, cinch straps, whatnot, old saddle blanket, use your own judgment. Simmer additional twenty-four hours.

6. Ladle as many servings as desired from pot but do not remove pot from fire. Allow to simmer continuously through following days and weeks, or until contents totally consumed. Stir from time to time, gently, when in vicinity. (DO NOT ABUSE BEANS.)

7. Serve Voluntary Poverty Hardcase Survival Pinto Bean Sludge® on small flat rocks that have been warmed in sun. If flat rocks not available, any convenient fairly level surface will do. Plates may be used, if obtainable. (WEDGEWOOD ONLY, PLEASE!) After serving, slather beans generously with *salsa*, ketchup, or barbecue sauce. Garnish with sprigs of fresh sagebrush. (Your guests will be amused and pleased.)

8. One cauldron of Pinto Bean Sludge, as specified above, will feed one starving artist for approximately two weeks. A grain supplement, such as rice, wheat, or maize, is needed for full protein complement.

9. The philosopher Pythagoras declared flatulence incompatible with thought and meditation. For this reason he forbade the eating of beans in his ashram. We have found, however, that thorough cooking ameliorates the condition, and custom (or solitude) alleviates the social embarrassment.

Second recipe:

Arizona Highways R.[1] K.[2] Stew®

½ cup rattlesnake grease à la blacktop
2 lbs sun-dried skunk (from the middle of the road)
¼ cup jackrabbit blood (dehydrated)
2 lbs squashed cottontail bunny
2 lbs flattened chipmunk (with tread marks)
1½ lbs macerated ground squirrel
1½ lbs laminated kangaroo rat
2 lbs elongated bull snake
2 lbs mashed house cat
2 lbs smashed dog à la asphalt
etc., etc., etc.

---

[1] road   [2] kill

We are visiting a bar in the town of Garlic (a.k.a. Ajo), Arizona. The bar is full of locals, mostly citizens of the Mexican and Papago Indian preference. My friend is dancing. John has approached several of the Papago ladies—short stout barrel-shaped women with cheerful brown faces and long rich lovely hair so black it looks blue—but they have all turned him down, laughing. Even the fattest of them, who looks like the Venus of Willendorf, has declined his courteous invitation. Therefore my friend Debris, untroubled, dances alone.

He dances like Zorba the Greek, like Anthony Quinn, in the middle of the empty floor, hands clasped behind his back, old pipe smoking in his mouth, the decayed and rotten slouch hat on his head. The jukebox is playing *Mi Corazón es su Corazón* by Gabriel Cruz y sus Conjuntos. Ranchero music—guitars and violins and trumpets. A barbarous racket. Debris dances solemnly forward, then back, twirls, spreads his arms like wings and turns his face to the ceiling. Eyes closed, dancing, he flies, he soars, he sails like an eagle across the empyrean of his soul. Alone in the universe, he makes it all his own. No one but me pays him any heed. Just another gringo drunk. But what a beautiful, happy, ontological gringo drunk. Only one pitcher of beer—and God entered his soul.

We drive into the desert beyond Garlic, beyond Why, beyond the ghost town of Pourquoi Non, beyond the far western borders of Hedgehog Cactus National Park where I had once been employed, for three elegant winters, as a patrol ranger. Under the moon we pass Carrico Peak, the Halcoss Range, the Bilhoy Range, past warning signs lettered in red on white, riddled with bullet holes, where we enter the Gunnery Range. This is the bleakest wasteland east or west of the Empty Quarter, a gaunt and spectral landscape littered with .50-caliber machine-gun shells, 88-mm cannon shells, unexploded rockets, and aerial tow targets stuck nose-down in the sand like twelve-foot arrowheads. Nobody lives here but the diamondback, the fatal coral snake, the Gila monster, the tarantula and the scorpion, and us, from time to time. Debris and I love the place. God loves it. The Air

Force loves it. And nobody else I know of but a Green Beret named Douglas Heiduk, who discovered it years ago.

The dirt road becomes impassable, a torture track of sand traps and volcanic rocks with flint-sharp edges, petering out in prehistoric Indian paths. A tribe called the Sand Papagos haunted the region until a century ago, lurking about the few known waterholes, ambushing bighorn sheep, Spanish missionaries, gold seekers, and other pioneers, and eating them. The one road through this desert, long since abandoned, was called the Vulture's Highway.

We stop the truck, shut off the motor, get out and vomit. Feeling better we open another jug. My friend Debris hurls an empty bottle at the stars and bellows through the silence, *Chinga los cosmos!*

Nobody answers. Far to the north we can see flares, bright as molten magnesium, floating down across the sky. We hear the mutter of gunnery, like distant thunder. It's only the Air Force, hunting the last of the Sand Papagos. Something to do on a Monday night. Watching those eerie lights, Debris crosses himself and recites an introit, "*Dominus vobiscum et tu spiritu, sancto oremus, pace . . . pace . . . pace. . . .*"

Once an R. C. always an R. C. His mother was Irish, her family name Early. He'd been an altar boy, of course, long ago and far away, in another country. (New Jersey.) Although he worships at an older and grander altar now De Puy expects to end up, as they all do, back in the arms of the Mother Church. Not by choice but because he feels he will have no choice. Frankly he wants to live—to exist—to *be*—forever.

Why?

Out of spite.

You owe the earth a body.

But not my soul.

I seem to hear Gregorian chants in the distance, coming from far beyond and above the desert mountains. Sound of the *Dies Irae.* I shiver in the chill night, the fantasy passes. We build our ritual little fire of mesquite twigs, spread out bedrolls on the ground, contemplate the flames. The Air Force goes to bed. The silence becomes complete.

But forever? I say. That's a long time.

Only an instant, says De Puy.

I fall asleep, by slow degrees, while my friend puffs on his pipe and explains to me the peculiarities of his quaint Roman religion. He talks; I dream.

I dream of a country church in Appalachia, painted white, shaded by giant oaks. There is a graveyard on the hillside nearby, most of the headstones at least a century old. Some of the graves are marked with rusted iron stars and standards that carry the shafts of tiny faded American flags. The stars bear the initials G.A.R.—Grand Army of the Republic. Roots and branches of the family tree. My three brothers and I are marching through the woods, rifles on our shoulders. It seems to be autumn; the dead leaves rattle beneath our feet. We march swiftly, easily, without effort, without fear, toward a joyously desired but unimaginable fulfillment. There are other men with us, ahead, behind, on both sides. We all march easily, swiftly, without effort, without speaking, toward the lights that glimmer off and on, like summer lightning, beyond the trees, beyond the dark ridge ahead. No one speaks. We move swiftly, easily . . .

De Puy is bustling about in the gloom, mumbling and grumbling, making the tea. Stars crowded over the west, opaline clouds on the east. One bird cheeps in the bush. The hackberry bush that grows by the dry wash, by the arroyo that snakes across the desert. I sit up in my sleeping bag, reach for my shirt and leather vest—the air is cold. Debris comes with the steaming mug, the maniacal grin, his mad eyes gleaming behind the glasses.

"*Allons-nous,*" he snarls.

"No!"

"But yes!"

"But for chrissake, Debris, it's still dark."

He shoves the mug of hot tea into my hand and points over

my shoulder toward the east. "Rosy fingers." He indicates the jagged pinnacles of the mountains, charcoal black and cobalt blue against the cadmium red of dawn. "*La motif,* it will not wait." Scarlet vermilion in his eyes.

I put on my hat and boots. We eat the Debris breakfast, the eggs and the cheese and the thick home-baked bread, washed down with about a quart each of the violent tea. Then the beer. Why always this nonsense of rocks, peaks, crags, sunrise skies, I ask him. Why can't you stay home, like other artists do, in a warm snug comfortable studio, and paint, well, say, what I would paint (if I didn't have better things to do), namely, a damn good-looking girl sprawled recklessly across a divan, her peignoir a pool of black satin oozing across the floor, and in her green-gold eyes the sullen glow of an insane insatiable lust! Eh? why not?

"You're spilling your tea," De Puy says.

"But why don't you?"

He smiles, puffing on the pipe, and quotes freely from the journal of Ferdinand Victor Eugène Delacroix: "'The energy which should have gone this morning into my painting I expended instead upon the recumbent form of the model.' I had," he adds, "about a year of that in England." He fidgets, glances at the sky, stands up. "Time to work."

I see that he is ready; the daypack on his shoulders holding the sketchbooks, jerky, canteen of water; his shirt pockets braced with a battery of Marvy Markers and Pentel felt-tips of various calibers.

"Or *schmierkunst,*" I say, "why not paint *schmierkunst?* Some abstract frenzy of the inner eye, like Pollock or Rothko or Gottlieb or What's-his-name? Why not a study of your neighborhood laundromat in photographic neorealism? Why not a bowl of fruit on a green felt table? Pears? Turnips? Apples? Poker chips? Okra?"

"I've done it all," he says, slashing at the air with his walking stick. "Now I must paint the real world. *Allons-nous!*"

Time to march.

Very well. We go.

Our job is to record, each in his own way, this world of light and shadow and time that will never come again exactly as it is today. And as we walk toward the sunrise, my friend Debris sings once again the little theme which *his* friends Gauguin and Van Gogh had also sung when they sauntered out each morning, a century before, into the rosy hills of Provence.

Allons! Allons!

Nous allons sur la motif!

Floating

Each precious moment entails every other. Each sacred place suggests the immanent presence of all places. Each man, each woman exemplifies all humans. The bright faces of my companions, here, now, on this Rio Dolores, this River of Sorrows, somewhere in the melodramatic landscape of southwest Colorado, break my heart—for in their faces, eyes, vivid bodies in action, I see the hope and joy and tragedy of humanity everywhere. Just as the hermit thrush, singing its threnody back in the piney gloom of the forest, speaks for the lost and voiceless everywhere.

What am I trying to say? The same as before—everything. Nothing more than that. Everything implied by water, motion, rivers, boats. By the flowing . . .

What the hell. Here we go again, down one more condemned river. Our foolish rubber rafts nose into the channel and bob on the current. Brown waves glitter in the sunlight. The long oars of the boatpeople—young women, young men—bite into the heavy water. Snow melt from the San Juan Mountains creates a river in flood, and the cold waters slide past the willows, hiss upon the gravel bars, thunder and roar among the rocks in a foaming chaos of exaltation.

Call me Jonah. I should have been a condor sailing high above the gray deserts of the Atacama. I should have stayed in Hoboken when I had the chance. Every river I touch turns to heartbreak. Floating down a portion of Rio Colorado in Utah on a rare month in spring, twenty-two years ago, a friend and I found ourselves passing through a world so beautiful it seemed and had to be—eternal. Such perfection of being, we thought—

these glens of sandstone, these winding corridors of mystery, leading each to its solitary revelation—could not possibly be changed. The philosophers and the theologians have agreed, for three thousand years, that the perfect is immutable—that which cannot alter and cannot ever be altered. They were wrong. We were wrong. Glen Canyon was destroyed. Everything changes, and nothing is more vulnerable than the beautiful.

Why yes, the Dolores too is scheduled for damnation. Only a little dam, say the politicians, one little earth-fill dam to irrigate the sorghum and alfalfa plantations, and then, most likely, to supply the industrial parks and syn-fuel factories of Cortez, Shithead Capital of Dipstick County, Colorado. True, only a little dam. But dammit, it's only a little river.

Forget it. Write it off. Fix your mind on the feel of the oars in your hands, observe with care the gay ripples that lead to the next riffle, watch out for that waterlogged fir tree there, clinging to the left bank, its trunk beneath the surface, one sharp snag like a claw carving the flow, ready to rip your tender craft from stem to stern. Follow that young lady boatman ahead, she knows what she's doing, she's been down this one before, several times. Admire her bare arms, glistening with wetness, and the deep-breathing surge of her splendid breasts—better fasten that life jacket, honey!—as she takes a deep stroke with the oars and tugs her boat, ferrywise, across the current and past the danger. Her passengers groan with delight.

Women and rivers. Rivers and men. Boys and girls against United Power & Gas. Concentrating too hard, I miss the snag but pivot off the submerged rock beyond, turning my boat backward into the rapids. My two passengers look anxious—

"For godsake, Ed, didn't you see that rock?"

"What rock?"

—but I have no fear. Hardly know the meaning of the word. God will carry us through. God loves fools, finds a need for us, how otherwise could we survive? Through all the perilous millennia? Fools, little children, drunks and concupiscent scriveners play a useful function, its precise nature not yet determined, in the intricate operations of evolution. Furthermore, I reflect—

"Watch out!"

"What?"

"Rock!"

"Where?"

—as we do another graceful pivot turn off a second rock, straightening my boat to face downstream again, furthermore, it seems clear at last that our love for the natural world—Nature— is the only means by which we can requite God's obvious love for it. Else why create Nature? Is God immune to the pangs of unreciprocated love? I doubt it. Does God love *us?* Well, that's another question. Does God exist? If perfect, He must. But nobody's perfect. I ponder the ontological dilemma.

"Watch it!"

"Who?"

"The wall!"

The strong current bears us toward the overhanging wall on the outside bend of the river. A sure deathtrap. Wrapped on stone by a liquid hand with the force of a mountain in its pressure, we would drown like rats in a rainbarrel pushed under by wanton boys with brooms. ("We are as boys to wanton sports . . .") Panic, terror, suffocation—not even our life jackets could save us there. Something to think about, I think, as I contemplate the imminent disaster, and meditate upon possible alternatives to a sudden, sodden, personal extinction. Walt Blackadar, I remember, world's greatest kayaker, died in similar fashion beneath a jammed half-sunken tree on the Payette River in Idaho.

"Jesus!"

"What?"

"Good Christ!"

God's love. God's elbow. We graze the wall and spin out into the sun. Not much damage: a slightly bent oarlock, a smear of powdery sandstone on the left gunwale, and my old straw hat left behind forever, snared on the branch of a shrub of some kind protruding from the rock. A last-minute pull with my oars—good reflexes here—has saved us from the deepest part of the overhang and propelled us into safety. I've said it before:

Faith alone is not enough. Thou must know what thou art doing. *His Brother* sayeth it: "Good works is the key to Heaven . . . be ye doers of the Word, and not hearers only . . ." (James 1:22)

Yes sir.

Flat water lies ahead. Our River of Sorrows, bound for a sea it will never reach, rolls for a while into a stretch of relative peace.

A good boatman must know when to act, when to react, and when to rest. I lean on the oars, lifting them like bony wings from the water, and ignore the whining and mewling from the two passengers seated behind me. Will probably be free of them after lunch; they'll find another boat. Nothing more tiresome to a thoughtful oarsman than critics.

I think of lunch: tuna from a tin, beslobbered with mayonnaise. Fig Newtons and Oreo cookies. A thick-skin Sunkist orange peeled in a crafty way to reveal a manikin in a state of urgent priapism. Salami and cheese and purple-peeled onions. Our world is so full of beautiful things: fruit and ideas and women and banjo music and onions with purple skins. A virtual Paradise. But even Paradise can be damned, flooded, overrun, generally mucked up by fools in pursuit of paper profits and plastic happiness.

My thoughts wander to Mark Dubois. Talk about the *right stuff*. That young man chained himself to a rock, in a hidden place known only to a single friend, in order to save—if only for the time being—a river he had learned to know and love too much: the Stanislaus in northern California. Mark Dubois put his life on the rock, below high-water line, and drove half the officialdom of California and the Army Corps of Engineers into exasperated response, forcing them to halt the filling of what they call the New Melones Dam. For a time.

In comparing the government functionaries of the United States to those of such states as the Soviet Union, or China, or Brazil, or Chile, we are obliged to give our own a certain degree of credit: they are still reluctant to sacrifice human lives to industrial purposes in the full glare of publicity. (Why we need a free press.) But I prefer to give my thanks direct to people like Mark

348

Dubois, whose courage, in serving a cause worthy of service, seems to me of much more value than that of our astronauts and cosmonauts and other assorted technetronic whatnots: dropouts, all of them, from the real world of earth, rivers, life.

One river gained a reprieve; another goes under. Somebody recently sent me a newspaper clipping from Nashville, in which I read this story:

> Loudon, Tenn. (AP)—Forty years of dreams and sweat have died beneath a bulldozer's blade as the Tennessee Valley Authority crushed the last two homes standing in the way of its Tellico Dam.
>
> The bulldozers arrived Tuesday hours after federal marshals evicted the last two of 341 farmers whose land was taken for the 38,000-acre, $130-million federal project.
>
> By nightfall the barn and white frame house that the late Asa McCall had built for his wife in 1939 and the home where postman Beryl Moser was born 46 years ago had been demolished. . . .
>
> "It looks like this is about the end of it," Moser said, as three carloads of marshals escorted him from his home. "I still feel the same way about it I did ten years ago: to hell with the TVA. . . ."
>
> The W. B. Ritcheys, the other holdouts, packed their furniture Monday. . . . All three families had refused government checks totaling $216,000 mailed to them when their land was condemned.
>
> Supreme Court Justice William Brennan on Tuesday rejected a plea by Cherokee Indians for an injunction to prevent TVA from closing the dam gates. Justice Potter Stewart and the 6th U.S. Circuit Court of Appeals in Cincinnati rejected the same request last Friday.
>
> The Cherokee contend that a lake over their ancient capital and burial grounds violates their First Amendment rights of religious freedom. . . .

Sandstone walls tower on the left, five hundred feet above this Dolores River. The walls are the color of sliced ham, with slick concave surfaces. Streaks of organic matter trail like draperies across the face of the cliff. Desert varnish, a patina of blue-black oxidized iron and manganese, gleams on the rock. A forest of yellow pine glides by on our right, so that we appear to be still in high mountain country while descending into the canyonlands. Bald eagles and great blue herons follow this river. A redtail hawk screams in the sky, its voice as wild and yet familiar as the croak and clack of ravens. The windhover bird, riding the airstream. Staring up at the great hawk, I hear human voices fretting and fussing behind my back, urging caution. A glance at the river. I miss the next rock. Can't hit them all. And bounce safely off the one beyond.

"Don't tell Preston," I suggest to my passengers. Preston— Preston Ellsworth—leader of this expedition, veteran river guide, owner and operator of Colorado River Tours, Inc., is one of the best in a difficult business. At the moment he is somewhere ahead, out of sight around the next bend. Though a sturdy and generous fellow, he might be disturbed by my indolent style of boatmanship. This sixteen-foot neoprene raft I am piloting from rock to rock belongs to him, and a new one would cost $2,300. And the rapid called Snaggletooth lies ahead, day after next.

Be of good cheer. All may yet be well. There's many a fork, I think, in the road from here to destruction. Despite the jet-set androids who visit our mountain West on their cyclic tours from St. Tropez to Key West to Vail to Montana to Santa Fe, where they buy their hobby ranches, ski-town condos, adobe villas, and settle in, telling us how much they love the West. But will not lift a finger to help defend it. Will not lend a hand or grab ahold. Dante had a special place for these ESTers, esthetes, temporizers, and castrate fence-straddlers; he locked them in the vestibule of Hell. They're worse than the simple industrial developer, whose only objective, while pretending to "create jobs," is to create for himself a fortune in paper money. The developer is what he is; no further punishment is necessary.

As for politicians, those lambs and rabbits—

"Watch it!"

Missed that one by a cat hair. As for the politicians—forget them. We scrape by the next on the portside, a fang of limestone under a furl of glossy water. Vicious loveliness, hissing at my ear. I glide into a trough between two petrified crocodiles and slide down the rapid's glassy tongue into a moderate maelstrom. I center my attention on the huge waves walloping toward us. We ride them out in good form, bow foremost, with only a stroke now on one oar, now on the other, to keep the raft straight.

We leave the forest, descending mile after mile through a winding slickrock canyon toward tableland country. It is like Glen Canyon once again, in miniature, submerged but not forgotten Glen Canyon. The old grief will not go away. Like the loss of a wife, brother, sister, the ache in the heart dulls with time but never dissolves entirely.

We camp one night at a place called Coyote Wash, a broad opening—almost a valley—in the canyon world. After dark one member of the crew, a deadly pyromantic, climbs a thousand-foot bluff above camp and builds a bonfire of old juniper and piñon pine. He is joined by a second dark figure, dancing around the flames. As the flames die the two shove the mound of glowing coals over the edge. A cascade of fire streams down the face of the cliff. Clouds of sparks float on the darkness, flickering out as they sink into oblivion. A few spot-fires burn among the boulders at the base of the cliff, then fade. The end of something. A gesture—but symbolizing what?

Maybe we should everyone stay home for a season, give our little Western wilderness some relief from Vibram soles, rubber boats, hang gliders, deer rifles and fly rods. But where is home? Surely not the walled-in prison of the cities, under that low ceiling of carbon monoxide and nitrogen oxides and acid rain— the leaky malaise of an overdeveloped, overcrowded, self-destroying civilization—where most people are compelled to serve their time and please the wardens if they can. For many, for more and more of us, the out-of-doors is our true ancestral estate. For a mere five thousand years we have grubbed in the soil and laid brick upon brick to build the cities; but for a million years before that we lived the leisurely, free, and adventurous life of hunters and gatherers, warriors and tamers of horses. How can we pluck *that* deep root of feeling from the racial consciousness? Impossible. When in doubt, jump out. Withdraw.

Ah yes, you say, but what about Mozart? Punk Rock? Astrophysics? Flush toilets? Potato chips? Silicon chips? Oral surgery? The Super Bowl and the World Series? Our coming journey to the stars? Vital projects, I agree, and I support them all. (On a voluntary basis only.) But why not a compromise? Why not—both? Why can't we have a moderate number of small cities, bright islands of electricity and kultur and industry surrounded by shoals of farmland, cow range, and timberland, set in the midst of a great unbounded sea of primitive forest, unbroken mountains, virgin desert? The human reason can conceive of such a free and spacious world; why can't we allow it to become—again—our home?

The American Indians had no word for what we call "wilderness." For them the wilderness was home.

Another day, another dolor. The dampness of the river has soaked into my brain, giving it the consistency of tapioca. My crackpot dreams fade with the dawn. Too many questions, not enough answers. Enough of this theopneustic glossolalia.

We are approaching Snaggletooth Rapid at last. A steady roar fills the canyon. My passengers, a new set today, life jackets snug to their chins, cling with white knuckles to the lashings of our baggage as I steer my ponderous craft down the tongue of the rapid, into the maw of the mad waters. I try to remember Preston's instructions: ferry to the right, avoiding that boat-eating Hole beyond the giant waves; then a quick pull to the left to avoid wrapping the boat upon Snaggletooth itself, a brute chunk of limestone rough as a broken axehead, gashing the heart of the current.

I grip the oars and shut my eyes. For a moment. The shock of cold water in the face recalls me to duty. A huge wave is rising over the port bow, about to topple. Pull to the right. The wave crashes, half-filling the boat. We ride down past the side of the Hole, carried through by momentum. The Tooth looms beyond my starboard bow, an ugly shark's fin of immovable stone. Pull to the left. We slip by it, barely *touching*—dumb luck combined with blind natural talent. The boat wallows over the vigorous vee-waves beyond. Wake up. I'm drifting beyond the beaching point. I strain at the oars—oh, it's hard, it's hard—and tug this lumpen-bourgeois river rig through the water and into the safety of an eddy. My swamper jumps ashore, bowline in hand. We drag the raft onto the sand and tie up to a willow tree.

Safely on the beach I watch (with secret satisfaction) the mishaps of the other oarsmen. And oarswomen. Nobody loses or overturns a boat but several hit the Tooth, hang there for awesome seconds, minutes, while tons of water beat upon their backs. They struggle. Hesitation: then the boats slide off, some into the current on the wrong side of the rock to go ashore on the wrong side of the canyon. No matter; nobody is hurt, or even dumped in the river, and no baggage is lost.

Recovered, reassembled, we eat lunch. We stare at the mighty rapids. We talk, meditate, reload the boats and push out, once again, onto the river.

Quietly exultant, we drift on together, not a team but a family, a human family bound by human love, through the golden canyons of the River of Sorrows. So named, it appears, by a Spanish priest three centuries ago, a man of God who saw in our physical world (is there another?) only a theater of suffering. He was right! He was wrong! Love can defeat that nameless terror. Loving one another, we take the sting from death. Loving our mysterious blue planet, we resolve riddles and dissolve all enigmas in contingent bliss.

On and on and on we float, down the river, day after day, down to the trip's end, to our takeout point, a lonely place in far western Colorado called Bedrock. Next door to Paradox. There is nothing here but a few small alfalfa farms and one gaunt, weathered, bleak old country store. The store is well stocked, though, with Budweiser (next morning we'll find among us a number of sadder Budweiser men), and also a regional brew known as—Cures? Yes, Cures beer, a weak, pallid provincial liquescence brewed, they say, from pure Rocky Mountain spigot water. Take a twelve-pack home tonight. Those who drink from these poptop tins will be, in the words of B. Traven, America's greatest writer, "forever freed from pain."

Three of the boat people are going on down the Dolores to its junction with the Colorado, and from there to the Land of Moab in Darkest Utah. My heart breaks to see them go without me. But I have a promise to keep. Preston Ellsworth has business waiting in Durango; the others elsewhere. Must all voyages end in separation? Powell lost three of his men at Separation Rapids, far down there in *The* Canyon. And Christopher Columbus, after his third voyage to the Indies, got in trouble with his royal masters and was sent back to Spain in chains, leaving his men behind on Hispaniola.

Which made no difference. There will always be a 1492. There will always be a Grand Canyon. There will always be a Rio Dolores, dam or no dam. There will always be one more voyage down the river to Bedrock, Colorado, in that high lonesome valley the pioneers named Paradox. A paradox because—anomaly—the river flows across, not through, the valley, apparently violating both geo-logic and common sense. Not even a plateau could stop the river. Their dams will go down like dominoes. And another river be reborn.

There will always be one more river. The journey goes on forever on our little living ship of stone and soil and water and vapor, this delicate planet circling round the sun which humankind call Earth.

Joy shipmates joy.

FROM

The Rites of Spring

(novel-in-progress)

Stump Creek, West Virginia, April, 1942.

The war? What war? Henry Lightcap, fifteen years old and lean and green as a willow sapling, had deeper things in mind. Henry loved the chant of the Spring peepers, 10,000 tiny titillated frogs chanting in chorus from the pasture, down in the marshy bottoms by the crick, that music of moonlight and fearful desire, that plainsong, that Te Deum Laudamus, that Missa Solemnis deep as creation that filled the twilight evenings with a song as old (at least) as the carboniferous coal beds beneath his homeland. (Grandfather Lightcap had signed a broad form deed to the mineral rights in 1892, but nothing ever came of it. Or ever would, thought Paw.)

Henry detested highschool with a sharp absolute loathing keen as his knifeblade but loved getting on the bus behind Wilma Fetterman, watching as she climbed the high steps, her short skirt riding up, his eyes fixed on the twin tendons behind her knees, the sweet virgin untouchable gloss of her forever inaccessible thighs. Henry, virgin himself, thought that he understood the mechanical principle of the human sexual connection but also believed, with the hopeless sorrow of his youth, that he himself would never, never, never be capable of the act because—well, because his penis, when excited and erect, rose hard and rigid as bone against his bellybutton. There was no room in there, no space whatsoever, for a female of his own species. The thing could not be forced down to a horizontal approach, as he assumed was necessary, without breaking off like the joint of a cornstalk. He told no one of his deformity. Not even his mother. But though it was hopeless, he continued to love watching Wilma Fetterman climb the schoolbus steps.

He loved the lament of the mourning doves, echoing his own heartache, when they returned each Spring from wherever they went in winter. He loved the soft green of the linwood trees, the bright green of the Osage orange, against the morning sun. He loved the red-dog road that meandered through the smoky hills, beside the sulfur-colored creek, into and through the covered bridge and up the hollow that led, beyond the last split-rail fence, toward the barn, the pigpen, the wagon shed, the ice house, the springhouse, and the gray good gothic two-story clapboard farmhouse that remained, after a century, still the Lightcap family home.

He loved his Berkshire pigs. He loved the beagle hounds that ran to meet him each evening. He loved—but intuitively, not consciously—the sight of the family wash hanging from the line, the sound of his father's axe in the woodyard as the old man split kindling for the kitchen stove. He even loved the arrogant whistling of his older brother Will—hated rival—as Will brought the horses up from the half-plowed cornfield, the team harnessed but unhitched, their traces dragging, their chains jingling, over the stony lane to the barn.

But most of all, and above all, and always in April, Henry loved the sound of a hardball smacking into leather. The *whack!* of fat bat connecting solidly with ball. And better yet, when he was pitching, Henry loved the swish of air and grunt of batter lunging for and cleanly missing Henry's fast one, low and outside, after he's brushed the hitter back with two consecutive speedballs to the ear.

He loved his brandnew Joe "Ducky" Medwick glove, personally autographed (at the Spalding factory) by Joe himself. He loved the feel and heft and fine-grained integrity of his sole uncracked Louisville Slugger, autographed by baseball's one and only active .400 hitter, the great and immortal Ted Williams.

Brother Will liked the game too, in his calm complacent way, but never lay awake at night dreaming about it, never dawdled away hours composing elaborate box scores of imaginary games in a fantasy league that existed only in the mind of Henry Lightcap.

Henry had his reasons. The rail-fence league was real.

Blacklick, a coal-mining town, was coming to Stump Creek for the first game of the season. Henry, self-appointed captain and prime organizer, had scheduled the game by ringing Kovalchick's Store—two longs and a short—one evening after school. He heard the click of receivers coming off the hooks up and down the line, then after a time the surly voice of old man Kovalchick coming to him through the miracle of the telephone from seven miles away.

"Yeah? Kovalchick's."

"Mister Kovalchick—?"

"Yeah? Speak up." He heard the old man bellow at unseen auditors. "Turn down that goddamn radio, I'm tryin to talk. Yeah, who's dis?"

"Mister Kovalchick, can I speak to Tony?"

"Yeah? That bum?" Henry heard the old man roar again. "Tony! Antonio! Some kid wants you. Yeah, you!" He heard the earpiece drop and bang against the wall. A pause, then the voice of Tony, twenty years younger but also suspicious, equally hostile, came over the line. "Who's talkin?"

Henry mentioned his name.

"What do you want, farmer?"

Henry stated his business.

Tony paused to absorb the information, then said, "Listen, farmer, we got a real ball team here. We ain't got time to fool around with a bunch of hillbillys."

Henry said he had a better team than last year.

Tony laughed, a short harsh bark. "Last year you had nothin. Nothin is always nothin. Anyhow our field aint ready. Somebody tore down the backstop for firewood."

Henry said Stump Creek had a good diamond, cleared and dragged, and the outfield in usable shape. (Gil Prothrow's cow pasture, mined with cowpies, but he didn't mention that.)

"Yeah? Well . . ." Tony K. hesitated again. "Naw, we don't play farmers; you ain't in our league. Goodby now . . ."

"Wait!" Henry risked a few bold words—a challenge.

"What? What'd you say, you crumb?"

Henry repeated the challenge, even made it a shade stronger.

A moment of silence at the other end of the line, then Tony's snarl of contempt. "We'll be there, Lightcap. This Saturday. Two o'clock. You furnish the balls—" Another brutal laugh. "—if you clodhoppers got any balls."

Henry agreed but added one further stipulation: no fair bringing any players older than fourteen. Will's our oldest player, he explained, and he's only thirteen and a half.

Tony nearly choked on his astonishment. "Jesus but you can lie. Will's sixteen and you know it and I know it."

All right, Henry agreed again. But nobody over sixteen, okay?

"Don't worry about a thing," Tony said. "We'll be there." He hung up. Henry waited, hearing the earphones go back on the hooks, then slowly replaced his own, his mind already racing ahead to work out his lineup.

He and Will picked the team, writing names down on a ruled paper tablet. Henry would take over the mound, Will handle the catching, as usual. Their little brother Paul could play right field, where he'd be mostly out of the way, not in a position to do much harm. Their best player and one genuine athlete, the sharp-eyed clean-cut Eagle Scout Chuck Tait, would sparkplug the team at shortstop, or take over first, or relieve the pitcher, wherever needed. That made four players, the heart and solid core of the Stump Creek nine. But where to find the other five? Stump Creek, W.Va., population one hundred twenty (counting dogs and girls), scattered for five miles along County Road 14, did not offer a wealth of talent.

They brooded over the problem and concluded that the best they could do was have the Adams brothers, Clarence thirteen and Sonny twelve, play second and third base, and let the Fetterman boys, Junior (his baptized, Christian name—the father's name was Bill), age thirteen, and Elman, age eleven or so, play the outfield. None of the four, as Will said, could hit a cow's ass with a snow shovel, but who else was available?

We're still one player short, Henry pointed out. We need somebody to start at first base. They thought about that for a while. Finally Will mentioned the name of Ginter.

"No . . ." said Henry.

"Who else?"

"Not Red Ginter . . ."

"Who else we got?"

"But Red," said Henry. "Red's seventeen."

"Yeah but he's still in fourth grade."

"That was three years ago."

"Well that's where he was last time he went to school."

"Tony would object."

"Tony's a liar. You wait and see. Every one of them Guineas and Polacks will be at least seventeen. You know what those Roman Cat-lickers are like—they drink blood in church every Sunday. You know—that Sacred Heart of Mary Church. Bunch of mackerel snappers."

"I dont believe that any more, Will. They're Catholics but they're human like us. More or less. Besides . . ."

"Besides what?"

"Red won't play."

"Ask him. Who else we got?"

"He can't play. He's big but he won't move, he won't run."

"He'll catch the ball if you throw it to him. He'll do for first base."

"Can't hit the ball. He swings the bat like he thinks he's mowing hay. Like it's a golf club. Strikes out every time."

"Yeah but he takes a mighty powerful cut at the ball." Will smiled, his dark eyes musing. "I saw him hit a ball four hundred feet on a line drive one time."

"I saw that. A fluke hit and anyway it went foul."

"He's the only one we got left, Henry."

Henry thought about it. "What about his little brother, Leroy? Maybe he could play."

"Christ," muttered Will, and he brushed back his shaggy black mop of hair and made a rotating motion with his forefinger close by his right ear. "Leroy's crazy as a moon-eyed calf. We don't even want him around."

They were silent for a minute, sitting there in the kitchen at the oilcloth-covered table, lit by the amber glow of the kerosene lamp, staring at their paper lineup of eight ballplayers, five of them children. "Then it's gotta be Red," Henry said.

"We got no choice, Henry."

"All right. But you go ask him."

"We'll go together," Will said. "And we'll take Elman and Junior with us."

"We should take the twelve-gauge too."

"We should. But we won't."

Swinging out from the schoolbus, late in the afternoon, Henry and Will walked half a mile homeward up the red-dog road, under the trees, then cut off up the hill through the Big Woods toward the adjacent valley two miles away. Once called Crabapple Hollow, it became known as Hardscrabble Holler when the Ginter family, coming from no one knew where, made it their family seat in the late 1800s, soon after the end of the War Between the States. (Virginia versus West Virginia.)

The Fetterman boys had declined to join them, mumbling various excuses: their Paw'd get mad, they had all them evening chores to do, something was wrong with their big sister Wilma who'd stayed out late the night before and come home with blood running down her leg, their dog Shep was sick, Maw needed them to set out the stringbean stakes and plant crowder peas, Uncle Homer was coming to show everybody his new Ford automobile, he was the one worked at Jim Stewart's Hardware Store in Shawnee who everybody said earned a hundred fifty dollars a month. Lies.

Will and Henry walked alone through the shade of the tall pines, a second growth but already uncut for fifty years—Joe Lightcap, their old man, logger and sawyer, had his mind on those trees; he cruised every stand of timber in the county and could estimate the board feet in a tree with one squint of his deep brown eyes. They passed the ruins of Brent's sawmill, abandoned half a century before. There was a scatter of slabs rotting in the goldenrod, the tattered remnants of antique power belting, the enormous hill of sawdust barely beginning, after so much time, to support the growth of a few weeds on the slopes of its sterile, smoldering immensity.

Here they struck a narrow footpath leading down the steep side of the ridge toward the eroded corn patches and over-grazed pastures of Ginter's farm. Halfway down they passed the gulch and tailings pile of a small coal mine, unworked for years. A dribble of sulfurous water leaked from the dark portal of the mine, where decayed locust props, warped beneath the overburden, shored up the roof of the tunnel. The entrance resembled a rotten mouth, spiked with fragments of teeth. There were many such small, one-man workings in the area; in one of these, as everyone knew but few dared mention aloud, old Jefferson Ginter kept his distilling equipment.

The farm buildings came in view, a collection of weather-blackened, unpainted, ramshackle structures with sagging roof-beams, then the Ginter house, a one-story slab shack with a rusted tin roof, built by the Ginters themselves, attached to a much older but sturdy, square-cornered log cabin. The Ginter coon hounds, smelling the Lightcap brothers from afar, began to bay, stretching their chains to the final link.

The path to the back porch of the house, where they were headed, was easily wide enough for two but Henry, slowing down, allowed Will to walk before him. Will was a year and a half older, a dark stolid solid fellow, not easily intimidated by any-thing, broad at the shoulders and thick in the arms, built—as everyone agreed—like a brick shithouse. Though only a sopho-more, he easily made first string right tackle on the varsity foot-ball team at Shawnee High School.

The back door of the house stood wide to the mellow April afternoon, opening into a dark interior. There was no screendoor and a number of Ginter chickens, moulting Reds and scraggly Leghorns, wandered idly in and out of the house, pausing to shit on the doorstep, pecking at ticks, ants, June bugs, dead flies, fallen shirt buttons, crumbs of tobacco, whatever looked edible, viable, biodegradable. A thread of blue smoke from the kitchen stovepipe rose straight up in the still air.

The dogs, four of them chained beneath the porch, barked with a hoarse and passionate intensity, rich with hatred, as Will and Henry made their cautious approach to the house. From inside the kitchen they could hear two semi-human voices engaged in fierce debate—the buzzsaw screech of a threatened woman, the baritone bellow of an outraged man.

"They're fightin again," says Henry. "Maybe we should come back later."

"They're always fightin," Will says. "Come on." And he marched firmly forward.

At that moment there was an explosion of hens through the open doorway, squawks of panic, wings flapping in urgent haste. The chickens were followed by a small yellow dog, also flying, or at least airborne, as if propelled by catapult from the interior. The dog cleared the porch without touching, landed running on the bare dirt of the yard—something pale and and soft clamped in its jaws—and scuttled like a wounded rat toward the security of the nearest outbuilding—a collapsed implement shed supported by the hulk of a broken-down John Deere manure spreader.

Will hesitated; Henry stopped behind him.

Old man Ginter appeared in the doorway, roaring mad. He roared after the disappearing dog: ". . . ever come back in here agin you docktail misbegotten yellowback hyena I'll fill your hinder end with birdshot so goldamn stiff you'll be shittin bee-bees through your teeth for a month."

Another screech of female indignation from within. Old Jeff Ginter, clutching a pint Mason jar filled with a clear, oily liquid, half turned to the unseen woman behind him and roared at her: "I don't care about no goldamn pet dog how many times I got to

tell you I don't want no goldamn dog in the house it haint
sanitary goldamn it all to hell and back. How many times I got to
tell you that dog of yourn haint no better'n the others. He got to
learn his place and a dog's place haint never inside a decent
Christian home goldamnit woman you raised in a barn? In a
cave? Under a goldamn manure pile?"

And then he saw Will and Henry, these two schoolboys in their
neat clean school clothes—bright sport shirts, fresh bib overalls—staring at him from across the beaten, grassless, dung-
spotted yard a hundred feet away. Old Ginter was wearing bib
overalls too, but his were worn through at the knee, unpatched
and unwashed, and instead of a shirt he wore a long-sleeved
Union suit buttoned to the neck, his winter underwear, once
white but now aged to a uniform grayish blend of sweat, dust,
woodsmoke, and ashes. Suddenly silent, he squinted at the boys
through bloodshot eyes under pale and shaggy brows, reached
inside the door and produced a shotgun, a veteran double-
barreled twelve-gauge bandaged at breech and forestock with
multiple wrappings of black friction tape. Cradling the weapon
in his left arm, at the ready, he snarled at the boys, "What're you
two a-doin here?"

Will gazed calmly at Ginter, waiting for Henry to speak. Henry
was the captain. When Henry realized that Will was leaving the
business up to him, he cleared his throat and tried to say something, starting off with a soprano squeak, "We come to see—" He
stopped, swallowed, gained better control of his voicebox, and
started over, this time in a firm adolescent tenor. "We come to see
Red, Mister Ginter. Is Red here?"

"What's that?" the old man shouted. "Speak up for Christ's
sake." The dogs were still barking, a steady uproar, from the end
of their taut chains beneath the porch. Ginter stepped forward
and roared down at them. "Shut up! You there, Buck! Bell!
Molly!" The dogs cringed, the barking subsided to a servile
whimpering. "Git the hell back there!" The dogs crept backward, tails lowered, into the shadows. Only one, a young spotted
Bluetick hound, dared a final snarl at the visitors. "You too,

Blue! Git the hell back under there." The fourth dog retreated, muttering quietly. Ginter looked at Henry and Will. He lifted the jar to his lips, took a sip, checked the bead at the rim, holding the jar up to the light, then lowered it and looked again at the boys. "Now what you want here? Speak up."

Henry swallowed and said, "We're lookin for Red."

"What you want him for?"

"We need him for the ball team, Mister Ginter. We got a game with Blacklick Saturday."

"My boys don't associate with them foreigners. They hain't no better'n niggers. Can't even speak decent English, them people. You ever hear them try to talk? Jabber and jibber at you like a bunch of cockeyed lunatics."

"We got a game. We need Red."

"Red's got better things to do than monkey around with you young snotnoses."

Henry felt Will go rigid beside him, about to turn and walk away. Before he lost his temper. Hastily, Henry said, "Look, Mister Ginter, we really need him." He tried flattery, though the lie sickened his soul. "Red's our slugger, Mister Ginter. Cleanup batter, number four slot." Lying through his teeth, he said, "We can't hardly play without Red . . ." He paused.

The old man swayed a little on the porch, looking down at them, considering Henry's mute appeal. He took another languid, loving sip from his pint of white lightning. He lowered the jar and said, "You boys oughta know better'n trouble honest folks with your foolishness. Some folks got to work for their livin." Squinting suspiciously, he asked, "When's this here game agonna be?"

"Saturday," Henry assured him.

"You sure it hain't the Sunday?"

"No sir, Saturday."

"Any child of mine plays that baseball game on a Sunday I'll peel his hide off his back with a drawknife'n hang him by the ears with it to yon ole butternut—" He gestured toward a nearby half-dead butternut tree, its lower limbs long since amputated for firewood. "—till sundown in July. Like I would a goldamn blacksnake. Till he stops wigglin. Ain't Christian play games on the Sunday."

"No sir it's Saturday."

Old Ginter relented. "They're out at the pigpen sloppin the hogs, him and Leroy." Leroy's name suggested an afterthought. "Now you mind and let Leroy play too or by God Red don't play neither. You hear me?"

Will and Henry glanced at each other in momentary despair. Will shrugged. They had no choice.

"Yes sir," Henry said.

They turned and walked toward the barn, Henry avoiding where he could the freshest applications of chickenshit. "Now you mind my words now," the old man shouted after them. They heard the resumed squawling of the woman inside the house and Ginter's answering bellow.

Behind the barn they found Red leaning on the pigpen fence, watching his little brother Leroy inside. Red was a hugely overgrown lad, far over six feet tall and more than two hundred pounds heavy, dressed like his father in overalls and undershirt. He wore patched rubber boots on his feet; the barnyard was a swampy mire, irrigated by random streams from the spring above the barn.

Henry greeted Red with formal politeness; Red ignored him, ignored Will, who said nothing but stood close by, ready for trouble. Will never did talk much—but then, like Red Ginter, he didn't have to. They stared at young Leroy.

Leroy was on his hands and knees inside the pen, creeping over the muck and dung toward a three-hundred-pound slime-coated sow. The sow lay on her side, eyes closed, giving suck to her litter of eight. Leroy was playing piglet. "Ernk, ernk," he grunted, lowering his belly to the ground and wriggling forward, "ernk, ernk, mumma . . ." His broad pink harelip was twisted in what was meant to be a porcine smile.

Red encouraged him, but there was no glint of malice in his dull, pale eyes. "Keep a-goin, Leroy. You jine 'em. And don't settle for hind tit neither."

Leroy squirmed closer. "Ernk ernk, mumma, gimme suck too." He was barefoot; the ragged overalls he wore seemed two sizes too large for him. The reddish hair on his head was so thin, fine, and short he appeared nearly bald. "Ernk, mumma," he crooned in soothing tones, "ernk, ernk . . ."

The great sow, lying peacefully in the April sun, at ease in the cool mud, opened one tiny red eye and saw Leroy inching toward her and her children. She grunted.

Leroy hesitated. "Ernk . . . ?"

The sow grunted again in alarm, in annoyance, and scrambled heavily to her feet. Leroy rose up to his hands and knees. The sow squealed with anger and maternal outrage and charged, lumbering forward like a leather locomotive. Her brood hung swinging from her tough teats, unwilling to let go. Leroy jumped up, turned—"Nom nam nun of a nitch!" he yelled, running toward the boys at the fence. "I gotta get the nom nam outa here!" He leaped for the top plank, caught it and rolled over on his belly, falling to the ground outside. The mighty sow crashed like a truck into the fence, almost breaking through. But the planking, spiked to square railway ties sunk three feet in the ground, held up one more time.

Leroy got up screaming with rage, wiped the mud from his hands onto his overalls, threw a few stones at the sow—she ignored them—and limped toward the house, bawling for his Maw.

When Red, still bland-eyed and unmoved, gave him some attention, Henry explained the purpose of the visit.

"I play first or nothin," Red says.

"That's okay, Red, that's where we need you."

"I bat first too."

"Well—you're our cleanup hitter."

"Bat first or nothin. Use my own bat too."

"Well . . ." Again Will and Henry looked at each other. No choice. "Okay, Red. Now the—"

"And Leroy bats second," Red went on.

"What?"

"If'n Leroy don't play I don't play."

"Aw come on, Red, you know Leroy can't play."

"Them's the rules, Lightcap. Leroy plays or I don't."

"He could be coach, Red. We'll need a coach at first."

"Leroy could be right field foul umpire," Will suggested.

"You heard me," Red says, picking up a bucket full of sour skim milk, potato peelings, corncobs, chicken entrails, turnip greens, chicken heads, eggshells, bacon rinds, assorted bones. He emptied the bucket into the wooden trough inside the fence. The huge sow shuffled in, snorting, and plunged her quivering snout into the swill. Red banged the bucket on her head to knock out the last bits and pieces of her dinner. Crunching on the bones and heads—best parts first—the sow gave the bucket no more response than the twitch of one hairy ear. The piglets hung from her udders, still suckling.

Henry and Will tramped homeward over the ridge, into the Big Woods, past the forgotten sawmill, through the gloom of the trees and approaching twilight. Mourning doves called from the shadowy depths. New bright fresh green spring leaves breathed in and out, in and out, silently, from the gumwood trees, the wild cherry, the beech and the locust and the poplar and the dog-wood. A horned owl hooted from the darkness of a hollow syca-more, calling for its mate. Another answered from a faraway pine.

"You hear that, Henry?" says Will, as they paused before the split-rail fence that marked the Lightcap frontier.

"Hear what?"

"The owls."

"The howls?"

"I said owls. What do you suppose they're saying to each other, Henry?"

Henry listened carefully. The owls were silent. He threw one leg over the top rail, then his other. He waited on the far side of the fence, listening. The owls called again, first one, then after a few moments of thought, the second.

Will grinned at his little brother Henry; the bright teeth shone in Will's brown honest face. Will said, "They're a boy and a girl owl."

"Baloney. How do you know?"

"Because the first owl says, 'Hoo hoo, wanna screw?' And the second owl she says, 'Hoo hoo, not you.'"

"Come on."

"No joke, that's what they're a-sayin."

"Bull-loney."

They went on, down the hill into Honey Hollow. And poor Henry, nursing in silence the secret of his grotesque, repulsive, disabling mutation, thought of Wilma Fetterman climbing into the schoolbus, of Elaine Kennedy draping her splendid cashmere-sweatered breasts over the back of her chair as she turned to tease him for a bit, of Betsy Shoemaker turning cartwheels in her cheerleader uniform at the pre-game pep rally. A pang of agony coursed upward through Henry's aching core, from the misaligned piston-rod of his groin to the undifferentiated longing in his heart. Never, never with a girl. He couldn't even get his fist in there. What was he supposed to do, make love to his own umbilicus? Pound a hole through his stomach?

The owls hooted gently after him through the green tender cruelty of April, down the hills of the Allegheny. The ghosts of Shawnee warriors watched them from the shadows of the red oaks.

A light rain fell Saturday morning, leaving pools of water on the basepaths, but the sun appeared on time at noon. Henry and Will and Paul filled burlap sacks with sand and paced off the bases. Chuck Tait came soon after with a bag of lime to mark the batter's box, the baselines, the coaching positions. They built up the pitcher's mound, chased Prothrow's cows into deep left and right field, and shoveled away most of the fresh cow patties from the infield. They filled in the pools with dirt, creating deceptive mudholes which only the home team need know about. They patched the backstop with chickenwire and scrap lumber. The Fetterman boys came with their gloves and a new bat, then the

Adams brothers with their gloves and two fractured, taped bats. (Both were cross-handed hitters.) No sign of the Ginters. There was time for a little infield practice and Will batted high-flying fungos to Paul and Elman and Junior in the outfield.

Henry thought he was ready for his pitching duties; he'd spent an hour every day for the past year throwing a tennis ball at a strike zone painted on the barn door, scooping up the ball one-handed as it bounced back to him down the entrance ramp. Precision control, that was his secret. He only had three pitches: an overhand fastball, not very fast; a sidearm curve which sometimes broke a little and sometimes didn't; and his newly-developed Rip Sewell blooper, a high floating change of pace which he pushed forward with the palm of his hand, no spin to it whatsoever, a tempting mushball of a pitch that rose high in the air and then drifted toward the plate like a sinking balloon. Weak pitches, all of them—but he had the control. He could hit the center of Will's catcher's mitt wherever Will called for it. And Will knew how to study the batter. They were ready, Red Ginter or no Red Ginter.

The Blacklick team arrived an hour late, Tony Kovalchick driving his father's twelve-cylinder 1928 Packard sedan. The three smallest boys sat in the trunk, holding up the lid with a bat. Seven large blond Eastern European coal miners, fingering rosaries and wearing sacred silver medals around their necks, heaved themselves like wrestlers out of the front and back seats. Stump Creek surrendered the field to the visitors for a thirty-minute warmup.

Tony and Henry compared scorecards.

"Your guys are too old," Henry complained. "Those are all highschool guys."

"That's our team," Tony says. "You wanta play baseball or you wanta go home and cry?"

"Carci, Watta, Jock Spivak—those are all football players."

"You got Will and Chuck, they're varsity. And who's this Red Ginter fella? Ain't he the one got in the fight at the Rocky Glen Tavern last Saturday night? Near killed some guy?"

"Not Red, you got him mixed up with somebody else." Henry pointed to a dark little fellow with a serious case of visual strabismus sitting on the Packard's runningboard. "Who's he? He's not in your lineup."

"That's Joe Glemp. He's our umpire."

"Umpire? He's cross-eyed!"

"Yeah, that's right. Don't make fun of him. He can't play ball worth a shit, but he's a pretty good ump."

"You're crazy. He can't see anything but his own nose. Anyhow Mister Prothrow's gonna be umpire." Henry looked around; old Gilbert Prothrow was nowhere in sight.

"The visiting team always brings the umpire," Tony said complacently. "You know that, Lightcap."

"You're nuts."

"It's in the rule book. Black and white."

"Not in any rule book I ever saw. Let's see this rule book."

"Let's see this Mister Prothrow."

Henry looked again. No Prothrow in view. But there came the Ginters, Red and Leroy, tramping up the dirt road, Red carrying his giant axe-hewn home-made hickory bat on his shoulder. The one with the square shaft, like a four-by-four.

Henry and Tony made a deal. Joe Glemp and Leroy Ginter would work as umpires, one calling the pitches from behind the plate, the other calling the plays in the field, and changing places each inning.

Leroy was not persuaded, not with Red behind him. Leroy meant to play baseball. Henry had to bully little brother Paul into taking the field umpire's position. He promised Paul that Leroy would soon get bored with the game, leaving a position open. Tears streaming down his rosy cheeks, Paul trudged slowly to his umpire's place in the vacant area behind second base. The Stump Creek nine took the field, Red Ginter on first nonchalantly taking Chuck Tait's rifle-shot throws from short, Henry on the mound, Will catching, the children at second, third, and scattered across the outfield among a number of grazing milk cows.

"Play ball!" hollered little Joe Glemp with surprising authority, masked and armored and hunkered down behind the broad back of Will Lightcap at home plate. Tony Kovalchick, batting right-handed, stepped into the batter's box, tapped some mud from his cleated shoes, made the sign of the cross before his chest, and dug in firmly for the first pitch. He gazed with insolent coal-dark eyes at the pitcher.

Henry, glove in his armpit, rubbed the sweet new unhit Spalding ball vigorously between moist palms and surveyed his team. All were in place, crouched for action, except Leroy in deep right field yelling hare-lipped obscenities at a thoughtful cow. No matter; Tony would pull to left.

Henry faced him. Tony was short but fierce, lively, eager, the pitcher, captain, and manager of the Blacklick team. Henry noticed at once that Tony was choking his bat by three inches. He waited; Will gave him the sign, fastball wide and low. Henry wound up and threw the ball exactly where Will wanted it, cutting the outside corner of the plate.

"Ball one!" shouted Glemp the umpire.

Will held the ball for a few moments to indicate his contempt for the call, then without rising tossed it back to Henry. Tony crowded the plate a little more. Will asked for another fastball, high and inside. Henry threw it precisely where wanted. "Ball—" began the umpire, as Tony tipped it foul back over their heads. "One ball, one strike," little Joe Glemp conceded.

He can't see but he can hear pretty good, thought Henry, rubbing the ball like a pro. Will called for the sidearm curve, low and outside. Backing off slightly (weakness!), Tony swung and tipped the pitch off the end of the bat. Two strikes. Now we got him, Henry thought, he's getting mad. Will called for the floater, mixing them up, and Henry threw it, Tony waited, watching the ball sail in a high arc toward him, and lost patience, and swung furiously much too soon, nearly breaking his back. He picked himself up, brushing the mud from his knees, and stormed darkly back to the visitor's bench. Will flipped the ball to third, Sonny Adams caught it, dropped it, passed it to Chuck who whipped it to Clarence Adams who caught it with stinging glove and passed it to Red and Red to Henry. One out.

A small fat Italian kid named Carci stood in the box, well away from the plate, twitching his bat nervously. He was a second-string center on the football team but proved to be afraid of a flying baseball, especially after Henry pitched his first fastball straight at Carci's upper lip, as instructed by Will. Luckily for the batter he had a retractable lip. Luckily for the pitcher the batter was a placid, abstracted intellectual, not too bright, who made no protest. His manager had to do it for him. Tony Kovalchick rose from the bench shouting but accepted Henry's apology for the wild pitch. He and Will struck Carci out with two more pitches, the batter drawing away from the plate as he swung, missing the ball by a foot. Two down.

Big Stan Watta, defensive lineman by trade, stood in the box. Stan was big but the next batter, Jock Spivak, fullback, was bigger. After a brief conference Henry and Will agreed to pitch to Watta and then, if necessary, walk the Jock. They returned to their places. Watta confronted Lightcap, standing close to the plate but relaxed, graceful, swinging his bat with practiced ease. Henry pitched him two fastballs low and inside. Watta ignored them, keeping his eyes on the pitcher. Two balls, no strikes. Will called for the sidearm slider, low and outside. Henry threw it, Watta stepped forward and drilled the ball smartly past Sonny at third, deep into left field. Watta trotted into second base with an easy stand-up double.

Jock Spivak stood deep in the batter's box, measuring the plate with his slugger's bat. Will and Henry, exchanging signs, stuck with their plan: a free pass to first for the big guy. (The next batter was a little pimple-faced punk known around Shawnee High School as Jerk-Off Panatelli—a fanatic onanist; his mother called him Pasquale. A sure and easy out.) But first they had to dispose of the menacing Jock.

Henry checked the runner at second, then threw the pitch high and outside into Will's guiding mitt. "Ball one!" cried the ump. Watta returned to second. Henry repeated the pitch, Will standing away from the plate to catch it. "Ball two!" Quickly now, impatient to get at the easy batter, Henry threw the third ball. "Ball three!" Jock spat on the plate, moved forward a bit, and grinned ferociously at the pitcher.

Henry threw it, neck high and a foot outside. Laughing, Jock stepped forward across the plate and smacked the pitch true, hard, and high into far right field. Leroy Ginter was out there, somewhere, barefoot, wiggling his toes in the squishy delight of a fresh cowpie. He was watching a young heifer at the fence, his mouth agape. The Stump Creek team hollered for attention.

Leroy turned, saw eighteen faces facing him, eight mouths yelling, then a towering fly ball beginning its descent toward his barely-haired-over head. He wiped the drool from his chin and ran a few steps to the left, a few to the right, slipped in another pile of cowshit and fell to his knees. "Nom nam nun of a nitch!" he screamed, throwing his glove at the falling ball. It bounced into the high weeds along the fence. Leroy made no move to retrieve it. Junior Fetterman ran over from center field and hunted for the ball. Stan Watta crossed home plate. Laughing all the way, Jock Spivak jogged toward third. Junior found the ball and pegged it to Chuck Tait at short, who relayed it to Sonny Adams at third. Sonny dropped the ball. Half sick with laughter, Jock headed for home, running now. Sonny threw the ball to Will, trapping Spivak between home plate and third. Spivak stopped but didn't stop laughing. Will faked a throw to third, Spivak reversed direction, hesitated, Will ran him down and tagged him out.

Blacklick one, Stump Creek zero, bottom of the first. The home team came to bat.

Red Ginter, about six feet four and two hundred twenty pounds, maybe seventeen years old, slouched into the batter's box with the squared-off log on his shoulder. He took a few practice swings, like a golfer at the tee, and waited for the first pitch. He wore the same overalls, the same sweat-and-grime-gray undershirt he'd been wearing all through the winter. Like his old man, young Red knew only two seasons, winter and summer, and was indifferent to daily fluctuations in temperature. Let the weather change, not him. He waited, peering indifferently at the pitcher from beneath his dangling, reddish forelock, his pale and freckled brow. His little close-set eyes, pallid and blandly blue, resembled the eyes of a carp fished from the stagnant mudholes of Stump Creek.

The pitcher, Tony Kovalchick, faced this agrarian atavist with equanimity. Shaking off his catcher's signal, he raised both arms above his head and began an elaborate, bewildering, Polish-American windup.

Ginter waited, legs far apart, waving his club in tight ominous circles behind his shoulder. The first pitch came in like a bullet straight down the middle, Ginter reared back, lifting his wrong, or hinder foot, and took a vicious cut at the ball, swinging eighteen inches beneath it. His bat scraped a groove through the dirt in front of the plate.

"Sta-rike!" yells Glemp, jabbing the air with his thumb.

The Blacklick catcher—squat square massive Dominic Del Poggio—chuckled as he flipped the ball back to Tony. The pitcher allowed himself a smile. Both could see already that this game was going to be such a laugher they might not make it through the fifth inning.

Untroubled, Red reassembled himself at the plate and casually awaited the second pitch. It came: a repeat of the first. He let it go by. No balls, two strikes.

Will and Henry glanced at each other; neither could find much sign of hope in the other's face. The sharp-featured pink-cheeked bright-eyed Eagle Scout, Chuck Tait, rolled his blue Scotch-Irish eyes at the sky, conveying his disgust to the clouds.

Another baroque windup. Teasing the batter this time—anything for a laugh—Tony threw a careless slider inside and much too low, almost in the dirt. Red swung down and up, digging another furrow through the dirt, and golfed the ball foul in a sharp hook toward deep left, where it struck a cow and caromed back toward fair territory. Left fielder Panatelli scooped up the ball and relayed it to the mound. The cow, hit on the side of the skull, stared for a moment with hurt, innocent surprise at the ballplayers, uttered one low moo-cry and sank to its knees, then to its side, where it remained for half an hour. The count at the plate, meanwhile, stayed the same: no balls, two strikes.

Red Ginter waited, the pale eyes flat and empty, his face showing less emotion than that of the unconscious cow. The pitcher and catcher, after quick consultation, played the next pitch safe: a fastball chest high across the center of the plate. The long-ball hitter's dream pitch. Red watched it go by. Three strikes and out.

The next batter was Leroy Ginter, as per the order insisted upon by his brother. Bare feet green with moist cowshit, Leroy clowned at the plate, switching from one side to the other and waving a little taped stick crazily at the pitcher. Kovalchick waited for the clown to settle down.

As Red slouched back to the bench Chuck Tait, the next batter, rose to meet him. "Look, Red," Chuck says, "you're swinging way under the ball." He imitated Red's underhanded swing. "Now watch: you have to level your stroke. Watch." He illustrated his words with a swift, beautifully smooth, perfectly level swing, in the manner of Williams and DiMaggio. "See? Like that." He gave a second demonstration, pure grace and sweet perfection.

Chewing on his wad of Mail Pouch, leaning on his club, Red stared down at Chuck from some ten superior inches, some forty extra pounds, and spat a spurt of tobacco juice onto Chuck's shoe. "You bat your way, baby-face," he says, "and I'll bat mine." He tramped past Chuck and took a place on the bench.

Chuck stared at the brown stain on his clean new sneakers and said nothing. But to Henry and Will, later, he grumbled, "No team spirit. None of your guys have the real team spirit."

Leroy struck out in three wild swings, two from the left and one from the right side of the plate. He slammed his bat on the plate—"Nom nan nun of a nitch!"—broke it again, and ran off toward the thicket beside the creek, where two heifers browsed on the elderberry bushes.

Chuck Tait took his left-handed stance at the plate and cracked the first pitch between first and second for a clean single. He danced back and forth on the base path as Will came to bat. Will let the first pitch go by and Chuck stole second. Will waited out a second pitch, then doubled Chuck home with a drive over third base. Henry Lightcap came to bat, anxious and eager, aware of Wilma Fetterman and some other girls watching the game—watching him—from the sidelines. Trying hard to be a hero, trying too hard, Henry popped out to second base.

Blacklick one, Stump Creek one, top of the second. Hating himself, Henry took his place on the mound, threw a few warmup pitches, and looked around. There was nobody in right field. Leroy, as expected, had disappeared. Thank God, he thought. He signaled little Paul to take Leroy's place, and faced the batter. The batter was Mike Gresak, not Panatelli; Kovalchick had wisely juggled his batting order. Henry pitched carefully, following Will's instructions, and got Mike to hit an easy grounder to second. But Clarence Adams bobbled the ball and Mike was safe at first.

The heavy-set, always dangerous Dominic Del Poggio now waited at the plate, batting left, ready for the pitch. Will, keeping one eye on Gresak far off first base, called for an outside pitch. Henry threw it, Gresak ran for second, Will caught the pitch and threw accurately to Chuck, covering the base, for what should have been an easy out. But Clarence, thinking the throw was meant for him, made a frantic leap for the ball and got run over by the base-runner, piling them both in the mud. A discussion followed.

Joe Glemp, peering sternly at his own nose, declared the runner safe on grounds of interference; furthermore, he penalized the home team by awarding Mike Gresak free passage to third base. The decision led to more discussion, prolonged and hectic. But the umpire stood his ground, would not be swayed by reason, common sense, the rule book, or threats of physical violence.

And Dominic still waited at the plate. He hit a high looping fly to right field which Paul Lightcap almost caught. Mike scored.

Dominic loped into second, smiling, and Charlie Kromko came to bat. Bearing down, Henry fooled the batter with a curveball that failed to break, with a fastball which Kromko mistook for a change of pace, and with his soaring blooper that the batter interpreted as a wild pitch. At the last moment, cursing, Charlie stepped forward, took a swing at it, and fell on his face. Dominic stole third as Sonny Adams sat down laughing.

Concentrating on his work, Henry threw two strikes past Jerk-Off Panatelli, low and inside, then jammed him with the inside curveball—it broke a little this time—which Panatelli swung at and hit with the handle of his bat, an easy roller straight toward Red Ginter at first base. Red waited for it, one foot on the bag, but the runner got there before the ball. Dominic scored.

The ninth batter in the lineup, Willie Hritsyk, hit a soft fly ball to Elman Fetterman in left field. Elman almost caught it. Two more runs scored. The stricken cow lurched to its feet and staggered off toward deep center field.

Henry confronted the laughing Tony Kovalchick and the meat of the Blacklick batting order. Following Will's strategic directions, pitching the corners, wasting a few, changing the pace, he struck out Tony, then Carci, and almost struck out Stanley Watta. Not quite. Watta smashed the intended third strike over second base and deep into center, where the ball splashed down in a cowpie as Junior Fetterman hurled himself at it. Paul Lightcap, backing up Junior, relayed the smeared ball to Elman to Clarence to Sonny: each player dropped it. Grinning grimly, sprinting all the way, Watta scored an inside-the-park home run. Jock Spivak, unable to control his laughing, struck out on three consecutive blooper balls.

The home team came to bat, bottom of the second, and the game, like the cow, lurched and staggered into the lengthening shadows of the afternoon. But Stump Creek was not outclassed. The Blacklick fielding proved as inept as Stump Creek's; Chuck Tait and Will Lightcap and even Henry managed to single, double, or triple each time they came to bat, for Kovalchick's pitching was steady and predictable: nothing but fastballs down the middle or else so high and outside that even Glemp the umpire, listening intently and obeying some primordial instinct toward objectivity, judged them balls not strikes.

The Adams boys, batting cross-handed and thus in danger of breaking their wrists, as everyone warned, succeeded in connecting with a pitch now and then, while Chuck and Will and Henry ran wild on the basepaths, detouring the mudholes, sliding greasily into second, into third, across home. In the third inning Junior Fetterman hit a double with the bases loaded; in the fourth inning Elman Fetterman, shutting his eyes and swinging for distance, popped a Texas Leaguer over the amazed shortstop Stan Watta's head. By the end of the fifth inning every player on the Stump Creek team had got on base at least once. Even Paul, the baby.

Every one, that is, but Red Ginter. Red struck out five times, watching the pitches with lacklustre eyes, never lifting the bat from his shoulder after his initial efforts at the plate in the first inning. Each Kovalchick pitch came whistling down the middle of the strike zone, fat and smug as a melon, and Red let them all go by, unwanted, untouched, unsmitten.

At the end of the fifth inning the score stood fourteen to twelve, Blacklick leading. The sun hovered close to the roof of Prothrow's barn, up on the green and pleasant hill to the west. Henry and Tony agreed to end the game after seven innings.

Clouds were gathering again, and the rainbirds sang.

The sixth inning was a high-scoring shambles. Each team batted around the order, scoring on fumbled grounders, wild throws, dropped fly balls, triples and doubles by Stan Watta, Jock Spivak, Mike Gresak, Tony Kovalchick, Chuck Tait, Will Lightcap, and Henry. As he stood on second wiping his brow with the felt of his cap, Henry thought for a moment he saw Wilma smiling at him. But he couldn't be certain, she sat so far away in the encroaching twilight, among a cluster of other girls, all of them smiling, laughing, most of the time. Laughing at me? he wondered—the pride in his two-base hit sank before the pain in his lonely heart.

Red Ginter struck out again, unmoving and unmoved as a great but lifeless snag of a tree.

Blacklick scored five runs in the top of the seventh, taking advantage of fly balls to the Fetterman brothers, bouncing grounders to the Adams brothers, a throw to first a little wide that Red would not condescend to reach for, and an intentional walk to Dominic Del Poggio, who replayed Jock Spivak's feat by stepping across the plate to hit the pitch-out over first and off Paul Lightcap's feeble glove in right field.

Nobody hit a genuine, bona fide, legitimate home run. The pasture fence, after all, was four hundred feet away at the nearest point. Beyond the fence lay the stagnant waters of Stump Creek. Beyond the creek stood a row of white oak trees—six of them—and beyond the trees was the cow-grazed, half-trampled, half-standing fodder of Prothrow's main cornfield.

Out of chaos, if too late, came a semblance of order. Henry and Will, aided by the general weariness of the batters, struck out the lower, weaker end of the Blacklick batting order one, two, three. After six and a half innings the score, agreed upon after much debate, seemed to be Blacklick twenty-one, Stump Creek sixteen.

In the gathering darkness and deepening gloom, with faint hearts, the home team came to bat for its last time. But Chuck Tait, leading off, intense and eager, hit the lead pitch inside first and down the foul line for a triple. His fourth hit of the game. Will doubled again, scoring Chuck, and Henry singled, scoring Will. Henry took second then third on wild throws by Panatelli in left and Carci at second. Blacklick twenty-one, Stump Creek eighteen, man on third and nobody out. Sonny Adams, learning to wait out the pitches from the tiring Kovalchick, walked. Clarence popped to second. One out. Junior Fetterman popped to the pitcher, Henry still holding third. Two outs and Elman Fetterman, Stump Creek's smallest, weakest hitter, stood at the plate. But Elman tried, he went down swinging, and the catcher—the massive, impassive, nerveless Dominic—somehow let the third strike get past him. He groped for the ball as all Stump Creek hollered at Elman:

"Run, Elman, run!"

Elman ran. Dominic found the ball, hurled it toward first, and hit Elman on the rump, propelling the boy face down into first base. Henry raced home, Sonny took second, and Elman stood up on first smiling happily with his second big hit of the day. Two men on base, two outs, and the score twenty-one to nineteen.

Top of the order, Red Ginter. Henry had to call him in from far left field, where he'd been hunting for Leroy. Red slouched toward the plate, holding his private bat by its rough-cut, heavy end, and took his stance. Feet spraddled far apart, like a plowman about to lift his plow around the end of a furrow, Red stared blankly at Kovalchick and waited for the first pitch, that inevitable but slowing fastball down the middle. Chewing his chaw, he stood there deep in the box, a glandular monster looming in the twilight, huge, terrific, terrifying, and impotent.

Will rose from his crouched position beyond third, where he was coaching the runners, and stared at the pitcher. Henry, watching from near first base, saw Tony Kovalchick touch the silver medal at his neck—St. Anthony—make the sign of the cross, and begin once more his fatigued but still fantastic windup. Red stopped chewing.

Kovalchick wound and then elaborately unwound, about to release the pitch—

"*Mackerel snapper!*" shouted Will, loud and clear.

—released the pitch, his body suddenly off balance, and threw wild into the dirt halfway between the pitcher's block and home plate. The ball dribbled crookedly toward the batter in little rabbity bounces.

"Ball one!" yelped the umpire, as Red stepped forward this time, not back, and swung boldly downward, like Sam Snead with a driving iron, and caught the ball with his slashing club as the ball made its last pathetic hop toward home plate. There was a flurry of dirt in the air, as if Red had dug too deep and missed, but all present heard the sharp *crack!* of hickory meeting hardball with magnum impact, a certain special unmistakable sound that every ballplayer and every fan recognizes instantly, as if engraved on memory and soul among those clouds of glory on the other side of birth, beyond the womb, before conception, in the source of all-being when God Himself was only a gleam in a witch-doctor's eye.

The sound of the long ball.

All faces turned toward the sky, toward the far-flung splendor of an Appalachian sunset, and saw Red's departing pellet of thread, cork, rubber, and frazzled leather rise like a star into the last high beams of the sun, saw it ascending high, higher, and still higher over Jock Spivak's despairing arms in the deepest part of center field, above the fence, over the creek and past the oak trees beyond the creek, where it sank again through twilight and disappeared (for two weeks) into the tangled jungle of Gil Prothrow's cornfield.

Sonny Adams, followed by Elman Fetterman, came trotting across home plate, dancing in delight. Blacklick twenty-one, Stump Creek twenty, Stump Creek twenty-one. The home team swarmed with joy around the runners.

Ah, but where exactly was the winning run? Where was Red? Red was nowhere. Red was everywhere. Red stood in front of home plate, leaning on his bat, watching his first hit of the game vanish into immortality somewhere southwest of Stump Creek. "Run?" he said. "What the hell you mean, run? Hit's a godamn *home* run, hain't it? What the hell I gotta run round them goldamn bases fer?" He spat a fat filthy gob of juice into the trenched soil at his feet. "Only little kids run round the bases fer nothin."

They yelled at him, pleaded, reasoned. He would not budge. Finally, when the screaming and hollering and debate became too loud he shouldered his bat in disgust and strode away down the red-dog road, headed for home. Ginter's home, that is.

Blacklick claimed a tie, twenty-one—twenty-one. Stump Creek claimed a de facto victory, twenty-two to twenty-one. The discussion raged for weeks and never was settled to the satisfaction of anybody, except maybe Red Ginter. And Leroy, who didn't care one way or the other. Old man Prothrow found Leroy that night bedded down in a stall on cowshit and straw, along with two heifers, when he checked his cow barn before turning in.

"No team spirit," Chuck Tait complained. "I don't think I'll play with you guys anymore. You hillbillys just don't have the right team spirit." Chuck was a town boy; he lived in the heart of Stump Creek, in a good solid brick house with plumbing and electricity. His father was village postmaster. Chuck joined the Army Air Force in 1943, learned to fly a Mustang P-51, and would return from the Pacific Theater later with captain's bars on his shoulders and a chest covered with ribbons. He started an insurance business and soon afterward evaporated, forever, into the state legislature.

Red Ginter joined the infantry, where he is now a master sergeant for life. Leroy joined the Salvation Army and became a major-general.

And Henry? Henry Lightcap fell in love. He fell in love that year with Wilma, with Betsy, with Elaine, and with eleven other girls. He knew his cause was hopeless but he tried. It was not Wilma or Betsy or Elaine or the others, however, but Mary, Tony Kovalchick's little sister, who provided the needed succor. One rainy night in May, in the back seat of Will's 1937 Hudson Terraplane, Mary Kovalchick showed Henry Lightcap a thing or two. Henry joined Mary. For a number of times. He never again went back, after that, to throwing tennis balls at barn doors or baseballs at Roman Catholics.

Will Lightcap, he stayed with the farm.

So it was, and so it all really happened down there in Shawnee County, in the Allegheny Mountains of West Virginia, about five thousand years ago.